Library of
Davidson College

# DANIIL KHARMS AND THE
POETICS OF THE ABSURD

By the same author

*V. F. Odoyevsky: his life, times and milieu* (1986)
*Pasternak's 'Dr Zhivago'* (1987)
*Daniil Kharms: The Plummeting Old Women* (trans.) (1989)
*The Literary Fantastic: from Gothic to Postmodernism* (1990)

# Daniil Kharms and the Poetics of the Absurd

Essays and Materials

Edited by
Neil Cornwell
*Senior Lecturer in Russian Studies*
*University of Bristol*

St. Martin's Press    New York

© Neil Cornwell 1991

All rights reserved. For information, write:
Scholarly and Reference Division,
St. Martin's Press, Inc., 175 Fifth Avenue,
New York, NY 10010

First published in the United States of America in 1991

Printed in Hong Kong

ISBN 0-312-06177-3

Library of Congress Cataloging-in-Publication Data
Daniil Kharms and the poetics of the absurd : essays and materials /
  edited by Neil Cornwell.
    p. cm.
  Majority of the essays translated from Russian.
  Includes bibliographical references (p.   ) and index.
  ISBN 0-312-06177-3
  1. Kharms, Daniil, 1905–1942—Criticism and interpretation.
2. Absurd (Philosophy) in literature.  I. Cornwell, Neil.
PG3476.K472Z65   1991
891.78'4209—dc20                                              91-7702
                                                                  CIP

# Contents

| | |
|---|---|
| An unpublished relic of Daniil Kharms<br>*Robin Milner-Gulland* | vii |
| Acknowledgements | ix |
| Note on Transliteration and Abbreviations | x |
| Epigraph: Aleksandr Galich, *Legenda o tabake* | xii |
| Notes on the Contributors | xv |

### PART I: INTRODUCTORY

1 Introduction: Daniil Kharms, Black Miniaturist    3
  *Neil Cornwell*

2 On Daniil Kharms    22
  *Iakov Druskin*

3 A Kharms Chronology    32
  *Anatolii Aleksandrov*

### PART II: GENERAL STUDIES

4 Daniil Kharms in the Context of Russian and European
  Literature of the Absurd    49
  *Jean-Philippe Jaccard*

5 The Anti-World of Daniil Kharms: On the Significance
  of the Absurd    71
  *Anthony Anemone*

### PART III: THE PROSE WORKS

6 Towards an Interpretation of Kharms's *Sluchai*    97
  *Robin Aizlewood*

7 Slobodan Pešić's Film *Slučaj Harms* and Kharms's *Sluchai*    123
  *Milena Michalski*

8 Elements of the Fantastic in Daniil Kharms's *Starukha*    132
  *Rosanna Giaquinta*

9  Some Features of the Poetics of Kharms's Prose:
   the story *Upadanie* ('The Falling')  149
   *Aleksandr Kobrinsky*

PART IV: THE POETIC WORKS

10 On One Enigmatic Poem by Daniil Kharms  159
   *Lazar Fleishman*

11 '*I Razrushenie*'  169
   *Daniil Kharms*

12 Kharms's '1st Destruction'  171
   *Jerzy Faryno*

13 Daniil Kharms's Poetic System: Text, Context, Intertext  175
   *Nina Perlina*

PART V: THE THEATRICAL WORKS

14 The Oberiuty and the Theatricalisation of Life  195
   *Tat'iana Nikol'skaia*

15 Kharms's Play *Elizaveta Bam*  200
   *Mikhail Meilakh*

16 *Yelizaveta Bam*: A Dramatic Work. A new translation
   from the definitive text by Neil Cornwell  220
   *Daniil Kharms*

PART VI: CONCLUSION AND APPARATUS

17 Beyond the Turning-Point: An Afterword  243
   *Robin Milner-Gulland*

18 Selected Bibliography  268
   *Neil Cornwell and Julian Graffy*

Index  278

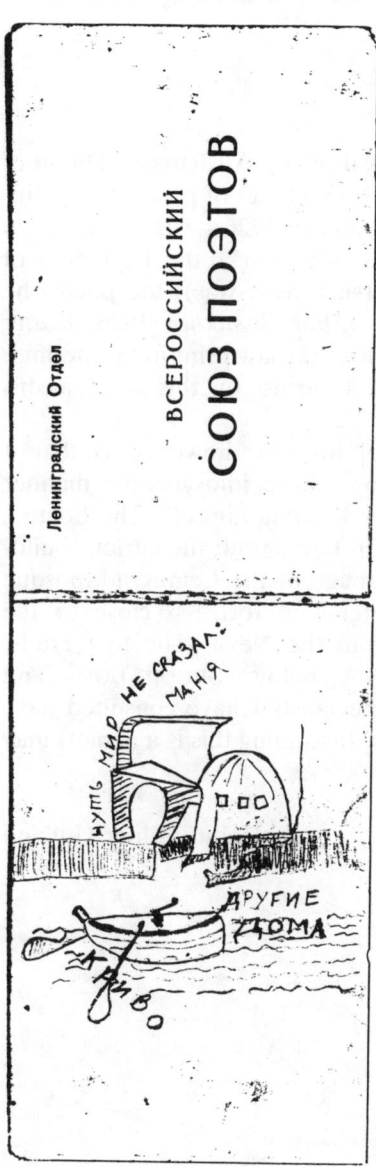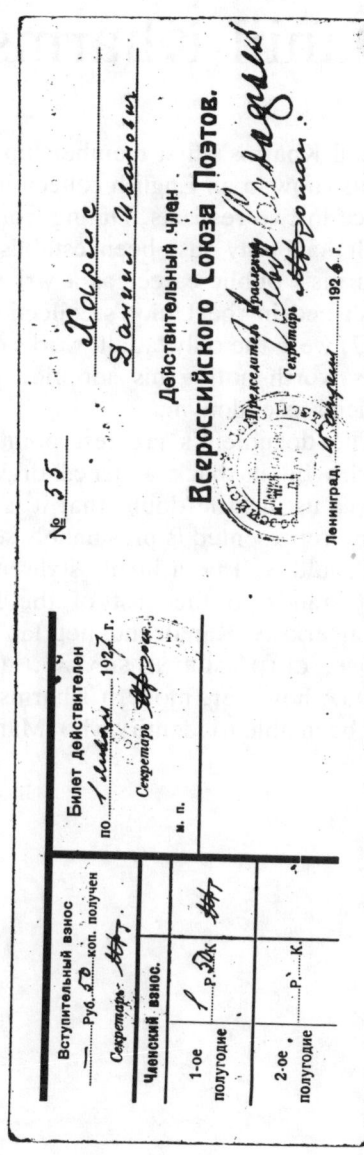

Membership Card (Leningrad Branch) of the All-Russian Union of Poets, dated 15 April, 1926, in the name of Daniil Kharms. On the back cover is a pencil sketch, presumably of the River Neva, bearing the words: 'Chut'mir ne skazal: Mania', 'drugie doma' and 'krivo'.

# An Unpublished Relic of Daniil Kharms

Daniil Kharms's first membership card of the All-Russian Union of Poets (now in an English collection) is an object of particular significance in two respects. Dating from early in 1926 – when the Union itself had only just been established – it marks the beginning of Kharms's public career as a writer (such as it was); the poems he published in the Union's collections (*Sbornik stikhov* 1926; *Kostër* 1927) were the only 'adult' works of his that saw print in his lifetime. It is worth noting his adoption of 'Kharms' by this stage as his 'official' pseudonym.

The document's greatest point of interest, however, is that it carries on its back a pencil drawing whose idiosyncratic manner leaves us in little doubt that it is by Kharms himself. The boating scene represented is presumably set in Leningrad; the curious building could well be a highly stylised image of the Leningrad mosque that stands to the east of the Peter-Paul fortress, close to the Kronverksky Kanal and not far from the Neva. The text reads, above, CHUT' MIR NE SKAZAL: MANIA: below, DRUGIE DOMA and KRIVO; however, modern Kharms specialists I have consulted have not been able to identify who 'Mania' (assuming this is a name!) may be.

Robin Milner-Gulland

# Acknowledgements

Thanks are due to the appropriate editors or journals, and of course authors, for permission to translate and reprint the articles here by A. Aleksandrov (the original is to be found in *Polët*, 1988: thanks in this case also to VAAP, Moscow, for permission to reproduce); J-P Jaccard (original noted in Bibliography as 'Jaccard, 1988a'), L. Fleishman (Fleishman, 1987) and M. Meilakh (Meilakh, 1987). These essays have all been edited, revised or supplemented for the present volume.

I should like to thank Ann Shukman for checking and improving my translations of articles from the Russian (as well as for doing her own); Marie Press for doing the same with my translation from the French; and Mikhail Meilakh for an invaluable consultation over my translation of *Elizaveta Bam*. Any remaining faults, however, must be mine alone.

Bibliographical assistance, general encouragement, or assistance with contributors or contributions has been rendered by Mikhail Meilakh, Julian Graffy, Robin Milner-Gulland, Anatolii Aleksandrov, Rosanna Giaquinta, Gerry Smith, Martin Dewhirst and Lazar Fleishman. Special thanks for her assistance, advice and inspiration at all stages of this project, from its initiation to its completion, must go to Ann Shukman.

N.C.
Bristol, May 1990

# Note on Transliteration and Abbreviations

The system of transliteration from Russian used in this collection is that of the Library of Congress (without diacritics, except for the letter 'ë'). Minor exceptions to this system are the retention in the main text (but not notes or bibliography) of the letter 'y' at the end of surnames (as in 'Vvedensky', or 'Tolstoy') and the omission of representation (again, in the main text) of the soft sign when occurring at the end of names (as in 'Gogol').

Titles of works by Kharms will normally be given in Russian, followed by English translation in brackets upon first use in each essay. Titles of works referred to by other authors in the main text will normally be given in English only. It should be noted that Kharms poems to which the author gave a title are referred to by that title in italics: poems without this distinction, however, are referred to by their first line, also in italics, but with quotation marks as well.

MAIN ABBREVIATIONS (used throughout text and notes)

| | |
|---|---|
| *Russia's Lost Lit.* | George Gibian (ed. and trans.), *Russia's Lost Literature of the Absurd – A Literary Discovery: Selected Works of Daniil Kharms and Alexander Vvedensky* (Ithaca and London: Cornell UP, 1971). |
| *Izb.* | Daniil Kharms, *Izbrannoe*, ed. George Gibian (Würzburg: jal-verlag, 1974). |
| *Sob. proizv.* | Daniil Kharms, *Sobranie proizvedenii*, ed. Mikhail Meilakh and Vladimir Erl' (Bremen: K-Presse, 1978– ), vols so far I–IV. |
| *Black Coat* | George Gibian (ed. and trans.), *The Man in the Black Coat – Russia's Literature of the Absurd. Selected Works of Daniil Kharms and Alexander Vvedensky* (Evanston, Ill.: Northwestern UP, 1987). |
| *Polët* | Daniil Kharms, *Polët v nebesa: Stikhi. Proza. Dramy. Pis'ma*, ed. A. A. Aleksandrov (Leningrad, 1988). |

Note on Transliteration and Abbreviations

| | |
|---|---|
| *Plummeting* | Daniil Kharms, *The Plummeting Old Women*, ed. and trans. Neil Cornwell (Dublin: Lilliput, 1989). |
| Vved. | Aleksandr Vvedenskii, *Polnoe sobranie sochinenii*, ed. Mikhail Meilakh (Ardis. Ann Arbor, 1980, 1984), vols I–II. |
| Oleinikov | N. M. Oleinikov, *Stikhotvoreniia*, introduction L. S. Fleishman (Bremen: K-Presse, 1975). |

For all other abbreviated references, see Selected Bibliography.

## ЛЕГЕНДА О ТАБАКЕ

*Посвящается памяти замечательного человека, придумавшего себе странный псевдоним – Даниил Хармс – писавшего прекрасные стихи и прозу, ходившего в автомобильной кепке и с неизменной трубкой в зубах, который действительно исчез, просто вышел на улицу и исчез. У него есть такая пророческая песенка:*

«Из дома вышел человек
С веревкой и мешком
И в дальний путь, и в дальний путь,
Отправился пешком,
Он шел, и все глядел вперед,
И все вперед глядел,
Не спал, не пил,
Не спал, не пил,
Не спал, не пил, не ел,
И вот однажды поутру,
Вошел он в темный лес,
И с той поры, и с той поры,
И с той поры исчез...»

Лил жуткий дождь,
Шел страшный снег,
Вовсю дурил двадцатый век,
Кричала кошка на трубе,
И выли сто собак.
И, встав с постели, человек
Увидел кошку на трубе,
Зевнул, и сам сказал себе –
Кончается табак!
Табак кончается – беда,
Пойду куплю табак,
И вот..., но это ерунда,
И было все не так.

Из дома вышел человек
С веревкой и мешком
И в дальний путь,
И в дальний путь
Отправился пешком...
И тут же, проглотив смешок,
Он сам себя спросил –
А для чего он взял мешок?
Ответьте, Даниил!
Вопрос резонный, нечем крыть,
Летит к чертям строка,
И надо, видно, докурить
Остаток табака...

Итак, однажды, человек
Та-та-та с посошком...
И в дальний путь,
И в дальний путь
Отправился пешком.
Он шел, и все глядел вперед,
И все вперед глядел,

Не спал, не пил,
Не спал, не пил,
Не спал, не пил, не ел...

А может, снова все начать,
И бросить этот вздор?!.
Уже на ордере печать
Оттиснул прокурор...

А в дверь стучат,
А в дверь стучат,
На этот раз – к нему!

О чем он думает теперь,
Теперь, потом, всегда,
Когда стучит ногою в дверь
Чугунная беда?!

А тут ломается строка,
Строфа теряет стать,
И нет ни капли табака,
А т а м – уж не достать!
И надо дописать стишок,
Пока они стучат…
И значит, все-таки – мешок,
И побоку зайчат,
(А в дверь стучат!)
В двадцатый век!
(Стучат!)
Как в темный лес.
Ушел однажды человек
И навсегда исчез!..
Но Парка нить его тайком
По-прежнему прядет,
А он ушел за табаком.
Он вскорости придет.

За ним бежали сто собак,
И кот по крышам лез…
Но только в городе табак
В тот день как раз исчез,
Начнем вот эдак – пять зайчат
Решили ехать в Тверь…
А в дверь стучат,
А в дверь стучат –
Пока не в эту дверь.

Пришли зайчата на вокзал,
Прошли зайчата в зальце,
И сам кассир, смеясь, сказал –
Впервые вижу зайца!

Но этот чёртов человек
С веревкой и мешком,
Он и без спроса в дальний путь
Отправился пешком,
Он шел, и все глядел вперед,
И все вперед глядел,
Не спал, не пил,
Не спал, не пил,
Не спал, не пил, не ел.
И вот однажды, поутру,
Вошел он в темный лес,
И с той поры, и с той поры,
И с той поры исчез.

На воле – снег, на кухне – чад,
Вся комната в дыму,
И он пошел в Петродворец,
Потом пешком в Торжок…
Он догадался, наконец,
Зачем он взял мешок…

Он шел сквозь свет
И шел сквозь тьму,
Он был в Сибири и в Крыму,
А опер каждый день к нему
Стучится, как дурак…
И много, много лет подряд
Соседи хором говорят –
Он вышел пять минут назад,
Пошел купить табак…

## А. ГАЛИЧ

# Note on Epigraph

Aleksandr Galich's song, 'Legenda o tabake' ('A Legend of Tobacco') (reproduced here by kind permission of Possev-Verlag, Frankfurt), used as the epigraph to this collection, quotes within its text, and embroiders considerably upon, one of Daniil Kharms's best known poems.[1] 'Iz doma vyshel chelovek' ('A man left his home', *Polët*, p. 249) was published by Kharms in the children's magazine *The Hedgehog (Chizh)* in 1937. With its motif of disappearance (a man leaves his home, walks off, enters a dark wood and is never seen again), this simple poem (subtitled originally 'a song') apparently caused Kharms much trouble in the extreme climate of 1937; the children's publishing house (Detizdat) stopped publishing him for a while (see *Polët*, p. 525) and hungry times arrived.[2] With hindsight, this poem, along with other Kharms texts, has assumed a prophetic tone. In Galich's version, the man becomes Daniil himself, a well-known pipe smoker, who pops out to buy tobacco, disappears and becomes an emblematic figure of the Gulag. Neither the circumstances described by Galich, nor those enacted in Kharms's poem, correspond all that closely to what happened in the case of Kharms's own arrest; nevertheless, the symbolism strikes a poignant chord on the late Galich's guitar.

N.C.

NOTES

1, 2  see notes to Introduction

# Notes on the Contributors

**Neil Cornwell** (editor), University of Bristol. Is the translator of Daniil Kharms, *The Plummeting Old Women* (1989) and the author of studies of V. F. Odoevsky (1986), Pasternak's *Doctor Zhivago* (1986), and *The Literary Fantastic* (1990).

**Robin Aizlewood**, School of Slavonic and East European Studies, University of London, is the author of *Verse Form and Meaning in the Poetry of Maiakovskii* (1989).

**Anthony Anemone**, Colby College, has written a PhD dissertation on Vaginov (1985) and is the author of a number of articles on the Leningrad avant-garde.

**Anatolii Aleksandrov** has been one of the Leningrad mainstays of Kharms publications since the 1960s and is editor of Daniil Kharms, *Polët v nebesa* (1988).

**Iakov Druskin** (1902–80). Philosopher and musicologist; a close friend of Kharms and Vvedensky, he was instrumental in preserving Kharms's archive and in the revival of Kharms publications. His memoirs of the Oberiuty were written in the 1970s.

**Jerzy Faryno**, Warsaw University. Has published widely on twentieth-century Russian poetry and poetics, especially on Tsvetaeva and Pasternak.

**Lazar Fleishman**, Stanford University. A specialist in twentieth-century Russian literature and cultural politics, he is the author of major studies of Pasternak.

**Rosanna Giaquinta**, University of Udine, is Kharms's Italian translator, a specialist in Soviet literary institutions of the 1920s and the author of several articles on OBERIU theory and practice.

**Julian Graffy**, School of Slavonic and East European Studies, University of London, is the co-editor of *Culture and the Media in the USSR Today* (London: Macmillan, 1989).

## Notes on the Contributors

**Jean-Philippe Jaccard,** University of Geneva, is the leading French-language OBERIU scholar and the author of several important articles on Kharms. He is completing a doctoral thesis under the title '*Tradition et modernisme dans l'oeuvre de Daniil Kharms*'.

**Aleksandr Kobrinsky,** Herzen Institute, a Leningrad scholar specialising in Oberiuty and avant-garde.

**Mikhail Meilakh,** freelance Leningrad scholar and translator. He has played a major part in promoting OBERIU studies since the 1960s, is the editor of the collected works of Vvedensky and co-editor of the on-going collected works of Kharms.

**Milena Michalski** is a London-based employee in East-West trade; she holds BA and MA degrees from the School of Slavonic and East European Studies and has research interests in early twentieth-century Russian literature, including Remizov.

**Robin Milner-Gulland,** University of Sussex, was the first western scholar to promote the Oberiuty, by re-publishing the OBERIU manifesto in 1970. He has since published a range of articles on Zabolotsky, Kharms, Vvedensky and Oleinikov and is the author of *A Cultural Atlas of Russia and the USSR* (1989).

**Tat'iana Nikol'skaia** is a Leningrad freelance scholar and librarian. She has published widely on the Russian avant-garde and experimental theatre.

**Nina Perlina,** University of Indiana, is a specialist on Russian literary theory and the author of *Varieties of Poetic Utterance: Quotation in 'The Brothers Karamazov'* (1985).

# Part I: Introductory

# 1 Introduction: Daniil Kharms, Black Miniaturist
## Neil Cornwell

Russian literature seems to enjoy a particular propensity, deriving, one may suppose, largely from historical factors, for throwing up 'new' writers from its past – writers with something unexpected to say to the modern reader. Such recently reclaimed writers may have languished in obscurity from some point of the nineteenth century, or have suffered from repression in the twentieth. In some cases, the existence of their main works may have remained unknown until decades after their death (as with Bulgakov's *The Master and Margarita*). In other instances, the very existence of both works and (even) author was virtually unknown or forgotten for many years. Such is the case with Daniil Kharms (1905–1942).

\* \* \*

'Daniil Kharms' was the principal – and subsequently constant – alias, pseudonym and pen-name combined of Daniil Ivanovich Iuvachëv. He was born in St Petersburg, a city which was also to change its name twice but which he was scarcely ever to leave, on 30 December 1905 (New Style: 17 December, Old Style). His mother, Nadezhda Ivanovna Koliubakina, an educationalist, ran a shelter for women who had been imprisoned. His father, Ivan Pavlovich Iuvachëv (1860–1940), was also a remarkable Petersburg personality in his own right. As a young naval officer, he joined the revolutionary 'People's Will' organisation, was arrested in 1883 for plotting to assassinate the Tsar and served his time in the fortress of Schlüsselburg and on the island of Sakhalin, where, having by now transformed himself into a Tolstoyan pacifist, he attracted the notice of the visiting Chekhov. Eventually he returned to St Petersburg, where he became a noted scientist and religious writer, publishing a number of books under his own adopted name of 'I. P. Miroliubov'.[3]

Kharms wrote a number of spoof autobiographical pieces about the circumstances of his own birth; he also recorded his father's subsequent attitude (as late as 1936) to his use of the name 'Kharms': 'Yesterday Papa told me that, as long as I am Kharms, my wants will continue to persecute me'.[4] On another bizarre 'family' level, he invented a brother, 'Ivan Ivanovich Kharms, former *"Privatdozent"* (visiting lecturer) at the University of St Petersburg' (*Polët*, p. 352; Gibian, *Black Coat*, p. 7).

The young Iuvachëv was educated at Peterschule, an establishment which gave its main instruction in German and also taught English, and later at the former Mariinskaia *gimnaziia* at Detskoe Selo (now Pushkin), under his maternal aunt, Natalia Ivanovna Koliubakina. Brief studies at electro-technical college and a course in cinematography followed (further details can be gleaned from Anatolii Aleksandrov's 'Chronology', translated here, and his introduction to *Polët*). The name 'Kharms' seems to have been devised while its bearer was still at school.[5] Among the large number of other pseudonyms which Iuvachëv employed or tried out were 'Daniil Dandan' and 'Kharms-Shardam'.

The predilection for the name 'Kharms' is thought to derive from an appreciation of the tension between the English words 'charms' and 'harms' (plus the German 'scharm', not to mention the actual German surname 'Harms'), but may also owe something to the similarity in sound to Sherlock Holmes: in his final year at school, he was said to be engrossed in Conan Doyle.[6] Sherlock Holmes, in any case, became a favourite pose later adopted by Kharms (pipe and deer-stalker being much in evidence in surviving photographs and sketches). A 1937 diary entry reads:

> I create a pose for myself and I have the character to keep to it. At one time my pose was that of an Indian, then Sherlock Holmes, then a yogi and now an irritable neurotic. The latter pose I would not like to sustain for my own sake. I'll have to think up a new pose.[7]

By 1925, 'Daniil Kharms' was established with his first wife, Ester Aleksandrovna Marcel-Rusakova, was a frequenter of Leningrad poetry readings and had been a professional poetry reciter. He gained admission to the Leningrad section of the All-Russian Union of Poets (one of the many groupings which preceded the formation in 1932 of the Union of Soviet Writers) and published a poem in a Poet's Union anthology of 1926 and another in an almanac of 1927. These two publications were to remain the only occasions that Kharms had been able to publish his 'adult' works during his whole lifetime. In

1926, Kharms and his friend Vvedensky wrote to Pasternak for help with publication (Vved. 2, p. 227),[8] and other projects for literary collections involving writers and critics more from the mainstream of Soviet literary life came to nothing (see Chronology). By 1928, Kharms and Vvedensky allowed themselves to be drawn into the realm of children's literature, which would afford them the only publishing opportunities open to them in the coming decade.

At first associated with such post-Futurist and *zaum*' (trans-sense) poets as Aleksandr Tufanov and Konstantin Olimpov, Kharms made the aquaintance in 1925 of Aleksandr Vvedensky (1904–41), who was to be his main friend and colleague for over a decade. Kharms and Vvedensky founded, or were closely associated with, a number of 'left art' avantgardist groupings of the second half of the 1920s. These included the largely theatrical 'Radiks' (presumably based upon the Latin *radix*, root), in which Kharms and Vvedensky associated with a group based at the Institute of the History of Arts, initiated by Georgii (or 'Gaga') Katsman, Boris (or 'Doivber') Levin, Sergei Tsimbal and the youthful Igor Bakhterev (born 1908, the last surviving figure from these circles); various other minor poets and musicians were fringe adherents.[9] Similarly, the 'Chinari' (a word invented by Vvedensky, based on *chin*, or 'rank'), sometimes regarding themselves as the (experimental) 'Left Flank' (*'Levyi flang'*), consisted for a while of Kharms, Vvedensky, Bakhterev and the subsequently famous poet, Nikolai Zabolotsky, with Konstantin Vaginov and Olimpov as loose associates.[10] Attempts were made to form an 'Academy of Left Classics' (see Chronology), bringing in the artists Malevich and Filonov, while Lidiia Ginzburg has recorded the proposed organisation of a 'Club of Semi-literate Scholars' (Kharms, Zabolotsky, L. Savelev (Lipavsky) and the comic poet Nikolai Oleinikov).[11] From the period of 'Radiks', becoming 'Left Flank', dates an irrecoverably lost show, named from a Vvedensky verse, entitled 'My Mother is all in Watches' (*'Moia mama vsia v chasakh'*: Vved. 2, pp. 230–7).

These loose groupings coalesced in 1927 into 'OBERIU' (the Union of Real Art: *'Ob"edinenie real'nogo iskusstva'*). This word, apparently invented by Bakhterev with the intention of avoiding any further -*izm* and achieving some distance, in name at least, from the now over-nuanced word 'left',[12] became the name under which this group of writers has come (sometimes, strictly speaking, anachronistically) to be known. The high point of the group's activities were the productions of the OBERIU spectacular 'Three Left Hours' (*'Tri levykh chasa'*) in 1928, which included comedy, verse, music, gimmicks and Kharms's absurdist play, *Elizaveta Bam*. OBERIU consisted of Kharms, Vvedensky, Zabolotsky, Vaginov, Bakhterev, Levin and Iurii Vladimirov, plus, more informally, Oleinikov, Lipavsky and Iakov Druskin (musician and philosopher).

Inheriting the legacy of Futurist art forms and Formalist aesthetics, the 'Oberiuty', then, considered themselves a 'left flank' of the literary avant-garde. The so-called 'OBERIU Manifesto' (published simply as 'OBERIU' in the Leningrad 'Posters of the House of Print' series, 1928) proclaims involvement in literature, fine arts, theatre and cinema, with a musical section under formation; it contains programmatic statements on social role, stressing again 'the left course in art', poetry, cinema and theatre, as well as notes on the leading Oberiuty participants. In poetry, the concentration was on broadening the meaning of the word (but not destroying it, as the *zaumniki* had done); in theatre and cinema, it was a matter of getting away from the traditional spotlight on plot, to allow other, more disparate, factors to come into play. The OBERIU approach claimed to be both revolutionary and universal: object, word and act were to be reinvigorated through 'collisions of verbal meanings'; logic and appearances would be challenged in depictions of a new relationship between art and life. In the case of *Elizaveta Bam*, for example, 'the dramatic plot is replaced by a scenic plot which arises spontaneously from all the elements of our spectacle'.[13]

Indeed, the almost one-to-one relationship between art and life became the hallmark of OBERIU activities. Their publicity antics and semi-scandalous public performances became, for a brief period, a highlight of Leningrad artistic life. A rooftop appearance on what is now the House of Books (*Dom knigi*) building to promote an OBERIU performance; simultaneous poetry readings and happenings; fancy-dress cavortings: all were grist to the OBERIU mill, in the traditions of the Cubo-Futurists in pre-revolutionary Russia and the Dadaists in Europe. Cinematic theory and practice, such as Eisenstein's 'Montage of Attractions', also come to mind. Iakov Druskin records:[14]

> At the end of the 1920s, Vvedensky said that Kharms does not create art, but is himself art. Kharms, at the end of the 1930s, used to say that the important thing for him was not art, but life: to make his life like art. This was not aestheticism: 'the creation of life like art' was, for Kharms, a category not of an aesthetic order but what would now be called an existential one.

## Introduction: Daniil Kharms, Black Miniaturist 7

Among the OBERIU catch-phrases were 'art is like a cupboard' and 'poems are not pies; we are not herring'; and a black, varnished cupboard indeed became a sign for art, when Kharms was wheeled in, on top of such an object, to read 'phonetic' verses to a bemused audience.[15]

Anecdotes abound of Kharms's activities, particularly in those years (see Chronology and the contribution to this volume by Tat'iana Nikol'skaia). Some versions of Kharms's lifestyle are disputed, such as the question of whether he ever kept a mysterious and purposeless machine in his flat.[16] There is evidence, though, that in addition to his more obvious artistic talents, Kharms enjoyed unusual abilities as, for example, a juggler, while his prowess in the billiard halls earned him the additional nick-name of 'Mister Twister'.[17] Socially, he was largely known as an eccentric, a clown or a dandy, and, to one memoirist, as 'the most original of originals'.[18]

However, as the 1920s gave way to the sombre thirties, Kharms's fortunes and his mood changed. Publishing possibilities, other than in children's literature, were non-existent; public performances by the Oberiuty were quickly frowned upon; bookings became rare occasions in small venues and then ceased. Cultural and political despair set in as his economic plight worsened. The time for propagating experimental modernist art, in the Stalinizing years of the late 1920s, or any reasonable expectation of tolerance towards such activities, had passed. By the 1930s, any such pretentions were positively dangerous. Even the sheltered pastures of children's literature, under the patronage of the redoubtable writer and translator Samuil Marshak, offered no guaranteed refuge. Although the early thirties seemed, at the time, a period of relaxation for writers after the end of the 'RAPP terror', this proved to be an illusion and, in any case, such a feeling of well-being probably did not extend to Kharms and his circle in Leningrad.

Hostile publicity had ensured the hurried disbandment of OBERIU as a group by 1930. However, Kharms and Vvedensky continued their 'playful' approach within children's literature, employing with considerable effect what had been a number of OBERIU-type devices. The OBERIU approach had been denounced from 1930 as 'reactionary sleight-of-hand' (see documents collected in the appendices to Vved. 2) and, at the end of 1931, Kharms, along with Vvedensky and others, was arrested and accused of 'deflecting the people from the building of socialism by means of his trans-sense verses'. However, the times then were still what Anna Akhmatova has called 'relatively vegetarian', and just a short period of exile in Kursk followed. In 1934 Kharms married Marina Vladimirovna Malich.

Work became ever harder to come by; Vvedensky moved to the Ukraine in the mid-thirties and things blackened still further when Oleinikov was arrested in 1937. At least one Kharms scholar (Vladimir Glotser) thinks Kharms was arrested again, presumably briefly, in that year too.[19].

It is not easy to attempt to gauge Kharms's literary reputation by the early 1930s (later he was likely to have been even less known). So little of his work had been published and the circles within which he operated were limited. We can glean, though, that he was somewhat in mode by 1932, being compared to Khlebnikov, and that he had been praised as a children's writer by no less a figure than Lunacharsky; he did not even meet Akhmatova before May 1940; however, Shostakovich was to be counted among his admirers and even contemplated composing to a Kharms text.[20]

Kharms tended to move from verse into prose as the 1930s wore on: poems and (usually verse) dramatic fragments gave way to very short stories, dialogues and philosophical (and even mathematical) pieces. His poverty and hunger were expressed in poetic fragments and diary entries: doom and gloom set in as Kharms felt drawn to Oblomov-like lethargy and to musing on immortality.[21] And yet this was the period in which Kharms wrote his most extraordinary prose miniatures, the 'Incidents' (*Sluchai*) cycle and his novella *Starukha* (*The Old Woman*). Here Kharms marshals all his powers for the creation of scenes of pointless violence, private terrorism and bizarre inter-relations, turning character and content, as well as context and communication, inside out. Wildly funny as his writing can be, it is often profoundly disturbing, not least when his private diaries and notebooks so resemble his fiction that any differentiation becomes virtually impossible: 'When I see a human being, I feel like hitting him in the face. It is so pleasant to hit a person in the face!' ('Kind Feelings', untitled in Kharms's notebook, *Black Coat*, p. 120). The main Kharmsian protagonist is an inadequate and practically brain-dead 'sub-person' (*nedochelovek*), to whom anything can and does happen and who represents, perhaps, in the words of Jean-Philippe Jaccard, 'a hypertrophied figure of the writer himself', condemned to an immobility anticipatory of actual death.[22] Such, no doubt, was the mood of the 1930s in Leningrad.

Thus did Kharms and Vvedensky survive the main purges of the 1930s. However, the outbreak of war brought new dangers: the arrest of Kharms came in August 1941, while that of Vvedensky took place the following month in Kharkov. Vvedensky died in December of that year and Kharms in February of 1942.

## Introduction: Daniil Kharms, Black Miniaturist 9

Kharms was arrested, reportedly, when the caretaker of the building in which he lived called him down to the yard for something: a Black Maria stood by and he was taken away, half-dressed, in his bedroom slippers (see Chronology). Various stories and theories surround Kharms's arrest, which was ostensibly for the spreading of 'counter-revolutionary defeatist agitation', while the part which may have been played by denunciations remains unknown. In the first place, Kharms was seen as a provocative eccentric, out of tune with the times, who affected anglicisms. Secondly, he was a suspect person by connection with his first wife, Ester Rusakova, sister-in-law of the writer Victor Serge and daughter of Aleksandr Rusakov (an old émigré revolutionary, subsequently accused of oppositionist tendencies).[23] Thirdly, his friends Oleinikov and Zabolotsky had been arrested in 1937 and 1938 respectively. Fourthly, he remained a marked man from his own earlier arrest(s).

Any of these factors would have been sufficient in the Soviet Union of 1937–9, or in a Leningrad facing likely German occupation in 1941. Recent evidence unearthed by Mikhail Meilakh, in the most ironic context of his own dealings with the KGB, suggests that the 1932 business may have been largely to blame: he and his associates had been convicted then of the dissemination of harmful, anti-Soviet literature in the children's sphere (cited here was Kharms's published story of 1928, in which two boys want to fly to Brazil: see Chronology).[24]

There exist also conflicting theories as to whether Kharms died in a Leningrad prison, or in deportation in Novosibirsk (see Chronology). However, Meilakh's account now deduces that Kharms's final macabre tussles with the NKVD, as grotesque as anything in his fiction, involved a feigned madness. The result seems to have been an acquittal on the 'criminal' charges, followed by deliverance into the tender mercies of enforced psychiatric care. Death, seemingly in a Leningrad prison hospital, ensued from either the treatment itself, or from starvation. Kharms may even have been, therefore, an early victim of psychiatric abuse.[25] It is doubtful whether any more information will now come to light.

\* \* \*

Kharms's archive, or a great part thereof, was preserved by Iakov Druskin (1902–80). From the 1960s, Soviet scholars began to work on it and, from this source and others, publications began to trickle out: occasionally in the Soviet Union, but more particularly abroad, in Eastern Europe and in the West. After Druskin's death, the archive was lodged in the Leningrad Public (Saltykov-Shchedrin) Library. From 1962, the children's works of Kharms began to be reprinted in the Soviet Union. Kharms began to be mentioned in memoirs, too, from the 1960s and the odd scholarly paper devoted to the Oberiuty appeared. Until Gorbachëv's policy of *glasnost'* took real effect, however (from 1986), only a small fraction of Kharms's literary production for adults had achieved Soviet publication. One Kharms scholar (Vladimir Glotser) blames the archivists for the prolonged neglect of the Oberiuty.[26] A flood of newspaper, magazine and journal publications of works by Kharms, particularly from 1987, has seen a considerable part of his *oeuvre* finally made available to the Soviet reader. This process culminated with a substantial volume of selected works at the end of 1988, edited by Anatolii Aleksandrov (*Polët*). There are still, at the time of writing, a number of his stories known in the West which seem not yet to have attained Soviet publication (in particular, some of the 'nastier' ones) and the poetry is so far there only partially known. There would also seem to be further works as yet unpublished altogether. However, the situation is fluid and a number of publications of substance are known to be in preparation.

In the West, along with sporadic publication of the Russian texts in émigré journals and elsewhere, there came a book-length selection in 1974 (*Izb.*) and translations began to appear (*Russia's Lost Lit.*). However, textual doubts surrounded many of these earlier printings. In 1978 an annotated collected works of Kharms began publication (*Sob. proizv.*), published in Bremen by the Verlag K-Presse (appropriately enough, the 'Kafka Press'), under the editorship, from Leningrad, of Mikhail Meilakh and Vladimir Erl. Three volumes appeared (two in 1978 and a third in 1980); the introduction was delayed for 'technical reasons', and the series underwent an abrupt (but fortunately only temporary) pause with the arrest of Meilakh in 1983, for activities apparently in part connected with his OBERIU publishing programme;[27] Meilakh also published in the USA a two-volume complete works of Vvedensky (Vved. 1–2). The K-Presse Kharms edition is scheduled to run to nine or ten volumes. Publication resumed, following Meilakh's release under the 1987 amnesty, and volume four has appeared (1988), completing Kharms's poetic output. The remaining volumes, featuring the prose, drama, letters and miscellaneous writings are still awaited. Fuller academic editions may also be expected from Soviet publishing houses.

## Introduction: Daniil Kharms, Black Miniaturist

Meanwhile, a Yugoslav film on Kharms has achieved some success (see Milena Michalski's essay), translations have appeared in a number of languages and Kharms at last begins to enjoy cult status amid the atmosphere of fragmentation which currently pervades the Soviet Union: OBERIU evenings, theatrical compilations and Kharms 'mono-spectaculars' have become almost commonplace.

\* \* \*

Definitive assessment of the achievement of Daniil Kharms must await full publication of his works and further surrounding materials, while the task of placing his *oeuvre* in the context of both Russian and European literature is still in the early stages. Some of the problems of approaching OBERIU poetry are outlined in essays here by Lazar Fleishman and Nina Perlina, while Meilakh's exposition of *Elizaveta Bam* prepares the ground for its consideration within the European theatre of the absurd (see also Jaccard, 1990). Regarding the prose, currently by far the best known body of Kharms's work (as recent translations demonstrate: *Black Coat* 1987; *Plummeting*, 1989), the situation is a little further advanced. As well as general essays (see the contributions here by Jaccard and Anthony Anemone), it is now possible (following the publication of *Pölet*, 1988; and Glotser, 1989) to begin considering *Sluchai* ('Incidents') as a cycle (Robin Aizlewood). Studies of *Starukha* (*The Old Woman*) are now almost plentiful (our contribution is made by Rosanna Giaquinta, in terms of the fantastic), while that here of '*Upadanie*' ('The Falling') by Aleksandr Kobrinsky will no doubt be the first of many to analyse a separate short story.[28]

Many of the issues broached here will require both further explanation and future exploration. The prose miniature – a form which Kharms may ultimately be judged to have made his own – has long been a genre more commonly found in Russian literature than elsewhere. Among the disparate writings that come to mind, various as they are, mention may be made, from the nineteenth century, of: the *feuilletons* of Dostoevsky, the prose poems (*Senilia*) of Turgenev and the shortest stories of Garshin and Chekhov; and, from the twentieth century, short pieces by Zamiatin, Olesha and Zoshchenko and, more recently, the aphoristic writings of Andrei Siniavsky [Abram Terts] and the prose poems of Solzhenitsyn. In spirit, Kharms clearly belongs to the Russian tradition of double-edged humour that extends from the word-play and irrelevancy of Gogol and the jaundiced mentality of Dostoevsky's underground to, in recent times, the intertextual parody of Siniavsky and the satirical absurd of Voinovich. Within the fruitful strand of Russian literature which sprang from a Futurist-Formalist base during the experimental high-point of Russian prose in the early twenties, Kharms has clear affinities (stylistic, linguistic, thematic and philosophical) with certain of the writings of Zoshchenko, Olesha and Platonov.

In a verse and prose sequence entitled 'Sablia' ('The Sabre', 1929), Kharms singles out Goethe, Blake, Lomonosov, Gogol, Koz'ma Prutkov and Khlebnikov for special admiration (*Polët*, p. 439); elsewhere, his approbation falls on Gogol, Prutkov, Meyrink, Hamsun, Edward Lear and Lewis Carroll; in his younger days he wrote out, in English, works by Blake, Kipling, Carroll and A. A. Milne.[29] On a general European plane, in terms at least of affinity or parallel, it seems scarcely necessary to mention the various modernist, Dadaist, surrealist, absurdist and other avantgardist movements. Borges wrote brief masterpieces in a somewhat different vein, while Beckett and Kafka are two names which frequently occur in comparison with Kharms. Jaccard (below) discusses some aspects of Beckett's work in this connection. Kafka's diaries (not to mention his fiction and his letters) are full of feelings of isolation in the face of 'totalitarian' pressures (actual or imagined) and share many Kharmsian obsessions: with the power of words, with parts of the body, with inkwells and with falling: 'When I sit down at the desk I feel no better than someone who falls and breaks both legs in the middle of the traffic of the Place de l'Opéra'.[30] Or, take the following remarks made by Kafka in a letter to Max Brod:

> If you only knew how much I have to do! In my four district headquarters – apart from all my other work – people fall, as if they were drunk, off scaffolds and into machines, all the planks tip up, there are landslides everywhere, all the ladders slip, everything one puts up falls down and what one puts down one falls over oneself. All these young girls in china factories who incessantly hurl themselves downstairs with mountains of crockery give one a headache.[31]

However, let us pause briefly on surrealism, particularly as represented by André Breton (who himself coined the term 'black humour'). Despite Druskin's view that 'the verses of Vvedensky and Kharms have nothing in common either with "literature of the subconscious" or with surrealism',[32] the prose of Kharms, at least,

## Introduction: Daniil Kharms, Black Miniaturist    13

bears quite close comparison with surrealist theory. The 'leftism' of OBERIU is arguably the counterpart of the subversion aimed at by the surrealists, even if the former did not so overtly share the Marxian and Freudian emphases of the latter. The failure of the narrator of *Starukha* to write his story within a story might be taken almost as a satire of surrealist automatism, and yet the narrative in itself might be a product of that very same phenomenon. Similarly, the surrealist belief in association may be reflected in Kharms's use of obsessive motifs, while a common approach to dialectical thinking can be seen both in certain of the writings produced and in the shared philosophical antecedents (involving in each case romantic thought and its predecessors in Hermetic and pre-Socratic philosophy). The literary antecedents of surrealism, which are acknowledged to include Swift, Sade and Carroll, bear at least a family resemblance to those of Kharms.

The Oberiuty would surely have shared many of the sentiments of Breton's essay 'Introduction to the Discourse on the Paucity of Reality', particularly with regard to the position of language: 'Does not the mediocrity of our universe depend essentially on our power of enunciation?'.[33] Kharms certainly also dreaded 'the deplorable inspectors who pursue us even after we leave school [and who] still make their rounds of our homes and our lives' (p. 26). Kharms would also have recognised, perhaps even as actuality, the 'resolution of those two seemingly contradictory states, dream and reality, into a sort of absolute reality, of *surreality*, so to speak', as propounded in Breton's 1934 lecture, 'What is Surrealism?' (p.126). He would also have shared the surrealist interest in the simulation of mental diseases and Dali's 'paranoiac-critical method' (pp. 136–7), while who, if not Kharms, might have been fulfilling the surrealist recipe for the future novel?

> When, however will we have the novel in which the characters, having been abundantly defined with a minimum of particularities, will act in an altogether foreseeable way in view of an unforeseen result? And, inversely, the novel in which psychology will not hastily perform its great but futile duties at the expense of the characters and events but will really *hold* between two blades a fraction of a second, to surprise there the germs of incidents? (p. 135).

Finally, the *Anthology of Black Humour* (1940), said to embody 'a deliberate critical attitude in surrealism', set out to challenge 'all forms of accepted belief' (p. 188). Breton later referred (p.246) to 'the psychic apparatus of *black humour* which, at a certain temperature, can alone play the role of a safety valve', 'an extreme means for the "ego" to surmount the traumas of the exterior world' (p. 204). Where was such a temperature reached, if not in Leningrad in the 1930s? The Surrealist Manifesto had declared (p. 125): 'What is admirable about the fantastic is that there is no longer a fantastic; there is only the real'. Kharms might have said the same of the absurd.

The Druskin 'school' of philosophy, in which Kharms participated, shared a concern for the (in)adequacy of language as a means of communication, which runs from Plato, through the romantics, to the extreme linguistic relativism of such twentieth-century exponents as Fritz Mauthner, whose nihilistic conclusions about the relativity of truth according to differing perspectives resembled those of Nietzsche.[34] In addition to such epistemological nihilism, Kharms must also have confronted the kind of existential nihilism familiar to us from Camus (see Jaccard). However, whether deriving from Druskin or elsewhere, there are hints in Kharms's fiction and diaries of mystical aspirations, at least, which may have been attempts to climb out from the nihilistic absurd. The story 'Pakin and Rakukin', for example, appends just such an ending to what is otherwise a typical scene of ludicrous Kharmsian persecution, and thereby concludes the *Sluchai* cycle; *Starukha* may be read as, among other things, an extended exercise in this direction.

As an interim indicator to Kharms as a European literary type, we might perhaps stress the combination, or the convergence, of three principal interlocking factors. The first involves Kharms's personal psychological propensities (including the extremes of splenetic feeling which he sometimes termed '*Ignavia*'[35]): or human nature, with a Kharmsian face. The second arises out of the currency of Russo-European avantgardist artistic trends: or the theory and practice of the human condition. Thirdly, but certainly not least, we have the grotesque historical reality of Kharms's environment: or the seemingly all-pervasive trauma of human repression.

Yet there remain qualities in Kharms which seem to defy categorization and comparison, qualities which perhaps come across through his adoption of what might be described as a poetics of extremism. One obvious example of this is his brevity. If many of his stories seem micro-texts of concise inconsequentiality, there remain others which incommode the printer even less: consider, for example, the following text, which begins '*Starichok chesalsia* ...' (*Izb.*, p. 120; translation mine):

An old man was scratching himself with both hands. In places where he couldn't reach with two hands, the old man scratched himself with one, but, to make up for it, very, very quickly. And, while he was at it, he blinked quickly too.

Another feature of Kharmsian extremism, frequently commented on in this collection, is his tireless quest for means to undermine his own narratives, or to enable them to self-destruct. Even more striking to many readers is the recurrence of Kharms's strange and extreme obsessions: with falling, accidents, victimization, mindless violence and sudden death.

A possible ancestry for such Kharmsian 'incidents' (whether within the *Sluchai* cycle or, in the broader sense, outside it) can be seen in a multitude of pre-existing genres: the fable, the parable, the folk tale, the children's story, the philosophical or dramatic dialogue, the comic monologue, pantomine (or *commedia dell' arte*), carnival and the silent movie (not for nothing did Max Brod describe Kafka's remarks in his letter (above) as Chaplinesque; not for nothing did the OBERIU declaration include a section on cinema). All seem to be present somewhere, in compressed form and devoid of explanations, description and other standard trappings. Kharms, indeed, seems to serve up, transform or abort the bare bones of the sub-plots, plot fragments and authorial devices of world literature, from the narratives of antiquity and classical European fiction to the metafictions of the present period: from *The Satyricon*, through Cervantes, to Calvino.

Of such intertextual antecedents, let us mention here only Knut Hamsun's *Mysteries*, a novel whose impact on *Starukha* has been previously noted; the following passage, part of one of the protagonist Nagel's fantasizing monologues, seems to contain the seeds of many a Kharmsian mini-story:[36]

... Imagine hearing someone brushing against the walls on a dark night. You're wide awake, sitting at a table smoking a pipe, but aware that your senses are somewhat blurred. ... you can see a shadow on the wall. ... You stand there facing the shadow and you are face to face with an unknown person – a man of medium height wearing a black-and-white woollen scarf around his neck, with incredibly blue lips. He looks like the jack of clubs in a Norwegian deck of cards. You're more curious than afraid and you walk right up to the fellow and give him a withering look. But he doesn't move, though you're so close to him you can see his eyes blink and know he's as alive as you are. Then you try to be friendly . . . And you leer at him. But he still doesn't move and you don't know what to do next. Then you take a step back, poke at him with the stem of your pipe, and say: 'Bah!' Still his expression doesn't change. That's going too far! Your anger mounts, and you give him a good whack. The man is definitely there in the room, though he doesn't react to your whack. He doesn't keel over but sticks both hands deep down in his pockets, and shrugs his shoulders, as if to say: 'Well, what is that supposed to mean?' 'What is that supposed to mean?' you repeat, and by now furious, you give him another whack in the pit of the stomach. After this, the man begins to fade away. You watch him slowly vanish, his form becoming more and more blurred, until at last there is nothing left but his stomach, which also eventually disappears. All this time he has kept his hands in his pockets, looking at you with that same defiant, scornful expression, as if to say: 'What's that supposed to mean?'

One possible originator for this Hamsun-Kharms line of bodily dismemberment is Edgar Allan Poe's 'The Man That Was Used Up'.

\* \* \*

Kharms's prose may be discussed within a framework of psychology, one of linguistics or of communications theory; or, indeed, with reference to surrounding reality. Another approach is by way of the theory of joke or comedy. This may be Freudian in slant; indeed, Kharms makes a rare appearance (to date) in general studies of literature in Elizabeth Wright's *Psychoanalytic Criticism* (1984), in which '*Golubaia tetrad' No. 10*' ('Blue Notebook No. 10', or 'The Red-Haired Man') features as the book's epigraph: moreover, 'Psychoanalytic criticism', we are informed, 'explores texts for the "free" association that tell of the struggle between a body and the society on which it depends'.[37]

The body also features prominently in Jerry Palmer's study of film and television comedy, *The Logic of the Absurd* (1987). The most common of 'the peripeteias of traditional farce' is here said to be 'the infliction of pain and/or indignity on the human body'.[38] Such a 'peripeteia' (or surprise, in Palmer's somewhat un-Aristotelian use of

## Introduction: Daniil Kharms, Black Miniaturist 17

the term) is the receiving of a pot of paint on the head, say while walking under a ladder, or the rather more Kharmsian brick, for no reason at all. With any intellectual involvement, to avoid or minimise such an occurrence, we are in the realm of the 'gag' (p. 45). Gags, which may be totally unpredictable or indeed totally predictable, when strung together with some degree of linkage, form a narrative. Other factors involved may include the dislocation of natural laws and/or narrative expectations, the exploitation of coincidence, of 'Murphy's law' ('if it can go wrong it will', p. 145) and of aggression, plus a tension, or balance, between plausibility and implausibility: 'the logic of the absurd demands ... that any event – in order to be funny – should be simultaneously surprising, implausible and plausible' (p. 136). Much, of course, depends on the balance between plausible and implausible: excessive implausibility may tip the absurd into nonsense, but there is likely to be a particular stress on all these factors in 'crazy comedy', as opposed to 'realist comedy' (p. 145).

We are, clearly, again very close to the universe of many of Kharms's shorter prose texts and we may well feel more at home with this kind of theoretical approach than with that of 'traditional literary theory which insists that the defining feature of comedy is its specific narrative rhythm and not its humorous qualities' (p. 143). The OBERIU history of performance art should also not be forgotten. We need here test the applicability of such an approach on no more than one Kharms text; let us take '*Stoliar Kushakov*' ('The Carpenter Kushakov': *Polët*, pp. 361–2; *Black Coat*, pp. 55–6).

Kushakov undergoes a series of falls (and pratfalls) on the icy street (surprise after surprise). The implausibility of coincidence is balanced against the plausibility of the slippery conditions, while the reader's awareness of repetition yields swiftly to a sense of predictability. The 'gag' of buying multiple bandages, to offset the predictability of falling, as suggested by the chemist, is refused by Kushakov on the grounds that 'I'm not going to fall any more'. Nevertheless, Kushakov becomes so covered in plasters that he is not recognised and faces the further (unexpected) surprise (or more genuine peripeteia) of being refused admittance to his flat. He spits and goes out to the street: we are not told whether or not he falls again, but the previous sequence seems to have been broken. The plausibility factor here is low enough to make the story clearly absurd, but it is nevertheless sufficient to keep it this side of nonsense.[39]

Such a model may be applied to Kharms texts, achieving varying results with regard to comedy, absurdity and nonsense, with appropriate allowance made, along the lines of the surrealist view of black humour, for contextual and thematic variables – notably the impingement of Stalinist reality – which may be particularly strong in certain texts. George Orwell's view that whatever is funny is subversive may not hold universally, depending on the particular constituents in the communication process, the ambiguities inherent in humour and the variability of context, circumstance and perception. However, there is little doubt that, in Stalinist Russia, Kharms's experimental prose would and should be construed as subversive. Notwithstanding this over-arching factor, Kharms was experimenting too, as even a casual familiarity with his prose will reveal, with contradictions in expectations and mixes of plausibility and implausibility (the 'wrong' mix as well as the right one: the 'over the top' and unfunny, as well as the hilarious), using different brands of discourse (content and context) and such Kharmsian authorial devices as the narrational self-destruct and the non-punchline.

Kharms, then, turned his surgical glance on both the extraordinary world around him and on its representations, past and present, in story telling and other printed forms. He thus operates, in the main, against an often precise, if somehow abstracted, Leningrad background; he reflects aspects both of Soviet life and its various literary forms; and he passes sardonic and despairing comment on the period in which he lived. He ventures also, in a ludicrous manner, into historical areas, parodying the ways in which well-respected worthies (Pushkin, Gogol, Ivan Susanin) are enshrined both in legend and in modern print. This practice doubtless stems from specific cases of the glorification of such figures in Soviet journalism: the relating of the work of Kharms to its contemporary sources is just beginning (see Fleishman's essay below).

In the modern idiom, apart from theatre of the absurd and theatre of cruelty, Kharms's fictions anticipate in some almost primeval way almost everything from the animated screenplay and the cartoon strip to the video-nasty. Its nearest literary counterpart is perhaps some of the work of American minimalist writing of the past decades. To adopt a broadcasting metaphor, the prose of Kharms, with its skeletal terseness, has the stark but compelling quality, perhaps, of 'steam' radio, as opposed to the comprehensive vacuousness on offer from the colour TV transmissions of fuller fictional forms. Once again, it is both the times and the environment in which he wrote that are striking here. Kharms, the black miniaturist, is an exponent not so much of the modernist 'end of the Word' (in a Joycean sense) as of a post-modernist, minimalist and infantilist 'end of the Story' (in a sense perhaps most analogous to Beckett). Such a trend is usually taken to be a post-war cultural phenomenon of the nuclear age. However, the Holocaust and Hiroshima may have been felt prematurely in the Leningrad of the bleak 1930s.

\* \* \*

As the pace of Kharms publications has increased, so has scholarly literature on the Oberiuty been growing. The present volume is intended as a significant contribution to this process. We here make available to the English reader substantial articles by Meilakh and Fleishman, previously published in Russian, as well as Aleksandrov's 'Chronology' (from *Polët*), along with an essay in a more European context by Jaccard (already published in French). The remaining offerings, by Russian, European, British and American scholars, were specially written for this collection. At a comparatively late stage we were supplied with a valuable essay-memoir by Iakov Druskin, friend and associate of Kharms, written in the 1970s and only partially published in Russian.

We cover in particular the prose, aspects of theatre and a little of the poetry, remaining fully conscious of the areas of Kharms's work still requiring fuller exploration: the poetry as a whole, the children's writing, and the philosophical pieces (not to mention the ideological tendencies underlying Kharms's work overall and the ideational influences thereupon). It is to be hoped that our example here will at least serve to point the way in these, and perhaps other, directions.

## NOTES TO INTRODUCTION

1. A. Galich, *Pokolenie obrechënnykh*, 3rd ed. (Frankfurt: Possev, 1975) pp. 124–8. Aleksandr Arkad'evich Galich (1919–77) was a Soviet playwright, turned dissident poet and balladeer, who died in emigration; for a detailed examination of his career, see Gerald Stanton Smith, *Songs to Seven Strings: Russian Guitar Poetry and Soviet 'Mass Song'* (Bloomington: Indiana University Press, 1984); and Alexander Galich, *Songs and Poems*, ed. and translated by G. S. Smith (Ardis: Ann Arbor, 1983), which does not include '*Legenda o tabake*'.
2. See Kharms's diary entries, an interim selection of which are printed in *Knizhnoe obozrenie*, 3, 19 January, 1990, pp. 8–9.

3. For more on I. P. Iuvachëv, see Aleksandrov, 1988b, pp. 8–10 (and references thereto); see also, however, Jaccard, 1989.
4. *Knizhnoe obozrenie*, 3, 1990, p. 8. For examples of autobiographical writings, see *Polët*, pp. 453–4, 455.
5. Glotser, 1988a, p. 129.
6. Bakhterev, 1984, p. 63; see also Aleksandrov, 1980, pp. 66–7.
7. *Knizhnoe obozrenie*, 3, 1990, p. 9.
8. Things may not have been helped by Pasternak being addressed as 'Boris Leont'evich' (rather than 'Leonidovich'). There is no mention of a reply. This may, or may not, account for Pasternak's being included in Kharms's diary list of 'what is bad' (*Knizhnoe obozrenie*, 3, 1990, p. 8).
9. Bakhterev, 1984, pp. 67–9.
10. Druskin, 1989, p. 103. Compare also the verb *chinit'*, in its various senses; the word *chinar* (plane tree); the verb *sochiniat'* (to compose); and the possible hint of Khlebnikov's *Changara-Zangezi*.
11. Ginzburg, 1989, p. 383. See also Robin Milner-Gulland, 'Zabolotsky's *Vremya*', *Essays in Poetics*, 6, 1 (1981) 86–98 (p. 92).
12. Bakhterev, 1984, pp. 86–7.
13. *Afishi Doma pechati*, 2, 1928, pp. 11–13. Reprinted in Milner-Gulland, 1970; *Izb.*, pp. 287–98; English translation in *Black Coat*, pp. 245–54.
14. Druskin, 1989, p. 108.
15. Bakhterev, 1984, pp. 89–90; Zhukova, 1983, p. 226. For descriptions of OBERIU evenings, see Bakhterev, pp. 89–91; and Olegri, 1982, pp. 199–200.
16. Compare Lifshits, 1969, pp. 241–3; and Druskin, 1985, p. 400.
17. Semënov, 1982, p. 264; Olegri, 1982, p. 199.
18. Semënov, 1982, p. 258.
19. Glotser, 1988a, p. 132; Glotser, 1988b, p. 16.
20. Ginzburg, 1989, p. 142; Semënov, 1982, p. 259; Kublanovskii, 1988, p. 10; Fëdorov, 1976.
21. *Knizhnoe obozrenie*, 3, 1990, p. 9.
22. Jaccard, 1988b, p. 740. On the *nedochelovek*, see the essay by Druskin, translated below.
23. See Fleishman's essay (translated here), note 22; Victor Serge, *Memoirs of a Revolutionary*, trans. by Peter Sedgwick (London: Writers and Readers, 1984) pp. 277–8.
24. Meilakh, 1989, p. x.
25. Meilakh, 1989. For a slightly divergent account (fuller than in the Chronology printed here), see Aleksandrov, 1990.
26. Glotser, 1988a, p. 129.
27. See Meilakh, 1989.
28. Even Kharms's shortest texts elicit comment; for example, on '*Starichok chesalsia* ...' (quoted below), see Nakhimovsky, 1982, p. 67.
29. *Knizhnoe obozrenie*, 3, 1990, p. 9; Aleksandrov, 1988b, p. 12.
30. *The Diaries of Franz Kafka, 1910–23*, ed. by Max Brod (Harmondsworth: Penguin, 1972) p. 29. On the topic of Kafka and totalitarianism,

see John Hoyles, *Modern Literature and Totalitarianism: European Writers, 1900–1950*, (Harvester: forthcoming); I am grateful to this study for several references to Kafka and to Breton. On Kafka and Kharms, see also Milner-Gulland, 1984. Another author to offer parallels with Kharms is Flann O'Brien (see Maxton, 1989).
31. Max Brod, *The Biography of Franz Kafka*, trans. by G. Humphrey Roberts (London: Secker & Warburg, 1947) p. 70.
32. Druskin, 1985, p. 381.
33. André Breton, *What is Surrealism? Selected Writings*, ed. by Franklin Rosemont (London: Pluto Press, 1978, reprinted 1989) pp. 17–28 (25). Page references to this edition follow in the text.
34. See Donald A. Crosby, *The Specter of the Absurd: Sources and Criticisms of Modern Nihilism* (Albany: State University of New York Press, 1988) pp. 23–6.
35. Jaccard, 1988b, p. 734; Gibian, 1987, pp. 9–10.
36. Knut Hamsun, *Mysteries*, trans. by Gerry Bothmer (London: Picador, 1976) pp. 123–4. Cf. the following passage (p. 233): 'I've had an odd and beautiful dream about you. I dreamed that you were in the middle of a swamp, that I had been tormenting and bullying you, and that you kept thanking me. You threw yourself down and thanked me for not having bullied you and tortured you even more. It was a lovely dream.' On Hamsun and *Starukha* (which labours some rather dubious parallels but ignores these passages), see Scotto, 1986. Further Kharmsian motifs may be found elsewhere in Hamsun's work: for example, the novel *Hunger* includes mention of a non-existent red-haired man, disparities with clocks and time, and instances of what Kobrinsky (in his essay below) calls 'quasi-nomination'. See also Aizlewood (1990) for further comments on Hamsun and Kharms.
37. Elizabeth Wright, *Psychoanalytic Criticism: Theory in Practice* (London and New York: Methuen, 1984), pp. xiii, 179.
38. Jerry Palmer, *The Logic of the Absurd: On Film and Television Comedy* (London: BFI Publishing, 1987), p. 44. Page references follow in the text.
39. For a summary of the OBERIU theory of nonsense, see Druskin, 1989, pp. 108–9.

# 2 On Daniil Kharms[1]
## Iakov Druskin

Artists can be divided into types according to whether their art is directly connected with life, or not. Kharms and Vvedensky were both keenly aware of the distinction. At the end of the 1920s, Vvedensky said that Kharms was not creating art, but was himself art. At the end of the 1930s, Kharms used to say that the most important thing for him had always been not art, but life: to make his life into art. This is not aestheticism since 'making life into art' was not an aesthetic category for Kharms, but, as we now say, an existential one.

Kharms had a sense of life as miracle and he wanted to make his life into a miracle. This is why miracles feature in many of his stories. Very typical is the story of the man who was capable of working miracles, but never in his life performed a single one; the consciousness that he *could* was enough for him.[2] Miracle, the understanding of life as miracle and as an absolutely purposeless one at that, miracle as miracle; this is the first and one of the foremost ideas which determined Kharms's writings, his life, the close tie between them, the very inseparability of his creativity from his life. Kharms thought that if not everyone, then at least most people were consciously or unconsciously seeking or expecting a miracle, not, I repeat, a miracle aimed at anything in particular, but a purposeless one. Purposelessness is in general one of Kharms's characteristic qualities; for example he could not stand any playing – whether cards or chess – for money. He would watch a game of chess, and he played chess himself, but if anyone began playing for money he would leave immediately. Miracle for him was similarly purposeless.

Miracle also had a second peculiarity for Kharms: very often his miracles are incomprehensible and this is connected with their purposelessness. Take one of his stories on the theme of miracle: a man decides that if he stands every day for an hour facing the cupboard eventually a miracle will occur. Days go by, perhaps weeks, and every day he stands in front of the cupboard and still there is no miracle. And so from boredom he examines the picture hanging on the wall and suddenly remembers: surely, this picture does not hang above the cupboard but on the wall behind it and to see the picture you would have to rise at least one or two metres in the air. The miracle had already occurred and he had not even noticed it happening. But there it was, he must be hanging in mid-air since he could see the picture hanging behind the cupboard. Kharms told me this story when the two of us were out for one of our walks; after Kharms's disappearance I found this sketch among his papers, written almost word for word as he had related it to me, and also a story based on the same theme which Kharms thought was unsuccessful (the story, not the theme), so he had not shown the story, or read it, to anyone . . .[3]

In any society, in any culture, there exists a range of conventions and restraints without which no society can function. Freud included rules of grammar and semantics among such conventions and restraints. But they also include rules of behaviour, for example, politeness, and many other things which, by habitual psychological association, in society, culture and art and in our general picture of life, are considered to be universally recognised, unquestioned and fixed (in Kierkegaard's terms).

There is a tale by Hans Andersen called 'The Emperor's New Clothes'. People create fetishes for themselves and then believe in them. Bacon called these idols. The few create the idols, but the many believe in them. Some cunning people thought up the idea of sewing a costume for the king which could only be seen by people who were clever. The king and all the people believed it and, although they could see the king was naked, they thought that they only saw him like that because they were stupid. Others were afraid of being called stupid and therefore kept quiet. And only the little boy said, 'But the king's got nothing on' and then everyone saw that the king was naked.

In some of his stories Kharms is like that little boy. He was not afraid to say, 'But the king's got nothing on'. This applies to many of the idols people create, but not, of course, to faith. Faith is not created by people. Kharms saw that mechanised life, when it becomes ossified in automatised ways of thinking, feeling and living, was worthless and empty; he saw the emptiness and senselessness of existence determined by phrases like, 'Everyone does it like that' and 'it's the done thing'. Kharms demolishes the fixities, that is to say the automatism of thought, feeling and everyday life. A person may live in religious, a-religious, or anti-religious automatism – and the first kind is no better and may be even worse than the last. Kharms exposes not the petty bourgeoisie, not the philistine, but the automatism of any kind of life, whether petty bourgeois or intellectual, be it super-educated, religious or anti-religious.

Religious automatism is actually anti-religious, the worst form of anti-religiosity is Pharisaism. It is not Kharms's stories which are nonsensical and alogical, but the life which he describes in them. The formal senselessness and situational alogicality in his work, and the humour, were a means of exposing life, of expressing the real nonsense of automatised existence, of some of the real conditions peculiar to every human being. So he used to say that there were two significant things in life: humour and sanctity. Sanctity was connected with the concept of miracle. He meant by sanctity authentic life, living life. He used humour to expose inauthentic, stagnant, dead life – life that is not life, but merely the dead shell of life, impersonal existence. And here once again is the connection between his writings and his life: in life he was the little boy who could see and who said, 'But the king has nothing on'.

Humour, as I have already said, was seen by Kharms as one of the two significant things in life. He did not like satire, however, precisely because of its partiality: satire is directed at something and on behalf of something – it ridicules, or negates something [...]⁴

Kharms was fascinated by evil, by the root of evil in human beings. He was, however, neither a philosopher nor a moralist, but a writer, though undoubtedly one with a philosophical bent. So even in his more horrific stories, he is not moralising, but laughing, while he exposes evil, narrow-mindedness and stupidity, and his laughter at times is no less horrific than the laughter of Gogol, whom he loved very much and whose work is linked with his own. One of the themes of his stories and poems is that of the complacent and self-satisfied sub-person [*nedochelovek*] who recognises no moral principles or values. Particularly horrific are some of these stories and poems written in the first person. They are funny when you start reading them. But gradually the laughter as it were dies down and finally turns to horror. They are written with such direct artistic conviction that sometimes it even seems as if the first-person, by whom the story is told, is the same as the author. Kharms was not of course the hero of these horrific stories and poems, though in some of the pieces Kharms's three main themes – life in miracle, the exposure of some of the aspects of life which are covered over by hypocrisy, and the sub-person – are so interwoven that a new kind of literary genre is the result. This genre is not easily defined: is it an entry in a diary, a philosophical conjecture, a short story, or a poem? The horrific in these pieces goes beyond the limits of art.

In 1936 Kharms wrote: 'I once saw a fly and a bedbug fighting. It was so terrible that I ran out into the street and made off the devil knows where. It is the same in this album. You write something nasty and then it's already too late.' (*Black Coat*, p. 121). This 'nastiness' he wrote of was something unpleasant, not funny but actually horrific. We are reminded of Gogol's attitude towards his negative heroes. But the comparison of Gogol with Kharms shows up not only the similarities but perhaps also the contrast between them.

In Kharms's writings the formal literary boundaries disappear: it is hard to decide whether some of his pieces are poetry or prose, autobiographical note, or short story, a new form or a stylisation, or an old form 'made strange'. And in the same imperceptible way laughter turns into lament, the comic into the horrific, what is normally regarded as something elevated becomes something low, and the relativity of human measures and standards of what is high and low, good and evil, is exposed.

Kharms had a naive, almost infantile cynicism. This is why sometimes he expressed the kind of thoughts which every person thinks deep down but keeps hidden even from themselves. Everyone thinks bad thoughts but, from an unconscious inner Pharisaism, they try to cover them up with a pseudo-poetic form. Kharms completely sincerely and naively failed to understand why this should be necessary, and in his stories and in conversation he exposed the lie of this pseudo-poetic form. In actual fact, this is not really cynicism, but the naivety of the wise child who has noticed that the king is naked. This boy has not yet been besmirched by human stupidity and prejudice, by the wisdom of the age; in a certain respect he is still Adam before the Fall. So he just does not understand why certain phenomena of physiological life should be hushed up, why it is considered cynical to speak of them. He says what other people think but consider indecent to utter, sometimes even to themselves. Kharms's interest in physiology, his stress on it and his naturalism, even, in some stories, notes and verses, is primarily of an infantile kind, like a child's interest in analurinary functions. Here once again Kharms is the boy who has spotted that the king is naked. Secondly it is connected with what Sartre called *la nausée*. But, in both cases, Kharms, unlike Sartre, knows when to stop so as not to plunge into vulgarity, not to exceed the bounds of the possible (which I think is how Malevich put it). Kharms used to say: you have to go right to the edge, to the abyss, to look over and know how to hold on without falling (the second temptation of Christ). In my case when I read some of his stories and poems, just a few, my head starts spinning and I feel sick, *la nausée*. Is this a shortcoming? If so, whose? Is it in me or in the stories? Or is that the way it is supposed to be? The feeling associated with inebriation of a kind of weakness, light-headedness and a little dizziness can be pleasant. But Kharms did not think so. In the same way he felt no physiological aversion: he used to say that he felt no aversion to formless, slimy creatures. He could pick up a slug and put it to his lips. This is why he could write about repulsive things in such a way that the story is not repulsive. He restrained himself at the bounds of the possible.

Kharms was also intrigued by conditions like rudeness (see 'A Nice Little Song about Fefelia', *Sob. proizv.* 4, 303) and viciousness ('Rakukin's Soul', 'Rehabilitation' and many other examples). His interest in them was purely existential. He was concerned with them not as abstract concepts, nor as psychological ones, but as noumenal realities, that is to say as the real states of a fallen soul, the realities which went beyond the confines of the soul. So this is not subjectivism, but absolute subjectivity. This can partly be found in Gogol, whom Kharms so admired, where it is a presentiment of our modern existential understanding of life. Pushkin after a reading from *Dead Souls* had said, 'How horrific our Russia is'. Nowadays we understand this more correctly, existentially: how horrific our life is, not only the story but human life in general. And this is what we can find in Kharms. His *Sluchai [Incidents]* are directed not against the Stalinist regime, but against any regime whatever. They were not anti-Soviet, but anti-political, anti-social. In other words, they were religious.

Apart from the purely philological problems and the religious and philosophical ones which arise in the study of Kharms, there is also another. How in his writings, particularly those concerning the subperson, is the authorial 'I' to be distinguished from the narratorial 'I'? That is to say, his sub-persons are not himself, though to some extent they are. His sub-persons are, partly, an admission of guilt. With Gogol the distance between him and his heroes is too great. With Kharms it is sometimes very slight. For instance he wrote a poem about liking meat and fat Jewish women, and he really did like meat and fat Jewish women. This near identity is in itself characteristic of Kharms with his Oedipus complex, his Nestorianism, his physiological propensities. He is not the lyrical hero of this poem, but all the same he is somehow bound up with him. How? Having linked the narratorial 'I' with the authorial one we should be able to determine this. It is important to do this with any writer, but it is particularly vital for an understanding of Kharms. In the case of Vvedensky it is far less important, though still significant [see his conversation with T. Lipavskaia about 'Kuprianov and Natasha' in the commentary to 'Kuprianov and Natasha', Vved. II, pp. 280-5]. In Kharms's case this is not only a meta-anthropological or a meta-theological problem, but a physiological one as well. We may recall his words on humour and sanctity, where humour touches on admission of guilt, repentance and sanctity. Sometimes it also touches on shamelessness, whether cynical or noumenal shamelessness, when a person stands naked and alone before God, just as God created them.

Besides, life passes into art and art into life. This perhaps explains the widespread anecdotes about Kharms: that he lived on milk only, that he built a kind of miraculous machine, and so on. Kharms used to say to me that art for him took second place, second place to *making his life* [emphasis here and below by Druskin]; that is to say, making it just as poetry and music is made. In his younger days, his ideal used to be Nagel, the protagonist of Hamsun's *Mysteries*. If Kharms had achieved this ideal in his life it would have been of little interest. But in 1932 the sense of failure set in: he began to understand that he would never achieve his ideal. Then he said, 'I am not as stupid, and not as talented as it seems'. And the non-realisation of his ideal was more interesting and better than the ideal. From the wreck he did create his life as art.

Kharms was not a miracle-worker and he could not perform miracles. Yet in this very inability of his the greatest miracle was revealed, the miracle of life, or, more exactly, the miracle of life-making. The year 1933 marked the crisis in Kharms's life-making, a crisis which evidently began in 1931 and 1932. He understood that he was not a miracle-worker and could not perform miracles and, once he had grasped this, then he worked a miracle, like the miracle-worker of his story, who, when he was completely disappointed in himself and his ability to work miracles, suddenly saw that the miracle had already occurred and was occurring. This is a short story, but at the same time it is also an autobiographical confession and philosophical treatise.

We could say a lot about the inner spiritual crisis in Kharms's life-making. It was not connected with any external circumstance. In brief, it was a victory in defeat, a perfection in imperfection, abundance in dearth. Perhaps in art as in life, only the medium is successful. We are reminded that in the history of European art the greatest works are either formally imperfect, or they are unfinished: *Don Quixote*, the Mozart Requiem, *Dead Souls, The Brothers Karamazov, The Critique of Pure Reason*, Fichte's *Theory of Science [Wissenschaftslehre]*.

There is evidently some sort of law: the higher a tower which a person builds, the nearer it is to heaven, and the harder it falls. But it is precisely in its fall that it affirms itself and is preserved for ever. The collapse of the Tower of Babel ensured its immortality.

I cannot claim that my account of the main features of Kharms's life-making is anywhere near exhaustive. In my account of the four features and especially of the first three, I allowed myself a degree of simplification. Kharms understood evil not as the normal moral-subjective psychological condition, but as a certain contradictoriness in the human reaction to life and in the hostile reaction of life to humanity, so that in certain of his writings, such as the poem 'Lead me with blindfold eyes' (*Sob. proizv.* 4, 311) it is not even clear what the evil is here: the man in his confrontation with life, or life itself, advancing on the man and repressing his personality. Evil here is neither subjective nor psychological, but substantial and ontological. I also over-simplified the second feature of Kharms's life-making. Kharms envisaged not only automatised life, impersonal existence. In his exposure of life he reveals the contradictory, alogical principle inherent in life itself, in each of us. I also simplified the first feature: miracle for Kharms is not external, as traditionally understood, but neither is it a simple metaphor, as when, for instance, we say that life itself is the greatest miracle. True, life is the greatest miracle, and this is rarely appreciated, but Kharms had in mind miracle in a more precise sense as a real ontological change in the structure of the soul, a change which carries over into a person's behaviour and lifestyle, even into their manner of dressing, so that ordinary life itself is changed. Kharms used to say that he had the gift of seeing the harmoniousness of a person. At home, when he was alone, Kharms liked to go around naked; he liked lying on the beach, but he could not stand the bath-house, where nakedness was somehow not for its own sake.

In 1938 Kharms got the idea of dividing people up into four categories: well-brought-up intellectuals, badly-brought-up intellectuals, well-brought-up non-intellectuals, that is representatives of the common people, and badly-brought-up non-intellectuals. This categorisation was not simply an interest in the social graces and good behaviour. For Kharms upbringing was a recognition of a certain order, elevated above the natural order of life. This is why he also divided the common people into two categories: the third category comprises those people who, although they do not know what we mean by good upbringing or best behaviour, yet have their own best behaviour and upbringing. This is what Kharms meant by the harmoniousness of a person, but in this case it is the harmoniousness of life. And just as human harmoniousness does not reside in regular facial features, so the harmoniusness of life, Kharms would say, is not to be found in the usual rules of decency and best behaviour, but rather in something else.

When Kharms and I were walking one sunny day past the Greek church, two boys aged about eight or ten were sitting on the church porch; they were well-dressed in velvet jackets and were very seriously burning holes in their jackets with a magnifying glass. Kharms was very taken with this scene and he said, 'Although I don't like children, I am quite struck by these boys'. He very much disliked badly-brought-up children, but he could scarcely have hated all children, though more than once claiming he did. When he performed with Vvedensky, or with Oleinikov, he used to go down marvellously with the children. He could hardly have managed this if he had hated children.

Harmoniousness of the person, according to Kharms, shows up when something unusual happens, or perhaps in some kind of ritual which sanctifies a person's external life. Harmoniousness of the persona is a certain formation of the soul; harmoniousness of life is the formation of ordinary life. This often coincides with good upbringing, but not always, and it is essentially something else. Rather, it is close to his recognition of the primacy of life over art. But in 1940 and 1941 he was no longer interested in this classification; he had gone further; he was no longer interested in the form of life but in its very essence, concentrated for him in one single saying, on which more below.

And once again, all this is not the traditional understanding of harmony. Thus he would say, 'Even a one-eyed man can be harmonious'. Kharms was rarely understood and this goes for his view of life, miracle and harmony, a view which he put into practice not only in his writings, but in his life, in life-making. The street urchins laughed at him but so did educated people, even his fellow writers as I once saw in the Maiakovsky Club. On such occasions, he would somehow wilt, climb down and yield the floor to human stupidity, narrowness and vulgarity.

We come on to his final period, the conclusion of his life-making. If a person's life, at least by the end, becomes a kind of hagiography, in the case of Kharms this was true to the highest degree. From 1934 or 1935 Kharms lived in expectation of some sort of culmination, in other words, he felt NOW to be eschatological: something had to happen. This *something which had to happen* was not a matter of material welfare, or even of creativity, but, in the words of his verse, a matter of 'intensive life'. It was more than a sense of fate or destiny. Fate, *fatum, kairos* are pagan concepts: but in the case of Kharms it was rather a sense of culmination, of the 'fullness of time'. And as it went on the stronger grew this sense of the approaching culmination and fullness of time. It was no accident that Kharms was greatly interested at that time in the *Dobrotoliubie*. He did not read very far, only as far as the saying, 'Ignite the misfortune around you' [*Zazhech' bedu vokrug sebia*].[5] He read no further because this was exactly what he needed. In the final month before his disappearance he kept repeating this saying all the time. He was not calling down misfortune on others, but on himself, in order through affliction to save himself from the dead husk of life within himself, to discover within himself the 'inmost heart of man'. In August 1941 misfortune struck, and then humour, or 'God's irony' (as Schlegel would put it), attained sanctity. In February 1942 Kharms died.

*Translated by Neil Cornwell*

NOTES

(supplied by the Editor. Author's notes have been included in the text)

1. This essay is published here for the first time, though some of the material in it is to be found in earlier Druskin publications (see Druskin 1985; Druskin 1989). Like these other posthumous publications from Druskin's notes and memoirs, it appears to have been written in the 1970s.
2. Reference to the novella, *Starukha* (*Polët*, pp. 398–430; English version, *Black Coat*, pp. 123–53).
3. This story, to the best of our knowledge, has yet to be published. It is

to be expected that this and other such pieces will be included in subsequent volumes of *Sob. proizv.*

4. We have omitted here half a page of discussion on satire as related to Zabolotsky's book of poetry, *Stolbtsy.*
5. A quotation from Bishop Feofan in *Dobrotoliubie.* The *Dobrotoliubie,* the Russian version of the *Philokalia,* was translated into Russian from the Greek by Bishop Feofan the Recluse.

# 3 A Kharms Chronology
## Anatolii Aleksandrov

**1905**

*17 (30 New Style) December*: born in St Petersburg (1, Glinskaia Street) as Daniil Ivanovich Iuvachëv. From the notebook of the writer's father, I. P. Iuvachëv, for 17 (30) December 1905: 'The priest came and we started to settle the question of what to call our son. Together, we decided to call him Daniil. In the first place, today is Daniil's day; 2) twelve days ago, between five and six in the morning, I dreamed of him; 3) by his name "God's judgement" I can call both my personal sufferings of fourteen days and "Russia's revolution"; 4) my favourite prophet, from whom I construct my philosophy . . .' (ChS).

**1915**

Enrols in first form of the technical high school, which formed a part of Peterschule (the main German school of St Peter in Petrograd).

**1919**

*Summer*: lives with his aunt (N. I. Koliubakina) in Detskoe Selo. First surviving manuscripts (in German) and drawings (Indian ink, pen) relate to this period.

**1922**

Earliest preserved poem by D. Iuvachëv, 'In July somehow, in our summer . . .' ['*V iule kak-to, v leto nashe* . . .'], signed with the pseudonym 'D. Ch.'.

*1 September*: begins studying in the penultimate class of the Second Soviet Labour School of Detskoe Selo. The school's Director was N. I. Koliubakina. 'His aunt was my teacher of Russian literature and the headmistress of the former Mariinsky High School in Tsarskoe Selo. She was in all respects an outstanding woman, clever, energetic [. . .], and as I was friendly with her and often called on her, I knew that she was worried about the fate of her nephew, whom she had taken under her protection while she was still headmistress and whom she hoped to direct on to the true path. He entered my class, I think about a year before finishing school and left school with us. He was already writing poetry and at a literary evening the following year read a few pieces, for example "I'll boot bums for madams" ['*Zadam po zadam za dam*'] and so on in this vein, to the horror of his aunt' (from the memoirs of N. Zegzhda. ChS).

**1924**
*14 July*: leaves Second Detskoe Selo School.
*Autumn*: enrols in Leningrad Electro-Technical College.
'I met Kharms in 1924, at which time I was working as a porter in the Svoboda factory on the Vyborg side ... When I called on Daniil for the first time, he took one look at my suit and said "that's no good", and dragged a better one out of his cupboard and said "wear that as long as you like" and suggested that we go down to the Philharmonia to a recital by a well-known pianist' (from the memoirs of G. N. Matveev. ChS).
*During 1924*: meets Ester Aleksandrovna Rusakova. 'I loved her for seven years. She was for me not only the woman whom I loved, but something more besides, which entered all my thoughts and activities. I conversed with Ester in a language other than Russian and wrote her name in Latin letters: ESTHER' (from a letter from Kharms to R. Poliakova).

**1925**
*First half of the year*: gives public readings of his own verses and those of Soviet poets at the Electro-Technical College, the State Steamship Line, the Turgenev Library, the Institute of the History of Arts and in other concert venues. The start of his friendship with A. Vvedensky. Meets the poets N. Kliuev and A. Tufanov. 'I went with him to poetry readings, at one of which, I recall, Tikhonov appeared. Daniil used to call on Kliuev, he liked Kliuev's eccentricities: his almost medieval set-up, his angelic voice and tongue, his appearance – as if butter wouldn't melt in his mouth, but he couldn't half let rip with the bad language. Once at Kharms's place I met his friend the trans-sense poet [*zaumnik*] Tufanov – a short chap, hunch-backed, with long hair and a frock coat ... I was there often and used to stay the night. I was studying at that time at the workers' faculty and was pretty bad at maths. Daniil used to help me. We read Nadson, Tiutchev and I don't remember the others ...' (from the memoirs of G. N. Matveev. ChS).
*9 October*: applies for admission to the Leningrad branch of the All-Russian Union of Poets. Kharms presented two notebooks of

poems to the admissions commission (IRLI: see also *Ezhegodnik*, 1978).

*17 October*: performs at an evening of Leningrad trans-sense poets, held at the Union of Poets. Vvedensky and Tufanov performed with him.

*End of the year*: moves, together with father and mother, to Flat 8, 11 Nadezhdinskaia Street (now Ulitsa Maiakovskogo). Lives at this address until mid-August 1941.

## 1926

*Beginning of January*: together with Vvedensky creates the 'School of Chinari' ['Shkola chinarei'].

*March*: accepted into Union of Poets.

*Spring*: meets N. Zabolotsky. Zabolotsky dedicates his poem 'The Uprising' ['*Vosstanie*'] in August of this year 'to Daniil Kharms, author of "The Comedy of the City of Petersburg" ["Komedii goroda Peterburga"]'.

*September*: applies for state courses at the Institute of the History of Arts: 'I request enrolment as a student on the film-studies courses' (LGALI). Kharms did not graduate from this course, nor from the Electro-Technical College.

*September*: the '*chinari*' appear in collaboration with the literary-theatrical group 'Radix' ['Radiks'].

*21 September*: 'we have started to write a play' (ZK no. 7, ChS). Kharms and Vvedensky write the play 'My mama is all in watches' ['Moia mama vsia v chasakh (detiam – podarok, uchiteliam – ogarok)']. 'In spite of the tortures of organizational confusion, work on the play and recruitment of the company came to a successful conclusion. Actors came from Lenfil'm, the Foregger "Mastfor" studio, from semi-professional troupes. I did sketches for the future décor, the musician Iakov Druskin selected music from scores he had procured of contemporary composers – Milhaud, Poulenc, Satie. We rehearsed at my place, in the dining room of my parents' appartment, at other times in the Vvedensky family drawing room' (I. Bakhterev, in *Vospominaniia o Zabolotskom*, p. 68).

*October*: rehearsals of the play take place in the Institute of Artistic Culture. (ZK no. 7, ChS).

*10 November*: ' "Radix" has collapsed' (ZK no. 7, ChS). Zabolotsky and the chief actor of the play 'My mama . . .', E. Vigiliansky, were called up for the Red Army.

*12 November*: reads his works at an evening at the Union of Poets. 'This Friday, the 12 November, I want to set up the firing order, which goes as follows: after our reading, Igor' Bakhterev will come on and make a senseless speech, quoting from unknown poets and so on. Then Tsimbal will come on and also make a speech, but with a Marxist slant. In this speech he will defend us, justifying our writings to various swine. Finally two unknown persons, holding hands, will go up to the table and declare: regarding what has been read we can't say much, but we shall sing something. And they will. Last, Gaga Katsman will go on and recite something from the lives of the saints. That will be good' (ZK no. 7, ChS).

*During 1926*: publication of an anthology of the Leningrad branch of the Union of Poets in which Kharms makes his debut as a poet with the poem 'An Incident on the Railway' [*'Sluchai na zheleznoi doroge'*].

**1927**

*9 January*: Kharms, together with Vvedensky and Bakhterev, performs at the circle of the friends of chamber music.

*16 February*: a meeting between the '*chinari*' and K. Malevich. discussions on the possibility of collaboration between the poets and the artists.

*25 March*: the creation of a union of artists seriously occupies Kharms. He proposes to his friends setting up an 'Academy of Left Classics'. Its goal: 'The fight against hack art. Against stagnation in form and feeling. The new form is the Revolution' (ZK 1927. ChS). 'Our most immediate tasks; 1.) to create a firm Academy of Left Classics. 2.) . . . to draw up a manifesto. 3.) To join the House of Print [Dom pechati]. 4.) Try to set up dances, to raise the sum of 600 roubles for the publication of an anthology. 5.) Publish the anthology.' (ZK 1927. ChS).

*28 March*: performance by the '*chinari*' (Kharms and Vvedensky) at a meeting of the literary circle of the Institute of the History of Arts.

*3 April*: the newspaper *Smena*, no. 76, 1927, published the article by N. Ioffe and L. Zheleznov, entitled 'Literary affairs (on the "*chinari*")'. This article described an incident which took place on the evening of the 28 March. A group of participants of the literary circle of the Institute of the History of Arts, among whom was Zheleznov, had sent a letter repeating the content of the newspaper article to the executive of the Union of Poets. This elicited an explantion from Kharms and Vvedensky:

'Statement to the Leningrad Union of Poets from the Academy of Left Classics. The reason for the scandal described, and its significance, were not as *Smena* interprets it. Even before the evening had started we had been warned that the assembled audience was in a somewhat rowdy mood . . . There was whistling in the hall, shouting and quarreling. Speakers whom no one listened to kept jumping up. This lasted for about five to seven minutes, until one of the *chinari*, D. I. Kharms, came on and pronounced his fatal words "Comrades, please note that I do not perform in stables or in brothels", after which he left the meeting. The noise lasted for some further time and ended in fights among the audience which did not involve us.

In view of what has been said above, we, the Academy of Left Classics, consider that our behaviour was fully appropriate to the reception which we were accorded; D. I. Kharms's sharp words, which referred to the meeting which was to take place and not to the Institute in general, as comrades Ioffe and Zheleznov would have it, we consider to have been particularly apt. *Chinar'* A. Vvedensky, *chinar'* D. Kharms' (IRLI).

*May*: 'The Academy of Left Classics' proposes to prepare for publication an almanac entitled 'Radix', with the following sections: 'theoretical' (including Shklovsky, Malevich, Lidiia Ginzburg), 'creative' (Vvedensky, Bakhterev, Zabolotsky, Kharms), 'painting', 'drawings'. This plan did not come to fruition.

*First Half of 1927*: Kharms plans the cover for his collection of verses to be entitled 'The *Chinar'* Daniil Ivanovich Kharms. The control of things. Inaccessible poems'. This project was not realised.

*23 November*: a *chinari* meeting: 'Agenda: 1.) To work out the principles uniting poets and artists. 2.) To work out the methods of internal work. 3.) To work out the methods of external work. 4.) To plan an evening called 'Three Left Hours' ['Tri levykh chasa']. 5.) To draw up estimates for that evening' (ZK 1927. ChS).

*12–24 December*: works on the play 'Elizaveta Bam'.

*December*: 'Oleinikov and Zhitkov have organized an association of "Writers of Children's Literature". We (Vvedensky, Zabolotsky and I) are invited' (ZK 1927. ChS).

*During 1927*: publication of the anthology 'Kostër', by the Union of Poets, which includes Kharms's 'Peter Iashkin's Verse' ['*Stikh Petra Iashkina*'].

**1928**
*January*: publication of the OBERIU declaration (Society of Real

Art [Ob"edinenie real'nogo iskusstval]) in the series 'Posters of the House of Print' [Afishi Doma pechati] (Leningrad, no. 2).
*24 January*: the Oberiuty theatrical evening, 'Three Left Hours', was held in the Leningrad House of Print. The first hour, according to the programme, consisted of a performance by the poets. 'Prelude. A conferring choir. The OBERIU declaration. Declaration of the literary section. Poems read by: K. Vaginov, Zabolotsky, Daniil Kharms, N. Kropachev, Igor' Bakhterev, Vvedensky. Your compère will ride around on a three-wheeler in improbable lines and figures'. Second hour – theatrical presentation – 'Elizaveta Bam'. Third – 'An evening meditation on the cinema, by Aleksandr Razumovsky', and then a showing of the film 'The Mincer' ['Miasorubka'] (a montage of scraps from various films).

'In the first, the literary hour, Kharms came out standing on a black lacquered cupboard, moved by my brother and his friend, who were inside it. Daniil stood aloft it, powdered, pale faced, in a long jacket, adorned with a red triangle, in his favourite golden cap with pendants hanging down, he stood like a fantastic sculpture or a minstrel of legendary times. He read 'phonetic' verses in a loud, somewhat sing-song voice. Suddenly, getting his watch out of his jacket pocket, he asked for silence and announced that, at this moment on the corner of 25 October (as Nevskii was then called) and 3rd of July Street (as Sadovaia was called) Nikolai Kropachev was reading his poems' (I. Bakhterev, in *Vospominanie o Zabolotskom*, pp. 89–90).

*25 January*: publication of L. Lesnaia's feuilleton 'Ytuerebo' ['ытуеробо'], on the 'Three Left Hours' evening, in the Leningrad *Krasnaia gazeta* (evening issue).

*February*: publication of the first issue of the children's magazine *Ëzh [The Hedgehog]* (organ of the Central Bureau of Young Pioneers) in Leningrad. Kharms was among the most active contributors to the magazine. Over the period of a year, ten works by Kharms were published in it, including the poem '*Ivan Ivanych Samovar*', the story 'The Mischievous Plug' ['Ozornaia probka'] (under the pseudonym D. Bash), and 'The Story of how Kol'ka Pankin flew to Brazil and Pet'ka Ershov didn't believe any of it' ['Rasskaz o tom, kak Pankin Kol'ka letal v Braziliu, a Ershov Pet'ka nichemu ne veril'].

*8 March*: Kharms called up for short-term service in the Red Army.
*12 December*: Kharms draws up programme for a new Oberiuty evening: '1st. Section. 1.) Lecture on round worms. 2.) Compère 1.

3.) B. M. Levin – prose. 4.) Compère 2. 5.) D. I. Kharms – poems. 6.) Gladiator trio. 7.) I. V. Bakhterev – forks and poems. 8.) Preparation. 9.) A. I. Vvedensky – poems and prose. 10.) Two romances from P. A. Vul'fius. 11.) Compère 3. 12.) Collective item. 2nd. Section. Theatrical performance 'A Winter Stroll' ['Zimniaia progulka']. Play by D. I. Kharms and I. V. Bakhterev, Players: E. I. Vigiliansky and A. Ia. Grin. 3rd. Section. Theatricalized debate. Evening hosted by E. I. Vigiliansky' (ChS).

*During 1928*: publication of the following children's books by Kharms: *Teatr (stikhi)* ['Theatre (poems)']. Illustrations by Pravosudovich. Moscow, GIZ; *O tom, kak Kol'ka Pankin letal v Braziliu, a Pet'ka Ershov nichemu ne veril (rasskaz)* [see 'February' above]. Illustrations by E. Evenbakh. Moscow-Leningrad, GIZ; *Ozornaia probka (rasskaz)* [see 'February' above]. Illustrations by E. Safonova. Moscow-Leningrad, GIZ.

**1929**

*In the course of the year*: the Oberiuty perform in clubs, educational institutions, student hostels in Leningrad.

*May*: Kharms draws up plan for an anthology: 'Poetry: 1.) Zabolotsky. 2.) Vvedensky. 3.) Kharms. 4.) Khlebnikov. 5.) Tikhonov; 'Elizaveta Bam'. Prose: 1.) Kaverin. 2.) Vvedensky. 3.) Dobychin. 4.) Kharms. 5.) Tynianov. 6.) Shklovsky. 7.) Olesha' (ZK 1929, ChS). 'In May 1929 I was in Moscow and V. Kaverin wrote to me there about "Archimedes' Bath": "The anthology which you know about (with Oberiuty participation) is being put together. There are grounds for supposing that it will be published by the Writers' Publishing House [Izdatel'stvo pisatelei]. You know the poetry section (even Tikhonov is a possible). The outlook is worse with the prose section, and that in particular is what we decided to trouble you about. Couldn't you call on Olesha and tell him about our venture? It would be very good if he would let the anthology have just a small thing, or even an excerpt from something bigger. Also represented in this section will be Dobychin, Khlebnikov, myself, Kharms and supposedly Tynianov. In the critical section are people extremely well known to you. They are thinking of writing (together with you) 'A Review of Russian Letters for 1929'. Apart from that, other contributors will be Bor. Mikh. [Eikhenbaum], Iur. Nik. [Tynianov], and Viktor Borisovich [Shklovsky] whom we are asking you to approach on this matter"' (L. Ginzburg, in *Vospominaniia o Zabolotskom*, p. 146). The anthology 'Archimedes' Bath' did not come out.

*12 December*: performance by the Oberiuty in House of Print.
*During 1929*: the following books for children by Kharms came out: *Vo-pervykh i vo-vtorykh (rasskaz)* ['Firstly and Secondly (a story)']. Illustrations by V. Tatlin. Moscow-Leningrad, GIZ; *Ivan Ivanych Samovar (stikhi)*. Illustrations by V. Ermolaev. Moscow, GIZ; *O tom. kak Kol'ka Pankin letal v Braziliu, a Pet'ka Ershov nichemu ne veril (rasskaz)*. Illustrations by E. Evenbakh. Moscow-Leningrad, GIZ, 2nd. edition; *O tom, kak starushka chernila pokupala (rasskaz)* ['How an Old Woman bought some Ink (a story)']. Illustrations by Z. Krimmer. Moscow-Leningrad, GIZ.

**1930**
*January*: publication begins in Leningrad of *Chizh [The Siskin]* (for younger children, 1930–41), a second children's magazine, at first thought up as a supplement to *Ëzh*. Kharms was among the regular contributors to the magazine, writing poems and stories and thinking up ideas for the illustrators. N. Gernet, chief editor of *Chizh*, recalled: 'every day Kharms got together with Shvarts, Oleinikov (who at one time was editor-in-chief of *Chizh*), Zabolotsky, Vvedensky, Bianki, Zhitkov, Charushin, Zoshchenko – and I didn't fully realise what an exceptional and rare happiness this was. I just listened with delight to the reading, the conversation, the bright ideas, the jousting, and I considered any day lost that was spent out of the editorial office . . .'
'And yet, of all that literary élite, Daniil Ivanovich was unique, the most amazing. In outward appearance he could best be characterized by the word – gentleman. Tall, handsome, beautifully mannered, invariably correct, neat, decent to the core, he possessed a perfect sense of humour and no less perfect a sense for words – and a literary ear' (Gernet).
*Beginning of April*: performance by the Oberiuty (B. Levin and Iu. Vladimirov) in a Leningrad University student hostel.
*9 April*: publication in the Leningrad paper *Smena* of an article about the evening at the Leningrad University student hostel, entitled 'Reactionary Jugglery (on a sally by literary hooligans')' signed by L. Nil'vich. After this article, according to the evidence of A. Razumovsky, the Oberiuty performances ceased.
*During 1930*: publication of the following children's books by Kharms: *Igra (stikhi)* ['A Game (verses)']. Illustrations by V. Konashevich. Moscow, GIZ; *Ozornaia probka (rasskaz)* [see above]. Illustrations by E. Safonova. Moscow-Leningrad, GIZ,

2nd edition; *O tom, kak Kol'ka Pankin letal v Braziliu, a Pet'ka Ershov nichemu ne veril (rasskaz)* [see above]. Illustrations by E. Evenbakh. Moscow-Leningrad, GIZ, 3rd edition; *O tom, kak papa zastrelil mne khor'ka (stikhi)* ['How Papa shot me a Polecat (verses)']. Illustrations by Iu. Vasnetsov. Moscow, GIZ.

**1931**
*The whole year*: spent devising games and mystifications, in which an indispensable participant was the artist A. I. Poret. She wrote: 'There was also the game of "monsters". D. I. had his ones, our family had theirs, and Glebova had a very valuable collection. We exchanged them, introduced them to our friends and tried to show them to good effect. D. I. tended his and cherished them and spent loads of time with them. For example, he had a principal monster – a beggar with a great long scythe, a huge shock of hair, in chains, barefooted, who walked along the Nevsky Prospect with an iron staff. Some sort of natural philosophers, antique collectors who had suffered ruin, wild-looking types' (Poret, p. 358).
*March-April*: writes poem '*Khniu*'.
*End of December*: 'A whole crowd of our friends – Kharms, Vvedensky, Andronikov, Safonova, Ermolaeva have been arrested' (first draft of A. Poret's memoirs of Kharms. ChS). 'I was most happy when they took away my pen and paper and forbade me to do anything. I wasn't worried that I was not doing anything through my own fault, my conscience was clear, and I was happy. That was when I was in prison. But if I were asked if I'd like to go there again, or to a situation like prison, I would say: no, I DON'T WANT TO' (note by Kharms. GPB).
*In 1931*: publication of one children's book by Kharms, *Million (stikhi)* ['A Million (verses)']. Illustrations by V. Konashevich. Moscow, GIZ.

**1932**
*23 April*: Resolution of the Central Committee of the All-Union Communist Party 'On the Restructuring of Literary-Artistic Organizations'.
*18 June*: Kharms freed from detention. 'Freedom, in the evening at Zhitkov's. 19 June: at Tsarskoe. 20 June: at Shvarts's, then at Lipavsky's. 21 June: at Zabolotsky's. 22 June: at Zhitkov's. Summer solstice. 23 June: Levin stayed the night. 24 June: by motorcar to Tsarskoe. 25 June: at Oleinikov's. Saw Sokolov off. 26

June: at Natasha's. 27 June: on the veranda. Don't feel too good. Have got very thin' (ZK 1932. ChS).
*13 July*: Kharms, together with Vvedensky, exiled to Kursk. 'We lived in two rooms. My friend occupied the smaller room and I had the quite big room with three windows. For whole days my friend went out and he would return to his room only to spend the night. I sat in my room almost all the time and if I went out, then it was either to the post office, or to buy myself something for dinner. On top of that, I caught dry pleurisy and this tied me to the place even more.

I like being alone. But a month went by and I got fed up with my solitude . . .' (note by Kharms. GPB).
*18 November*: Kharms and Vvedensky return to Leningrad.
*20 November*: 'Went with Vvedensky to an exhibition of all the artists. The only good one was Malevich' (ZK 1932. ChS).
*21 November*: 'Evening at Zhitkov's, where Oleinikov and Zabolotsky were too. Oleinikov has now become a fine poet and Zabolotsky is publishing his book of poems' (ZK 1932. ChS).

**1933**
*During the course of the year*: Kharms participates in discussions at L. Lipavsky's apartment. Apart from Kharms and the host, taking part in the 'conversations' (as the participants themselves called their meetings) were Vvedensky, Druskin, Zabolotsky, Oleinikov.

'My interests: writing poetry and recognising various things from poetry. Prose. Illumination, inspiration, enlightenment, superconsciousness – everything which has anything to do with this. Ways of achieving this. Finding my own system of achieving it. Various types of knowledge, unknown to science. Zero and number. Numbers, especially those not tied by order to sequence. Signs, letters. Types of print and handwriting. Everything which is logically senseless and absurd. Everything that causes laughter. Humour. Stupidity. Natural thinkers. Omens, old-fashioned ones and those re-invented by anyone. Miracle. Tricks (without apparatus). Human, private interrelations. Good behaviour. Human faces. Smells. Overcoming squeamishness. Washing, bathing, the bath. Cleanliness and filth. Food. Preparing certain dishes. Decorating the dining table. Furnishing a flat and a room. Clothing, male and female. Questions of the wearing of clothes. Smoking (pipes and cigars). What people do when they are on their own. Notebooks. Writing on paper in ink or pencil. Paper, ink, pencil. The daily record of events. Notes on the weather. Phases of the moon. A view of the sky and the water. The wheel. Sticks, walking canes, rods. An ant-hill. Small smooth-haired dogs. The Kabbala. Pythagoras. Drama (my own). Singing. Church service and singing. All kinds of rites. Pocket watches and chronometers. a plastron. Women, but only those who are my type. The sexual physiology of woman. Silence.' (note by Kharms, made in the 'Conversations' diary. ChS).

'I like to stroll by the Neva, in the Field of Mars, in the Summer Garden, over Troitsky Bridge, in Catherine's Park, at Tsarskoe Selo. I like to walk by the sea: at Ol'gino, Lakhta, Sestroretska and Kurort. I like walking alone. I like finding myself among considerate people' (ZK 1933. ChS).

*From the middle to the end of the year*: work on a cycle of stories for readers of *Chizh*, about Professor Trubochkin.

*From September to the end of the year*: 'epistolary affair' with the actress Klavdiia Pugachëva.

**1934**

*During the whole year*: thinks up themes for illustrations for *Chizh*. 'In *Chizh* there used to be a regular character called "Clever Masha", extremely popular among the children, they kept writing her letters and phoning her. Few people knew that Masha had been invented by Daniil Ivanovich at one of our editorial meetings at Oleinikov's. Afterwards lots of people thought up her adventures, but the first Masha was Daniil Ivanovich's' (Gernet).

*Second half of the year*: work is begun on the philosophical-literary work 'Sushchestvovanie' ['Existence'] (unfinished). Manuscript signed 'Daniil Dandan'.

*In 1934*: Kharms was accepted into the newly-organized Union of Soviet Writers. Gets married to Marina Vladimirovna Malich.

**1935**

*17 May*: Kharms attends the civil obsequies for Kazimir Malevich, where he reads his poem '*Na smert' Kazimira Malevicha*' ['On the death of Kazimir Malevich']. Signs his manuscripts 'Kharms-Shardam'.

**1936**

*Second half of the year*: the free translation by Kharms of the verse novel 'Plikh i Pliukh', from a work by Wilhelm Busch, was published in *Chizh*, nos. 8 to 12. Various jokes by Kharms in verse and prose were published in *Chizh* under the name 'Karl Ivanovich Shusterling'. 'Karl Ivanovich Shusterling, an old chap with a bald spot. Very plump. With goggle eyes. Short' (note by Kharms. IRLI).

*August–September*: 'This fugue (Handel's second fugue) has pride of place in my repertoire. For a month I have been playing it twice each day, but as a result I can now play it fluently. Marina is not very favourably disposed towards my practising, and since she hardly ever leaves the flat I practise not more than an hour a day, which is very little. Apart from the fugue, I play Palestrina's 'Stabat mater', in the choral arrangement, a minuet by John Blow (18th century), 'Oh, the field, the field' from *Ruslan*, the E-major chorale from 'The St John Passion' and now I am learning the C-minor aria from a Bach partita' (from letter to B. Zhitkov, *Polët*, p. 493). The artist B. Semënov remembers musical evenings at the Kharms flat: 'At the table would be seated the well-known musicologist Ivan Ivanovich Sollertinsky, the acclaimed organist E. M. Braudo. Here I managed to hear at close quarters the remarkable *Lieder* singer Anatolii Dolivo, and also the best interpretor of Monostatos in *The Magic Flute*, Nikolai Chesnokov' (Semënov, p. 271).

**1937**

*7 January*: wrote the story 'Byl odin ryzhii chelovek' ['The Red-Haired Man']. It was subsequently to open the cycle 'Sluchai' ['Incidents'].

*27 March*: beginning of the cross-city correspondence with Ia. S. Druskin.

*March*: publication in *Chizh* no. 3 of the poem 'Iz doma vyshel chelovek...' ['A man walked out of his house'], after which nothing by Kharms was published in the magazine for about a year.

*In the second half of the year*: publication in the journal *Detskaia literatura* (no. 18) of L. Kon's article 'On Humour'. The author inveighed against the 'sabotage' being carried on by the pre-school magazine *Sverchok* ['The Cricket'] (the editor of which was N. Oleinikov) and the translation of Busch's tale, which Kharms had done. 'Our children want to know who is their friend, and who their enemy', said the article.

*28 September*: a note in the 'blue notebook':

This is how hunger begins:
The morning you wake, feeling lively,
Then begins the weakness,
Then begins the boredom,
Then comes the loss
Of the power of quick reason,
Then comes the calmness –
And then begins the horror.

*31 October*: 'I am interested only in "nonsense" [*"chush'"*], only what makes no practical sense. Life interests me only in its absurd manifestation. Heroism, enthusiasm, daring, morale, hygiene, morality, sentimentality and ardour are hateful words and feelings for me.

But I fully understand and respect: rapture and delight, inspiration and despair, passion and restraint, debauchery and chastity, sorrow and grief, joy and laughter' (note by Kharms. GPB).

*At the beginning of the year*: publication in book form of: W. Busch, *Plikh i Pliukh*, a free translation by Daniil Kharms, Moscow-Leningrad, Detizdat.

**1938**

The name of Kharms again appears in *Chizh* (no. 3) after a year's interval.

*During the year*: literary-musical evenings are held in Kharms's room. 'I had already heard a lot about Kharms's room. They used to say that the whole of it, from floor to ceiling, was drawn over and written over with poems and aphorisms, of which one was always quoted: "We are not pies". But this information must have applied to some earlier period: I didn't find anything of the sort. There was just a sheet of squared paper, torn from an exercise book, pinned to the wall, with a "List of people particularly respected in this house" (of whom I can remember Bach, Gogol, Glinka and Knut Hamsun), and a silver pocket watch hung on a nail with a notice stuck beneath it: "This watch has a special superlogical significance". Between the windows stood a harmonium and on the walls I noticed an excellent portrait of Kharms painted by Mansurov, an old lithograph depicting a moustached colonel from Nicholas I's time and an abstract painting in the spirit of Malevich, black and red, of which Kharms used to say that it expressed the essence of life. This picture had also been painted by Mansurov' (V. N. Petrov, 'Memoirs of Kharms'. ChS).

## 1939
*May-June*: 'Starukha' ['The Old Woman'] finished.
*September*: the journal *Detskaia literatura*, no. 9, carries the article 'On "Funny Poetry"' by V. Trenin, in which the children's poetry of Kharms and Vvedensky is analysed and positively evaluated.
*During 1939*: Kharms is treated in the psycho-neurological hospital located on the Fifteenth Line, Vasil'evskii Island, Leningrad. He puts together the 'Sluchai' cycle.

## 1940
The artist V. A. Grinberg paints a half-length portrait of Kharms.

## 1941
*22 June*: invasion of Soviet Union by Nazi Germany. 'The last time I saw Daniil Ivanovich was in 1941, two or three days before war broke out. We were sitting on the roof by my garret window. He was serious and preoccupied as never before. "Leave town as soon as possible. Go away!, he said, – There's going to be war. Leningrad can expect the fate of Coventry". He had no thought of going away himself. I then, like many people, hoped until the last day that there would not be war, in spite of the threatening signs. But I believed him. It always seemed to me that Daniil Ivanovich knew and foresaw much that we did not yet know . . .' (Gernet).
*23 August*: arrest of Kharms. He was charged with the standard offence of spreading defeatist propaganda.
'Before the end of August, I think, in 1941 the janitor ['dvornik'] came and asked him to step down into the yard for something. A Black Maria was standing there. They took him away half dressed with just slippers on his bare feet.

I had seen Daniil Ivanovich two or three days before his arrest. I had always known that he was very clever, that his eccentricity was a mask, and that he never was the buffoon that some considered him to be. That evening we drank cheap red wine, and ate white bread. Our conversation was mainly on the war. Daniil Ivanovich believed that the Germans would be smashed and thought that Leningrad in particular – the staunchness of its population and defenders – would decide the outcome of the war' (L. Panteleev, 'Iz leningradskikh zapisei', *Novyi mir*, 1965, no. 5, p. 149).

*24 August to 7 December*: Kharms is held in the NKVD's inner prison in Leningrad.
*7 December*: on the basis of the findings of a judicial-medical examination, Kharms was discharged from criminal responsibility and sent for enforced treatment to the psychiatric wing of the deportation prison hospital (Prison No. 2). From this prison, prisoners were taken out of Leningrad (even during the blockade).
*End of December*: 'The news has just been confirmed that Dan. Iv. is in Novosibirsk. If you have any material possibility, then help him. From you it is nearer and more sure to get through. For my part, I am doing all I can, but it is more difficult for me because of the distance . . . The address is: Novosibirsk, NKVD, the prison, prisoner Dan. Iv., send it in my name. I shall be endlessly grateful to you . . . If there is any chance of finding out from where you are about how to send warm things and what the state of his case is – he is mentally disturbed, you see, and the thought of this is driving me mad' (from a letter from Marina Malich to Natal'ia Shan'ko. TsGALI)

**1942**
*2 February*: death of D. I. Iuvachëv-Kharms. This news came to Prison No. 1 ('Kresty'). The place of Kharms's death is not stated in the communication. It is not known whether he died in Prison No. 2 or in a prison train on the way to Novosibirsk.

*Translated by Neil Cornwell*

ABBREVIATIONS FOR SOURCES USED IN CHRONOLOGY

ChS: *chastnoe sobranie* (private collection)
Ezhegodnik, 1978: see Aleksandrov, 1978
GPB: Manuscript Section of the Saltykov-Shchedrin State Public Library
Gernet: see Gernet, 1988
IRLI: Manuscript Section of the Institute of Russian Literature AN SSSR (Pushkinskii Dom)
Poret: see Poret, 1980
Semënov, 1982
TsGALI: Manuscript Section of the Central State Archive of Literature
ZK: *zapisnye knizhki* (note books of D. Kharms)

# Part II: General Studies

# 4 Daniil Kharms in the Context of Russian and European Literature of the Absurd
## Jean-Philippe Jaccard

> It has been said that I am a writer of the absurd; there are words like that around, it's a fashionable word which will be fashionable no longer. In any case, as of now it is vague enough to mean nothing any more and to define everything with ease.   Ionesco[1]

The purpose of this essay is to show that there are in the work of Daniil Kharms the necessary elements to permit him to be inscribed in a tradition which we have decided to call, for reasons of convenience and usage, *the absurd*, a term which will require further definition. What can be said without any more ado is that Kharms's *oeuvre* is not a chance phenomenon and that it may be approached in the Russian or European literary contexts. In fact, a certain vision of the world and of the laws which govern it, a certain linguistic rapport, as well as certain connections in the literary works themselves – these are the three main points of this study – have produced, in the twentieth century, works which resemble each other in a striking manner, even when their authors could not have known or read one another, whether for reasons of language or of temporal distance.

The lines which we shall follow deal, moreover, with a bond existing between Kharms (1905–42) and certain tendencies linked with the notion of the absurd in France. It is in this way that we shall be able to isolate from works habitually classified among this order a certain number of general categories which allow parallel treatment of literatures lacking any familiarity one with the other.

THE IRREMEDIABLE DIVORCE

The concept of 'literature of the absurd' is extremely vague and often permits the ranging under the same term of a whole series of disparate works which often have no common denominator but their obscure nature. Besides, a primary definition of the absurd as simple violation of the laws of logic is inadequate due to being too restrictive. It is that definition, moreover, which has all too often allowed comparisons with English 'nonsense', even if it is quite evident that the limericks of Lear and certain verses of Kharms do present a number of common traits.

When one pronounces the word 'absurd' in the French-speaking world, one always has in mind, first and foremost, Camus and his essay *The Myth of Sisyphus*, published in 1942.[2] In a more literary context, one thinks of the 'Theatre of the Absurd', an expression used to designate the drama of the 1950s and 1960s, of which the best known authors are Eugène Ionesco, Samuel Beckett and Arthur Adamov. The link which unites these two tendencies is a certain relationship between man and the world. The absurd, according to Camus, is 'essentially a divorce', it 'is not in man (. . .), nor in the world, but in their common presence'.[3] There is no question in these lines of addressing the philosophical problems that Camus links to this proposition, namely suicide or hope as a means of escaping the 'sentiment of absurdity' which resides in man, but it is, on the other hand, necessary to insist on this notion of divorce, which will be developed in his novel *The Outsider*, published the same year. This notion is central in the work of Kharms, whose characters are attacked by an environment which is the same as that which will lead Meursault to the guillotine. But if this confrontation is a basic given of the absurd, its presence is not sufficient to categorise as 'absurd' the work which performs it. If Kharms and Kafka have so often been compared, it is crystal clear that they have that quality in common. The arbitrary arrest by Ivan Ivanovich and Pëtr Nikolaevich of Elizaveta Bam in the play of that name,[4] written in 1927 and performed in 1928, strangely resembles that of Joseph K by Franz and Willem in *The Trial*, published just one year earlier.[5] And in both texts the scene is repeated at the end, thus enclosing the plot within a fatal circularity. The theme of arrest, moreover, is extremely recurrent in Kharms. In *Pomekha* ('The Drawback'),[6] written in 1940 (hardly a year before the writer would be subjected to the same fate), he sees a man in a black coat, accompanied by two armed soldiers and the inevitable caretaker, burst into a room where Pronin and Irina are engaged in the preliminaries to love-making; the coercive forces of society intervene in the most intimate actions of the individual.

The twentieth century was to develop this type of victim figure, which, not only society and its policemen, but the universe at large, crush mercilessly. Henri Michaux's Plume bears an astonishing resemblance to certain characters of Kharms.[7] The short story *Plume at the Restaurant* begins with the following lines:[8]

> Plume was dining in a restaurant when the head waiter came up, looked at him severely and said to him in a low and mysterious voice: 'What you've got there on your plate is *not* on the menu'. Plume apologised immediately.

Despite his desperate attempts to justify himself, the unfortunate Plume has to make successive appeals to the manager of the establishment, the chief of police, the head of criminal investigation and the fire brigade before the secret service takes the 'affair' in hand and beats our 'hero' up.[9] There is a short text by Kharms which bears a striking resemblance to that of Michaux:[10]

> Petya walks into a restaurant and sits down at a table.
> The waiter brings the menu and puts it in front of Petya, Petya looks at the menu.
> Petya: Give me, if you can, the boeuf-bouille.
> Waiter: I won't.
> Petya: (with a frightened look at the waiter): Boeuf . . .
> Waiter: I'm just going to have to throw you out.
> Petya: (threateningly): What do you mean?
> Waiter: All right, all right. Out you go.
> Petya: I'm not going. I'm an engineer. (reaches from his pocket and offers the waiter some sort of document)
> (The waiter takes the document in his hand, examines it and says):
> Waiter: How do I know this is you? Perhaps it's a stolen document you've got.
>
> [1933–1937]

Nineteenth-century Russia also has its retinue of the humiliated and offended, of buffoons who are either ridiculous or are afraid of so being, and of characters who are arbitrarily pursued for a crime which they have not committed. It is by no means idle speculation to stress a direct descent from Gogol to Kharms, by way of Dostoevsky. And it is no accident if one should frequently come across minor characters in Kharms bearing the name and patronymic Ivan Iakovlevich, that is to say the same as those of the barber in *The Nose*, and that he should be lost during the course of the story, liquified with terror before an agent of the law.[11]

Most of the characters of Kharms are descendents of Akakii Akakievich and precursors of Plume: what little substance they have will be pulverised mercilessly by a hostile environment, as with 'the man of average size' [or 'medium height' Ed.] in *Sud Lincha* ('A Lynching') by Kharms.[12] A certain Petrov, who is making a speech to the crowd, breaks off suddenly to note a few words in his notebook. The man of average size asks him what he has written. When he refuses to comply a fight breaks out, during which Petrov manages to escape. The crowd, which needs to vent its urges, turns on the man of average size:

> The crowd gets excited and, for lack of any other victim, seizes on the man of average size and tears his head off. The torn off head rolls down the pavement and gets stuck in a drain. The crowd, having satisfied its passions, disperses.

In *Son* ('A Dream'),[13] Kalugin, after several repetitions of an obsessional nightmare involving a militiaman, sleeps for four days and four nights straight off,[14] from which he emerges so emaciated that he can no longer be recognised at the bakery. The text finishes with these words:

> And a sanitary commission, going round the flats and catching sight of Kalugin, decided that he was insanitary and good for nothing whatsoever and ordered the porter to throw Kalugin out with the rubbish. They folded Kalugin in two and threw him out as rubbish.

Meursault will be guillotined, K . . . stabbed in a quarry, Poprishchin from *Diary of a Madman* is locked up in an asylum like Beckett's Molloy, Kalugin is thrown on a rubbish heap, the man of average size is massacred by a crowd, while the fate of the narrator of *Starukha* ('The Old Woman'),[15] who has just lost the suitcase in which he has enclosed the corpse of the old woman whom he found dead in his flat, remains uncertain . . . . One could multiply these examples but, as we have already said, even if this relationship of conflict is a basic given of the absurd, it will in no way be its dominant trait. In fact, if Camus's character is seized with the 'sentiment of absurdity', *The Outsider*, by the same token, is not a novel of the absurd. Camus wrote *on* the absurd, but he is not a writer *of* the absurd. If such were the case, it would be impossible to 'imagine Sisyphus happy' (the final words of the essay) and even less so *The Rebel* . . .

We shall now see that the notion of divorce must be extended to all levels of a work for it to be classifiable as *absurd*.

## A FRAGMENTED WORLD

**The real**

It emerges from the preceding lines that the world is an accumulation of people, objects and facts, linked by pure convention; by structures of the spirit which are more or less conscious, man invents for himself a universe which seems to him to be ruled by logical and immutable laws. But as for the absurd outlook on the world, it isolates each part of the world and negates the links between them. This is exactly what Viktor Shklovsky was expressing when, in his short article on Kharms, he wrote:[16]

> The world is linked not only by causal connections. Things which have arisen separately and have found themselves side by side appear logical. But children and poets see them otherwise.

Ionesco, in his *Notes on the Theatre* of 1953, admirably expresses the process of this painful lucidity:[17]

> In this world, at times, I am as though at a show; these are, let it be said, rare moments of quietude. Everything which surrounds me is spectacle. Incomprehensible spectacle. Spectacle of forms, of figures in movement, of lines of opposing force, deeply dividing, knotting, unravelling. What strange machinations! Not tragic, but stupefying. Astonishment is my fundamental world sentiment. Not tragic, all right, very well; perhaps comic, strangely comic, certainly derisive, this world. All the same, upon lengthier contemplation, I feel caught by a certain pain, by heartbreak. This pain itself astonishes me; this heartbreak itself plunges into the strange. Infinitely surprised that such things exist, and such events and such passions, and such colours and such sorrows of the night and of the day however precarious, transparent, imperceptible: fruits of nothingness. And all these figures which move inter-collide, in order to destroy each other reciprocally.

This fragmented characteristic of the real is frequently met with in Gogol. There are to be found in his work numerous examples of demonic machinations, of which the individual is the victim. Piskarev, in *Nevskii Prospekt*, represents a typical example in this respect. The beautiful woman encountered on Nevskii Prospekt immediately provokes in him visual delusions: 'all before him was enclosed in some sort of a mist'.[18] Further on, the young lady's practice of the oldest profession in the world will be laid at the door of 'the terrible will of some infernal spirit, thirsting to destroy the harmony of life'.[19] Later, when Piskarev is plunged into a fateful worldly soirée, the fragmentation of the world drives him to madness, reinforced, precisely in the form of visual deformations, by subsequent doses of opium:[20]

> ... it seemed to him that some demon or other had crumbled the whole world into a mass of different pieces and all these pieces were senselessly, irrationally mixed together.

Poprishchin of *Diary of a Madman*, for his part, who has attained the stage of perceiving his own madness as a form of lucidity, remembers that 'before, everything was before [him] in some sort of a mist'.[21]

Kharms has himself expressed this irremediable divorce in his piece *O vremeni, o prostranstve, o sushchestvovanii* ('On Time, space and existence'),[22] in which he develops the idea that the world exists only from the moment that it is conceived as heterogeneous:

1. A world which is not can not be called existing, because it is not.
2. A world consisting of something unified, homogeneous and continuous can not be called existing, because in such a world there are no parts and, once there are no parts, there is no whole.
3. An existing world must be heterogeneous and have parts.
4. Every two parts are different, because one part will always be *this* one and the other *that* one.
5. If only *this* one exists, then *that* one cannot exist, because, as we have said, only *this* exists. But such a *this* cannot exist, because if *this* exists it must be heterogeneous and have parts. And if it has parts that means it consists of *this* and *that*.
6. If *this* and *that* exist, this means that *not this* and *not that* exist, because if *not this* and *not that* did not exist, then *this* and *that* would be unified, homogeneous and continuous and consequently would also not exist.
7. We shall call the first part *this* and the second part *that* and the transition from one to the other we shall call *neither this nor that*.
8. We shall call *neither this nor that* 'the impediment'.
9. Thus: the basis of existence comprises three elements: *this, the impediment* and *that*.

10. We shall depict non-existence as zero or a unity. Therefore we shall have to depict existence by the number three.
11. Thus: dividing a unitary void into two parts, we get the trinity of existence.

Throughout the reasoning of Kharms we encounter this idea that the world exists in opposites: for each of its parts there exists one (perhaps the same, or its negative equivalent) which will cancel it out, reducing in this way the existence of everything to a position of equilibrium equivalent to zero. Kharms's texts are all constructed on this principle, whether poetry, prose or drama: by means of the juxtaposition of diverse textual elements (words, narrative motifs, retorts, syllables etc.), this writer reproduces the incoherence of the world within the very texture of his writing.

**Language**

> Verses should be written so that, if they are thrown as a poem against the window, it will smash.
> Daniil Kh-Kharms[23]

It is quite possible to approach in this way the *zaum'* poetry of Kharms and of his direct predecessors, Velimir Khlebnikov, Aleksey Kruchënykh and the poet in whose company he was to take his first steps in the world of literature, Aleksandr Tufanov.[24] The linguistic sign, the bearer at the same time of this fundamental duality and of the arbitrariness of its relation to the world, is in fact itself an object capable of conflicting with other objects of the same type, sometimes in a painful manner. In fact syntax is merely a sum of conventions of the same type as those which make us see a coherent universe. And these conventions are worth no more than those which oblige us to use special cutlery for fish. It would take far too long to engage in a detailed analysis of the tendencies connected to this attitude, for this would involve grappling with the totality of European poetry of the beginning of the twentieth century. Moreover, such a discussion would be specious, in that *zaum'* poetry is above all an attempt to discover meaning by new means, and not the account of a fracturing of the world such as is presupposed by the notion of the absurd.[25] Indeed, it is not by chance that the poetry of Kharms subsequently approximates more to the form of prayer than to the destructive Dadaism of a Tristan Tzara. The quest for a new perception of the world is clearly expressed in the few words of introduction to Kharms contained in the OBERIU declaration of 1928:[26]

> DANIIL KHARMS – poet and dramatist, whose attention is concentrated not on the static figure, but on the clashing of a series of objects, on their interaction. At the moment of action, an object acquires new specific outlines, full of effective sense. An action, transformed in a new manner, retains in itself a 'classical' imprint and at the same time it represents a broad sweep of OBERIU-type attitudes . . .

However, a mistrust *vis-à-vis* words and the affirmation of their incapacity to express anything of the world but its incoherence is a fundamental element of the theatre of the absurd, and Ionesco has always had plenty to say on this. In *Notes and Counternotes* we read the following analysis of his anti-play *The Bald Prima Donna* (1948), described, in the sub-title of the article as 'a tragedy of language':[27]

> . . . the language was dislocated, the characters were decomposed; the speech, which was absurd, had been emptied of content and the whole thing ended with a quarrel, the motivation for which was impossible to know, for my characters spewed forth not responses, nor even bits of clauses, nor words, but syllables, or consonants, or vowels! . . .

In the short unpublished sketch of Kharms which follows, one finds exactly the same process of decomposition and explosion of language:[28]

KOKA BRIANSKY: I'm getting married today.
MOTHER: What?
KOKA BRIANSKY: I'm getting married today.
MOTHER: What?
KOKA BRIANSKY: I said I'm getting married today.
MOTHER: What did you say?
KOKA BRIANSKY: To-day – ma-rried!
MOTHER: Ma? What's *ma*?
KOKA BRIANSKY: Ma-rri-age!
MOTHER: Idge? What's this idge?
KOKA BRIANSKY: Not idge, but ma-rri-age!
MOTHER: What do you mean, not idge?
KOKA BRIANSKY: Yes, not idge, that's all!
MOTHER: What?

| | |
|---|---|
| KOKA BRIANSKY: | Yes, not idge. Do you understand! Not idge! |
| MOTHER: | You're on about that idge again. I don't know what idge's got to do with it. |
| KOKA BRIANSKY: | Oh blow you! *Ma* and *idge*! What's up with you? Don't you realise yourself that saying just *ma* is senseless. |
| MOTHER: | What did you say? |
| KOKA BRIANSKY: | *Ma*, I said, is *senseless*!!! |
| MOTHER: | sle? |
| KOKA BRIANSKY: | What on earth is all this! How can you possibly manage to catch only bits of words, and only the most absurd bits at that: sle! Why sle in particular? |
| MOTHER: | There you go again – sle. |

*Koka Briansky throttles his mother. Enter his fiancée Marusia.*

The word is fragmented in this short dialogue. This dislocation allows the creation of an abnormal rhythm of which a physical perception is possible: the play of the phonemes 'b', 'a', 'k' [in the original], if the scene is effectively performed, must be heard by the audience as the rhythm of a percussionist.[29] The mother responds each time by taking up only a fraction of what has previously been uttered and consequently, while remaining within the traditional form of dialogue, the result is collisions and ruptures in its logical unfolding. And this puts in danger the entirety of the rules which subtend it. Its self-destruction is evident and it is moreover the reason why Koka Briansky perfects the agony by neutralizing his interlocutor, that is to say one of the very conditions of the existence of dialogue.

The whole human tragedy is there present: if language is incapable of expressing the real world, does that mean that the latter is itself incomprehensible, or perhaps that it does not even exist? Ionesco continues with these words:[30]

> ... For me, it was about a sort of collapse of the real. Words had become sonorous crusts, denuded of sense; characters also, of course, had been emptied of psychology and the world appeared to me in a weird light, perhaps in its true light, beyond interpretation and arbitrary causality.

Would the absurd then not be this paradoxical and incoherent manner of saying that nothing exists, but that we must still speak of it, for to speak is not to die just yet? That anyway is what Beckett says in a few terrifying verses drawn from *Mirlitonnades* (1976–8):[31]

> flux cause
> que toute chose
> tout en étant
> toute chose
> donc celle-là
> même celle-là
> tout en étant
> n'est pas
> parlons-en

We shall now see that this human dismay in the face of the world and this constriction of the word will be encountered down to the very narrative structure of texts, themselves condemned henceforth to prostration and death.

## TOWARDS ALMOST LESS THAN NOTHING

> Ivan Iakovlevich turned pale . . . but at this point events become completely enshrouded in mist, and of what happened next absolutely nothing is known.[32]

Thus ends the first chapter of Gogol's *The Nose*, And this is just one example among numerous others which make Gogol's *oeuvre* a vast system of onslaughts upon canonical prose. The discourse of the narrator is incessantly threatened with disintegration; from the impossibility of expressing what there is to say to purely and simply forgetting events to be narrated, there is a whole gamut of procedures which mutilates narrative discourse and puts in peril the very validity of the literary enterprise. For example, in *The Overcoat*, after a short introductory description of Petrovich the tailor, one reads the following commentary:[33]

> Of this tailor, of course, one ought not to say much, but since it is already established that in a tale the character of each personage should be fully spelt out, then there is nothing else for it; we'll just have to cough up here over Petrovich.

The description of a new character, to all intents and purposes customary in traditional prose, is ridiculed from the outset by an adroit game of self-reflection on the part of the narration.

We have seen the astonished – frightened even – glance of man upon the world; we have seen how this divorce is reflected in the impossibility of language being capable of expressing this world; now we have the astonished glance which literature turns upon itself.

In *Evenings on a Farm near Dikanka*, the story *Ivan Fëdorovich Shpon'ka and his Aunt* provides perhaps the most spectacular example of this process, since the plot is presented from the beginning as unfinished. The novella begins by recounting how it has become a novella: 'This story has a story behind it'.[34] The narrator, as is often the case with Gogol, has a memory which he himself compares to a sieve. That is why he asks the person who has recounted the events to him to write them for him. Unfortunately his wife will use the sheets of the final chapter for cooking purposes and he himself will forget to ask the author over again for the ending: 'There's nothing to be done, we'll just have to publish it without the ending'.[35] We have in this novella just about all the characteristics of the authors who can be ranged in this tradition which we have classified as the *absurd*, with all the reservations which we have made. The figure of Shpon'ka is just as crushed by his setting as is Plume. In his dream, he is stricken, faced by women, with the same anguish as is Kalugin, in Kharms, faced by the militiaman. It should suffice to compare extracts from the two texts to persuade ourselves of this. First Gogol:[36]

> Suddenly someone grabbed him by the ear. 'Ow! who's that? – 'It's me, your wife! – said some voice or other noisily to him. And he suddenly woke up. [. . .] He inadvertently turned over and saw another wife, also with a goose's face. He turned back again – there stood a third wife. Back – yet another wife. At this point he felt sick. He rushed out into the garden; but in the garden it was hot. He took his hat off and looked at it; in his hat too sat a wife. Sweat started to run down his face. He reached in his pocket for his handkerchief – and in his pocket was a wife; he took a cotton thread from his ear – and there sat a wife . . .

And now Kharms:[37]

> Kalugin went to sleep and had a dream, that he was sitting in some bushes and past the bushes strolled a militiaman.
> Kalugin woke up, scratched his mouth and went to sleep again, again dreaming that he was walking past the bushes and in the bushes a militiaman had concealed himself and was sitting.
> Kalugin woke up, put a newspaper under his head, so as not to wet

the pillow with spittle and again went to sleep and again dreamed that he was sitting in the bushes and past the bushes strolled a militiaman. [...]

And so on, to the point of becoming 'insanitary'!

In both dreams an obsessive image returns and invades the subject's imaginary space to such an extent that he suffers physical attacks. It is therefore not only the exterior world which subdues Kalugin and Ivan Fëdorovich, but the whole interior universe of the two figures, to the extent that it is no longer possible really to speak of them as 'characters', since the former is coarsely thrown on the rubbish heap, while the latter does not even have the right to the end of his story.

We may note again that the impotence of Shponka is linked to his own speech:[38]

> At this point he stopped, as though he couldn't get hold of the proper word any more. There's nothing to prevent me here saying that he was not generally the greatest with words. Perhaps this was from timidity and, it could be, from a desire to express himself more elegantly.

Later Ivan Fëdorovich, who has just pronounced a short sentence of extreme platitude, is 'pleased to have uttered such a long and difficult sentence'.[39] In Kharms too one finds numerous figures who similarly find themselves silenced. This is the case with Kuznetsov, in an untitled text dating from 1935.[40] This character goes out with the intention of buying glue but, passing a building site, he gets a brick on the head. In order to revive his spirits, Kuznetsov recites to himself his identity and what he has to do:

> – I, citizen Kuznetsov, went out of my house and went to a shop in order to ... in order to ... Oh, what's wrong with me! I've forgotten why I went to the shop!

He receives a second brick on the head straight away, then a third and a fourth. With each brick he repeats his sentence, but each time a bit is curtailed, so that he forgets first where he wanted to go, then why he had gone out, then where he had gone out from and, finally, who he is:

> – Well, now! said Kuznetsov, scratching the back of his head. I ... I ... I ... Who am I? Have I really forgotten what my name is? What a business! What is my name, then? Vasilii Petukhov? No. Nikolai Sapogov? No. Pantelei Rysakov? No. Well, who am I then?

The loss of ego goes hand-in-hand with loss of speech; after the fifth and last brick, there remains of Kuznetsov no more than a sound denuded of sense ('O-go-go!') and a distraught flight, far from himself.

These problems of elocution are also extremely common in the work of Beckett. All the spectres which haunt his works are victims of it. And it could be said that, in a general manner, this reflection on speech is a fundamental question posed by this great writer. This assumes striking proportions in the short 'play' *Not I* (note the negation of the 'I' contained in the title), which puts on stage as its main character 'Mouth'. This figure, by little scraps of phrases, often agrammatical, broken by ellipsis, recounts her own story, which is that of transition from the unintelligible to discourse, a discourse which gradually gets carried away and which nothing could channel any further:[41]

... no idea what she's saying! ... and can't stop ... no stopping it ... she who but a moment before ... but a moment! ... could not make a sound ... no sound of any kind ... now can't stop ...

The 'mouth has gone mad' and the brain also is in 'total delirium'. It is the infernal struggle to render the world coherent, to give it *sense*. But speech is not capable of this ....:[42]

... so on ... grabbing at the straw ... straining to hear ... the odd word ... make some sense of it ... whole body like gone ... just the mouth ... like maddened ... and can't stop ... no stopping it ... something she-... something she had to-... what? .. who? .. no! .. she! ..

The question therefore arises: in this 'steady stream', is there a 'tiny little thing' which Mouth ought to pronounce? 'Keep on trying', she tells herself, but the curtain is already coming slowly down and her last words are:[43]

... April morning ... face in the grass ... nothing but the larks ... pick it up–

After that the voice becomes unintelligible again, as at the beginning of the play, before going definitively silent. And if, as in *Ivan Fëdorovich Shpon'ka and his Aunt*, one has no right to an ending, it is evidently because an ending does not exist ...

It should be stressed that it is not simply a matter of a plot which fizzles out. The false dénouement is only an episode in a narrative which never stops dying, in the same style as the discourse: the chapter called 'The Road' in *Ivan Fëdorovich Shpon'ka and his Aunt* begins with the words: 'Along the road nothing remarkable happened'.[44] This procedure is almost a rule with Kharms. The most striking example is the beginning of this unfinished text:[45]

> At two o'clock in the afternoon on Nevskii Prospekt, or rather on Prospekt 25th October, nothing special happened. No, no, that person beside the Coliseum had stopped simply by chance.

The technique consists then in announcing a narration or an explanation which will not take place. The short text by Kharms called *Simfoniia No 2* ('Symphony No. 2')[46] is typical: several times over, the narrator begins to recount the story of a new character who, each time, for one reason or another, leaves the text. For example:

> Il'ia Pavlovich was born in 1893 in Constantinople. When still a small boy he was brought to Petersburg and here he passed through the German school on Kirochnaia Street. Then he worked in some shop or other, then he did something else and, at the start of the revolution he emigrated. Well, forget him. I'd do better to tell you about Anna Ignat'evna.

Everything started with great precision, with the date and place of birth, and the reader could expect a narrative within the rules. But, immediately, this begins to crumble before collapsing completely one line later: the character is lost. So much the worse for us. Of the candidate for the story which follows, the narrator confesses to knowing almost nothing and immediately abandons her to her absence of fate in order to speak of himself. One is, at this point, in the same mist as at the end of the first chapter of *The Nose* and these successive plotlines terminate themselves like that of Shpon'ka. On his own account, the narrator decides to recount an event (a *sluchai*) which has happened to him:

> And so a funny thing happened to me with Marina Petrovna, which I want to talk about. The incident was quite usual but, all the same, amusing, for Marina Petrovna, thanks to me, went completely bald, like the palm of your hand. It happened like this: once I arrived at Marina Petrovna's and she – bang! – and she went bald. And that's all.

In saying that he is going to tell us how Marina Petrovna became bald, the narrator promises us a story. And this story is reduced to repeating what we know already.

Exactly the same thing is to be found in Gogol's *The Carriage* (one example among others), when the narrator decides to tell us which *sluchai* had obliged his hero Chertokutsky to leave the cavalry:[47]

> It's highly likely that he would have dissipated in other provinces too a fame advantageous to himself, if he had not gone into retirement from a certain incident [*po odnomu sluchaiu*] which would usually be called an unpleasant story: whether he had given someone a slap in the face years ago, or he had been given it, I am not entirely sure, but the point is that he was asked to retire.

As in the case of Il'ia Pavlovich, development of the narration is prevented by a weak memory (the same thing as with the narrator of *Ivan Fëdorovich Shpon'ka and his Aunt*) and, as with Marina Petrovna, we have been told that a *sluchai* will be recounted, yet we have been told nothing really at all. We are in the same mist. Well, forget about us . . .

In fact there is a global doubt which little by little installs itself over the particular work and over literature in general. The proportions which this doubt assumed in the texts of Beckett are sensational. In the long diatribe of Malone, which is just as much in its death-throes as is he who utters it, one reads:[48]

> But what matter whether I was born or not, have lived or not, am dead or merely dying, I shall go on doing as I have always done, not knowing what it is I do, nor who I am, nor where I am, nor if I am.

*Ivan Fëdorovich Shpon'ka and his Aunt* finishes cruelly with the following words: 'Meanwhile, in his aunt's head there ripened a completely new scheme, about which you will learn in the next chapter',[49] a chapter which, as has already been made clear, does not exist. This is ultimately logical, since the degenerating speech of the protagonist, in the same way as that of the narrator without memory, oriented the tale towards silence from the beginning. And these two lines deliver a serious blow to literature, which, in the twentieth century, is to develop this technique, pushing it, without any pun, to the point of the *absurd*.

We find this device of incompletion again in the work of Kharms, in the story *Piat' neokonchennykh povestvovanii* ('Five Unfinished Narratives')[50] The title immediately announces this quality: the failure to finish a story is elevated to the level of a genre. The first of the five stories is interrupted, in full 'sequence', with the words:

> We cease narration on the subject of the blacksmith and the unknown man and begin a new narrative about four friends and a harem.

The second story begins with the classic 'Once upon a time . . .' ('*Zhil-byl* . . .'), only to be interrupted in the same manner several lines further. The three following morsels of text bring in to play the same figure, a philosopher, and it is no longer a question from then strictly speaking of *rasskazy*, but rather of philosophical pseudo-arguments. The fifth and last 'story' can be summed up in a sentence:

> The philosopher strolled under the trees and kept quiet, because inspiration had abandoned him.

There is neither narration, nor speech any more. But huge silence . . .

In Beckett, the theme of incompletion is permanent: his texts are as dying as his characters; this is seen, for example, in the panting of the Voice in the short radio play *Cascando*, which begins as follows:[51]

> -story . . . if you could finish it . . . you could rest . . . sleep . . . not before . . . oh I know . . . the ones I've finished . . . thousands and one . . . all I ever did . . . in my life . . . with my life . . . saying to myself . . . finish this one . . . it's the right one . . . then rest . . . sleep . . . no more stories . . . no more words . . . and finished it . . . and not the right one . . .

Of course, the story of Maunu which the Voice is attempting to tell, will not finish. Henry declares the same thing in *Embers*:[52]

> I usen't to need anyone, just to myself, stories, there was a great one about an old fellow called Bolton, I never finished it, I never finished any of them, I never finished anything, everything always went on for ever.

The first speech of Clov, in *Endgame* [!] begins as follows:[53]

> Finished, it's finished, nearly finished, it must be nearly finished.

After that, the play will never finish finishing. Hamm will say:[54]

> I'll soon have finished with this story. (*Pause.*) Unless I bring in other characters. (*Pause.*) But where would I find them?

Life is only an 'old lost endgame', in which the partners serve merely to 'give their cue', for it is essential to speak, in order not to die. Beckett's texts are all dying, always at the limit of non-being.

Likewise, the stories of Kharms have a general tendency of expressing the impossibility of being of the stories. They attack fundamentally all the narrative conventions which would permit them simply to exist. In the celebrated *Golubaia tetrad' No. 10* ('Blue

Notebook No. 10'),[55] a character is announced, who will be physically eliminated within a few lines: he has no eyes, neither ears, nor hair, nor nose, etc. And, consequently, 'it is better that we should not say anything more about him'. The story breaks off, for want of participants. In *Simfoniia No 2*, as we have seen, the characters leave the text one after the other, taking with them each time what could have been related about them. It only remains for the narrator to speak of himself, and even this will not be attained.

All traditional categories are therefore mocked, starting with the most elementary ones, such as time, though it is essential in narrative development. In *Krapp's Last Tape* by Beckett, the action takes place on 'A late evening in the future'.[56] It brings to the stage a figure who re-listens for the nth time to his life, which he has recorded on magnetic tapes, from which he consequently is able to manipulate at will the temporal unfolding, by jumping bits or going back.

With Beckett, everything merges into a dense mist, like the story of Ivan Iakovlevich: 'The old fog calls',[57] says Malone in *Malone Dies*, a novel which, let it be said in passing, is itself also constructed from a number of beginnings of narratives. From novel to novel, from play to play, his works progress towards non-being by the systematic negation of everything which had characterized until then a certain type of 'literature': his characters are a class of talking vegetables, for whom the slightest gesture is a suffrance: time is concentrated entirely in the idea of the finish never finishing; narrated events are derisory and incapable of forming a plot; the syntax itself is often defective, the reflection of a dying discourse, itself as incoherent as the thought which it tries unsuccessfully to express.[58]

> Did I say I only say a small proportion of the things that come into my head? I must have. I choose those that seem somehow akin. It is not always easy. I hope they are the most important. I wonder if I shall ever be able to stop.

In a word, the work is entirely orientated towards the 'never . . . more' in the last words of *Malone Dies*, for 'nothing is more real than nothing'.[59]

Destruction threatens everything, down to the essential tool of writing, the small bit of lead which Malone uses to note down his states of mind:[60]

> What a misfortune, the pencil must have slipped from my fingers, for I have only just succeeded in recovering it after forty-eight

hours (see above) of intermittent efforts. [...] I have spent two unforgettable days of which nothing will ever be known [...]

Further:[61]

> Perhaps I should throw away my lead [pencil]. I could never retrieve it now. I might be sorry. My little lead. It is a risk I do not feel inclined to take, just now.

Rarely had literature had such a fright since the wife of the narrator of *Ivan Fëdorovich Shpon'ka and his Aunt* had utilised the last chapter of the novella for cooking, unless in the work of Kharms, when, in *Khudozhnik i chasy* ('The Artist and the Clock'), the story breaks off and ends with these words:[62]

> Heck! I would have written more, but the ink-pot has suddenly disappeared somewhere.

In short, in this tradition of the absurd, literature is in the process of becoming that *unnamable* which was to give its name to the last novel of Beckett's trilogy.[63] And this leads not towards anti-literature, but towards *non*-literature.

And so, one should naturally ask whether it is plausible to have in one's hands a literary work and to affirm at the same time that literature is no more. The reply must of course be negative. It is clear that if we read Beckett or Kharms we experience, to take up an expression from Barthes, a certain *'plaisir du texte'*.[64] From where does this pleasure emanate? We have seen that the absurd is, more than a painful statement of divorce between man and the world, a certain type of parodic process pushed to the limit. The absurd is the incoherence of the world, elevated to the level of the means of expressing this incoherence. And it is perhaps in this single correspondence of the said and the saying that, at the same time, the *'plaisir du texte'* and the secret of the longevity and the productivity of the genre reside.

NOTES

This essay is a revised version of Jaccard (1988a)
1. E. Ionesco, *Notes et contre-notes*. (Paris: Gallimard [1966] 1979) p. 297.
2. Cf. Martin Esslin, *The Theatre of the Absurd* (first published New

York, 1961). Despite the intellect displayed in his survey, Esslin groups under this title all sorts of authors, some of whom are rather distant from what is covered by the notion of the absurd.
3. A. Camus, *Le mythe de Sisyphe*, (Paris: Gallimard [1942] 1973) p. 48.
4. The play *Elizaveta Bam* was first published by G. Gibian in *Izbrannoe* (1974). Preferable is the version published by M. Meilakh at Stanford (1987) and, with V. Erl', in Riga (1988). In English, see Gibian's versions of 1971 (and 1974) and 1987, plus the new translation by N. Cornwell offered in the present volume.
5. It is impossible to affirm that Kharms had read this novel, all the more so as it did not then enjoy the readership that it has today, but the close chronological proximity of the two texts remains astonishing. It can, moreover, be added that Kharms studied at Peterschule (*'Glavnoe nemetskoe uchilishche sv. Petra'*), where foreign languages were taught, and that he thereby knew German and English.
6. Published by I. Levin in *Kontinent* 24, 1980, pp. 289–91 (see also *Plummeting*, pp. 80–2). This is just one example among many. See, in the same publication, the text *Shapka* (pp. 283–4), which also tells of an arrest, involving this time an old man tackled by a militiaman and 'some citizen or other in a grey suit'.
7. Michaux spoke later of Plume as a *'personnage-tampon'*, who receives blows in place of the author, placing himself between the latter and the world. A number of the characters of Kharms seem to play a similar role.
8. H. Michaux, *Un certain Plume* (Paris: Gallimard, 1930); reprinted in id., *L'espace du dedans (pages choisies 1927–1959)* (Paris: Gallimard [1966] expanded 1973) p. 83.
9. The play *Elizaveta Bam* is constructed on the same principle. At the beginning, she is arrested although no crime has been committed. When the first scene is repeated at the end, crime has taken place. Elizabeth Bam has not committed it, but that does not matter: the play which originated in nothing at all serves to justify an arbitrary act and, consequently, to justify itself. In Michaux's text too, Plume, unjustly accused from the outset, finds himself by the end guilty of having nothing to say.
10. Manuscript Section of the State Public Library (Leningrad), fond 1232, m.s. 348. The text is probably unfinished. In a variant, quite different but equally close to Michaux's text, the waiter does not understand the order and repeats incessantly and imperturbably 'What do you wish to order?'. When he finally manages to repeat the strange words ('bëf–bui'), he leaves the dining room perplexed and a new waiter brings the menu, thus repeating the opening scene (a circularity recalling that of *Elizaveta Bam*).
11. N. Gogol', *Sobranie sochinenii v vos'mi tomakh* (Moscow, 1984) vol. 3, p. 43.
12. *Izb.* (1974), p. 93; *Pölet*, p. 376; *Black Coat*, p. 66.
13. *Izb.*, pp. 54–5; *Pölet*, p. 367; *Black Coat*, p. 80.
14. It is worth pointing out an error in the text published by Gibian. The sentence runs as follows: '*Kalugin spal chetyre dnia i chetyre nochi*

podriad . . .', not '*Kalugin spal chetyre nochi podriad* . . .'. This error is repeated in my article (see Jaccard, 1985, p. 279).
15. *Pölet*, pp. 398–430; *Black Coat*, pp. 123–53; published for the first time in the Soviet Union in *Novyi mir*, 4, 1988, pp. 142–56. On the echoes of Russian literature in this novella, see Chances (1985), tracing parallels with works by Pushkin, Dostoevskii, Gogol' and Chekhov.
16. V. Shklovskii (1967).
17. Ionesco, op. cit., p. 295.
18. Gogol', op. cit., vol. 3, p. 14.
19. Ibid., p. 17.
20. Ibid., p. 18.
21. Ibid., p. 178.
22. Published in Jaccard (1985), pp. 304–7, with an error in point 27 which I now take the opportunity of rectifying: '*Vremia, ispytyvaia prepiatstvie prostranstva* [not *proshedshego*], *raskalyvaetsia na chasti, obrazuia troitsu sushchestvovaniia*'.
23. Published by V. Erl', 'Iz zapisnykh knizhek', *Avrora*, 7, 1974, 78; in this publication, the signature with the initial double consonant is omitted.
24. Aleksandr Tufanov (1877– 194?), the prime mover of 'Zaumnyi orden', in which Kharms appeared, then co-founder, with Kharms and Vvedenskii among others, of the first version of 'Levyi Flang' in 1925. He is the author of three books (all three self-published with low print-runs): the first, *Eolova arfa* (St Petersburg, 1917) is neo-Symbolist in inspiration, while the two following ones, *K zaumi* (Petrograd, 1924) and *Ushkuiniki* (Petrograd, 1927) seem rather a repetition and a radicalisation of the system of consonantal phoneme semantics established by Khlebnikov and Kruchënykh.
25. This is what Apollinaire also had said, in *Calligrammes* (1918):

'O bouches l'homme est à la recherche d'un nouveau langage
Auquel le grammairien d'aucune langue n'aura rien à dire'

(Paris: Gallimard, 1974, p. 180).
26. 'OBERIU', *Afishi Doma pechati* (Leningrad), 2, 1928, pp. 11–13. Reprinted in Milner-Gulland (1970); and in *Izb.*, pp. 285–98, under the (non-original) title of 'Manifest OBERIU'; also in *Black Coat*, pp. 245–54.
27. Ionesco, op. cit., p. 252.
28. Manuscript Section of the State Public Library (Leningrad), fond 1232, ms. 345 (1933). The passage quoted is preceded by '*1 deistvie*', suggesting that the text was to have been longer. Moreover, the text is preceded by a crossed out passage with the title '*Piesa*', announcing the character '*pisatel' Shvarts*' (probably Evgenii Shvarts, with whom Kharms collaborated on the magazines *Chizh* and *Ezh*), the marriage with Marusia, as well as a second act. The stage direction '*dushit mat*'' is preceded by '*brosaetsia na mat*'', crossed out.
29. This short scene has been staged by M. Levitin at the Teatr Miniatiur in Moscow, as part of the review 'Kharms, Charms, Shardam ili shkola klounov', which assembles a number of the texts of Kharms and which has had a successful run, now into years. In order to overcome the

incompletion of the text, Levitin had the excellent idea of repeating it several times before Koka Briansky cracks, underlying simultaneously the lack of communication between characters and the circularity of the dialogue (which, as we have seen, is a trait of the absurd).

30. Ionesco, op. cit., p. 252.
31. Samuel Beckett, *Poèmes suivi de mirlitonnades* (Paris: Les Éditions de Minuit, 1978) p. 36.
32. Gogol', op. cit., vol. 3, p. 43.
33. Ibid., p. 127.
34. Ibid., vol. 1, p. 238.
35. Ibid., p. 239.
36. Ibid., p. 262.
37. *Izb.*, p. 54; *Pölet*, p. 367.
38. Gogol', op. cit., vol. 1, p. 246.
39. Ibid., p. 256.
40. Published by I. Petrovichev in *Russkaia mysl'* (1985); reprinted and analysed in Jaccard (1985), pp. 292–3; *Plummeting*, pp. 22–3.
41. Samuel Beckett, *The Complete Dramatic Works* (London: Faber, 1986) p. 380.
42. Ibid., p. 381.
43. Ibid., p. 383.
44. Gogol', op. cit., vol. 1, p. 243.
45. Beginning of an unpublished text of about one page (preserved in the Manuscript Section, State Public Library, Leningrad), unfinished and crossed out in blue pencil. In about 1940, it would seem, Kharms took up, corrected and annotated his texts in red or blue pencil, sometimes taking care to date the correction.
46. *Izb.*, pp. 98–9; *Black Coat*, p. 53; reprinted and analysed in Jaccard (1985), pp. 290–1.
47. Gogol', vol. 3, p. 154.
48. Samuel Beckett, *Molloy, Malone Dies. The Unnamable* (London: Calder & Boyars [1959] 1973) p. 226 [hereafter: Beckett, Trilogy].
49. Gogol', vol. 1. p. 263
50. Published by I. Levin, *Soviet Union/Union Soviétique* (1980), p. 231; *Polët*, pp. 498–9; *Plummeting*, pp. 43–4.
51. Beckett, *Complete Dramatic Works*, op. cit., p. 297.
52. Ibid., p. 254.
53. Ibid., p. 93.
54. Ibid., p. 118.
55. *Izb.*, p. 47: *Polët*, p. 353; analysed in Jaccard (1985), pp. 289–90; *Plummeting*, p. 27; *Black Coat*, p. 57.
56. Beckett, *Complete Dramatic Works*, p. 215.
57. Beckett, Trilogy, p. 182.
58. Ibid., p. 254.
59. Ibid., p. 193.
60. Ibid., p. 222.
61. Ibid., p. 254.
62. Published by I. Petrovichev in *Russkaia mysl'* (1985); reprinted in Jaccard (1985), p. 292; *Plummeting*, p. 25.

## General Studies

63. S. Beckett, *L'innommable* (Paris: Minuit, 1952); English translation by the author in Beckett, Trilogy (1959).
64. R. Barthes, *Le plaisir du texte* (Paris: Seuil, 1973).

*Translated from the French by Neil Cornwell*

# 5 The Anti-World of Daniil Kharms: On the Significance of the Absurd
Anthony Anemone

Among the various interpretations of the prose of Daniil Kharms put forward since the rediscovery of the OBERIUTY in the 1960s and 1970s, three approaches in particular have proven especially influential. The first approach may be called international in that it locates the 'key' to Kharms's prose in its parallels to twentieth-century European literature of the absurd. While George Gibian was careful to describe the OBERIU's Russian context as well as to point out some of the important differences between Kharms and writers such as Kafka and Beckett, he was also the first to argue that the OBERIUTY 'belong to the history of the European literature of the absurd' (Gibian, 1974: 32). More recently, Lazar Fleishman has noted the remarkable resistance of OBERIU poetry to critical analysis, and contrasted it to the relative ease with which literary scholars have assimilated the OBERIU prose and theatre to the norms of European literature of the absurd.[1] While parallels with European literature of the absurd can illuminate the general phenomenon of OBERIU literature,[2] this approach is limited by its ahistoricity and its inability to account for the specific Russian and Soviet cultural traditions and contexts with which Kharms's texts are inextricably connected.

A second interpretation of the OBERIU focuses on the parodic intertextual relationship between their works and the Russian literary tradition.[3] According to this view, OBERIU texts are said to prepare the ground for a new literature of the avant-garde through the systematic 'destruction', 'rewriting', or 'decanonization' of a moribund literary canon (Flaker, 1969; Chances, 1985; Vishevsky, 1986). The assumptions of this approach are cogently expressed in a recent article by Anatolii Vishevsky: 'The *oberiuty* aimed at creating their own world of literary reality, different from and contrasting to that of preceding literary traditions. But before creating the new world, they had to "destroy" the old one. The weapon they chose for this purpose was literary parody' (Vishevsky, 1986: 355). While literary parody certainly represents a central element of OBERIU texts, this approach is often flawed by its mechanistic and narrow formal explication of the intertextual problem, which it tends to construe as the one-sided and destructive parody of an outmoded literary tradition. Readings from this perspective suffer from two related problems: they tend to project everywhere the same self-referential message of the destructive and purifying aspects of literary parody and are, therefore, unable to articulate any positive programme. While such readings can show, for example, how a typical OBERIU text might 'destroy' a particular literary device, genre or tradition, they have considerably more difficulty describing the new 'literary reality' for the sake of which the old has been destroyed.

A third reading, less well represented in the secondary literature, sees the thematic 'key' to Kharms's prose in the author's use of the absurd to explore the nature of good and evil. The roots of this interpretation can be found in the following characterisation of Kharms by Iakov Semënovich Druskin (1902–80), a close friend and collaborator of the OBERIUTY (see p. 24 above):

> Kharms was interested in evil, in the root of evil in man. But he wasn't a philosopher or moralist: rather, he was a writer, but a writer with a definite philosophical bent. Therefore, even in his frightening stories he doesn't moralize, but rather laughs as he reveals evil, narrow-mindedness, and fatuity. And his laughter is at times no less terrifying than the laughter of Gogol, whom he greatly admired and with whom his creative work is closely related.

Such an approach has several distinct advantages over the two interpretations outlined above. For example, by locating the connection between laughter and terror in the problem of evil, it grounds Kharms in a specific Russian tradition of moral satire ('laughter through tears'). Also, by emphasising the essentially ethical concerns of Kharms's absurdism, this approach is capable of contextualising the intersection of his prose texts with the political and literary realities of Leningrad life in the 1930s, thus avoiding the hermetically-closed readings characteristic of purely formal analyses. Finally, such a reading encourages a more complete and complex image of Kharms and his fictional universe, which is too often seen as no more than a parody of the life, language and worldview of the Soviet urban philistine of the 1930s.[4] Many stories which have been ignored or relegated to the margins of Kharms's corpus because they did not accord with the standard image of the playful and eccentric humorist now appear central to his literary programme. Testing this hypothesis on a more representative body of Kharms's prose texts, then, would seem to be one of the urgent tasks facing Kharms criticism today.[5]

Recently, a young Soviet scholar has taken up the challenge of developing such a contextualizing approach to the works of Kharms and the OBERIUTY. Anna Gerasimova's 1988 article, 'OBERIU: The Problem of the Comic' provides, perhaps, the best general introduction to the poetics of the OBERIU, which she sees as a unified literary phenomenon, and points the way out of the current critical impasse. Building on unpublished works by Druskin and Leonid Savelich Lipavsky (pseud. L. Savel'ev; 1904–41), another close friend and associate of Kharms and Vvedensky,[6] Gerasimova argues that the comic should be seen as the key to the OBERIU 'worldview' and draws a convincing sketch of the organic connections between the outwardly very different works by Oleinikov, Zabolotsky, Vvedensky and Kharms. In her most important insight, Gerasimova describes Kharms's movement from poetry to prose as the transfer of the dominant semantic experimentation of his early poetry to the sphere of ethics, where actions replace words as the material to be explored.[7] According to Gerasimova, Kharms's prose represents an ethical experiment in which the author sets out to explore the limits of human behaviour in a world with no firm ethical values, a Dostoevskian world where 'all is permitted.' Kharms's 'black humour', she continues, derives from the absence of any ethical differentiation between good and evil, ugly and beautiful, the usual and the miraculous, even between life and death. In the absence of such values and distinction, cause and effect are replaced by the laws of caprice and accident, and the end result is the nullification of all emotion and meaning: in other words, an absurd world' (Gerasimova, 1988: 75–7).

Characteristic of Gerasimova's provocative analysis is her ability to succinctly describe the formal elements of Kharms's prose style, while subtly directing the reader to the crucial connections between Kharms's texts and Stalin's Soviet Union of the 1930s. For the Soviet reader in particular, her reading of such typically Kharmsian themes as cruel and unmotivated violence against the weak and innocent, the moral equivalence of life and death, and the breakdown of language, logic and cause and effect, as part of a general disillusionment with the creation of a new Soviet reality and a 'new Soviet man'[8] is startlingly original. Gerasimova's Kharms, far from a creative but harmless eccentric, is a writer who used the literary techniques of the absurd to dramatise the central social, ethical and philosophical problems of his age. While this approach promises a breakthrough in our understanding of Kharms's role in the literary processes of the 1930s, Gerasimova has only scratched the surface of an issue which represents, perhaps, the central thematic 'key' to Kharms's late prose: the ethical significance of the Kharmsian absurd. The challenge, then, is to show how a thorough analysis of the absurd in Kharms's prose can lead to a fundamental revision of the familiar image of the author as a playful and eccentric parodist.

While almost all the critics would agree that the absurd (*alogichnost'*, *obratnost'*, *bessmyslitsa*) plays the central role in Kharms's humour, there exists considerably less consensus as to how the absurd should be interpreted.[9] Perhaps the most common interpretation sees the absurd as a tool of a general 'defamiliarisation' (*ostranenie*). The targets of Kharms's 'defamiliarising' absurd include almost everything: traditional literary genres and styles, cult figures, the 'mechanical' language, perception and existence of the urban Philistine, and the absurdities of life itself. Kharms's purpose, according to this point of view, is to remove the blinders of automatic perception from the reader's eyes and allow him to perceive the true essence of his language, art, literature, and life. This reading is supported by the OBERIU manifesto which defines the aesthetic function in basic formalist terms, as the liberation of words and objects from the clichéd and traditional associations that have accumulated through overuse and which blind us to their true essences (Milner-Gulland, 1970: 70). While some critics stress Kharms's subversion of our 'ordinary' understanding of reality (Vishevsky, 1986: 257), others ascribe the absurdity of Kharms's stories to life itself:[10]

> In his stories and poems one is confronted with what is often called absurdity, alogic. But it is not his stories which are absurd and alogical, but rather the life which he describes in them. For both the formal absurdity and alogic of situations in his works, as well as his humor, were a means of revealing life itself, an expression of the real absurdity of a mechanized existence, of various real states which are characteristic of every person. (Meilakh and Aleksandrov, 1967: 102–3)

One of the most interesting interpretations of the effects of 'defamiliarisation' in Kharms's prose belongs to Viktor Shklovsky. According to Shklovsky, the Kharmsian universe is constructed not on 'causal' (*prichinnye*) relations, but rather on 'habitual' connections (*privychnye sviazi*). His is a world of inertia, of 'common sense', which, in Shklovsky's witty and apt formulation, is 'usually nothing but the totality of the prejudices of an age' (Shklovskii, 1967: 16). Once the usual semantic, logical and moral relationships and associations are broken down by the grotesque action of the text, the world, which the reader had assumed to be solid, natural and unchangeable, loses its former stability and becomes unintelligible and absurd. Despite the brilliance of Shklovsky's formulations, his reading founders on its inability to specify the historical and social targets of Kharms's defamiliarisation, its failure, in other words, to ground his understanding of the absurd in the cultural web of Soviet society of the 1930s. To a greater or lesser extent, this failure is characteristic of all formal readings which refuse to engage the literary work's content as seriously and profoundly as they do its form.

To advance this line of analysis, what is needed is a critical approach which, while illuminating the historical and cultural context of Kharms's fictional universe, also provides a theoretical point of view broad enough to integrate the complex and contradictory elements of his prose into one literary system. Recent work by Soviet scholars on the semiotics of Russian culture points the way to a solution to this problem. In their *World of Laughter in Ancient Russia* ('*Smekhovoi mir*' *Drevnei Rusi*), Likhachëv and Panchenko develop the Bakhtinian notion of a Carnivalised 'anti-culture' to provide a provocative reading of the phenomenon of the 'holy fool in Christ' (*iurodstvo*) in medieval Russian culture. Central to their argument is the anti-system, that is, a semiotic system where the traditional fixed relationships between signifiers and signifieds of some dominant semiotic code are systemmatically disrupted or inverted. By rejecting the conventions, logic and limitations of the dominant culture, the anti-system provides a temporary escape from that culture; it opens up a utopian space, a world of desire and imagination that the authors call an anti-culture (Likhachëv and Panchenko, 1976: 3-4). By destroying the semiotic system of an official culture, parody is one way of creating such an anti-culture: 'One of the purposes of parody is the total destruction of the semantic system, of the world regulated by signs, and the complete construction of an unregulated world, a world of "anti-culture", a world which is in all respects absurd' (Likhachëv and Panchenko, 1976: 16). Among the side-effects of this semiotic destabilisation are a general loss of stability, a sense that everything is fantastic and unreal, and a total confusion of significance. In this 'anti-world',[11] Likhachëv and Panchenko have written, 'all signs signify the opposite of that which they signify in the "normal" world' (16–17).

While Likhachëv and Panchenko have been justly criticised for overstating the parallels between European carnival and the 'comic culture' of medieval Russia (Thompson, 1982; Lotman and Uspenskii, 1984), their notion of the anti-system provides a valuable tool for a semiotic analysis of Kharms's absurd prose texts. Their interpretation, for example, of the seemingly meaningless and absurd behaviour of the 'holy fool in Christ' as an ethical critique of the immorality of Russian society[12] is relevant to an analysis of the relationship of Kharms's absurd heroes and situations to the real world of Soviet Leningrad in the 1930s. In addition, through its transformation of wise men into fools and madmen into truth-tellers,[13] the spectacle of *iurodstvo* foregrounds issues of the transparency and referentiality of language and the stability of identity, which play a prominent role in Kharms's absurd prose as well. Finally, Likhachëv and Panchenko's characterisation of the anti-world of *iurodstvo* as delicately balanced between the comic and the tragic[14] is equally apt as a description of Kharms's absurd world. The worlds of medieval Russian *iurodstvo* and Kharms's absurd world are also related in that, despite their comic or absurd surface, they both demand an ethical reading from their audience. The person who understands the significance of such texts will not laugh at the comic and seemingly absurd heroes and actions – laughter is for the ignorant and the sinful – but will react to the ethical and moral lessons encoded in that behaviour: 'To cry over the comic – that is the positive end towards which the holy fool strives' (Likhachëv and Panchenko, 1976: 103–4). According to Likhachëv and Panchenko, the effect of *iurodstvo* can be described as a form of 'defamiliarisation' in the ethical sphere: 'it is as if the spectacle of the holy fool renews the "eternal verities", revives the passions' (105) and 'is the opposite of routine' (109). The purpose of the spectacle of the holy fool, in short, was to restore to medieval Russian society an accurate perception of its actual ethical, or rather unethical, conduct;[15] to one who does not understand this moral imperative, the actions and words of the holy fool must seem absurd and meaningless.

Interestingly, Lotman and Uspensky's revisions to Likhachëv and Panchenko's interpretation of medieval Russian 'comic culture' (Lotman and Uspenskii, 1984) shed additional light on Kharms's prose of the absurd. For example, the connection between the comic and the frightening, which Lotman and Uspensky see as unique to the cultural and religious system of Russia in which laughter always comes from the devil, represents as well a crucial element of Kharms's absurd universe: 'In the West European carnival the formula runs: "if it's funny, it's not to be feared" – since laughter removes a man from the confines of the serious medieval world where he is a victim of social and religious "terrors" (prohibitions). In Russia laughter, from the Yuletide and Shrovetide rituals to *Evenings on a Farm near Dikan'ka* by Gogol', is both "funny" and "scary"' (42). Rejecting the model of a 'comic culture' as foreign to the Russian tradition,[16] Lotman and Uspensky suggest that the anti-world of medieval satire and parody is rooted in pagan traditions of what they call 'magical anti-behavior' (43–4).

The potential of concepts such as the 'anti-world' and 'anti-behaviour' for a radical revision of traditional readings of Kharms is enormous. Such an approach, for example, can account, not only historically, but also theoretically, for such characteristic, but seemingly unrelated, features of his prose as his vision of an absurd and apparently meaningless world, the identification of life and art, the uneasy transitions from the comic to the tragic, the ambivalent role of the hero, the breakdown of language, and the nihilistic rejection of literary tradition. According to this view, Kharms's literary universe could be described as an inverted image of reality, where the systematic disruption of the normal laws of existence – physical, logical, semantic, aesthetic, moral – results in a world of arbitrary relations based on chance and caprice, where identity and meaning are rendered problematic and unstable (Flaker, 1969: 81). Having broken the chain between signifiers and signifieds, Kharms portrays a world of empty and arbitrary signs: a world where, in semiotic terms, 'all is permitted'. The balancing act performed by Kharms's texts between the comic and the tragic and the ambivalence of the Kharmsian hero[17] add to the reader's sense of unease for, despite the comic appearance of Kharms's texts, a serious ethical impulse is never far from the surface. The OBERIU philosopher L. Lipavsky's description of the structure of the typical OBERIU text as a 'hieroglyph', that is, a text which purposely locates a serious meaning beneath a comic surface in order to trick the inattentive reader (Gerasimova, 1988: 53), is relevant here as well. To revert to Bakhtin's terminology, Kharms's world is structured on the model of a carnivalised world (*Mundus inversus*), and it represents the culmination of a carnivalesque tradition in Russian literature which, in the works of Gogol and the medieval institution of *iurodstvo*, provides crucial cultural models for Kharms's absurdism.

At the centre of Kharms's topsy-turvy fictional universe is his subversive treatment of the Russian literary tradition. As several critics have pointed out, many of Kharms's stories are characterised by a deliberate and thoroughgoing repudiation of the generic and stylistic conventions of traditional literary discourse (Flaker, 1969; Nakhimovsky, 1982; Chances, 1982; Vishevsky, 1986). The term 'anti-story' has even been applied to stories such as *Vstrecha* ('A Meeting') (nd) and *Golubaia tetrad' No. 10* ('The Blue Notebook No. 10') (of 1937), which seem to act out the impossibility of traditional narrative (Chances, 1982: 181–92). While the targets of such playful texts are usually not difficult to identify, the rather predictable readings that result from formal analyses of their sources tend to oversimplify the various levels on which Kharms's absurdism actually functions. An additional key to the author's intentions in such stories which, surprisingly, has been little used by critics is the OBERIU manifesto's section on the theatre, written by Kharms himself and based on his own *Elizaveta Bam*. In it, Kharms contrasts the traditional 'realistic' theatre of the bourgeoisie, in which the various 'theatrical elements' (character, action, movement, sets, music, lighting, etc.) are subordinated to the 'tyranny' of dramatic plot, to the revolutionary theatre of the OBERIU, where these 'theatrical elements' are 'liberated' to play a role equal in importance to the play's theme. One could easily extend this approach to Kharms's 'anti-stories' in prose: on purely formal grounds, the absurdism of Kharms's prose is motivated by a similar 'decentering' of plot and dramatic theme and the 'liberation' of what were traditionally considered secondary textual elements. But Kharms's repudiation of the conventionality and artificiality of bourgeois literary realism can also be read on the level of political allegory; the subversive absurdism championed in the OBERIU manifesto may be taken as an expression of the author's solidarity with the repudiation of the bourgeois order brought about in the political realm by the revolution.

The corrosive effect of the Kharmsian absurd touches the authority of two of the central figures of the Russian literary past in such familiar carnivalised texts as *Pushkin i Gogol'* ('Pushkin and Gogol') of 1934 and *Anekdoty iz zhizni Pushkina* ('Anecdotes from the Life of Pushkin', 1936?). While these stories are typically interpreted as witty exercises in the debunking of established literary classics,[18] absurdist contributions to a genre with roots that predate the revolution and continue to the present day,[19] or as parodies of the Philistine cult of the classics,[20] they also raise interesting questions about the complex structure of Kharms's absurdism. Having stripped the two authors of their talent, individuality and verbal ingenuity, the texts transform them into puppets, mechanically repeating the same pointless words and actions in an idiotic and never-ending 'balagan.'[21] 'Pushkin' and 'Gogol' are emptied of their traditional associations[22] – Kharms's Pushkin is not the father of Russian literature but of four idiot sons, who can't keep from falling out of their chairs – and are transformed into comical playthings manipulated by the author. This absurd world can be analysed in several ways. A Bakhtinian reading would emphasise the 'ambivalence' of Kharms's laughter: how, rather than 'destroying' the objects of laughter, Kharms's parody of Pushkin and Gogol brings them back to life through the 'positive, regenerating, creative meaning' of laughter (Bakhtin, 1968: 71). A neo-formalist reading would similarly foreground the connection between the absurd world and the 'regenerative' effects of the text's 'defamiliarisation' of the familiar outline of Russian literature: by rejecting all the usual associations with Pushkin and Gogol, the text forces the reader to confront the clichés and received opinions which substitute for direct and personal knowledge of the authors and their works.

In addition to the defamiliarisation of Russian literary classics, one can glimpse Kharms anticipating one of the central problems of contemporary post-structuralist linguistic theory, the division of the signifier from the signified (Eagleton, 1983: 127–50). These texts can be said to achieve their comic effect, essentially, through the simple device of disrupting the usual transparent one-to-one correspondence between signifier and signified. The commonsensical confidence that we can summon up the essence of some meaning through the use of language[23] is exploded by Kharms's awareness that meaning is never absolutely present in our language, but is rather 'scattered or dispersed along the whole chain of signifiers' (Eagleton, 1983: 128). The distance between the parodic Pushkin who performs for Kharms and the historical figure we all think we know exemplifies the impossibility of ever capturing the original or absolute meaning of any signifier. While Kharms's attack on the Philistine cult of Pushkin in the Soviet Union is obvious and intentional (Levin 1980: 273), a reading which ignored the linguistic and epistemological issues raised by such texts would be incomplete. In a slightly different context, Milner-Gulland describes how Kharms's (and Vvedensky's) distrust of the resources of language make them quintessentially modern writers:

> these are writers of specifically modern kind, who cannot take the referential abilities of language for granted, who indeed are somewhat painfully if often ebulliently aware that the world of words is never truly in contact with – though equally never entirely separate from, as out-and-out *zaumniki* would hold – the world of things. Between phenomena, abstract or concrete, and ourselves we have only words to mediate – yet they are signs without substance, glued together [...] by conjunctions, by grammar and by syntax that build a structure truly corresponding to nothing outside our own heads. What is philosophical about this, of course, is that we are investigating the meaning of meaning, admittedly indirectly but possibly in the most convincing manner, through semantic experimentation.
> 
> (Milner-Gulland 1984: 32–3)

Kharms's rejection of the authority of the Russian literary tradition is just the most fully articulated part of a general modernist and irrationalist critique of mimetic realism, philosophical positivism and bourgeois liberalism. If mimesis is rejected because it betrays art's true transcendent nature, 'real art' is conceived of as a revolutionary aesthetic of liberation from the authority and the conventions of everyday life, where seemingly objective and unchanging laws of contingency, determinism, and cause and effect reign unchallenged. It is valuable precisely because it offers an alternative to the standard bourgeois notions of what is 'real' or 'realistic'. 'You will perhaps assert that our plots are "unreal" and "illogical?" But who said that "everyday" logic was necessary for art?' (Milner-Gulland 1970: 70–1). The key to the work of art is the 'new' logic of free play: in order to be 'free', the OBERIUTY cultivate the playful, the subjective, the individual, the alogical and the absurd in both their lives and their art, which equally are seen by the artist as material for the exercise of a liberating absurdism.[24]

> The writer put an equal sign between life and art. His creative work developed out of personal genres, such as letters, diary entries, and jokes. But the biographical and the personal are oddly combined with the fantastic, resulting in the creation of a particular world, located in a state of wonderous weightlessness, in which the most unexpected situations arise. (Aleksandrov, 1973: 296)

For Kharms and the other authors of the 1928 OBERIU manifesto, the total repudiation of everything associated with the traditional authority of the bourgeoisie was an eagerly sought-after badge of revolutionary merit as well as proof of the group's radical political sympathies: 'In the area of art, the proletariat cannot be satisfied with the artistic methods of the old schools [. . .] its artistic principles go much deeper and undermine the very roots of the old art' (Milner-Gulland, 1970: 69). And yet, while there is no reason to assume that the young authors of the OBERIU manifesto were anything but sincere in these sentiments, as Kharms's prose develops and evolves in the 1930s, this optimistic vision of the absurd as a revolutionary rejection of the literary and political authority of the past will undergo significant revision. Kharms begins to rethink this position as the negative results, in literature and in life, of the radical liberation from the traditions of the past gradually come into clearer focus. The prose texts of Kharms's last years are crucial because in them we can observe the confidence and militancy of the OBERIU manifesto gradually ebb away and be replaced by a darker, more tragic, if still occasionally playful,[25] awareness of the dark side of unrestrained freedom, both aesthetic and ethical. In fact, one could go further and asert that Kharms gradually becomes aware that his role, as an artist, was one of complicity in the creation of a monstrous social order. This transformation can be charted in the changing function and significance of the Kharmsian absurd anti-world, which loses its former connection with the joy of liberation, creativity, and potential meaning, and increasingly becomes associated with the dark tragedy, mindless violence, and total egoism of life in a world without moral authority or limits. If total freedom from tradition and the past results, in the realm of aesthetics, in the destruction of the story and the birth of the anti-story, its ethical consequences, the birth of the monstrous anti-heroes who populate the stories we now turn to, are considerably more alarming for the author, and reader, to contemplate.

In the stories discussed above, Kharm's absurd touches, primarily, the literary and historical context of the text, and the effect on the reader is broadly comic, without shadows or any obvious darker significance. In stories such as *Ol'ga Forsh podoshla k Alekseiu Tolstomu* ('Aleksei Tolstoy', 1934) *Tetrad'* ('The Notebook', 1938), and *Pomekha* ('The Drawback', 1940), Kharms can be seen moving away from a purely comic viewpoint and towards a more complex and nuanced appreciation of the tragic circumstances of contemporary reality. Despite the presence of such comic attributes of the anti-world as the 'pseudo-person' (*nedochelovek*), the inadequacy of the heroes' speech, the lack of correspondence between signifier and signified and cause and effect, unmotivated and absurd mechanised action and speech, and the total absence of emotional affect, these stories betray Kharms's growing interest in ethical and moral questions that bear centrally on the relationship between the individual and society. As such, they represent the beginning of a new stage in Kharms's creative evolution. The story 'Aleksei Tolstoy', for example, provides a clear example of Kharms's use of the anti-world as an instrument of literary and social criticism and a useful contrast with the parody of Pushkin and Gogol. The story is short, little more than a note, and I quote it in its entirety:

> Ol'ga Forsh walked up to Aleksei Tolstoy and did something. Aleksei Tolstoy also did something.
> 
> Then Konstantin Fedin and Valentin Stenich ran out into the yard and began to look for an appropriate stone. They didn't find a stone, but they found a shovel. With this shovel Konstantin Fedin smashed Ol'ga Forsh in the face.
> 
> Then Aleksei Tolstoy stripped naked and, running out to the Fontanka, he began to neigh like a horse. Everyone said: 'That's a major contemporary writer who's neighing.' And no one bothered Aleksei Tolstoy.
> 
> (Levin, 1980: 273; *Plummeting*: 20)

The author's grotesque treatment of well-known Soviet writers and critics mimics the discourse of the holy fool. On one level, it functions as a kind of ethical defamiliarisation, forcing the reader to confront the debased and brutal norms of literary discourse in Soviet literature of the 1930s. Kharms's purpose, like that of the holy fool, is primarily ethical: to change society's behaviour by restoring to it a clear perception of its actual immorality. Through the presentation of an anti-world, where normal and acceptable behaviour for writers includes bashing each other in the face with shovels and rocks, running naked through the streets and neighing like horses, where, in other words, writers have been transformed into wordless brutes, Kharms invites the reader to consider the beastly behaviour of real writers in the real world of Soviet literature. This critique takes on added force when we realise that it was composed in 1934, when the regimentation and brutalisation of official Soviet literary life was taking a great leap forward in the First Congress of Soviet Writers (Levin, 1980: 273).

One constant element of Kharms's absurd anti-world with no obvious ethical significance is the disruption of the laws of physical nature and logic. The results of the suspension of cause and effect can be seen, for example, in stories such as *Gospodin nevysokogo rosta* ('A Gentleman of Medium Height', 1939–40) and *O tom, kak menia posetili vestniki* ('How I was visited by Messengers', 1937). After a brick crushes his skull and lodges in his brain, the hero of 'A Gentleman of Medium Height' reassures the crowd of bystanders: 'No need to worry, Ladies and Gentleman. I've already had this habit. You see, I have a little stone sticking out of my right eye. That was another incident. I'm already used to this. Now it's all the same to me.' (*Kontinent* 24: 1980: 284). The *balagan* – inspired chronotope of 'A Gentleman of Medium Height,' especially the absence of physical and emotional reaction to violence, so typical of life in Kharms's anti-world, renders the violence harmless. A slightly different version of Kharms's disruption of the normal logic of cause and effect can be seen in 'How I was visited by Messengers'. The narrator of this parody of the philosophical tale gets caught up in an absurd situation when he attempts to verify a mystical visitation through the use of logic and reason: 'And then suddenly I was amazed: what kind of phenomenon can be caused by a broken clock and a draft in the room?' (*Polët*, 1988: 503). In the end, the disruption of the narrator's peace of mind disappears just as suddenly and inexplicably as it appeared. If 'A Gentleman of Medium Height' can be described as a story of cause without effect, then 'How I was visited by Messengers' is an effect without apparent cause. The patently unreal situations and characters of stories like this reassure the reader of the distance between the real world he inhabits and the anti-world of Kharms's characters, and ensure that the effect of such stories on the reader is basically comic, if uncanny.

A common reading emphasises just this apparent absence of an ethical or moral dimension to such stories. Flaker, for example, describes the effects of what we might call the 'domestication' of violence in Kharms's prose: 'Nothing significant happens in the world of Kharms's stories, and even if people die or kill each other, these "events" are not perceived as significant because they don't provoke any moral or ethical problems or questions' (1969: 79). And yet, while overt moralistic reactions to violence are indeed absent from such stories, one must beware of reading this as an unambiguous avoidance of moral issues. In fact, one could easily argue that even in these texts an ethical element is present, if implicit. A story like

*Proisshestvie na ulitse* ('An Event on the Street', nd) (*Izb.*: 65–6; *Black Coat*: 59), for example, which foregrounds the total absence of sympthetic reactions to another's sufferings provides an example of Kharms's implicit moralism.

> One day a man jumped off a tram, but so clumsily that he was run over by a car.
> The traffic on the street came to a stop and a militiaman began to investigate how the accident happened.
> The driver was explaining something for a long time, pointing with his finger at the front tires of the car.
> The militiaman felt these tires and wrote down in his notebook the name of the street.
> Suddenly, a rather large crowd gathered.
> Some citizen with dull eyes kept falling off the curb.
> Some woman kept looking over another woman, while that one in her turn would look over the first woman . . . (65)

While one result of the absurd reactions of the militiaman and the crowd to the spectacle of a man run over by an automobile is certainly to neutralise the reader's sense of danger, to conclude that the story defuses ethical and moral issues would be a misreading. The characers and situations of this story are typical of Kharms's prose in that they are presented as isolated and powerless individuals, subject to meaningless violence, personal attacks and accidents for which no one can be held ultimately responsible. No one, including the distant or invisible author, sympathises with them, and they have no one and nowhere to turn to for help and support. Adrift in a cruel, impersonal and inexplicable world, Kharms's characters are totally alienated from each other and incapable of establishing any meaningful contact with others. On a purely formal level, their alienation is a function of the lifeless and mechanical repetitiveness of their actions and their speech: 'the sense of a mechanical repetition of gestures [. . .] strengthens even more the feeling of the cruel indifference of separate and lonely people' (Flaker, 1969: 79–80). But, the ethical consequences of this vision of an anti-world, where all sense of connection and sympathy between people has been eroded, cannot be ignored and must be related to the concrete social milieu of the Soviet Union in the 1930s. The distance between a world where individuals calmly and passively observe the sufferings of others, and a world where the strong cold-bloodedly prey on the weak is quickly and effortlessly traversed in Kharms's texts of the 1930s.

Without a doubt, the ethical concerns of Kharms's anti-world are most strikingly and convincingly developed in a series of dark stories from the last years of his life where the boundaries between the comic and the serious are totally erased. One way to understand this dramatic shift in tone is suggested by Likhachëv and Panchenko's description of the transformation of medieval Russia's 'comic culture' in the time of Ivan the Terrible (Likhachëv and Panchenko 1976: 61– 75). As connections between the real world and the absurd anti-world become more pronounced, as the arbitrary and absurd violence, the wilful distortion of language, the hopelessness and helplessness of the individual in Stalin's Soviet Union in the 1930s come to resemble more and more closely conditions in the anti-world, the comedy of the absurd disappears and is replaced by an unspeakable horror and terror. As the horrors of the anti-world depicted in his texts are gradually matched, and even exceeded, by the actual horrors of Stalinism, and the link between the absurd and the comic is broken, Kharms's texts acquire the tragic tone and ethical significance which they had previously lacked.

In stories such as *Vsestoronnee issledovanie* ('Comprehensive Research', 1937), *Griaznaia lichnost* ('A Nasty Character', 1937) and *Reabilitatsiia* ('Rehabilitation', 1941), Kharms creates a horrifying double image of reality, a world of total egoists, whose only law is the satisfaction of their own will. Following Dostoevsky, Kharms creates a world in which the relationships between characters are all forged out of the general struggle for survival and power, or what one critic has called the 'moral dialectic' (Wasiolek, 1964: 39–59). The only possible relation between characters in this anti-world is that of master to slave or victimiser to victim, and one character's sufferings, rather than arousing sympathy, is another's fondest desire. While Kharms, unlike Dostoevsky, offers no solution to the problem, his ethical position is no less clear for remaining unstated. While the violations of common-sense logic, the inscrutable motivations, and the semantic reversals in these stories may, at first, be taken as signs of the familiar Kharmsian absurd, this impression is certainly deceiving: taken together, these stories add up to a stinging indictment of the ethical and moral climate of the Stalinist period and, one could argue, represent Kharms's most lasting achievement in prose.

The structure of 'Comprehensive Research' is typical. The story is constructed on the simple premise that in the anti-world, instead of healing the sick, doctors investigate the phenomenon of death by killing the healthy. After he gives Ermolaev the poison pill, the murderous doctor explains his action in the following way: 'Yes, we doctors must comprehensively research the phenomenon of death' (*Kontinent*, 24, 1980: 293; *Plummeting*: 39). The crucial break between signifiers and signifieds, noted above as a central concern of post-structuralist theory, is foregrounded in the semantic inversion of the anti-world in this text, where 'doctor' means 'murderer', 'patient' equals 'victim', and there is no discernible difference between 'medicine' and 'poison'. Ordinary language is manipulated and distorted by the doctor,[26] who not only wilfully and purposefully distorts the meaning of Ermolaev's words, but hides his own murderous intentions behind affectionate and misleading expressions such as 'good friend' (*druzhochek milyi*), 'a reliable remedy' (*sredstvo vernoe*) and 'a research drug' (*issledovatel'skaia piliulia*). The political issues raised by the text – the Orwellian dimensions of this sinister manipulation of language, betrayal by an authority figure, arbitrary and pointless violence against the unsuspecting and defenceless in the name of science – and their relevance to the actual conditions of life in Stalin's Soviet Union are clear.

What is interesting and important is how stories like 'Comprehensive Research' dramatise Kharms's new awareness of the dark side of the radical liberation from traditional notions of aesthetics, linguistics, ethics and logic which the 1928 OBERIU Manifesto welcomed and identified as the key to truly revolutionary art. Kharms's murderous doctor, in fact, adheres closely to the existential logic of OBERIU art which situates creativity and freedom in the rejection of the norms of 'everyday logic' (*zhiteiskaia logika*) or, in Shklovsky's increasingly disturbing phrase, 'the totality of the prejudices of the age' (Shklovskii, 1967: 16). The doctor's 'accomplishment' is to understand that traditional ethics is, likewise, nothing but the totality of prejudice, tradition and convention, and to act on this knowledge. While his actions exhibit the logical consistency of the psychopathic murderer, and therefore cannot be called absurd, they are completely immoral. Unlike the creative and playful absurdism of the artist, the anti-logic of the doctor is aggressive and destructive and leads him, like Dostoevsky's Underground Man, to assert his freedom through sadistic actions. 'Comprehensive Research', then, can be said to mark a crucial transition in Kharms's prose and the beginning of a serious reevaluation of the consequences of the avant-garde rejection of traditional aesthetics. It parodies the physical and linguistic violence and immorality of Stalinism, while simultaneously exploring the danger that language, liberated from the constraints of

# The Anti-World of Daniil Kharms 87

referentiality, can become a murderous weapon in the hands of immoral brutes. 'Comprehensive Research' even implies a connection between the rejection of conventional aesthetic norms and linguistic referentiality and the breakdown of traditional ethical principles in society at large. In this sense, then, Kharms implicates himself, and the entire avant-garde, in the allegorical murder of Ermolaev, as well as in the quite real crimes of Soviet society.

'Rehabilitation' one of Kharms's most terrifying stories, represents, perhaps, the apotheosis of these themes. The total absence of ethical stability in Kharms's universe, the sense that in this anti-world 'all is permitted', is again conveyed primarily through the disruption of ordinary language and the substitution of an alternative, murderous anti-logic for 'normal' (*zhiteiskaia*) logic. The agent of this disruption is an unnamed first-person narrator who concludes his justification and explanation of his unspeakable crimes to the reader with the following words:

> Well, OK: in all this (I will agree) one can see a certain cruelty on my part. But to consider it a crime that I sat down and defecated on my victims is simply, if you will excuse the expression, absurd. Defecating is a natural need and therefore not at all criminal. In this way, I understand the reservations of my defence attorney, but I am hoping for complete vindication.
> 
> (*Russica −81*: 360; *Plummeting*: 28)

The ideological force of the narrator's rhetoric, as he attempts to portray his horrible crimes as natural occurrences, provides one possible key to the text. In a summary of Roland Barthes's analysis of ideology in language, Terry Eagleton describes 'signs which pass themselves off as natural, which offer themselves as the only conceivable way of viewing the world' as 'authoritarian and ideological' (Eagleton, 1983: 135). According to Eagleton/Barthes 'one of the functions of ideology [is] to "naturalize" social reality, to make it seem as innocent and unchangeable as Nature itself. Ideology seeks to convert culture into Nature, and the natural sign is one of its weapons' (Eagleton, 1983: 135). That realism, the literary ideology that corresponds most closely to this 'natural attitude',[27] has traditionally been the only acceptable idiom of official Soviet literature is, of course, related to its ideological status as the privileged discourse of authoritarianism. While the monological discourse of the narrator of 'Rehabilitation' can be said to be oriented towards the 'natural sign', the author's discourse works in a counter-direction. Through the presentation of a psychology that completely rejects 'normal' logic, Kharms's discourse subverts the notion that reality is constant, unchangeable and natural: its functions, as we have already stated, as a form of defamiliarisation. By holding the brutality, horror and sheer absurdity of reality up to ridicule, Kharms signals his refusal to accept an unacceptable reality as natural or inevitable.

Further, as in 'Comprehensive Research', the implied complicity of the artist in the crimes of the real world represents a crucial, and disturbing, subtext of the story. For through the act of imaginatively reshaping and recreating his experience in a work of fiction that is not limited by the morality, logic and laws of everyday life, the pathological first-person narrator of 'Rehabilitation' is, in fact, playing the role of an artist.[28] 'Rehabilitation,' then, can also be read as Kharms's confession of the radical avant-garde's role in the moral collapse and indiscriminate violence of Stalinism. The seemingly incongruous image of the narrator humbly bowing his head and praying at the end of Kharms's greatest story, *Starukha* ('The Old Woman', 1939), sums up the author's repudiation of the youthful nihilism of the OBERIU Manifesto as well as his ultimate acceptance of responsibility for its social consequences. 'I bow my head low and quietly say: In the name of the Father, the Son and the Holy Spirit, now and in the ages to come. Amen...' (*Polët*, 430). We might summarise the lesson of 'The Old Woman' by paraphrasing Il'ia Levin's observation about the role of the miraculous in Kharms's stories: in the absence of a higher moral authority, 'life is transformed into a nasty eternity of absurd cruelty and violence'.[29]

Kharms's stories are often seen as 'humorous paradoxes': as quirky and original, but essentially light-weight comic exercises in the realm of black humour and the absurd: as, in the words of George Gibian, 'what if' stories – 'What if a woman dies in one's apartment? What if one forgot the proper sequence of numbers?' (Gibian, 1974: 39): as satires of Philistine manners and language in the manner of Zoshchenko. While some of Kharms's stories do indeed fit this model, there is little doubt that this interpretation is possible only through a very selective and partial reading of the corpus of his writings. While the complex evolution of Kharms's absurdism, as I have tried to show, cannot be reduced to one simple formula, three general stages in its development must be emphasised: first, a revolutionary and nihilistic attack on the authority of bourgeois traditions in art and politics; second, in the exploration of what have come to be called post-modern problems of language and meaning; and, most importantly, an ethical critique of the Utopian project in modern Russian history and of the role of the avant-garde in preparing the way for the violence and immorality of Stalinism. According to this view, Kharms is most significant for his profound critique of the radical experiment in creating a new world through the total rejection of tradition and traditional authority undertaken in the Soviet Union in the 1920s and 1930s. The central thematic issue of his mature prose concerns the desperate situation of the defenceless individual in a world without traditional ethical limits, a Dostoevskian world where all is permitted and where the only law is the rule of the strong over the weak. By subverting the official ideological discourse that depicts this reality as inevitable and natural, Kharms's anti-world forces the reader to confront the absurdity, cruelty and brutality of Stalinism in the real world. Stylistically, his work is most important for its apparent merging of the absurd with the rational, the abstract with the concrete; a synthesis, if you will, of the nameless world of Kafka and the specific world of Stalin.[30] In this sense, then, the most useful context for Kharms's work should be sought in the works of other contemporary writers who saw the central problem of Stalinism as ethical and philosophical, and who approached the problem through a fantastic mixture of realism and absurdism, uneasily balanced on the border between comedy and tragedy, with common roots in the ambivalent humour of carnival: writers, for example, such as Bulgakov, Zamiatin, Olesha and Platonov.[31]

NOTES

1. 'Even though the prose (and dramatic) works of Kharms and Vvedenskii lent themselves with relative ease to the categories available to literary scholars and were immediately recognised as a phenomenon analogous, and chronologically prior, to the literature of the absurd, the poetic texts of the OBERIUTY have proven incompatible with the existing critical apparatus of literary historians.' (Fleishman, 1987: 248).
2. Surprisingly, there does not yet exist an adequate critical treatment of this theme in the secondary literature devoted to Kharms and the OBERIU.
3. For a discussion of the non-parodic influence of the Russian fairy tale on Kharms's prose, see Nakhimovsky, 1982: 77–80.
4. 'The works of Kharms's stories is the world of the "mean", of mediocrity, a filthy, Philistine world.' Flaker, 1969: 81.

5. The intensive work being carried out by Soviet and Western scholars in the recently opened Kharms archive in the Saltykov-Shchedrin library in Leningrad, and the expanded possibilities for publishing the results of this research in the Soviet Union, are responsible for the sense that Kharms scholarship is poised on the threshold of a major breakthrough. Examples of important new work are the first book-length collection of Kharms's writings (*Polët v nebesa*) and recent articles by V. I. Glotser (Glotser, 1988; 1989).
6. While works by both Druskin and Lipavskii have been used extensively by M. Meilakh in the commentaries and notes to his editions of Kharms and Vvedenskii, most of their voluminous philosophical and critical works from the archives of the Saltykov-Shchedrin Public Library in Leningrad remain unpublished. (For recent publications, see Druskin, 1985; and Druskin 1988.)
7. Compare this analysis with the much weaker version put forth recently by A. Kobrinskii: 'Gradually, Kharms's alogic gains more and more concrete forms, his works increasingly tend towards narrative, and he begins to write prose. And he no longer simply reflects the absurdity of life, the vulgarity of ordinary, limited consciousness. Now, like an artist, he himself creates and shapes life. In his poems, plays and stories from the middle to the end of the 1930s, the idea of the author's opposition of the absurdity of the everyday, the "leaden abominations" of life, in the name of the higher truth of art comes increasingly to the forefront' (Kobrinskii, 1988: 204).
8. As long ago as 1969, Flaker suggested the possibility of an 'extra-literary' interpretation of some of Kharms's stories: 'the constant presence of a policeman in the dreams of Kalugin [in the story 'A Dream'] points to new possibilities for extra-literary readings of several stories.' [the story *Son*] (Flaker, 1969: 81). The obvious implications of this observation, unfortunately, have been ignored by Soviet scholars before Gerasimova.
9. Compare, for example, the accounts given by Flaker, 1969; Aleksandrov, 1973; Levin, 1980; Nakhimovsky, 1982; and Kobrinskii, 1988.
10. The arrests of Kharms and Vvedenskii in 1931 and the accusation that they were part of an anti-Soviet monarchist organisation centred at *Detizdat*, is but one example of the absurdities of real life in the 1930s. During the interrogation, it was asserted that the OBERIUTY composed their absurd literary works for the purpose of distracting Soviet workers from the building of socialism (Levin, 1980: 272).
11. Anatoly Vishevsky used the concept of the anti-world to describe the role of literary parody in Kharms's *Komediia goroda Peterburga* (Vishevsky, 1986: 364).
12. Through his consistently ridiculous and, according to the normal rules of society, inappropriate behaviour, the holy fool can be said to live in an anti-world, which is characterised by the total breakdown of the usual semiotic correspondences that rule 'normal' reality. By behaving in the 'real world' according to the norms of this unreal and absurd 'anti-world', the holy fool engages in an indirect, but thorough-going, critique of the existing social reality. For example, by taking Christ's

teachings on the subjects of wealth and poverty, or chastity and love absolutely literally, the holy fool of medieval Russia emphasises the disparity between Christian ideals and social reality in a nominally Christian society. Thus, the holy fool not only disrupts the semiotic system of medieval Russian society, but also asserts the possibility and desirability of another, more genuinely Christian social structure. In other words, the laughter of the holy fool functions as a utopian device, representing a liberation from the conventions which rule social existence, as well as a signpost towards a better world.

13. 'The holy fool is a sham madman, a voluntary fool who hides holiness and wisdom beneath a mask of stupidity. The people mocked by him are sham wisemen' (Likhachëv and Panchenko, 1976: 150).
14. The holy fool, as Panchenko writes, 'balances on the border between the comic and the serious, personifying in himself the tragic version of the world of laughter' (Likhachëv and Panchenko, 1976: 93).
15. This points to what is, perhaps, the central difference between medieval European carnival and Russian laughter: for while the 'fool in Christ' steps outside of society in order to revile the debased morality of that society, he is simultaneously functioning as a member of that larger community. His jeremiad is meant to reinforce, not undercut, the official values and morality of church and state.
16. 'Neither blasphemy, which took a "fateful delight . . . in trampling on the cherished sacred objects", nor a magical laughter, which is connected with the seeking of aid from the "black", inside-out world, belong strictly speaking to "laughter culture," since they totally lack its main element, comicality' (Lotman and Uspenskii, 1984: 43).
17. 'Having represented his friends in a comic light (in general, perfectly harmlessly), Kharms also doesn't spare himself' (Aleksandrov, 1973: 297).
18. Alice Stone Nakhimovsky, for example, describes the humorous effect of these stories as the result of the surprising discontinuity between content and tone: 'The content of the anecdotes is trivial or absurd, but the tone, [. . .] is one of admiration for a great man' (Nakhimovsky, 1982: 70).
19. For examples of the genre, see Vazarin, 1914; Kruchënykh, 1924; Siniavskii 1975; and Zarikovskii, 1982.
20. 'All the vulgarity of the Philistine who makes a myth of the Russian poet and his life but, in essence, is opposed with every fibre of his being to the poet who created the harmony of the Russian literary language and Russian poetry' (Flaker, 1969: 80). Aleksandrov suggests that the *Anekdoty* may be seen as a sort of 'laughing double' of a serious article Kharms wrote on Pushkin's childhood for the journal *Chizh* (Aleksandrov, 1978: 79).
21. One critic has described the combination of poetry reading and theatrical performance of the OBERIU 'evenings' as a sort of '*balagan*' (Aleksandrov, 1968: 297).
22. 'The concrete object, freed from its literary and everyday slough, becomes the property of art' (Milner-Gulland, 1970: 70).
23. That the theme of the breakdown of communication is more often

than not expressed through dialogue is a provocative irony about the works of the OBERIUTY, and one that deserves further study. For an interesting discussion of the role of dialogue in the works of the OBERIUTY, see Aleksandrov, 1968: 302.

24. 'Kharms's life, at least in the twenties, was spectacle: "Kharms is art," Vvedenskii said of him' (Nakhimovsky, 1982: 8). See also Milner-Gulland, 1984: 24.

25. 'The principle of "play" at the basis of art (art that could neverthless be in total effect profound or tragic) must have been a factor that originally brought Vvedensky close to Kharms' (Milner-Gulland, 1970: 67).

26. For a discussion of the comic, Chekhovian treatment of the impossibility of effective communication in early stories such as *Tiuk*, see Flaker, 1969: 70.

27. 'In Barthes's view, there is a literary ideology which corresponds to this "natural attitude", and its name is realism. Realist literature tends to conceal the socially-relative or constructed nature of language: it helps to confirm the prejudice that there is a form of "ordinary" language which is somehow natural. This natural language gives us reality "as it is": it does not – like romanticism or symbolism – distort it into subjective shapes, but represents the world to us as God himself might know it. The sign is not seen as a changeable entity determined by the rules of a particular changeable sign-system: it is seen rather as a translucent window on to the object, or on to the mind. It is quite neutral and colourless itself: its only job is to represent something else, become the vehicle of a meaning conceived quite independently of itself, and it must interfere with what it mediates as little as possible. In the ideology of realism or representation, words are felt to link up with their thoughts or objects in essentially right and uncontrovertible ways: the word becomes the only proper way of viewing this object or expressing this thought' (Eagleton, 1983: 135–6).

28. Kharms's dark vision of the Russian artist's criminal complicity in the murderous violence of Stalinism should not, of course, be confused with Thomas Mann's Felix Krull and the theme of the artist as confidence man, liar, i.e. fiction-maker.

29. 'For Kharms, faith in the miraculous constitutes the meaning and purpose of life. Without this faith, life is transformed into a nasty eternity of absurd cruelty and violence' (Levin, 1980: 274).

30. According to the OBERIU Manifesto, this concern with the concrete distinguishes the OBERIU poetics of 'real Art' from the poetics of *zaum*': 'There is no school more foreign to us than *zaum*'. Poets of the real, concrete to the marrow, we are the first enemies of those who would emasculate the word and transform it into a weak and absurd mongrel' (Milner-Gulland, 1970: 70).

31. Paradoxically, one result of a reading of Kharms's prose that emphasises the tragic ethical consequences of Soviet Utopianism makes the negative reaction to his work in the Soviet Union, to a certain extent, understandable. If Kharms's finest works are indeed concerned with unresolved ethical problems that lie at the base of the Soviet way

of life: if his pessimistic vision of the future is a dystopia, a world of total egoism, violence, cruelty and destruction, where communication, sympathy and love are impossible, then the seemingly hysterical criticism of the author of the article entitled 'Reactionary Juggling', that the 'meaningless poetry' of the OBERIUTY represented a 'protest against the dictatorship of the proletariat' (Nil'vich, 1930: 81), is perhaps, closer to the truth than most subsequent critics have granted.

REFERENCES

The works cited in this essay are to be found in the main Bibliography to this volume, except for those here given below.

Bakhtin, Mikhail, *Rabelais and his World* (Cambridge: MIT Press, 1968).
Eagleton, Terry, *Literary Theory: An Introduction* (Minneapolis: University of Minnesota Press, 1983).
Esslin, Martin, *The Theater of the Absurd* (Woodstock, NY: Overlook Press, 1973).
Kruchënykh, Aleksei, *500 novykh kalamburov iz Pushkina* (Moscow: 1924).
Likhachëv, D. S. and A. M. Panchenko, *'Smekhovoi mir' Drevnei Rusi* (Leningrad: 1976).
Lotman, Iu. M. and B. A. Uspenskii, 'New Aspects in The Study of Early Russian Culture', in *The Semiotics of Russian Culture*, ed. Ann Shukman (Ann Arbor: Michigan Slavic Contributions no. 11, 1984) pp. 36–52.
Nil'vich, L., 'Reaktsionnoe zhonglerstvo (Ob odnoi vylazke literaturnykh khuliganov),' *Smena*, no. 81 (1930): 81.
Siniavskii, Andrei, *Progulki s Pushkinym* (London: Overseas Publishers, 1975).
Thompson, Ewa, 'D. S. Likhachev and The Study of Old Russian Literature', in *Russian Literature and Criticism: Selected Papers from the Second World Congress for Soviet and East European Studies*, ed. Evelyn Bristol (Berkeley: Berkeley Slavic Specialties, 1982) pp. 245–54.
Vazarin, Z. V., *Nigde eshchë do sikh por ne pechatnye anekdoty pro A. S. Pushkina* (Tiflis: 1914).
Wasiolek, Edward, *Dostoevsky: The Major Fiction* (Cambridge: MIT Press, 1964).
Zarikovskii, A., 'Istorizmy', *Literaturnaia gazeta*, 12, 34 (1982): 16.

# Part III: The Prose Works

# 6 Towards an Interpretation of Kharms's *Sluchai*
Robin Aizlewood

Kharms's cycle *Sluchai*, although only recently published as a single entity,[1] has long been recognised as of central importance, along with *Starukha*, in his later prose and indeed in his work as a whole. *Sluchai* certainly provides a central focus for much of Kharms's prose, so that many other texts can be related to it, but among the great number of short prose pieces that make up a major part of his later work it also represents a unique approach to the creation of a large compositional unit, in effect a book: the texts were written out in a special notebook, with a title page, dedication and table of contents (see *Polët*, 528), and, furthermore, the composition as a whole reveals an order which makes it far more than a collection of pieces.[2]

The title *Sluchai*, which is also the title of the second story in the cycle, can be interpreted in several ways in accordance with its various meanings, principally as 'chances', 'cases' and 'happenings'.[3] First and foremost, by foregrounding the category of chance, the title embodies a central tenet of Kharms's (and OBERIU) poetics:[4] in the 'confrontation of verbal senses' ('*stolknovenie slovesnykh symslov*') and 'confrontation of a series of objects' ('*stolknovenie riada predmetov*'), in the 'semantic' and 'situational absurd' ('*bessmyslitsa*'),[5] the normal matrix of logical relations that governs life and language is vitiated and the laws of chance, on the face of it, take over; but the resultant combination of words, concepts, objects in an apparently unmotivated or contradictory way is still centrally concerned with questions of meaning and cognition, albeit meaning that may be beyond rational articulation.[6] A sequence of 'chances' invites speculation as to the possibility of an order behind, an order other than the laws of cause and effect and logic which ordinarily make sense of the world: thus for Kharms in the OBERIU article the interrelation of objects is stressed alongside their confrontation (Milner-Gulland, 1970, 71, 73), while in a letter to K. V. Pugachëva (16 October 1933) he defines art as the creation of order, a 'purity of order' which is simultaneously creation of the world and reflection of it, and this 'purity of order', incomprehensible in rationalist terms, is the essence

97

of art (*Polët*, 482–3). In this respect the meaning of '*sluchai*' as 'cases' comes into play, because it invites reference back to a higher order of which the cases are examples. This meaning is reflected in Kharms's orientation towards the fable or parable, although his use of these forms has a parodic aspect too; the same meaning is also found in the title '*Chetyre illiustratsii togo, kak novaia ideia ogorashivaet cheloveka, k nei ne podgotovlennogo*' ('Four Illustrations of How a New Idea Disconcerts a Man Unprepared for It'). In this connection it is important to note that the very world '*sluchai*' has a sense of bringing together in its prefix; indeed, one of the meanings of the word listed by Dal' is 'meeting' ('*vstrecha*'),[7] which is also the title of one of the stories in the cycle. Finally, in its meaning of 'happenings', the title *Sluchai* embodies the orientation towards action and events (sometimes inverted into a lack of events as in the minimalist '*Vstrecha*', 'A Meeting') which is characteristic of Kharms's stories and which in an obvious way links them to the genres of folk tale, children's story, anecdote, etc.; more generally the title carries with it a definition of genre derived from any small forms, literary or non-literary, which typically recount 'what happened' (apart from those already mentioned this might include the '*protokol*', the police or judicial record [see Gerasimova, 76]). The title *Sluchai* brings with it more specific literary associations as well. There is certainly an echo of Gogol, whose Petersburg is the antecedent world of strange occurrences: Gogol more typically uses the word '*proisshestvie*', which is found in the title of Kharms's '*Proisshestvie na ulitse*' ('An Event on the Street'), but *The Nose*, for example, begins with the verb '*sluchit' sia*' as well: 'On March 25 in Petersburg there occurred ['*sluchilos'*'] an unusually strange happening ['*proisshestvie*'].[8] Among other literary associations there is also an echo of Chekhov's use of '*sluchai*' in titles, as in *Sluchai iz praktiki* where '*sluchai*' serves both as an emblem of Chekhov's plotlessness, a feature taken by Kharms to an extreme in stories like '*Vstrecha*', and as a 'case' that provokes a consideration (very apposite to Kharms) of the absurdity of human life in the context of evil.[9]

The cycle as recently published consists of thirty texts, although the table of contents lists one more, '*Proisshestvie na ulitse*', which was apparently removed from the notebook in which the texts were written out, if not from the table of contents (*Polët*, 529). The texts form a string, or montage, of heterogeneous pieces: this principle, which was earlier embodied in the composition of *Elizaveta Bam*,[10] is a compositional variant of the principle of chance combination, the confrontation of objects and senses (see Fleishman, 1975, 6–8). The heterogeneity of *Sluchai* is of medium (prose, drama, verse) as well as of genre: twenty-two of the pieces that make up *Sluchai* are prose stories of some sort, but there are also seven dramatic sketches or dialogues and one, '*Okhotniki*' ('The Hunters'), which starts as a story but soon switches into dramatic dialogue. The sketches and dialogues essentially maintain the dominance of prose as the basic medium of the cycle, so that the verse, on the two occasions when it occurs, works as a defamiliarising exception, perhaps as the 'slight imperfection' ('*nebol'shaia pogreshnost'*') which figures prominently in Druskin's thought and was adopted by Kharms.[11] The two instances of verse are drawn from opposite ends of the spectrum: the first is the four-line dialogue '*Petrov i Kamarov*' which is written in the rhyming couplets of the folk *raëk*; the second occurs within '*Chetyre illiustratsii*...' when the stage directions in the second 'illustration' unexpectedly switch into classical verse with partial rhyme (everything else is in prose):

| | |
|---|---|
| Художник тут же побледнел как полотно, | The artist immediately turned white as a sheet, |
| И как тростинка закачался, | swayed like a reed, |
| И неожиданно скончался, | and unexpectedly died. |
| Его выносят. | He is carried out.[12] |

In an especially striking defamiliarisation Kharms here uses the free iamb, a classical dramatic measure in Russian verse, for stage directions, which normally stand on the edge of literature in prose (the past tense of the first three lines transforms them into narrative verse but the last line, though it does revert to the present tense of stage directions, is still iambic in rhythm).

Among the individual titles several genres are indicated, sometimes rendered absurd in confrontation with the form or content: the story entitled '*Sonet*' ('A Sonnet'), for example, applies a verse genre to a prose text, while the content of '*Nachalo ochen' khoroshego letnego dnia*' ('The Beginning of a Beautiful Day') belies not only this title but also the genre subtitle, the musical term '*Simfoniia*'. Among the prose genres indicated by title are '*sluchai*' itself, '*istoriia*' and '*anekdoty*', but other genres include the folk tale and the fable (both are found as titles of stories not in the cycle) and the historical sketch (relevant only to '*Istoricheskii epizod*' ('An Historical Episode') and untypical in general); this range of genres shows Kharms's orientation towards the margins of literary/non-literary discourse. The dramatic sketches and dialogues also draw on a variety of popular forms, such as vaudeville and the *balagan* as well as the *raëk*, but at least one sketch, '*Tiuk*' ('Clunk'), involves parody of the Chekhovian tradition.[13] At the same time, however, these forms may combine unexpectedly with the (Socratic) tradition of the philosophical dialogue, as in the parodied debate of '*Matematik i Andrei Semënovich*' ('The Mathematician and Andrei Semënovich') or in '*Makarov i Petersen*', which sets out as a quasi-philosophical discussion concerning the fulfilment of desires but soon descends into theatricality and parody. In fact, except for the dialogue '*Petrov i Kamarov*', all the dramatic pieces include stage directions, and only '*Chetyre illiustratsii . . .*' with its four sections does not include a final indication of the curtain falling. This overt theatricality, emphasised by the invocation of performance in the title of '*Neudachnyi spektakl"* ('An Unsuccessful Show'), unsettles the reader through a confrontation of prose narration and theatre.

While some of the titles indicate genre, more typically they indicate the subject, for example: '*Opticheskii obman*' ('An Optical Illusion'), '*Stoliar Kushakov*' ('The Carpenter Kushakov'), '*Sunduk*' ('The Trunk'), and so on; but in some cases definition turns into description in a way that again plays at the margin of literary and non-literary discourse: such titles are '*Son draznit cheloveka*' ('Sleep Teases a Man'), '*Chto teper' prodaiut v magazinakh*' ('What They Sell in the Shops These Days'), and '*Mashkin ubil Koshkina*' ('Mashkin Killed Koshkin') (in this last example the title is also the last line of the story). The most distinctive type of title, however, is one combining two names (or nouns representing people). No less than seven pieces have this kind of title: four are sketches or dialogues, in which the title comes from the participants ('*Petrov i Kamarov*', '*Pushkin i Gogol"*, '*Matematik i Andrei Semënovich*', '*Makarov i Petersen*'), but the same formula also occurs in the title of the last story, '*Pakin i Rakukin*', while two other titles include a linking verb ('*Molodoi chelovek, udivivshii storozha*' ('A Young Man Who Astonished a Watchman') and '*Mashkin ubil Koshkina*'). The recurrence of this kind of title foregrounds the problems of communication (in the dialogues) and, more generally, relations between people: in *Sluchai* these are consistently turned into their opposites, and it seems that the basic relationship is one of confrontation and even killing ('*Mashkin ubil Koshkina*'); the other verb highlighted – to 'surprise'/ 'amaze' ('*udivit"*) – is a key one in the Kharmsian world and stands as an emblem of its unsettling quality. Thus one of the most habitual syntactic formulations ('A and B', where A and B are persons) becomes defamiliarised and subject to a confrontation of senses: on the one hand even the conjunction 'and' is unsettled, on the other hand what it is to be human is questioned; indeed, Druskin defined the theme of the 'subhuman man' ('*nedochelovek*') as one of the three main themes in Kharms (Druskin, 1989, 112–13). In this respect the three lines of '*Vstrecha*', which seemingly have nothing to say, acquire a far wider resonance because of the very lack of anything untoward:

> Now one day a man went to work, and on the way he met another man who, having bought a Polish loaf, was setting off on his own way home.
> And that's all. (*Polët*, 378)

The opening story in *Sluchai* is the famous '*Golubaia tetrad' No. 10*' ('Blue Notebook No. 10' or 'The Red-Haired Man'). It can and has been seen as a perfect example of the Kharms story that destroys itself as it goes along, thereby becoming a parody of narration as such, as well as of itself (see Jaccard, 1985, 289–90, 293–94).[14] In this way '*Golubaia tetrad' No. 10*' introduces parody as a general principle of the cycle. At the same time, however, the story also establishes a contrary, non-parodic relationship to Russian literature, because the motif of losing parts of the body links to Gogol', especially to 'The Nose' (the nose is 'also' lost here), and also to Dostoevsky (see Fleishman, 1975, 8).

As well as establishing a relationship to literature, however, '*Golubaia tetrad' No. 10*' also establishes a reading that relates to the context of the times. The interplay of these two readings comes into focus when the story's form as a fable is taken into account. The fable plays a key role in *Sluchai* and indeed is important in Kharms's work generally. The story actually entitled '*Basnia*' ('A Fable'), which is not included in *Sluchai*, ends with a moral which does not articulate the point of the text but rather addresses the reader's response to it: 'Reader, think about this fable and you will feel ill at ease' (*Izb*. 122). This moral, while parodying the way a moral traditionally works, also works as a meta-moral by asserting the unsettling, defamiliarising principle upon which Kharms's work rests and which is very closely tied to his use of humour, his 'laughter through tears'.[15] At the same time '*Basnia*' shows how the fable, being composed of a text and a moral, readily invites confrontation of the two in accordance with

OBERIU poetics (see Fleishman, 1975, 10–11). The fable's importance for *Sluchai* comes from the fact that both the first two pieces, '*Golubaia tetrad' No. 10*' and '*Sluchai*', are fables in form, so that the fable provides a framework for the interpretation of the cycle as a whole, in particular through its typically situational reference. Thus, while '*Golubaia tetrad' No. 10*' can be read parodically, since on one level its moral literally has nothing to say, it can also be read non-parodically if viewed against the situation of the times:

> There lived a red-haired man who had no eyes or ears. He didn't have any hair either, so that it was a convention to call him red-haired.
> He could not speak since he didn't have a mouth. He also didn't have a nose.
> He didn't even have any arms or legs. He didn't have a stomach, and he didn't have a back, and he didn't have a spine, and he had no innards at all. There was nothing! So it isn't clear who is being talked about.
> We had better not talk about him any more.
> (*Polët*, 353; *Plummeting*, 27; *Black Coat*, 57)

Against the background of Stalin's Russia the text of the fable can be interpreted as an account of someone who becomes a non-person, an account that is defamiliarised and made funny by treating it absurdly literally, while the moral reads quite straightforwardly: such people are best not talked about. On this reading not only is the 'him' of the last line still a person, rather than being semantically void, but also the 'we' asserts a community of author/narrator and reader through communication; on this reading too the penultimate sentence comes uncannily close to the standard formula professing ignorance. The dismantling of the subject may seem absurdly literal here, but later in the cycle it takes the form of real dismembering: in '*Sud lincha*' ('A Lynching') the crowd tears off the head of the man of medium build, while in '*Okhotniki*' Oknov tears off Kozlov's leg (and maybe more). There is another way, however, of reading the dismantling, namely, as a process which happens on paper: in accordance with the practice of the times a person can be removed piece by piece from printed existence, or be rubbed out on a photograph; moreover, when people become numbers on a file then the elimination of their existence on paper is equivalent to their death. In this way the engimatic title '*Golubaia tetrad' No. 10*', when taken out of the context of Kharms's blue notebook (see *Sob. proizv.*, IV, 155), could be taken to refer to a numbered file. The motif of people as pieces of paper features explicitly in '*Otets i doch*'' ('Father and Daughter', not included in *Sluchai*), where Natasha buries her father's death certificate instead of the real person,[16] but it also recurs, by implication, in '*Son*' ('A Dream'): this is a defamiliarised account of arrest and disappearance in which Kalugin's sleep/dream is in fact a nightmare awake (the deprivation of sleep is inverted into an inability to wake up) and in the end, having returned home as a non-person so that he is not 'recognised', he is declared 'anti-sanitary', 'folded in half' (i.e., as a piece of paper) and 'thrown out as rubbish' (*Polët*, 367; *Black Coat*, 80–1).

The two readings of '*Golubaia tetrad'* No. 10' established so far both treat the text as a coherent whole, but it should also be read according to the OBERIU compositional principle, that is, as a montage or sum of heterogeneous parts put together as it were by chance. This motif is already present in the dismantling of the subject as if the body were an aggregate of parts (see Fleishman, 1975, 7–8), and when the text is similarly dismantled further avenues of interpretation and understanding are opened up. When read this way the dominant motif of the story, the repetition – nine times – of 'he didn't have...', becomes an assertion of absence or lack; from here this motif extends throughout the cycle where what is missing, be it cause, communication, humanity, is crucial.

When the repeated 'he didn't have...' is removed, what is left is as follows:

> There lived a red-haired man... it was a convention to call him red-haired... he could not speak... there was nothing... it is not clear [literally: not understood] who is being talked about... we had better not talk about him any more.

In addition, apart from the adverbs 'also' and 'even' (possibly Gogolian in its resonance), there are the conjunctions 'so that' (twice) and 'since' which, though logical in their immediate sentences, beg the question of cause and effect more generally. In the reduced text the first theme raised is that of meaning and language in the form of a divorce between signifier and signified, since red-haired has lost its referential meaning and become a name by convention; immediately, therefore, we see an extension of the motif of absence or lack. This divorce between signifier and signified is a recurrent theme in Kharms where words can lose their accepted reference and turn into their opposites (see Anemone, above): the names Pushkin and Gogol lose their reference, sleep in '*Son*' is in fact a nightmare awake, and in '*Kassirsha*' ('The Cashier'), which is not included in *Sluchai*, even the word 'dead' loses its meaning, so that when the police are asked to take away the 'dead cashier' they take away the cashier, but the one who is alive (*Izb.* 80; *Plummeting*, 63). Thus fundamental categories such as life/death, waking/dreaming, and identity all become unsettled.

Following on directly from the theme of language and meaning is the theme of communication: speech is the only faculty explicitly mentioned in relation to the parts of the body, and communication is highlighted in both the last two sentences. As Ann Shukman has shown, a key to the understanding of the absurd in Kharms lies in his breaking of conditions of communication;[17] in terms of Jakobson's communication schema some of Kharms's stories would seem to lack the 'context' (understood as a referent, something outside to which the message refers) which is needed for communication to take place,[18] and on one level this seems to be the case with '*Golubaia tetrad' No. 10*' because the subject (the referent) has been dismantled to the point of non-existence (Shukman, 61). In fact another of Jakobson's conditions, the code, is also threatened, because of the divorce of signifier and signified in 'red-haired'. In terms of the Bakhtin school's model of communication part of the 'context' (understood now as circumstances rather than as referent) which determines the meaning of an utterance is the interlocutors' shared knowledge and evaluation (often unspoken),[19] and yet typically in Kharms there is a void where this evaluation could be expected (Shukman, 62–3). Thirdly, many of the eight additional axioms that Revzin and Revzina added to Jakobson's schema,[20] such as the assumption of causal explanation or the semantic coherence of the text, may be broken either locally or generally, and yet, most significantly, the axiom of truthfulness, that there should be some correspondence between the text and reality, is typically fulfilled by the realia that locate many of Kharms's pieces in the world of the times (Shukman, 65–8). But, as we have seen, the key to understanding '*Golubaia tetrad' No. 10*' lies not in its relation to recognisable objects, places, or concierges, which, though well represented in Kharms's texts, are not present here, but in its relation to reality at a higher, situational level; it is this situational aspect, the 'situational absurd', that provides the link between the topographical realia and the portrait of an illogical world, a world out of joint, in a more general way.[21] When the story is understood as a defamiliarised account of someone who becomes a non-person, then Jakobson's context, which might seem to have disappeared, can be restored, and in so doing 'we' restore the conditions of communication and a community of author/narrator and reader is asserted. By extension, therefore, we can go on to restore other factors necessary for communication when these are found to be lacking:[22] for a start, in '*Golubaia tetrad' No. 10*', once the reality of the subject is accepted, he can be re-assembled and his identity and defining characteristic ('red-haired') restored,[23] so that the divorce between signifer and signified is overcome. This is an example of that 'reversibility' ('*obratnost'*') which is central to the poetics of both Kharms and Vvedensky (see Jaccard, 1985, 271–3; Vved., II, 287–8, 304, and elsewhere).

The relation between communication and existence is a recurrent theme in Kharms which is explicitly stated in *Elizaveta Bam* by Ivan Ivanovich: 'I speak in order to be' (*Polët*, 187).[24] Moreover, the existential significance of communication can be related to Kharms's attitude to the word, which is itself capable of transforming into an object: 'It seems that these lines of verse, having become a thing, could be lifted off the paper and thrown at the window, and the window will shatter. That's what words can do' (*Polët*, 483–4; *Plummeting*, 90).[25] The vital importance of communication is directly expressed in both the famous poem '*Iz doma vyshel chelovek*' ('A Man Left Home') and the untitled story '*Zhil-byl chelovek, Zvali ego Kuznetsov*' ('There Once Was a Man'), both of which end with an appeal to the reader to communicate in order to restore identity and existence:

| | |
|---|---|
| Но если как-нибудь его | But if you ever |
| Случится встретить вам, | happen to come across him, |
| Тогда скорей, | then hurry, |
| Тогда скорей, | then hurry, |
| Скорей скажите нам. | then hurry to tell us. |

(*Polët*, 249)

and:

> Please! If anyone meets a man on the street who has five bumps on his head, then remind him that he is called Kuznetsov and that he needs to buy some carpenter's glue and mend a broken stool.[26]

The apparently cautionary moral at the end of '*Golubaia tetrad' No. 10*' seems to run counter to these direct appeals, and on one level the contrast can be seen to articulate the inevitable tension at that time between the preservation of self and others and the need to keep communication alive.[27] On another level, however, the final line of '*Golubaia tetrad' No. 10*' disguises the fact that there is no need to say any more, because, once the context and hence communication are restored, the reader, in communion with the author, has implicitly resurrected the red-haired man. Moreover, since this is only the first story and the cycle continues, the caution is reversed and communication continues upon the understanding established here.

'*Golubaia tetrad' No. 10*' can thus be read against the contexts of both literature and reality and, beyond that, it can be seen to raise the themes of meaning, identity, communication, and existence; but still beyond that it opens up yet further questions of gnoseology and ontology. These questions arise out of the statement 'There was nothing', which seems to round off the dismantling of the subject but which lacks any reference to him, and the sentence following: 'So that it is not clear [literally: not understood] who is being talked about'. Nothingness, emptiness, and disappearance are recurrent motifs in Kharms which, as Meilakh points out in relation to *Elizaveta Bam*, may be interpreted in accordance with Eastern or Western terminology; at the same time these motifs relate in a variety of ways to the poetics of Kharms and Vvedensky (Meilakh, 1987, 202–4 and below; Smirnov, 1988, 698–700). In particular, nothingness in the form of emptiness of sense leads into the area of cognition beyond reason where, in Vvedensky's famous words, 'the star of absurdity [*bessmyslitsa*] burns' (Vved. I, 100), or, in the words of '*Golubaia tetrad' No. 10*', 'it is not understood' ('*neponiatno*'). The gnoseological and ontological problems opened up here are illuminated by a passage in which Druskin gives a brief exposition of his own thinking but which could be read as a commentary on '*Golubaia tetrad' No. 10*' as well:[28]

> I am interested in the final division. By this I understand the following: I am left on my own . . . . I am alone because there is no external understanding: I understand nothing. This does not mean that there is no inner understanding, that is, that no-one understands anyone. But in order for there to be real inner understanding and not hypocrisy, first there must be complete non-understanding, I must be left on my own: I and God. Having said this, I can see: not I, but God, I am no more. But how can I say that I do not exist ['*menia net*']? And again I repeat – I do not exist; the first part of the sentence negates the second, but both are correct. I call this the final division: I am divided myself, I myself observe my absence

and do not understand it. But only through this non-understanding is it possible to arrive at inner understanding, a certain non-understanding *is* understanding, the rest is false.

(Druskin, 1985, 393)

This exposition of the way to inner understanding may help to explain the comment 'against Kant' which Kharms placed under the text of '*Golubaia tetrad' No. 10*' in the Blue Notebook itself (see *Polët*, 528–9): understanding for Kant rests on the phenomenological world, but Kharms's 'nothing' opens up, for those who will pass beyond understanding, the noumenal world of the spirit. The possibility of passing into other worlds is raised in later pieces in the cycle ('*Sunduk*', '*Molodoi chelovek, udivivshii storozha*', '*Makarov i Petersen*', '*Fedia Davidovich*', where the entry is along the corridor in a communal flat, and '*Pakin i Rakukin*') as well as in Kharms's work more generally, and it relates also to Lipavsky's notion of neighbouring worlds and 'messengers' ('*vestniki*') (see Druskin, 1985, 391–2).

Since on the existential level the nothingness that overcomes the red-haired man is death, '*Golubaia tetrad' No. 10*' both articulates human incomprehension of death and opens the question of immortality, which in an entry from his private writings Kharms defines as the aim of any human life:

1. The aim of any human life is one thing: immortality.

1a. The aim of any human life is one thing: the achievement of immortality.

2. One person aims at immortality through the procreation of his kind, a second performs great deeds on earth so as to immortalise his name, and only the third leads a correct and saintly life in order to achieve immortality as eternal life.

3. Man has only 2 interests:
the earthly: – food, drink, warmth, woman and rest and
the heavenly: – immortality.

4. All that is earthly bears witness to death.

5. There is one straight line on which all that is earthly lies. And only that which does not lie on this line can bear witness to immortality.

6. And therefore man seeks a deviation from this earthly line and calls it beauty or genius.[29]

The point at which it is possible to depart from the earthly line in '*Golubaia tetrad' No. 10*' is at 'nothing': the way to immortality, as to understanding, is opened, though not articulated (*Starukha*, however, does end with the miracle of faith).

The second piece in the cycle is the title story '*Sluchai*' ('Incidents') itself (characteristically displaced). Like '*Golubaia tetrad*" it is a fable, a fact that is signalled in the second sentence by the name Krylov:

> One day Orlov stuffed himself on ground peas and died. And Krylov, when he found out about this, also died. And Spiridonov died of his own accord. And Spiridonov's wife fell off the sideboard and also died. And Spiridonov's children drowned in the pond. And Spiridonov's grandmother took to drink and went off. And Mikhailov stopped combing his hair and got eczema. And Kruglov drew a picture of a lady with a whip in her hands and went mad. And Perekrestov received four hundred roubles by telegraph and gave himself such airs that he was kicked out of his job.
>
> Good people don't know how to get on [literally: how to put themselves on a firm footing]. (*Polët*, 354; *Black Coat*, 64)

If '*Golubaia tetrad' No. 10*' can be read against the background of the times as a fable about someone who becomes a non-person, '*Sluchai*' invokes the situation in which death or disaster affects a chain of related (or unrelated) people, as indeed happened to Kharms's group of friends among innumerable others. But the situation is defamiliarised and made funny by the circumstances of death (overeating, the sideboard) as well as by the way the chain continues into eczema and beyond; the circumstances of Krylov's death, however, relate to the real danger of knowledge. The accidental nature of this string of disasters describes very accurately an absurd world where the abnormal became normal and one death could lead to others without reason, simply by the force of chance or circumstance; as defined in *Starukha*, there is 'infection by corpse poisoning' (*Polët*, 420). The link between all these events and people might only be established in a way similar to that in which Kharms relates a series of seemingly unconnected events and people in '*Sviaz*" ('The Connection', *Polët*, 500–02; *Black Coat*, 88–90), a text which is not included in *Sluchai*; then, perhaps, the link between all the deaths and what happens to Mikhailov, Kruglov, and Perekrestov would become clear.

Whereas '*Golubaia tetrad' No. 10*' opens up far-ranging questions of meaning, identity, and beyond, '*Sluchai*' addresses much more specifically the question of evaluation, that often unspoken factor which is vital for communication. The question of evaluation is raised by the fable form itself and then explicitly in the moral: 'Good people...' (compare 'better' in *'Golubaia tetrad' No. 10'*); such evaluative epithets, as generally in Kharms, are almost completely absent in the rest of *Sluchai* ('good' only comes to prominence again in the title of the penultimate piece *'Nachalo ochen' khoroshego letnego dnia'*). Within the text of the fable the same question arises at the juxtaposition (confrontation) of the tragic initial sequence and Mikhailov's eczema, followed by Kruglov's bizarre madness and Perekrestov's bad behaviour and loss of his job. The moral itself, while seemingly coherent if read independently of the text, becomes incoherent when applied to it: on one level this works parodically, since the moral should follow on from the text, but on another it creates a confrontation of senses and the moral, like the text, becomes an accidental sequence. The relationship between the epithet 'good' and the noun 'people', which might ideally be a fixed or natural one, is here arbitrary: which of the people in the text are good is impossible to define, but Perekrestov, whose case immediately precedes the moral, certainly seems otherwise, while Orlov at the beginning dies (on the face of it) from gluttony. The epithet 'good', once divorced from its noun, becomes free to invoke evaluation in general, and the reader is confronted by a text which describes a situation ruled not by good but by a combination of chance and evil. In this way *'Sluchai'* both foregrounds the role of chance in life and death and introduces the problem of evil in man, which Druskin identified as one of the three main themes in Kharms (Druskin, 1989, 112) and which will subsequently be exemplified in individual cases; but, in an inversion of the traditional roles of author and reader in the fable, it is the reader who has to recognise evil as such and restore meaning to human goodness (compare the unsettling moral of *'Basnia'*).

But if the moral is now read independently of the text and the literal meaning is invoked, then it characterises the period very precisely as a time when human goodness does not know how to get on, as a time when there is no firm ground under foot, echoing Mandel'shtam's lines:

Мы живем, под собою не чуя страны,
Наши речи за десять шагов не слышны.[30]

The absence of firm ground under foot becomes one of the key motifs of the cycle, taking the form of continued stumbling and falling; indeed, in the final sentence of the whole cycle Rakukin's soul even stumbles after death (*Polët*, 397), and subsequently this motif is realised in the title of the late story '*Upadanie*' ('The Falling'). Both falling and its inverse, flying, are recurrent motifs in Kharms's earlier work too, but of equal or greater significance for *Sluchai* is the recurrence of the motif of falling in his private writings of the later period, for example:

> Few people fall as low as I have done. One thing is beyond doubt: I have fallen so low that now I can never raise myself again. (12 Jan. 1938).[31]

The motif of falling is also found in one of the 'prayers' of his later verse:

| Избавь меня Боже от лени, падения и мечтания. | Save me O God from idleness, falling and daydreaming. |

(*Sob. proizv.*, IV, 43)

Falling here stands for moral and spiritual decline, and in a religious context this readily gives rise to associations with the Fall: one of Kharms's dramatic sketches is called '*Grekhopadenie. Ili poznanie dobra i zla*' ('The Fall. Or Knowledge of Good and Evil').[32] Against this background and in the context of the theme of evil, the recurrent motif of falling and stumbling in *Sluchai* could be seen as a symbol or, in Lipavsky's terminology, hieroglyph (see Druskin, 1989, 109) of the state to which man has sunk and hence of his fallen state and the consequent spread of evil in the world. As with communication and identity in '*Golubaia tetrad' No. 10*', the reverse process of rising, the restoration of good over evil, is invoked by its opposite; by extension the same reverse process should be applied to the negative bias of vocabulary in the cycle, especially in the description of human feelings, behaviour, attributes, and even physical features. Finally, in connection with this thematic complex, the motif of the earth at the end of *Starukha*, immediately prior to the miracle of faith, is of great significance: the steps of the train carriage 'do not reach the earth' so that the narrator has to leap off and then he observes a caterpillar 'crawling along the earth' (*Polët*, 429, 430; *Black Coat*, 153); in other words, he has refound the earth and can then make the leap of faith.

The motif of falling is immediately foregrounded in the third piece, '*Vyvalivaiushchiesia starukhi*' ('The Plummeting Old Women'), in which a series of old women fall from a window 'out of excessive curiosity' (*Polët*, 356; *Plummeting*, 11). This is no longer a fable in form (the fable only returns much later in the satirical '*Chto teper' prodaiut v magazinakh*'), but the familiar situation of leaning from a window to see what is going on is here taken to an extreme that is easily read against the background of the times as a cautionary tale about the dangers of excessive curiosity (compare the cautionary moral of '*Golubaia tetrad' No. 10*' and the death of Krylov in '*Sluchai*'). Another situation, however, is also invoked, because falling from a window can be suicide to avoid arrest, as indeed is contemplated by Elizaveta Bam (see *Polët*, 175; and below), in which case the 'excessive curiosity' need not be that of the old women. The final sentence of '*Vyvalivaiushchiesia starukhi*' then addresses the problem of evaluation once more, but now from a different angle as the narratorial 'I' operates within the space of the story rather than as the implied authorial voice of the first two texts:

> When the sixth old woman fell out I got fed up with watching them, and I went to Mal'tsevskii market where they say a blind man has been given a knitted shawl. (*Polët*, 356)

The indifferent attitude of the narrator to the spectacle of death, which has already been apparent in his use of the word 'shatter' ('*razbit'sia*') to describe the old women's demise, assaults 'our' values and provokes the reader to restore what is missing; it also takes the cycle a stage further by foregrounding the reaction of an observer to what is happening (at the same time the theme of communication – 'they say' – seems to operate, through the present tense, both inside and outside the space of the story). This reaction/lack of reaction is realised in the motif of seeing/not seeing which is immediately present in the figure of the blind man and is subsequently taken up in '*Opticheskii obman*' and elsewhere. It seems that only the blind get presents and protection (the shawl) in this world because only they cannot see what is going on; moreover, the shawl is a knitted one and therefore displays a coherence which the shattered old women and the world they inhabit lack. The metaphorical blindness on display, however, is the narrator's moral and human indifference to what he describes.

The theme of the observer's and more generally the community's moral and human blindness is now expanded in both '*Proisshestvie na ulitse*' (the story which has an uncertain status in the cycle) and the following '*Sonet*'. In '*Proisshestvie na ulitse*' accidents on the street become a spectacle in which the fate of the victim is ignored, while in '*Sonet*' memory loss concerning the sequence of numbers after six causes dispute among the community until another spectacle happens to distract them:

> We would have argued for a very long time but fortunately just then some child tumbled off a bench and broke both its jaws. This distracted us from our argument.
> And then we dispersed to our various homes.
> (*Polët*, 357; *Plummeting*, p. 13)

In this story the narrator becomes a participant and instigator, not just an observer, and the first person plural 'we', which previously invoked the community of author and reader, is now operating within the space of the story too. Neither the narratorial 'I' nor 'we' figure again in the cycle, so that Kharms seeks to confront the reader with his own reaction to the events not just as distanced reader but also as potential observer and participant. Moreover, the indifference shown by the community is now generalised beyond the more specific tragedies of the times to encompass indifference to human tragedy in general, using the archetypal example of the suffering of children; memory loss thus affects human and moral values as well as the sequence of numbers. Nevertheless, the relation between the specific and the general is shown by the fact that the memory loss affects the number chain at the exact point – six – where the narrator in '*Vyvalivaiushchiesia starukhi*' became fed up watching the old women (also an archetypal example of the defenceless in society). Thus by the end of '*Sonet*' Kharms has established a basis for the interpretation of *Sluchai* in the most general human terms.

The opening texts have revealed a logical progression in the introduction they provide to the cycle, moving from the general inwards while at the same time broadening the reference: this is the order of art asserted by Kharms. At this point, however, the cycle shifts into a composition of diverse variations, a shift marked by the defamiliarising effect of the four-line *raëk* '*Petrov i Kamarov*' (notice also the motif of dispersal at the end of '*Sonet*'), and in the final part of this essay I will look at the way this composition works. Firstly, certain regularities can be observed in the arrangement of the pieces according to medium (prose/drama) and length. There is a certain tendency for the pieces towards the end (from '*Okhotniki*' onwards) to be rather longer, around two pages in length, whereas the average length before is about a page; at least some of these pieces were written as late as 1939,[33] and this may reflect the general tendency in Kharms's prose towards greater length. It is also notable that the dramatic pieces are found more in the middle of the cycle: five of the seven come in the space of nine texts, from '*Matematik i Andrei Semënovich*' (13) to '*Tiuk*' (21). Both these features, as we shall see, can be related to the compositional order of the cycle. Whereas the first four texts develop linearly, the sequence of texts in the main body of the cycle rests more on the principle of juxtaposition or alternation according to opposition or unlikeness. This is a variant of the principle of confrontation of objects/senses, and it also relates directly to one of the philosophical axes of the Kharmsian world, the principle of existence *in contrario* and the dynamic balance of opposites set in motion by an obstacle or 'slight imperfection' (see Jaccard, 1985, 270–7). The juxtaposition of unlike may operate at the level of form or content: thus, the dramatic pieces in the middle of the cycle typically alternate with stories, and the parodied folk-tale '*Poteri*' ('Losing Things') is followed by '*Makarov i Petersen*' with its theme of disappearance into other worlds. The principle of alternation operates within the texts too: in '*Opticheskii obman*', for example, Semën Semënovich alternately does and does not see a peasant in a pine tree, while in '*Son*' Kalugin's first four dreams also proceed in the same way.

Alternation and confrontation, however, are complemented by interrelation (as in the OBERIU article), and the embodiment of these principles in a composition of diverse variations can be related in turn to the principle of transformation, which plays a central role in the poetics of Kharms and Vvedensky.[34] The operation of these principles can be illustrated for example by the stories '*Stoliar Kushakov*' and '*Sunduk*', although any two consecutive pieces could be taken. '*Stoliar Kushakov*' begins with the formula 'Once upon a time there was . . .' ('*Zhil-byl*') and is readily interpreted as a parody of elements of the folk tale, in particular the search motif (also parodied in '*Poteri*'): the hero is going out to buy some carpenter's glue (a symbol, or hieroglyph, of the search for something to make the world hold together) but he suffers a series of falls, after each of which he goes to the chemist (the wise fairy) to get a plaster until gradually his whole face is covered, so that when he gets home he is not recognised. The reason for Kushakov's falls is explicitly given: 'There was a temporary thaw, and it was very slippery on the street' (*Polët*, 361; *Black Coat*, 55), but in the context of the cycle this is a realisation of the lack of firm footing, and the result for Kushakov is a variant of what happens to the red-haired man: his face becomes obliterated by plasters until he is no longer recognised, a non-person, and his identity is threatened (a further transformation of this theme occurs in '*Son*', and also, outside *Sluchai*, in the story about Kuznetsov, whose sortie to buy carpenter's glue similarly ends in a loss of identity). In this way '*Stoliar Kushakov*' combines motifs from both '*Sluchai*' and '*Golubaia tetrad' No. 10*', as well as providing a variation on the theme of memory loss. At the same time the theme of communication continues, since Kushakov refuses to listen: 'I don't want to hear anything' (*Polët*, 361; *Black Coat*, 56). The parodic aspect of the text might introduce a further dimension that is lacking, in that one interpretation of the search in the folk (wonder) tale is that it is a search for the soul,[35] whereas Kushakov is looking for a practical solution (the glue).

This lacking dimension, which was opened in '*Golubaia tetrad' No. 10*', is now immediately expanded in the following story '*Sunduk*', where the man with a thin neck climbs into a trunk and then passively experiences and narrates the struggle of life and death as he suffocates (an 'accidental' link between the two texts is thus the neighbours' jibe 'Tell us another one' ['*Rasskazyvai*'] at the end of '*Stoliar Kushakov*' [*Polët*, 362]). As the moment of death arrives the motif of not understanding also arises: 'Now something has happened, but I cannot understand exactly [literally: namely] what' (*Polët*, 363; *Plummeting*, 15). The story also continues the theme of existence and communication, since the man keeps talking even when suffocating and maybe dead.[36] The ending then rests on a grammatical paradox which fixes the shift into an area beyond rational understanding: 'That means life has overcome death [or: death has overcome life] by means unknown to me' (*Polët*, 364; *Plummeting*, 16); as Kharms himself commented on the original manuscript, in Russian either word could be the subject or object (*Polët*, 530). These two stories also illustrate the way that an 'accidental' element may assist in linking the pieces of *Sluchai* through the order of art: in this case it is the neighbours' jibe 'Tell us another one' at the end of '*Stoliar Kushakov*'; another example is the memory loss concerning the sequence of numbers which links '*Vyvalivaiushchiesia starukhi*' and '*Sonet*'.[37]

The cycle approaches a preliminary resolution of the themes of human relations and communication at (or following) '*Vstrecha*'; this is marked by a break in the alternating sequence of dramatic sketches and stories. First the theme of communication is taken to an extreme in two consecutive dramatic pieces, '*Neudachnyi spektakl'*' and '*Tiuk*'. In '*Neudachnyi spektakl'*' a communal attack of vomiting renders the very act of utterance ineffective but the resultant statements, interrupted by vomiting, acquire a far-reaching existential significance: 'In order not to be...', 'I would be...' (*Polët*, 379; *Black Coat*, 54). Then in '*Tiuk*' communication is related to the absence of a link between cause and effect, since, in a vicious circle, Evdokim Osipovich's promises not to say '*tiuk*' have no effect, just as the axe has no effect on the log and its sound effect is supplied by Evdokim (there is an echo here of *The Cherry Orchard*). These two dramatic sketches are followed by two stories, '*Chto teper' prodaiut v magazinakh*' and '*Mashkin ubil Koshkina*', which reduce the theme of relations between people to the starkest violence and killing. In '*Chto teper' prodaiut v magazinakh*' communication in the form of argument and interruption leads straight into violence and killing which, with a cucumber as the weapon, is presented like a scene from popular comedy; this, however, is then advanced as a symbol of current achievement in the moral: 'That's what big cucumbers they're selling now in the shops' (*Polët*, 382; *Plummeting*, 21). The situational reference of this moral is immediately reinforced in '*Mashkin ubil Koshkina*' where the game of cat and mouse is inverted and 'comrade' Mashkin kills 'comrade' Koshkin (the misspelling, as with the name Kamarov, works as a 'slight imperfection' but also carries an echo of Dostoevsky's Prince Myshkin);[38] at the same time this story with its emblematic title (repeated in the last line) distils the theme of human relations to its negative essence. This concentration of the cycle in a preliminary resolution is broken by a return to the theme of sleep in the story '*Son draznit cheloveka*' (a repetition with variation of the earlier '*Sluchai s Petrakovym*' ['Petrakov']) which works as a defamiliarising relief, and then the cycle continues with a renewed diversification, although already in a different key: it is at this point that the texts become longer and more diverse ('*Istoricheskii epizod*', '*Anekdoty iz zhizni Pushkina*', the mixed medium of '*Okhotniki*') before the final two texts round off the cycle in circularity.[39]

Circularity of composition provides yet another parallel with *Elizaveta Bam*, where the first scene is repeated and then resolved in the last, and it is a recurrent feature in Vvedensky too. The last two pieces, '*Nachalo ochen' khoroshego letnego dnia*' and '*Pakin i Rakukin*' correspond symmetrically to the opening pieces '*Golubaia tetrad' No. 10*' and '*Sluchai*'.[40] '*Nachalo ochen' khoroshego letnego dnia*' echoes '*Sluchai*' both thematically and formally: like '*Sluchai*' it both highlights evaluation ('good') and is composed of a string of sentences describing a collection of people, who are linked, here, by the accident of time and place. In effect this piece presents an aggregate of the human (or, rather, subhuman) characteristics depicted throughout the cycle. There are no deaths, but the level of life is so low that the 'human herd' is an appropriate designation and the grotesque and/or everyday happenings are arranged without reference to any system of values: a mother is rubbing her pretty (*'khoroshen'kaia'*) daughter's face against a wall, bag-swinging women are queueing for sugar, and to complete the picture a drunken peasant is standing in front of the queue with his trousers open, uttering 'not nice [literally: not good] words'; this evaluative adjective is then immediately placed in confrontation with the final sentence: 'In this way a good summer's day was beginning' (*Polët*, 394; *Black Coat*, 52). The confrontation of 'good', now without the 'very' of the title,[41] and 'not good' opens a gulf in evaluation: either 'good' turns into its opposite, if applied to what is described in the text, or else the title and final sentence apply to the summer's day divorced from what is going on. The subtitles '*Simfoniia*' is also missplaced as a description of a chain of accidental events, and yet, just as '*Sluchai*' serves as the title of the whole cycle, so '*Simfoniia*' could serve as its subtitle, for the order of art has transformed the montage of pieces into an orchestrated whole (see note 39).[42]

The final story, '*Pakin i Rakukin*', then echoes '*Golubaia tetrad' No. 10*' as well as bringing together many other strands, both formal and thematic, from the cycle as a whole: now the break-up of the body is played out between two people as Pakin exercises his power over Rakukin, using only words, until the latter distorts his body (like Koshkin in '*Mashkin ubil Koshkina*') in such a way that his neck eventually snaps; moreover, since the scene is played out principally in dialogue, albeit one-sided, the text could be at least partially transformed into a dramatic piece, as happens in '*Okhotniki*', and so prose narration and drama are fused. At the moment of Rakukin's death the point of view unexpectedly becomes that of an external observer for the first time since the beginning of the cycle:

> If one looked from Pakin to Rakukin, it was possible to think that Rakukin was sitting without any head. Rakukin's adam's apple was sticking up in the air. One couldn't help thinking that it was a nose.   (*Polët*, 396; *Plummeting*, 46)

The loss of the head can signify the move into the world of cognition beyond reason, while the reference to the nose, as in '*Golubaia tetrad' No. 10'*, provides a symmetrical reference to Gogol. The move into another world is finally made explicit with the arrival of the 'angel of death' to take Rakukin's soul, still spiteful and stumbling, 'round the turning in the distance' into the next world (*Polët*, 397). The angel of death, who is the central, unnamed figure behind *Sluchai*, appears from behind the cupboard, which is one of the emblematic objects of OBERIU art, as in the famous slogan 'Art as a cupboard'; the purity of order in art, which is both creation and reflection of the world, opens areas beyond death and understanding.

## NOTES

1. See *Polët*, pp. 353–97; *Sluchai* should also be about to appear in the next volume, volume V, of the definitive edition of Kharms's work, *Sob. proizv.*
2. Concerning the creation of the cycle, see also Glotser, 1989, pp. 208–9. *Sluchai* includes texts written from 1933 to 1939, but Aleksandrov speculates that Kharms may have intended to expand the cycle (*Polët*, 528) and Glotser considers it 'completely obvious' that the cycle was continued (Glotser, 208); while it is indeed obvious that other texts relate to *Sluchai*, the suggestion that they could simply be added to it treats the cycle as a collection rather than a composition. For an introduction to the cycle's thematic and compositional unity, see Kobrinskii, 1988.
3. The title is usually translated as 'incidents' (see, for example, *Plummeting*) or 'happenings', but Milner-Gulland has pointed out the appropriateness of 'cases' as well (Milner-Gulland, 1984, p. 36, n. 16).
4. The term OBERIU has a specific reference to the literary grouping of 1927–30 which included Kharms, Vvedenskii, Zabolotskii, and others, but has also come to refer more generally (and loosely) to the literary tendency that is personified especially in Kharms and Vvedenskii (concerning the history of OBERIU and its narrowness as an appellation for Kharms and Vvedenskii, see Meilakh, *'Predislovie'*, to Vved. I, pp. xvi–xxiii). Of far broader significance for Kharms and Vvedenskii is the group known as *'Chinari'* which consisted of Druskin, Lipavskii, Vvedenskii, Kharms and Oleinikov and *de facto* Tamara Lipavskaia, Vvedenskii's first wife, as well (concerning this group, see Druskin, 1985); substantially the same material, with some additions, some deletions, and in a different order, has now also been published in the Soviet Union: see Druskina, 1989; and Druskin, 1989.
5. The terms 'confrontation of verbal senses' and 'confrontation of a series of objects' are found in the article introducing OBERIU (originally *Afishi Doma pechati*, 1928, no. 2, 11–13; first reprinted in

Milner-Gulland, 1970; also reprinted in *Izb.*, pp. 287–98); the terms 'semantic absurd' and 'situational absurd' are used by Druskin to characterise the work of Vvedenskii and Kharms (Druskin, 1985, 384).

6. Even the composition of OBERIU itself is presented in this way in their article: 'People talk about an *accidental* combination of *different* people. ... Our organisation [*ob"edinenie*] is free and voluntary. ... Each of us knows himself and each knows what links him to the others' (Milner-Gulland, 1970, 71). Concerning the OBERIU poetics of chance, and its relationship to the poetics of Pasternak and Khlebnikov, see Fleishman, 1975; see also Gerasimova, 1988, pp. 54–5. A recurring notion in Druskin's work on Vvedenskii, substantial extracts from which (especially from '*Zvezda bessmyslitsy*') are included in the commentary in Vved., II, is that of the 'unaccidental accidental' (Vved., II, 277, 299, and elsewhere); concerning the gnoseological aspect of the absurd, see Druskin, 1985, 381–4; see also his '*Stadii ponimaniia*' (published in Druskin, 1985, 405–13) where the stages of understanding proceed from the individual work (by Vvedenskii) to the work of that author as a whole and then on to encompass the five 'Chinari' as an interrelated unity. Concerning the philosophical aspect of Kharms and Vvedenskii as an investigation of the meaning of meaning, see Milner-Gulland, 1984, 32–3.
7. Vladimir Dal', *Tolkovyi slovar' zhivago velikorusskago iazyka*, second edition (St Petersburg and Moscow, 1882; reprinted Moscow, 1980), IV, 226.
8. N. V. Gogol', *Polnoe sobranie sochinenii* (Leningrad, Moscow, 1937–52), III, 49 (all translations are my own).
9. Concerning Kharms and Chekhov, see Chances, 1982. Concerning similarities between *Sluchai* and Kuzmin's cycle of mini-stories, '*Pechka v bane: kafel'nye peizazhi*' (1928), see Cheron, 1983, pp. 96–7; the word 'sluchai' also occurs in the title of Kuzmin's '*Piat' razgovorov i odin sluchai*' (1926).
10. See Meilakh, 1987, 172–3 (translated in this volume).
11. See Jaccard, 1985, 273–7; apart from the publications mentioned above (notes 5 and 6), the major publication of Druskin's work is Druskin, 1988.
12. *Polët*, 372; *Plummeting*, 12.
13. See Flaker, 1969, 79; translated in *Plummeting*, pp. 32–3.
14. The most detailed study of Kharms's use of parody (in *Komediia goroda Peterburga*) is Vishevsky, 1986.
15. Concerning the comic in Kharms, its ethical dimension and its relation to the carnivalised laughter of the medieval Russian tradition and *iurodstvo*, see Gerasimova, 50–5, 75–7; and Anthony Anemone's essay in the present volume; on the moral purpose of Kharms's humour, see also Druskin, 1989, 112.
16. 'Otets i doch'', *Voprosy literatury*, 1987, no. 8, 271–2.
17. Shukman, 1989; Kharms's violation of communication rules is also considered, though less systematically and only in relation to *Elizaveta Bam*, in Stelleman, 1985, 339–40; see also Jaccard, 1990.
18. Roman Jakobson, 'Closing Statement: Linguistics and Poetics', in

T. Sebeok (ed.), *Style in Language* (Cambridge, Mass.: MIT Press, 1960), pp. 350–77 (p. 353).
19. V. N. Voloshinov (M. M. Bakhtin), 'Discourse in Life and Discourse in Poetry' (*'Slovo v zhizni i slovo v poezii'*), translated by John Richmond, in A. Shukman (ed.) *Bakhtin School Papers* (Oxford: Russian Poetics in Translation, 10, 1983), pp. 5–30, especially pp. 10–13; V. N. Voloshinov (M. M. Bakhtin), 'The Construction of the Utterance' (*'Konstruktsiia vyskazyvaniia'*), translated by Noel Owen, in ibid., pp. 114–38, especially pp. 123–6.
20. Revzina and Revzin, 1971, 242.
21. Concerning the relationship of Kharms's prose to the general historical context of Stalinism, see Anemone, above. The identification of more specific references to the historical context has been suggested by Fleishman as a key to some of Kharms's poetry too: see Fleishman, 1987 (translated in the present volume, below). An example of this kind of reading can be seen in Zolotonosov's recent article about the intelligentsia in which he notes, with reference to *'Chetyre illiustratsii...'*, that only Kharms's absurd is adequate to define the fate of the intelligentsia at the time (Zolotonosov, 1989, 51–2). In fact *'Chetyre illiustratsii'* has a more specific situational reference as well:

Writer: I am a writer.
Reader: In my opinion you're s--t!

For a few minutes the writer stands dumbstruck by this new idea and falls dead. He is carried out.           (*Polët*, 372; *Plummeting*, 12)

The second and third 'illustrations' repeat the scene between an artist and a worker and a composer and Vania Rublëv, but the fourth scene involves a chemist and a physicist, and so can no longer be seen simply in terms of the relationship between the intelligentsia and the mass of the population; instead, these 'illustrations' can be read additionally as a defamiliarised but brutally literal account of denunciation, both public and private, and in this connection the words 'new idea' in the title can readily be interpreted as 'new ideology' as well.
22. This procedure should evidently be related to Faryno's recent proposal that, in respect of the standard communication model, the poetics of the historical avantgarde (the post-Symbolist generation) should be seen not negatively as anti-text etc., but positively, as an inversion of that model which calls for an orientation towards the conditions that generate the text – the context, code, and addresser (Jerzy Faryno, 'Deshifrovka', *Russian Literature*, 26 (1989), 1–67).
23. The role of names and defining characteristics in Kharms, and their relationship to identity, is extremely interesting and could make the subject of a separate study. Name creation, starting of course with his own name, was one of Kharms's favourite activities (Poret, 1980, 354–5); the motif of name changing is characteristic not only of Kharms but also of the OBERIU/'Chinari' more generally (as, for example, in Oleinikov's poem *'Peremena familii'*).

24. As Meilakh points out, this declaration of *homo loquens* reworks earlier (Cartesian, Socratic, etc.) existential definitions (Meilakh, 1987, 243-4, 198, and below). The whole question of the philosophical background to Kharms and the 'Chinari' has yet to be studied, except as presented in the writings of Druskin: in the first instance their thought should be related to the Russian anti-rationalist and Christian tradition, while Kierkegaard emerges as a central authority for Druskin (see Druskin, 1988). Certain parallels with Existentialism, of which Kierkegaard can be seen as a precursor but from which he is also distinguished, suggest themselves as well: for example, the theme of language and being in Heidegger, the theme of 'nothing', and so on. Returning to the theme of communication, an interesting comparison and contrast can be made with Beckett (concerning this theme in Beckett, see Jaccard, 1988a, 157-8, and the translation (above) in the present volume).
25. Concerning the transformation of word into object in Vvedenskii, see Vved., II, 279, 286, and elsewhere.
26. Published as '*Zhil-byl chelovek*', Russkaia mysl', 1985, viii; also in Jaccard, 1985, 292-3; and *Plummeting*, 22-3. Most interestingly, both these direct appeals rework the parodied moral in the Prutkovian fable:

>   Однажды нес пастух куда-то молоко,
>   Но нес ужасно далеко,
>   Что уж назад не возвращался.
>   Читатель! Он тебе не попадался?

>   'One day a shepherd was carrying some milk somewhere, but he carried it so terribly far that he did not come back any more. Reader! Has he turned up with you?':
>   Koz'ma Prutkov, *Polnoe sobranie sochinenii* (Moscow-Leningrad, 1965, 2nd. edn.), p. 89.

27. Alisa Poret testifies that Kharms would not show his work to anyone (Poret, 357).
28. One of Druskin's recurrent themes is the creative interpenetration of thought among the 'Chinari' (Druskin, 1985, 389, 401, and elsewhere); this phenomenon acquired an additional dimension when Druskin became the surviving custodian and primary interpreter of their heritage.
29. *Russkaia mysl'*, 1988, xii.
30. 'We live, not feeling the country beneath us, our speeches are not heard beyond ten paces': Osip Mandel'shtam, *Sobranie sochinenii v trëkh tomakh*, ed. G. P. Struve and B. A. Filippov, 2nd. edn. (Washington/New York, Inter-Language Literary Associates, 1967-9), I, 202.
31. *Russkaia mysl'*, 1988, xii.
32. Published *Iunost'*, 10, 1987, 95. Druskin relates absurdity to the Fall, which has taken man away from the divine, alogical Word (Druskin,

## Towards an Interpretation of Kharms's Sluchai     121

1985, 408–9); he also refers to Kharms's words that one needs to approach the abyss, stand right on its edge, look down, but not fall (Druskin, 1985, 385).

33. Both *'Istoricheskii epizod'* and *'Fedia Davidovich'* are dated 1939, but no other texts were dated in the cycle itself, although some dates can be established from manuscript copies (see *Polët*, 389, 391, 528); the numerous recent publications of Kharms's prose sometimes conflict over dating, and further clarification of this and other textological matters must await the forthcoming volume V of the collected works (*Sob. proizv.*).

34. Concerning the role of transformation in the composition of *Elizaveta Bam* and its relation to the motif of emptiness, see Meilakh, 1987, 201–4, and below; more generally, transformation can be related to Kharms's assertion of the 'fluidity' of his thought (quoted by Aleksandrov, *Polët*, 36). Concerning transformation in Vvedenskii, see Vved., II, 279, 286, and elsewhere.

35. Concerning Kharms's parodic use of the folk tale, see Nakhimovsky, 1982, 77–9; Nakhimovsky cites a very interesting extract from Kharms's papers in which he had recorded Propp's observation that 'everything that plays itself out in the fairy tale, plays itself out in the soul; ... its hero is the soul' (Nakhimovsky, 1982, 79).

36. Compare in *Lapa*: 'In order to appear living he speaks all the time' (*Sob. proizv.*, II, 92).

37. Compare the way that in *Elizaveta Bam*, according to the OBERIU article, individual extracts not only stand on their own but also move the play forward 'independently of their will' (Milner-Gulland, 1970, 73–4).

38. Kharms makes parodic use of Prince Myshkin in *Komediia goroda Peterburga* (Vishevsky, 359).

39. There are striking parallels between *Sluchai* and the compositional principles which Kharms identifies in Chopin's music in the review *'Kontsert Emilia Gillel'sa v klube pisatelei 19-go fevralia 1939 goda'* (published in Jaccard, 1985, 308–11). Kharms identifies three main (repeating) phases in any piece by Chopin: these are the 'accumulation' (*'nakoplenie'*), which proceeds towards a resolution and can then be repeated with variations, the 'cutting off' (*'otsekanie'*), which can provide a break and change of direction, and the 'free breathing' (*'vol'noe dykhanie'*), which provides relief after a concentrated accumulation.

40. Kobrinskii states that *'Nachalo ochen' khoroshego letnego dnia'* was moved by Kharms from penultimate to twenty-first position in the cycle (Kobrinskii 1988, p. 69), but this has not been mentioned elsewhere and I have treated the order of the cycle as given in *Polët*; if this text were moved, it would come between the successive dramatic sketches *'Neudachnyi spektakl'*' and *'Tiuk'* at the point where the cycle approaches its preliminary resolution.

41. The subversive effect of the 'very' in the title has been pointed out by Meilakh (Mikhail Meilakh, 'Neskol'ko slov o proze Daniila Kharmsa', *Raduga*, 1988, no. 7, 38).

42. In view of the compositional order and circularity of the cycle it is clear that it cannot be approached as a collection of pieces which could readily be expanded or extended; on the other hand, the compositional principles of diverse variation and alternation might allow for the inclusion of other texts but only in such a way as to maintain the cycle's balance and purity of order.

# 7 Slobodan Pešić's film *Slučaj Harms* and Kharms's *Sluchai*
## Milena Michalski

That evening the dog saw terrible things. He saw the great man plunge his slippery, rubber-gloved hands into a jar to fish out a brain...
*The Heart of a Dog*, M. Bulgakov

'Slučaj Harms', directed and co-written by Slobodan Pešić (born in Belgrade in 1956), was the official Yugoslav entry at the 1988 Cannes Film Festival. Despite references in the Yugoslav press to the 'Caméra d'Or' prize, it was shown not in competition, but in the Festival's non-competitive category 'Un Certain Regard' on 13 May 1988.[1]

The title is well-chosen. In Russian, the noun '*sluchai*' can mean incident, occasion, chance and case. These same connotations exist in Serbo-Croat too. In English, the translation is simply 'The Kharms Case' and in French 'Le Cas Harms'.[2] Only the German word '*der Fall*' can accurately render '*sluchai*' as case, event, accident – even having the additional meaning 'fall' which is also pertinent to Kharms's *Sluchai*.

In the context of Kharms's writing however, '*sluchai*' is the name given to the literary genre he invented.[3] A '*sluchai*' is a short piece, usually narrative, sometimes dialogue or philosophical discourse. Or so one is led to believe at first. After abrupt openings, these pieces seem to disintegrate, often even disappear. A narrative is suddenly aborted, either because it transpires that the subject is non-existent, or because the narrator loses interest, or because the narrator is physically unable to continue. A dialogue may turn into a fight, or the speakers find they cannot communicate. What promised to be a reasoned treatise degenerates into illogical nonsense. These are just a few characteristics, yet already it is clear that underlying the '*sluchai*' are uncertainty, anomaly and dislocation.

On the page, the '*sluchai*' are often visually striking. Some are only a couple of lines long. Others have extremely brief, numbered paragraphs, or physical descriptions in brackets, such as stage directions.

The '*sluchai*' not only contain non-sequiturs; they also lack a context, and often start *in medias res*. In style, the '*sluchai*' seem stark and devoid of extraneous, background detail.

Kharms's '*sluchai*' are powerful precisely because only a minute percentage of the information absorbed in any real situation is presented. In the film, however, events do not occur against a blank backdrop (the cinematic equivalent to Kharms's writing), but in detailed settings: characters are fully portrayed by actors, not merely their silhouettes.

Pešić has also removed another disturbing feature of Kharms's '*sluchai*': the detached narrator. The traditional role of the narrator is to interpret to some degree the events in a story, to act as an ordering link between the story and the reader. Kharms's narrators often seem to have no objection to whatever takes place, however grotesque or violent. Pešić might have used a deadpan voice-over to create the same effect; but it was not his aim to create a filmic *Sluchai*.

Nor is the film a biography of Kharms – despite its title, its opening with biographical detail and the suggestion in the 'Prologue' that the viewer is about to witness a report on a 'deviant' writer. Instances from the author's life are used only sparingly; the greater part of the film puts Kharms's art into his life, making him an embodied character to whom the incidents in his *Sluchai* and other pieces of writing happen (see below for examples).

This raises two questions: 1) If not the writer, what is 'Slučaj Harms' about? 2) If the film is neither a biography nor a *Sluchai* on screen, how, if at all, does it contribute to the study of Kharms? In this essay I shall address these questions – arguing, first, that the film uses Kharms and his material as the basis for a film about politics and spirituality, and, secondly, that by finding ways to fill the gaps in Kharms's text the film casts light on his writing by emphasising that what is most important in the '*sluchai*' is that which is absent.

## THE FILM

'Slučaj Harms' begins with a 'Prologue' in which a nameless scientist warns of the dangers of free and alternative thinking. Artists are said to exemplify this, and he refers to such individuals as 'cases' to be scientifically abolished. It is significant that he uses the word '*sluchai*'. Immediately after this a caption appears giving a biographical outline of Kharms's life. Evidently Kharms is just such a '*sluchai*'.

The next scene is called the 'Beginning'. It shows a boy running through the streets of St Petersburg as the October Revolution happens around him. The scene ends with his dashing into the house in which Kharms is later shown to be living. The boy finds the house occupied by revolutionary guards, indicating that the Revolution has taken over all areas of life.

The 'Middle' could be called 'Slučaj Harms' proper. Shown by itself it would seem like a merely random choice of Kharms's miniature works on film.[4] When viewed in the light of the 'Prologue', however, it becomes a manifestation of what is considered 'deviant' art. The 'Middle' section is the longest and ends abruptly with the arrest of Kharms.

Biography and literature are interwoven. For example, Kharms is shown putting on a false moustache to go to the theatre, something the real person was known to do, just as his non-functional machine in the film was an authentic feature of the author's room. Conversely, although Zabolotsky was a fellow poet and friend in real life, Irina Mazer, who appears with Zabolotsky and is portrayed as Kharms's lover, is, as far as we know, merely a character from Kharms's story *'Pomekha'* ('The Drawback': *Polët*, 348–50; *Plummeting*, 80–2).

The 'Epilogue' comprises two brief scenes. In one, Irina Mazer is persuaded to accept delivery of a parcel which is found to contain the writer's brain. In the other, the camera moves back from an unconvincing shot of Kharms flying past her window to reveal that he is hanging on a wire, at the same time showing the whole film set, including other actors, technicians, lights and props.

## 'SLUČAJ HARMS' AS POLITICS

The 'Prologue' and the scene called 'Beginning' are not drawn from Kharms's life or his writing. These scenes are pure Pešić. Therefore, they should form a point of departure for analysis of the film. Both make it clear that, whilst the film's subject is Kharms, the director's major concern is politics.

The function of the 'Prologue' is to introduce the world of the film. It is expressly a message to the viewer, communicating what will not be directly shown in the film, but to which all ideas and events in the film relate. In the nameless scientist's monologue in the 'Prologue', the world we see is reduced to a statement concerning the dangers of free and alternative thinking, the dangers of art not dedicated to the discovery of scientific truth. Pictures of Stalin, Pavlov and Michurin dominate the desk, and the whole atmosphere is claustrophobic. It is clear that the monologue is delivered from a position of Stalinist 'scientific socialism'. It is no accident that the setting feels like a cross between a laboratory and a prison.

The conflict is one of attitudes to the world. In the world forming the background of the film, science is the slave of authority. Its function is not to interpret the world, simply to make it less threatening for those already in power. Art is acceptable only as long as it serves the same ends. The 'Prologue' indicates to the viewer that the focus of the film is largely political. That it is, above all, an artistic critique of scientific socialism as a concept, and an attempt to recreate the atmosphere of terror, repression and instability under Stalin.

Precisely because the 'Prologue' is the key to understanding this film it is not in the spirit of Kharms's *Sluchai*, for they have no explicitly outlined context. They present incidents, but they do not comment upon or explain them. The 'Prologue' is removed from the rest of the film world in terms of space and time, both of which are unspecified. The 'scientist' could exist in any communist state, at any time.

The 'Beginning', however, is the start of the time continuum which also includes the 'Middle' and the 'Epilogue'. It depicts a few minutes of 1917, and it forms the transition from the 'Prologue' to the action of the film. The 'Beginning' also relates the mood of the real world and times in which Kharms lived to the imaginary world and timelessness of his *Sluchai*. Moreover, setting the scene in 1917 indicates that the Bolshevik revolution, the Soviet system and, perhaps, subsequent systems spawned by its communist ideology are Pešić's concern.

Two creative forces are at work here: the author, Kharms, and the director, Pešić. Kharms began collecting his *Sluchai* in 1937 (although some writing goes back to 1933). Given the political climate at that time, the mood of terror, repression, violence and lies, it is obvious that although Kharms has developed this atmosphere still further, the inspiration for his '*sluchai*' was reality.

Kharms tells of people suddenly and inexplicably disappearing, of objects and facts altering from one moment to the next, of gratuitous violence and groundless persecution. Pešić uses Kharms and his writing as vehicle for a critique of communist systems in which power may be arbitrarily exercised, including, no doubt, his own Yugoslavia.[5] The date and the scientist's speech make it clear that the director's target is communism.

## THE ANGEL

The characters Kharms writes about have no individuality and often either no name or identical names;[6] they are essentially replaceable. In Pešić's film, however, the main characters have names, have character traits and, certainly Kharms and Zabolotsky were living individuals. Simply to be able to see facial expressions lessens the impersonality of relations in Kharms's pieces. The main difference between the '*sluchai*' themselves and the surrounding film is that the film makes rational connections, which the '*sluchai*' do not.

The '*sluchai*' may be grouped together as writings, but there is no explicit linking of incidents or characters. In the film, however, Pešić has introduced his own artistic device in order to bridge the gaps left by Kharms. This is the function of the angel looking for the beam. The traditional role of the author is to order, interpret and connect. Kharms rejects this; Pešić does not, although he is sometimes obscure. The angel is the embodiment of the inner life which Kharms's characters lack. It represents individuality, spirituality and creativity, as well as simply providing a means of tying random scenes in. It offers the comfort of some higher meaning and order, inaccessible, perhaps, to those in this world, but which may, nonetheless, exist. The possibility of something beyond the world perceived by man lessens the fear of arbitrariness and senselessness.

By introducing the angel, therefore, the film removes a significant element of unease by switching the mode of the world of the '*sluchai*' from the absurdly dislocated, to the elusively spiritual. Whereas the world portrayed in Kharms's *Sluchai* is a meaningless and godless world, in Pešić film both meaning and God are present as concepts traditionally associated with the angel.

Pešić also introduces the beam, which is what the angel is looking for, and why he asks for Kharms's help. Neither Kharms nor the viewer is ever told why the beam is so important to the angel, only that he was carrying it when it suddenly disappeared. Much to Kharms's bafflement, the angel is extremely anxious that the beam should be destroyed.

The beam could be part of the burden he must bear as a writer. A clue to its symbolic significance may lie in the fact that it cannot be destroyed by fire, as is later echoed in the phrase 'manuscripts do not burn'.[7] The beam is linked with literature once more when Kharms is mocked for being a writer by profession, and it is sarcastically suggested that this might be his pen. The beam has also been seen symbolically as Kharms's Staff of Life.[8] Certainly, its connection with the angel indicates a religious dimension. Perhaps writing is to be understood as an activity which has in common with religion the human being's inner spiritual life.

Evidently, the beam is a noteworthy addition to the film. Yet Kharms receives it in the most mundane way – by registered post. He does have to sign for it, however, just as Irina Mazer later signs for the package containing Kharms's brain. In neither case is there any melodrama, yet both incidents are significant. Because there is no explanation of these bizarre deliveries the spirit of Kharms's writing is captured. All the same, delivery by registered mail is surely not just the director's whim. It means that they must accept their burdens, accept responsibility, however unwittingly.

The angel's appearance is a device by which Pešić makes cohesive and meaningful otherwise random and disparate elements drawn from Kharms's *Sluchai*. Its presence suggests that the seemingly incomprehensible incidents of the '*sluchai*' can be understood if a metaphysical, unifying force is present. In his film, Pešić gives the otherwise apparently nonsensical '*sluchai*' two contexts in which they become explicable and even normal: one is political, the other, spiritual. *Sluchai*, happening against the backdrop of an arbitrary exercise of power, in a violent state in which there are no fixed rules and where people suddenly disappear, become comprehensible. Similarly, the presence of an angel implies that strange little happenings may have meaning.

The opening scenes make it clear that Pešić's intention is to make a political film. The artifice revealed in the final scene where Kharms is seen as an angel suggests that Pešić intends the viewer to conclude that the angels are a fiction.[9] If not angels, then the only plausible explanation for a world in which the alogical, alienating and arbitrarily violent '*sluchai*' are normal is political.[10]

## POLITICAL AND SPIRITUAL ALIENATION IN KHARMS

Even though 'Slučaj Harms' is more about communist political systems than about Kharms, its relevance for Kharmsists is clear: it emphasises that what is important in Kharms's *Sluchai* is that which is not there. From the above interpretation of the film it emerges that external context and inner life are absent in the '*sluchai*'. The film raises the issues of politics and spirituality. It is for the Kharms scholar to decide whether politics (as Pešić suggests) and spirituality (which he seems to reject) help analysis of the 'sluchai'.

It is not difficult to see Kharms's writing as a reflection of the political world in which he lived. His formulating of the *Sluchai* cycle coincides with the period in Soviet history where the Stalinist terror was most excessive.[11] This was a time when people would suddenly disappear, arrested by the NKVD, when friends and neighbours ceased to trust one another and stopped communicating for fear they might be informed on. It was a period in which what was correct or true one day became false the next. Individuals were alienated from one another and society. Open spiritual activity was impossible. This was a world in which human values had been eliminated and replaced with the exercise of unchecked power, the only rationale for which was its own preservation. Pešić has made explicit the implicit parallels and links between this real world, in which there is a void in place of human interaction and spiritual connectedness, and the absurd world of Kharms's *Sluchai*.[12]

The world portrayed by Kharms is one of automatised, estranged people who cannot find a common language and cannot understand one another; it is not a world of individual human characters.[13] There is no description of any emotional response – indeed, there is indifference to death, characters simply walk away from it and no action is taken. In *'Proisshestvie na ulitse'* ('An Event on the Street') the policeman is not interested in the victim but in the driver's mistakes. Three people have accidents in the street which stresses the automatised repetition, reinforcing the feeling of cruel, 'indifference of disconnected and solitary people'.[14] The total lack of participation by people in the fate of another man is underlined in stories like *'Stolyar Kushakov'* ('The Carpenter Kushakov': *Polët*, 361–2; *Black Coat*, 55–6). The most personal and frightening works are those in which one character is trapped by another's arbitrary exercise of power; examples are *'Pakin i Rakukin'* and *'Fedia Davidovich'* (*Polët*, 395–7, 390–1; *Plummeting*, 45–6, 74–5).

The alienation evident in the *'sluchai'* may be regarded as a reflection of the society in which Kharms lived. That society destroyed personal, political and spiritual relations. Likewise, Kharms has removed these features from his stark prose creations. It is this which makes them so striking. The way in which 'Slučaj Harms' presents the *'sluchai'* detracts from their power. But Pešić's work is of more general relevance than either a cinematic *Sluchai* or a filmed biography would have been.

In using Kharms and his *'sluchai'* to address questions of spirituality and politics the director has made a film about the effects, realised or latent, of communist rule after its Stalinist refraction. It is of relevance not only to Russia at that time, but also to its subsequent manifestations there and elsewhere. By relating political and spiritual themes to the *'sluchai'*, the film casts light on Kharms's writing, thereby articulating and showing the importance of that which is absent.

## NOTES

1. *Politika* (Belgrade), 22 May 1988, 14; *Borba*, (Belgrade), 17 May 1988, 8.
2. 'The Harms Case', *Variety*, Special Cannes Issue, 18 May 1988, 42; F. St., 1988.
3. The singular and plural forms of the nominative and accusative of the Russian noun *'sluchai'* are here all transliterated simply as *'sluchai'*. For the most part my source for the *'sluchai'* is *Polët* (1988). See also Robin Aizlewood's essay in the present volume (above) and references thereto.
4. Amongst others, this section includes the *'sluchai'* *'Fedia Davidovich'* and *'Neudachnyi spektakl''*: *Polët*, 390–1 and 379; *Plummeting*, 74–5; *Black Coat*, 54.
5. Marcel Štefančič, jr., 'Harms Case', *Mladina*, 27 May 1988, 44. This article suggests that the film is less about Russia or Yugoslavia specifically, than about the concept of communism put into practice.
6. For example characters have no names in 'The Plummeting Old Women' and identical names in 'The Falling': see *Plummeting*, 11, 78–9; *Polët*, 356; *Soviet Union/Union Soviétique*, 1980, 235–6.
7. In this phrase, 'Manuscripts do not burn', Pešić alludes to Bulgakov's novel, *The Master and Margarita*.
8. 'The Harms Case', *Variety* (see note 2).
9. One reviewer finds the epilogue comforting, rather than disturbing, for it is about art and the viewer and no longer about the relationship between the writer as an artist and as himself, or the work and the world in which it is rooted: Milan Cvijanović, 'Slučaj Harms', *Ju Film Danas*, 2–3, 1988, 104.
10. Aleksandrov has suggested that Kharms's writing is informed *'printsipom alogichnosti'*, but the same cannot be said of Pešić's film: Aleksandrov, 1973, 296–7.
11. Kharms's personal life and career were by now in a worse state than ever. His diary notes show the hopelessness of his mood. See *Delo*, (Belgrade) XXXV, 7, July 1988, 112–19.

12. It is interesting to note the extension of Kharms's literary theory from the plane of objects to that of humans. According to Kharms, objects have contingent and necessary meanings. The former are relative, defined by 'connectedness' with other objects and humans; even if these connections are violated, objects retain their 'quintessential' meanings. Its continued existence when conventional links are denied affirms the object's absolute nature, its true meaning. If this idea is transposed to the '*sluchai*' (compiled a decade after Kharms gave expression to these theories) one might argue that the same principle operates at the human level: where 'connectedness' is destroyed, the absolute nature of the 'objectified' individual remains. Continuing existence in the absence of connectedness gives the individual a necessary, inalienable meaning. See Kharms, 'Predmety i figury otkrytye Daniilom Ivanovichem Kharmsom' (1927), *Soviet Union/ Union Soviétique*, 5, 1978, 2, 299–300. W. Kasack points out that people in Kharms's world are alienated not only from one another, but also from themselves: see Kasack, 1976, 77.
13. See Flaker, 1969.
14. Ibid., 78.

# 8 Elements of the Fantastic in Daniil Kharms's *Starukha*
Rosanna Giaquinta

> Où serez-vous demain, Èves octogénaires,
> Sur qui pèse la griffe effroyable de Dieu?
> Charles Baudelaire, *Les petites vieilles*

The long tale *Starukha* ('The Old Woman'), which Kharms wrote in mid-1939, represents probably the highest expression of his prose writing. In fact it is here that the concise, incisive motifs of the *Sluchai* ('Happenings') collection of mini-stories reappear in a plot of far greater complexity.

The *povest'* (long tale) may be analysed in double perspective: the first relative and the second absolute. The perspective which begins with the relativity of the text requires identification of the historical and literary roots of the tale as parody. The absolute perspective, on the other hand, leads us to an immanent reading of the text in itself, in an attempt to lay bare the possible layers of meaning by analysis of textual elements and narrative technique.

The relationship of Kharms's tale to its most important precursors, namely *The Queen of Spades* by Pushkin and *Crime and Punishment* by Dostoevsky, is an essential element for an accurate evaluation of the work in question and this has already been widely studied.[1] We would add only two points to the work of previous critics. The first concerns the derivation of Kharms's hero in *Starukha* from Dostoevsky's underground man: apart from fairly precise textual elements which match up, we can and must place the tale in the context of its wider psychological and spiritual genealogy, the neurotic aspects of which we shall discuss shortly. The second point is that between the unnamed Kharmsian hero (or anti-hero) and his predecessors, Hermann and Raskol'nikov, there is a substantial difference – the latter pair have strong motivation for falling prey to obsession and madness. They are determined in a very precise way, they have an idea, an aim, no matter how high or sordid it may be.

The hero of *Starukha* on the contrary finds himself quite unwillingly in a nightmare; he is forced to take the blame in consequence of a situation for which he is not responsible.

As far as the second possible level of analysis is concerned, we may proceed only with great caution and by hypothesis, given the open structure of the ending of the work,[2] which leaves open to the reader different interpretations of the facts. The aim of this study is thus to furnish some working hypotheses in particular by means of the analysis of the use of fantastic elements in the text. These elements are indeed strictly functional in the creation of a text which we may define as grotesque at a formal level and absurd at a conceptual one.

I

In the field of theoretical studies on the fantastic there reigns without doubt a certain confusion. The overwhelming tendency is to give a negative definition of the fantastic which, as R. Caillois (1965: 22) notes, means everything which is removed from reproducing what is real. This tendency can be traced from H. P. Lovecraft's broad review of 1927, which sees the fear of the unknown as the source of all supernatural and fantastic manifestations in artistic creation, through to Todorov's classifications of 1970. In his *Introduction à la littérature fantastique* Todorov on the one hand offers a psychological key for recognising the fantastic, the reader's hesitancy before the narrated facts; on the other hand he reduces fantastic phenomena to two single categories: those remaining within the subject and those projected to the outside world: '*les thèmes du* je' and '*les thèmes du* tu'. It is not too much to say that all successive works dedicated to the subject refer in some way back to Todorov and in particular tend to refute his anxiety to classify everything. As a matter of fact, the fantastic is not in itself a genre, but rather embraces several genres (see Rabkin, 1976: 117) and above all extends well beyond the period dealt with by Todorov. Kafka, as Todorov notes, treats the irrational as if it were real and hence destroys the formal and pyschological diaphragm which separates the reader from the text. In so doing, he opens the way for today's treatment of the fantastic, which is rather more disturbing than that created by nineteenth-century literature (the function of which was to console or subvert). Yet it is precisely this kind of fantastic writing which remains outside Todorov's analysis.

Moving on to the modern period, there are few definitions of the fantastic which are acceptable: *'une intrusion brutale du mystère dans le cadre de la vie réelle'* (Castex, 1951: 8); *'le fantastique se nourrit des conflicts du réel et du possible'* (Vax, 1960: 5); *'le fantastique est rupture de l'ordre reconnu, irruption de l'inadmissible au sein de l'inaltérable légalité quotidienne'* (Caillois, 1965: 161); *'le fantastique représente une expérience des limites'* (Todorov 1970: 99); 'an overt violation of what is generally accepted as possibility ... the narrative result of transforming the condition contrary to fact into "fact" itself' (Irwin, 1976: 4). A position partially more precise is assumed by Rosemary Jackson (1981); by giving what is in essence a purely functional role to the fantastic, she sees the latter in terms of an unresolved tension between the imaginary and its symbolic potential. It might be better, however, to adopt the methodological caution of Christine Brooke-Rose (1981), who, in her sophisticated analysis of the structure of fantastic narration, avoids any definition at all, on the basis of the very modern inability to define the real and therefore, logically and inescapably, its opposite.

The sequel to Todorov's work, which would ideally be dedicated to the modern period, is thus yet to be written. From a theoretical point of view, we may be sure only of the absolute uncertainty of the fantastic perspective in its relationship with the real and, in literary terms, of the ambiguity of a narrative mode which overcomes the limits of both technique and genre.

From a strictly Russian perspective things are different or, rather more precisely, theoretical precepts of the fantastic itself differ. One of the first observations on this subject is by Goncharov, who distinguishes between the realistic fantastic mode and the romantic fantastic one. He writes, in fact that the writer can 'enliven real life by means of fantasy', or 'embellish fantasy with real life, according to time and place, so that it should be neither too phantasmal, nor transparent'.[3]

This functional vision contrasts with the far better-known one of Vladimir Solov'ëv, to be found in his 1899 introduction to *Upyr'* (*The Vampire*) by A. K. Tolstoy. Here we can find several elements reflecting symbolist theories:

> The essential interest and significance of the *fantastic* in poetry is governed by the conviction that all that happens in the world, and particularly in human life, depends, its present and evident causes apart, also on some sort of other causality – more profound and universal, but less clear. It the connections in life between every-

thing existing were as simple and transparent as twice two are four, then this would exclude everything fantastic.

And later:

And therein lies the distinct element of what is *authentically fantastic*: this never presents itself, so to speak, in *naked* form. Its symptoms should never provoke a forced faith in the mystical sense of the events of life, but should rather give an indication, an *allusion* of this sense.[4]

The fantastic is thus, for Solov'ëv, not an aesthetic value, but one which discloses and alludes, and, through yet another definition of what the fantastic is not, we may interpret the connections between things in a way which is different from that which presents itself at first sight. The relationship between the real and the unreal is also, particularly for the Symbolists, the one between the real and the apparent, where the real is always found at a deeper level. In this there is much from German Romanticism which, as we can see in Hoffmann, through the creation of 'subjective wonder' (Castex, 1951: 103), roots the fantastic in the depths of men's minds; indeed the early Russian nineteenth century was entirely under Hoffmannian influence.[5]

Taking the fantastic so seriously is thus a peculiar characteristic of a symbolist vision which was little given to self-irony, at least as far as the relationship with the real is concerned. In his study of the grotesque, Iurii Mann, on the contrary, begins with a formal analysis and distinguishes two possible functions of the fantastic: it can be either the consequence or the result of certain circumstances, or the starting-point of an action, a premise which is not real (Mann, 1966: 78). In the first case especially, the fantastic, through exaggeration, works towards the grotesque effect.

What strikes the reader most in modern treatment of the fantastic is – from Kafka to Borges, from E. A. Poe to García Márquez – the absence of a diaphragm which saves him from direct involvement; just like the hero of an absurdist tale, the reader encounters and clashes with the mystery without any opportunity to adapt progressively. We would assume that the absurd is not an effect ('absurd' effect), not the result of a narrative situation, not the product of an atmosphere built on specific techniques of expectation and suspense, but an element, a condition predating the narration which we cannot dispense with. In particular, the reader of Kharms cannot but note the total absence of motivation in both this *povest'* and the ministories. The upsetting of causal relationships is an essential element in Kharms's prose, just as it is in his philosophical thought. In this connection we should not forget the series *Nekotoroe kolichestvo razgovorov* ('A Certain Quantity of Conversations') by Aleksandr Vvedensky (Vved. I, 142–56), which constitutes a stylisation of philosophical dialogue dedicated to the inconsistency in relationships of cause and effect, and appearance and reality.

*Starukha*, then, lacks any initial motivation. The brief meeting of the hero with the old lady in the courtyard is not enough to explain either her intrusion or her death. In terms of what the reader is able to understand subsequently, the problem of time, alluded to from the very first page by means of the old lady's handless clock, is, if anything, significant:

> ... and I ask her, 'What time is it?'
> 'You look', the old woman says to me. I look and I see that the clock has no hands.
> 'There are no hands', I say.
> The old woman looks at the face of the clock and says to me, 'It's a quarter to three'.
> 'Oh, I see. Many thanks', I say, and go away.
> (*Polët*, 398; *Black Coat*, 124)

We see that the hero is not able to read the blank face which the old woman shows him. She, however, can do so with quiet assurance and here anticipates her own role as symbol of death.

It is nonetheless a fact that the appearance of the old woman in the hero's room is determined by no apparent cause. Nor is her death, inexplicable and improbable, accounted for subsequently. An explanation of the causes of the events is not simply postponed, nor is the mystery unravelled regressively; there is only a chain of effects without causes. With a bigger or smaller symbolic component, according to the story, this is the primary characteristic of the absurd in Kharms. We find sequences of non-events: '*Golubaia tetrad' No. 10*' (Blue Notebook No. 10), '*Vstrecha*' ('A Meeting') etc.; sequences of events quite out of proportion to the causes which give rise to them: '*Reabilitatsiia*' ('Rehabilitation'), '*Vyvalivaiushchiesia starukhi*' ('The Plummeting Old Women'), '*Tiuk*' ('Clunk') etc.; and sequences without determining causes: 'Sluchai' ('Incidents'), 'Grigor'ev i Semënov' (Grigor'ev and Semënov), 'Nachalo ochen' khoroshego letnego dnia', ('The Beginning of a Beautiful Day') etc. It is perhaps only *Starukha* and 'Sviaz'' ('The Connection') which attain a philosophical value beyond the absurd itself. If in 'Sviaz'' the (absurd) sequence is organised in a circular structure and hints at a different and higher causal relationship, in *Starukha* the inner teleological movement which, despite an absence of motivation, underpins the development of events, will be seen to have a meaning; and this meaning, though not unique or unambiguous, is certainly possible. We see that rational causality is substituted by a different one which, having read the whole tale, we may define as 'mystical causality' (Vax, 1960: 32).

P-. G. Castex was probably the first critic to note that incursions of the fantastic into real life are linked to states of sickly consciousness,[6] when the mind is prey to nightmares or delirium. In the case of *Starukha* we are faced with a morbid state of consciousness which is certainly not occasional but rather permanent – that Kharmsian hypochondria which Aleksandrov (1968) had already named '*Ignavia*'. Without wishing yet to consider the elements of this hypochrondria symptoms of spiritual malaise (*Ignavia* is the loss of God) they certainly show the presence of what we could call a depressive neurosis on the part of the hero-narrator. Typical of this neurosis are persecution complex, desire for revenge and need for self-assertion. These elements are not essential, but are always present in the psyche of the hero of the Kharmsian 'underground'. Images recur obsessively of the invalid with the mechanical leg which produces an aggravating, hammering noise, and of the children at play. The hero's desire for revenge is directed principally against the children: he feels annoyed, spied upon and derided by them. The children make 'disgusting noises' (*Polët*, 399; *Black Coat*, 125); they are 'awful' (414/138); 'stinking little boys' (427/150); and in their disturbing effect they are just like the dead:

> 'And what do you think are worse: dead people or children?', I asked.
> 'I guess children; they bother us more often.' (414/138)

The hero's determination to make a name as a writer despite his colleague and rival Sakerdon Mikhailovich also belongs to a series of trivial and morbid items which hark back to the Dostoevskian prototype. It is a typical neurotic transition from lack of will power to hyperactivity:

> I'll take paper and pen and I'll write. I feel tremendous strength inside me. . . .
> I sit and rub my hands with glee. Sakerdon Mikhailovich will burst with envy. . . . Quickly, quickly to work! Away with all dreams and laziness. I'll write for eighteen hours straight off.
> I tremble all over with impatience. I can't figure out what I should do: . . .
> (*Polët*, 400; *Black Coat*, 125–6)

It is not by chance that this apparent psychic change does not lead to any concrete result:

> . . . I pick up my pen and write:
> 'The miracle-worker was tall'.
> I can't write any more than that.
> (*Polët*, 401; *Black Coat*, 127)

In his caustic critique of fantasising, Elémire Zolla writes that the man guilty of this act is a victim of split personality who is easy game for the Romantic fantastic. This hypertrophy of the conscience, the Romantic expansion of the senses, gives rise, from Hoffmann's characters onwards, to hallucinatory states approaching madness and possession. These states of over-excitement would seem to promise a quite exceptional expansion of the self's capacities in both a cognitive and an active, creative sense. The border between the self and the world (that is, between perception and conscience) is questioned; also the borders between reality and fantasy and reality and madness are determined by the hero's mental and nervous states, as already mentioned.[7] Moreover the passivity of the protagonist becomes obvious in his behaviour when the old lady arrives in his room; disconcerted, he weakly attempts to oppose her orders, but ends up supinely subject to a kind of psychological vampirism in the way he gives in to her and slides into unconsciousness. The masochistic nature of fantasising noted by Zolla is expressed in the subjection of the hero and we should consider it as one of the psychological implications of the icy inhumanity present in Kharms's stories.

In his famous study, *The Uncanny* (*Das Unheimliche*, 1919), Freud deals with several painful aspects of the fantastic in literature and reviews a whole series of situations and images which are half-way between life and fiction. Although he says that in general 'a great deal that is not uncanny in fiction would be so if it happened in real life' (Freud: 249), he does assert that the writer who works in the field of commonly-held reality 'accepts as well all the conditions operating to produce uncanny feelings in real life; and everything that would have an uncanny effect in reality has it in his story' (Freud, p. 250). This is the case (at least in the symptoms if not in the causes) of the painful fantasy of *Starukha*, where we can see not only the hero's unjustified sense of guilt, but also the fact that the unmotivated events acquire a threatening sense of fatality and inevitability. The evident Freudian observation that for many people everything concerning death, dead bodies and the return of the dead is frightening finds a clear expression in the horror felt by the Kharmsian hero. We find an amplification of the fantastic effect and a shift towards the grotesque in the words of the hero and of Sakerdon Mikhailovich concerning the misdeeds of the dead (413–14/137–8; 419–20/143–4). The horrific effect of single parts of the body which have a life of their own, usually those parts capable of expression,[8] is in Kharms reduced through ridicule by using a technique linked directly to the grotesque of his prose. The old woman 'crawled towards me on all fours' along the floor (418/143), a bruise on her chin grows following the kick with his boot that the hero gives the already dead women (405/130; 424/147); similarly, her denture seems to move quite of its own accord: it first sticks half-way out of her mouth (403/128–9) then slips into her nostril, flies into a corner when the hero hits it (405/131) and finally disappears (423/147).

We can see that the expressions used by Kharms suggest active power in the dead old woman. For the narrator she is, like all the dead, capable of anything: 'the old woman was lying quietly' (421/145); 'the old woman was lying there, quiet as before, face down on the floor' (423/146). The use of active intransitive verbs seems to lend to the old woman a lasting will of her own, not to mention the expressions we find which refer to the hero's fears of any uncontrolled actions by her: 'and what if the old woman crawled out of the room?' (422/146).[9]

Having crossed the threshold of death, the body eludes all norms; death as a concept half-way between the physical and the psychic world opens the way in the fantastic for limitless possibilities in the creation of events beyond even the most elementary rationality, insofar as the boundary between the real and the unreal has been overcome.[10] In literary terms, the boundary between the real and the imaginary wavers and becomes indistinct; the fantastic elements are treated in the same stylistic key as the real ones and the elements of concrete reality are, for all their sordidness, transferred to the level of the imaginary.

Such a real/unreal confusion is typical of dreams. The Kharmsian text shows clear evidence of this when the hero convinces himself that he only dreamed the arrival or at least the death of the old hag: he wonders, as he reviews what happened, exactly when the dream ended. The dream used as a device for creating a grotesque effect recurs several times in Kharms and sometimes as the only dimension to a mini-story.[11] In the case of *Starukha*, the dream of the hero (404/ 129–30) is presented as a symbolic dream centred on aspects of reality just experienced. It is one of those dreams which imply 'a metaphysical communion between man and the forces beyond him' (Kent, 1969: 88) and which in Russian literature have very significant roots in German Romanticism and in the literary *topos* of the dream as a manifestation of self-expansion. Here the dream is largely a nightmare and the hero's self very definitely cannot expand but rather is oppressed by foreboding and by the symbolic image of Sakerdon Mikhailovich who 'is not the real Sakerdon Mikhailovich, but one made out of clay' (404/130).

If in Hoffmann we are in a world which has already accepted the dream as a part of itself, with Kafka – and with Kharms – we are in a world which is so accustomed to nightmare that we can no longer distinguish it from the real. We have already noted that Todorov (1970: 181) wrote of Kafka that '*il traite l'irrationnel comme faisant partie du jeu*'. Paraphrasing Borges, we can say that in Kharms we see 'a contagion of reality', because fantastic projections and irrational elements return to the plane of trivial things, which is perfectly characteristic of the Leningrad *byt* of the Thirties. If indeed we may identify what is real in a dehumanised society only through a series of approximations and negative definitions, then it will consequently be impossible to define the limits of what might be called the 'unreal'; and the Kharmsian absurd is concealed not in playing on words or in linguistic nonsense, but before all else in cross-sections of an everyday life both hostile and incomprehensible.

Another Hoffmannian motif in Russian literature of the fantastic (Gogol in particular) is the contrast between the hero as artist and the philistine world which surrounds him.[12] In Kharms this motif is further defined in that the hero is a writer who writes a tale on a *chudotvorets* (a miracle-worker) who can perform miracles but doesn't do so. In the use of the technique of the tale within a tale Kharms condenses the main theme of his *povest'*: the fantastic is not only threatening and absurd but can also be wonderful and miraculous. However it is a question of a potential miracle (on the part of the *chudotvorets*) and the expectation of a miracle (on the part of the hero: 'My God, don't miracles happen sometimes?' (418/142). In his extremely interesting memoirs of the *Chinari*, Iakov Semënovich Druskin recalls Kharms's interest in the miracle 'in itself'. In the case of the internal tale in *Starukha*, Druskin emphasises the fact that for the *chudotvorets* the knowledge that he is able to work miracles is sufficient and that it is not really necessary for him to use his powers (Druskin, 1985: 384). In fact in Kharms's tale the motive would seem to be interwoven with its opposite in that the potential of the miracle is implicitly denied because the hero/writer is unable to express the idea he has in mind, or in other words is unable to express the very idea of the potential miracle. It is not by chance that the *chudotvorets* is living in our times and, through being evicted from the flat he lives in, is victim of an event very much part of everyday life. Thus we see that not only does the miracle-worker die without ever having worked any miracle, but also the hero of *Starukha*, who is about to embark on a task of modern hagiography, does not manage to go beyond the first banal words of description. After the hero's first creative moment the tone abruptly becomes pedestrian – the hero, unable to write anything, remains at the table until he starts 'feeling hungry' (401/127).

Another interesting aspect concerns the description of the *chudotvorets* himself, who 'was tall' (ibid.), just like Kharms. Druskin notes that Lipavsky, the other theoretician in the group, used the expression *vestnik* (messenger), as the literal translation of the Greek ἄγγελος, to indicate a being from an imaginary world, in part like us, in part profoundly different. This concept inspired Druskin to write a brief poetical-philosophical piece entitled *Vestniki i ikh razgovory* ('The Messengers and their Conversations'), which he read at Lipavsky's house and which evidently influenced Kharms too. Kharms subsequently wrote in fact the tale '*O tom, kak menia posetili vestniki*' ('On How the Messengers Visited Me', c. 1938–40).[13] This too is the story of a miracle *manqué*, of messengers (who stop time) whose presence is perceived but who cannot be identified and who then disappear. In this tale too there is a sharp lowering of tone, again in terms of a desire for food. Kharms's aspiring to miracle is even clearer in a note in his diary quoted by Druskin, who read it many years later: 'Druskin has read *The Messengers*. I am a messenger' (Druskin, 1985: 392). This aspiring to miracle is therefore a wish to identify with it and to be an active dispenser of grace: Kharms is a messenger, the miracle-worker is of great height and he too is Kharms himself.

To return to our outline of the fantastic, we may thus make a distinction which is fundamental in the work of Kharms. There exist two trends: one, so to speak, negative and the other positive. The fantastic elements linked to the real and the everyday are those which correspond to death, anguish and the horrific, that brutal incursion of mystery into real life which we have already highlighted, following Castex. The intrusion of death into the hero's room has all the characteristics not only of the inexplicable, but also of the inevitable. The old lady introduces herself with the words 'I have come' (401/ 127), as if her arrival was expected and taken for granted; the narration subsequently plunges into the total inability of the hero to react and his inevitably passive acceptance of what happens.

The other trend of the fantastic is the positive one, that is to say that of the marvellous, of miracle and faith. It is not by chance that we are still in the sphere of the potential, of desire and of anguished expectation. The hero, hoping that the old woman has disappeared during his absence, wishes for a miracle (418/142). In Kharms, in the stories in general and in particular in *Starukha*, the dissolution of reality is not accompanied by participation in another sphere of reality. The fantastic is portrayed as an aspect of, or a clue to, the modern grotesque, which is both destructive and without hope;[14] the reality of the miracle is only longed for, not realized. The end of *Starukha* does not give rise to much hope, for salvation is possible but improbable and the miracle in everyday life may not even happen.

The elements of the fantastic in this *povest'* are strictly related to the absurd. It is precisely because of the lack of a logical, causal connection between events that we must see in these the manifestation of an arbitrary law, inexplicable but necessary. All the elements of the tale are connected (even beyond recurrent images and correlations between situations) and play a part together in destroying the structure of reality.[15] The modern view of the marvellous is always negative, 'it is *our* world which changes into an *alien* world'.[16] Dream is nightmare and there is no concession to genuine comedy, nor to its purifying role (*samokazn'*, self-punishment, *kazn' smekhom*, punishment through laughter). Alongside this there has been a shift in modern literature from total realism to the absurd – and in the very terms of the real, which cannot be incontrovertibly defined. It is worth quoting here the words of Iurii Mann (1966: 156):

> the reflection of chaos from the point of view of chaos led, incidentally, also to a thinning of semantic links between the 'grotesque' and the 'real' – to the point when they were threatening to break.

The break in Kharms has already occurred, for chaos has already poured into the real.

While for Todorov the element which above all others shows we are in the presence of the fantastic is the hesitation of the reader before the text, in the modern fantastic, from Kafka onwards, we find on the contrary an attitude of scientific dispassion. The irrational is treated as if it were real and techniques used to create the effect of illusion and marvel are sidelined. The removal of the psychological diaphragm of hesitation and the marvellous not only changes the relationship between the narrator and the reader, but also – and *Starukha* is an excellent example of this – means that the absurd cannot signify anything but itself.[17]

II

To complete the picture, let us summarise some other structural elements of the *povest'*.

In the first place we have the already mentioned correlations within the text. Apart from the correspondence between the position of the body of the old woman on the floor and that of Sakerdon Mikhailovich (amply treated in Nakhimovsky, 1978), we have the essential correlation between the internal and external stories, which is nothing less than a metaphor for the paralysis of the sacred and the impossibility of miracle; the paralysis of the sacred is thus also the paralysis of the artist, who is not a 'messenger'.

We have noted also the use of recurrent images (the invalid with the mechanical leg, the shadow of the chimney on the roof opposite which is cast on the narrator's face) and the presence of a plot which may effectively be called a plot, despite the philosophical digression in the dialogue with Sakerdon Mikhailovich and the open ending.

This differentiates *Starukha* from most of Kharms's other tales, not just the *Sluchai* mini-stories, but also the longer ones written at the end of the 1930s.

The first-person narration creates the illusion of autobiography. As is well known, in Kharms many details belonging to his own personal life and to Leningrad *byt* in general are often present. The first-person narrative technique creates an essential ambiguity, in that the reader is driven psychologically to follow the narrator-protagonist either in his guise of hero with whose psychology we identify, or as a narrator whose story we accept as it is, without being able to verify it using our reason. On this subject Todorov (1970: 182) concludes that the reader, if he identifies with the character, also excludes himself from the real; but this cannot happen with *Starukha* since the false autobiographical nature of the narration is no less than 'chaos seen from the point of view of chaos'. The reader's identification with the hero is limited to the psychological plane of perception (the hypochrondriac atmosphere, the passivity) and does not affect the cognitive one (the reader cannot plausibly interpret the events), nor that of the action (the hero's acts of rage cannot be sympathised with, nor can his kneeling at the end be foreseen or explained). One of the determining factors of the fantastic is ambiguity itself (Brooke-Rose 1981: 304), which has the essential function of distancing and defamiliarisation; hence we see in *Starukha* the wavering between the pathological mental states of the narrator-hero and the objective and depersonalised rendering of his acts. While in a fantastic tale not written in the first person there exists between the narrator and the reader a kind of agreement that both remain in the dark, or that an explanation is promised or expected, in first-person narration the narrator/reader relationship is complicated by the very connection between psychology and knowledge. In Kharms and Vvedensky the absurd is always knowledge in that it can open not only the doors of horror, but also those of faith.

This duplication of levels – the everyday and the fantastic, the everyday and the absurd, the everyday and the spiritual – becomes in literary terms an objective description of the absurd, in which, regarding the spiritual (faith, miracle, creation, love), a process of constant lowering of tone at an ordinary and a trivial level is carried out. This stylistic technique has as an immediate result that of discrediting firstly the real (where unlikely things happen) and secondly the spiritual (which appears unable to manifest itself). The debatable nature of the real is at the centre of the work of both Kharms and

Vvedensky (we may mention here once again *Nekotoroe kolichestvo razgovorov*), in the sense that the cognitive moment is the necessary step in the transition to the mystical one.

## III

In conclusion we can state that the whole *povest'* is a figurative extension of the philosophical dialogue which takes place between the hero and Sakerdon Mikhailovich. Hence we see that elements referring to the 'content' become themselves formal, structuring factors, and vice versa: the fantastic elements are a function of the absurd and thus of the cognitive aspect of Kharms's work. The anti-aesthetic nature of the tale is connected both to the constant presence of the everyday in all its horror and to what we may call in Freudian terms the aesthetic/anti-aesthetic dimension of pain and anguish; the wish for a miracle leads to the appearance of an anti-miracle (the horrific fantastic and the arrival of the old woman) and hence the aspiration to faith is the cause of the subversion of the laws of the real.

The two levels of the everyday and the extraordinary are knitted together in the philosophical dimension and in the problem of God, which is none other than the question of guaranteeing immortality. Since 'there cannot be a self without a metaphysical framework',[18] the real/supernatural relationship is structured in *Starukha* through a series of relations/oppositions: guilt/grace; non guilt/grace; mystery/knowledge; mystery/miracle; miracle/faith; and, lastly, knowledge/faith. In Dostoevsky there exists a vital, direct relationship between guilt and grace. In Kharms this relationship is altered and becomes non-guilt/grace; but while in Dostoevsky the freedom of the individual is the determining factor, in Kharms this freedom can no longer exist, since freedom of choice is repressed – both by society (external necessity) and by an internal necessity. Grace is in any case indispensable, but for Kharms it is almost impossible.

Something must be said about the similarities that have often been suggested between Kharms's work (and of OBERIU in general) and Surrealism. In particular it is Kharms's very use of the fantastic, the grotesque and the 'black' strand in his fiction which might suggest this comparison. In reality, the cognitive function of the Kharmsian absurd, which we have already underlined, renders any comparison impossible. As Druskin states explicitly, the absurd is a poeticalgnosiological technique which has nothing in common with the surrealist playing with the unconscious.[19] In Kharms (and in Vvedensky) everything is deeply semanticised; there is no play but there are the eternal 'accursed questions' (*prokliatye voprosy*) – everything is a question of life and death. For example, Kharmsian dreams are never pure liberation of the unconscious, but always have a function which is cognitive and meaningful, which reveals and forewarns. If the surrealist 'mystery' remains such because its resolution is neither necessary nor foreseen, in Kharms we are faced with a mystery which is rather more elusive, ambiguous and incomprehensible but perhaps, through miracle, penetrable.

It is Todorov who once again makes a particularly helpful observation regarding the linguistic dimension of the supernatural:

> seul le langage permet de concevoir ce qui est toujours absent: le surnaturel. Celui-ci devient donc un symbole du langage, au même titre que les figures de rhétorique, et la figure est, on l'a vu, la forme la plus pure de la littéralité.    (Todorov, 1970: 87)

This, indeed, is the only road which the hero of *Starukha* seems able to follow, and this road is that of the word which guides him towards the supernatural: prayer.

NOTES

This article had already been written before the author could read the studies on the literary fantastic by Neil Cornwell (1988 and 1990: see References below), which attempt to dispel some of the confusion surrounding this subject. Here we do not claim to participate in theoretical discussions, but simply wish to approach Kharms's *povest'* from this particular point of view. (R.G.)

1. See M. Jovanovič [Iovanovich], 'Situatsiia Raskol'nikova i eë otgoloski v russkoi sovetskoi proze (Parodiinyi aspekt)', *Zbornik za slavistiku*, 21 (1981) 45–57; Chances, 1985; Cassedy, 1985; Sazhin, 1985. On Dostoevskii, see Bem, 1936; Petrovskii, 1971a and 1971b. The Raskol'nikov situation is de-ideologised in Kharms (Jovanovič, 1981: 48) and restructured in less tragic terms than in the Dostoevskian prototype.
2. See Chances, 1985: 358.
3. *Goncharov i Turgenev* (Leningrad, 1923), p. 32.
4. Solov'ëv, 1909; 376–7 (author's stress).

5. See the broad study by Passage, 1963.
6. Castex, 1951: 8. Note the entry in Kafka's diary for 24 November 1911: 'It is now that you come, evil thoughts, now, because I am weak and have an upset stomach. You pick this time for me to think you.' (Kafka, 1972: 126).
7. The problem of the conscious self is also treated by Kharms in terms, which could be defined as schizophrenic, of the relationship between the self and thoughts, which is not always a happy one. In *Starukha*, the hero tries to re-enter his room and sees (or thinks he sees) the old woman crawling over the floor towards him. Terrified, he cannot enter; a fully-articulated dialogue with his own thoughts begins as he debates whether the dead move or not (419–21/143–4). Particularly interesting is the fact that the hero's thoughts treat him 'mockingly' (420/144). Elsewhere in Kharms, something similar happens on a purely semantic plane: a 'battle with meanings' takes place in the poetic conscience, in which the poet requires the help of God (*'Molitva pered snom'*, 1931, *Sob. proizv.*, III, 22).
8. See Vax, 1960: 27; Freud, 1978: 244.
9. Also: ' "she might bite my finger"; I started to think: "Perhaps the dead old woman crawled around the room and looked for her teeth? Maybe she even found them and put them back into her mouth?" ' (423/146–7).
10. See Freud, 1978: 244 – 'an uncanny effect is often and easily produced when the distinction between imagination and reality is effaced'.
11. See Flaker, 1969: 81.
12. See Passage, 1963: 228–30.
13. Published *Kontinent*, 24 (1980) 285–6.
14. See Kayser, 1968: 22.
15. See Todorov, 1970: 50 – '*dans le monde surnaturel il n'y a pas de hasard, règne au contraire ce qu'on peut appeler le "pan-déterminisme"*'. On the real/absurd relationship in Kharms's work, see Jaccard, 1985.
16. Bakhtin, 1986: 341. He argues with Kayser on the nature of the grotesque, believing that Kayser's work is centred solely on the modern grotesque, ignoring the medieval and Renaissance grotesque of popular origin.
17. On the tautological nature of the fantastic, see Todorov, 1970: 98, 170.
18. This is a problem which features in Dostoevskii – see Kent, 1969: 90.
19. Druskin, 1985: 381; see also Flaker, 1969: 79. We may return here to Zolla, who stresses Artaud as a special case in the context of surrealism, because he takes everything so seriously.

# REFERENCES

The works cited in this essay are contained in the main Bibliography, except for those listed here below.

Bakhtin, M. M. (1986): 'Tvorchestvo Fransua Rable i narodnaia kul'tura srednevekov'ia i Benessansa. Vvedenie (postanovka problemy)' (1965), in his *Literaturno-kriticheskie stat'i* (Moscow, 1986) pp. 291–352.

Bem, A. L. (1936): ' "Pikovaia dama" v tvorchestve Dostoevskogo', in A. L. Bem (ed.), *O Dostoevskom: sbornik statei* (Prague, 1936) pp. 37–81.
Brooke-Rose, C. (1981): *A Rhetoric of the Unreal* (Cambridge: Cambridge University Press, 1981).
Caillois, R. (1965): *Au coeur du fantastique* (Paris: Gallimard, 1965).
Castex, P.-G. (1951): *Le conte fantastique en France de Nodier à Maupassant* (Paris: José Corti, 1951).
Cornwell, N. (1988): 'Critical Approaches to the Literary Fantastic: Definitions, Genre, Import', *Essays in Poetics*, 13, 1 (1988) 1–45.
Cornwell, N. (1990): *The Literary Fantastic: From Gothic to Postmodernism* (Hemel Hempstead: Harvester Wheatsheaf, 1990).
Freud, S. (1978): 'The "Uncanny" ' (1919), in *The Standard Edition of the Complete Psychological Works of Sigmund Freud*, vol. XVII (London: Hogarth, 1955) pp. 218–52. 1978 reprint cited.
Irwin, W. R. (1976): *The Game of the Impossible: A Rhetoric of Fantasy* (Urbana: University of Illinois, 1976).
Jackson, R. (1981): *Fantasy: The Literature of Subversion* (London: Methuen, 1981).
Kafka, F. (1972): *The Diaries of Franz Kafka 1910–1923*, ed. Max Brod (Harmondsworth: Penguin, 1972).
Kayser, W. (1968): *The Grotesque in Art and Literature* (1957) (Gloucester, Mass., 1968 edition).
Kent, L. J. (1969): *The Subconscious in Gogol' and Dostoevskij and its Antecedents* (The Hague: Mouton, 1969).
Lovecraft, H. P. (1945): *Supernatural Horror in Literature* (1927) (New York: Abramson, 1945).
Mann, Iu. (1966): *O groteske* (Moscow, 1966).
Passage, C. E. (1963): *The Russian Hoffmannists* (The Hague: Mouton, 1963).
Petrovskii, Iu. A. (1971a): 'Spetsificheskie funktsii tragicheskogo i komicheskogo v romane Dostoevskogo "Prestuplenie i nakazanie" ', in *Nauchnaia konferentsiia posviashchënnaia 150-letiiu so dnia rozhdeniia F. M. Dostoevskogo i N. A. Nekrasova. Kratkoe soderzhanie dokladov* (Novgorod, 1971), pp. 8–11.
Petrovskii, Iu. A. (1971b): 'Tragicheskoe i komicheskoe v tvorchestve Dostoevskogo 1846–1864gg.', in ibid., pp. 4–7.
Rabkin, E. S. (1976): *The Fantastic in Literature* (Princeton: Princeton University Press, 1976).
Solov'ëv, Vl. S. (1909): 'Predislovie k "Upyr'iu" grafa A. K. Tolstogo' (1899), in *Sobranie sochinenni Vladimira Sergeevicha Solov'ëva*, vol. IX (St Petersburg, 1909: reprinted Brussels, 1966), pp. 375–9.
Todorov, T. (1970): *Introduction à la littérature fantastique* (Paris: Le Seuil, 1970).
Vax, L. (1960): *L'art et la littérature fantastiques* (Paris: P.U.F., 1960).
Zolla, E. (1964): *Storia del fantasticare* (Milan: Bompiani, 1964).

# 9 Some Features of the Poetics of Kharms's Prose: The Story *'Upadanie'* ('The Falling')
Aleksandr Kobrinsky

The story 'The Falling' [*Upadanie*] was finished by Kharms on 7 September 1940,[1] and relates therefore to the final period of its author's creativity (1940–1). It is well known that this period saw Kharms's definitive transition from verse to a prose which retained the best of the features elaborated in the 1930s. In this respect, the story 'The Falling' is a particularly important one and for this reason it has been chosen for analysis here.

## SPATIAL AND TEMPORAL STRUCTURE OF THE STORY

The main feature of 'The Falling' is the diversification of the temporal co-ordinate of the chronotope, while its spatial unity is preserved. The story's space is closed and symmetrical, limited to two buildings, in the first of which are the observers, while the fall of two men begins and continues from the roof of the second. The manuscript contains a first draft entitled 'Near by and far off' [*Vblizi i vdali*],[2] which underlines the position of the author in the space of the story: the author-narrator is evidently situated alongside the observers, the latter being given in close-up.

The original title seems to underline the existence of two time-flows, topologically coinciding with the near and distant planes of action. The beginning of the story, apart from the fact itself of the fall of two people from a roof, also fixes the initial moment of this fall. The articulation of this phase of the action, equating it in significance with the action itself, becomes a formal signal for the imminent breakdown of the time-flow:

> Two men fell from a roof. They both fell from the roof of a five-storey newly erected building. Seemingly a school. They had

moved down the roof in a sitting position to the very edge and at that point *started* to fall. [our emphasis: A.K.]

Thus the slowing down of time also begins.

This fall is noticed by a certain Ida Markovna, standing at her window in a building opposite. She tears off her shift and begins to rub the steamed up window-pane with it, 'the better to make out who was falling out there from the roof'. At this moment, the thought enters her head that 'those falling might, from their vantage point, be able to glimpse her naked – and goodness only knew what they might think of her', and she jumps back from the window. 'At this juncture', remarks the narrator, 'those falling from the roof were sighted by another personage who lived in the same building as Ida Markovna, only two floors below. This personage was also called Ida Markovna'. Here the phrase 'at this juncture' [*v eto vremia*] is particularly important, as it draws attention to the sequentiality, and not the simultaneity, of the actions of the two Idas. The second Ida Markovna, having caught sight of those falling from the roof (the fall is still going on), tries to open her window. It does not open, being nailed up. Then Ida Markovna rushes for her pincers, pulls out the nail and flings open the window. Having flung the window open, she sees that those falling are still descending, or 'flying towards the ground' [*podletaiut k zemle*].

The heterochrony of what is happening is striking: the observers' time ('near by'), obviously, coincides with real time, whereas the fallers' time ('far off') is dragged out to the utmost, and slowed down. As a result, what would be, in a normal system of co-ordinates, such a rapid action as falling from the roof of a five-storey house turns out in the story to be equivalent in duration to a great number of actions which are carried out by the observers. It is curious that in the original draft Kharms put even greater stress on the non-correspondence of the time-flows, bringing into the text a remark by Ida Markovna, addressed to an old woman who happened to be beneath: 'Hey, old woman, there are two men falling on you from up there!'. However, in the final text of the story as well, the author's intention to underline this heterochrony by various means can be seen: originally the 'upper' Ida Markovna rubs the window in order 'the better to make out who *was starting to fall* out there from the roof'. In the final version, the word 'starting' is removed, which indicates that the fall had begun earlier. Finally, in what is the most expressive moment: before the fallers hit the ground, a 'smallish

## The Poetics of Kharms's Prose: Upadanie 151

crowd' has already managed to gather below, a 'diminutive militiaman' is *unhurriedly* approaching the location of the expected event, and a caretaker is bustling about, 'shoving people and explaining that those falling from the roof could smite the heads of those gathered beneath'.

Let us note these further characteristic features of Kharmsian prose: the militiaman, the caretaker and the crowd. They exist in the 'near by' time-flow and mark it in a particular way. The image of the caretaker (sometimes transformed into a watchman) first appeared in Kharms's work in a poem of 1933, called 'Constancy of Merriment and Filth' [*Postoianstvo vesel'ia i griaz'*]:

And the caretaker with his black moustache
stands for years at the gates
and scratches with his filthy hands
under his filthy hat the back of his head.
(*Polët*, p. 157, dated 14 October 1933; *Sob. proizv.*, 4, p. 17)

It reappears through the rest of Kharms's *oeuvre* ('The Fate of a Professor's Wife', 'Father and Daughter', 'The Young Man who saw a Watchman', 'The Drawback' etc.). Just as widespread in the work of Kharms is the image of the militiaman ('The Dream', the novella 'The Old Woman', 'Myshin's Triumph' etc.) and of the crowd ('A Lynching', 'An Event on the Street' etc.). The function of the caretaker/watchman/militiaman as representative of 'a complex of the repressive forces of society' has been noted by Jean-Philippe Jaccard.[3]

In this way, we may also note the sharply negative colouring which real time, the time of the 'sub-man' or 'non-man' (*nedochelovek* – Ia. S. Druskin's term), assumes in connection with the presence of these attributes. It will be shown below how the semantics of 'near by' time is made explicit in the images of the observers. For the moment, let us note that the fall from on high, and the crowd gathered below to await this fall, imply a definite parodic understanding of such important spatial symbols in Russian literature as the tower ('up'), the square ('down') and, connected with those, the idea of the dethroning of the pretender which Bakhtin writes of in some detail in relation to Dostoevsky and Pushkin.[4] We may note that Kharms's story is carried over onto this allegorical-parodic plane by the last sentence: 'Just as on occasion we, falling from heights we have attained, may strike the dreary cage of our future'.

It would be logical also to connect Kharms's discrediting of real time with Bakhtin's theory of time in folklore and literature. If folkloric time is entirely indivisible, then in literature, when:

> ... the time of personal, everyday, family events was individualized and separated from the time of the collective historical life of the social whole, when there appeared various scales for measuring the events of *private* life and the events of *history* ... in the abstract time remained indivisible, but plotwise it divided into two.[5]

In 'The Falling', it is as though social time in general switches itself off, is displaced by private time (this is characteristic of almost all the work of Kharms, with rare exceptions), but the latter takes on a duality peculiar to literary time. In this process, a method of a logical deformation is used, as a result of which time ceases to be indivisible, even in the abstract.

## ON THE PHENOMENON OF QUASI-NOMINATION

The phenomenon which we are here calling 'quasi-nomination' expresses the real discrepancy between the conventional sign and the signified, of which was said, back in 1928 in the OBERIU manifesto: 'The concrete object, once its literary and everyday skin is peeled away,' may look not at all as we are *accustomed* to see it in life.[6] In Kharms's prose the 'indifference' of the nominative units to their denotations turns into the destruction of nomination as a linguistic phenomenon. However, unlike Vvedensky, in whose works this destruction is explained by the organic impossibility of expressing certain basic categories (time, God, death); Kharms, as it were, transfers the centre of gravity (and, consequently, the reasons for the breakdown of nomination) into a world of the absurd.[7] Simplifying somewhat, we can say that Vvedensky reveals for us the poverty of verbal means of expression, in the face of the limitless depth and inexhaustibility of the world, while in Kharms everything happens the other way round: language becomes the victim of the impoverishment of life, of the emptiness of its manifestations.

Quasi-nomination is thrown into particular relief when the discrediting of the word as a nominative unit occurs directly, by contact. It is organised in exactly this way in the story 'Blue Notebook No. 10' [*Golubaia tetrad' No. 10*] (or 'The Red-Haired Man') from the *Incidents* cycle.[8] The only positive feature of the 'hero', the red colour of his hair (all the other features are negative), is already discredited in the following sentence: 'Neither did he have any hair, so he was called red-haired theoretically' [*uslovno*]. The destruction of nomination here occurs at the expense of an infringement of the law of formal logic – of the excluded third. In fact, a person may either be red-haired or not red-haired; Kharms brings in a third, logically impossible condition: that of being red-haired 'theoretically' (or 'conditionally'). Beginning with the annihilation of the authenticity of the feature, Kharms to all intents and purposes annihilates the man himself and, together with him, as Jaccard correctly notes, 'transforms the whole story into nothing'.[9]

Quasi-nomination is just as graphically apparent in the Kharms story 'The Four-Legged Crow' [*Chetveronogaia vorona*].[10] In the title itself there is an implicit denial of the concept of a 'crow' ('four-legged'!). But this is only the start; in the opening sentences the concept of 'four-leggedness' which had just been introduced is destroyed: it turns out that this crow 'strictly speaking ... had five legs, but it is not worth talking about this'. The concept of 'four-leggedness' turns out to be the same kind of 'dummy' as is 'red hair' in 'Blue Notebook No. 10'.

In the story beginning 'A certain man, not wanting to feed himself any more...', we are told how the protagonist, Ivan Iakovlevich, comes into a shop to buy himself some groceries. And here, before our eyes, there occurs a process of reducing usual names to nonsense. 'Salami' smells like cheese, it is not in the least like salami and the name does not signify anything. The protagonist goes to the fish counter, but it turns out that 'the fish counter had moved temporarily to where the wines had been before, and the wine counter had moved to confectionary, and confectionery to dairy products...'. Needless to say, at these counters it was impossible to buy anything. The nominative qualities of the words 'fish', 'wine', 'confectionery' and 'dairy' have ceased to correspond to any real concepts; here we have quasi-nomination. In the given instance it serves as a modelling device for a definite economic situation of the 1930s.

We are here dealing with a world in which people and objects have ceased to be what they were originally. In 'The Falling', Kharms personifies the idea of the standardisation of personality in the identical names of his observers – both of whom are called Ida Markovna. They have a completely similar inner world (that is to say an empty one) and the first impulse of each upon seeing the fallers is an urge to see better 'when those falling from the roof should strike the ground'. The difference between the two female figures resides only in their spatial position: they are divided only by two floors. And not by chance in the revision process Kharms removed the sentence: 'The naked Elena Markovna [as the women were originally called] stood on the wicker tripod [three-legged stool] and earnestly thought about *what assistance she could render those falling from the roof* [our emphasis, A.K.]. The name ceases to be an attribute of fully-fledged personality, but 'stiffens up' and turns into a meaningless hieroglyph.[11]

It is interesting that the significance of quasi-nomination as an artistic device in the prose of Kharms should be neatly confirmed by an analysis of authorial revision to the draft manuscript of 'The Falling'. Originally we had: 'Ida Markovna jumped back from the window and hid behind a pot-plant'. Then Kharms removed the last three words and in the final version the sentence reads as follows: 'Ida Markovna jumped back from the window and hid behind the wicker tripod *on which there had at one time stood a pot-plant*' [our emphasis, A.K.]. It is important to Kharms to emphasise that the objects in this world (in this case a wicker tripod) are no longer fulfilling their functions but have also dissolved into the general absurdity. The significance of Kharms's revisions becomes particularly apparent when we recall a phrase from his 1939 work 'A Treatise more or less summarising Emerson': '... if there are no flowers in a flower vase, then this vase becomes nonsensical and, if the vase is removed, then the little round table becomes nonsensical...'.[12] In exactly the same way the wicker tripod, on which there has long been no pot-plant, becomes nonsensical.

The natural result of this is, firstly: the already mentioned unification and standardisation of people ('both Ida Markovnas – the one in a dress and the other naked – having leaned out of their windows, were squealing and kicking their legs about'); and, secondly: the rapprochement (to the point of full identification) between the animate and the inanimate worlds. Typically in this way, to the draft version of the phrase '... those falling from the roof were flying towards the ground...', Kharms put in, after the words 'from the roof' the additional 'whistled' [*so svistom*], thus grotesquely accentuating the functional proximity of people and objects, who/which, being thrown off a roof, would fly down with a whistle.

*Translated by Neil Cornwell*

# NOTES

1. First published in *Soviet Union/Union Soviètique*, 7, 1–2, 1980, 235–6; Soviet publication in *Knizhnoe obozrenie*, 1, 1988, 7; English version in *Plummeting*, pp. 78–9.
2. The manuscript is in the Kharms archive of the Saltykov-Shchedrin State Public Library, Leningrad.
3. Jaccard, 1985.
4. M. Bakhtin, *Problemy poetiki Dostoevskogo*, Moscow, 1969, pp. 196–8.
5. M. Bakhtin, 'Formy vremeni i khronotopa v romane', in his *Literaturno-kriticheskie stat'i*, Moscow, 1986, p. 242.
6. See 'OBERIU', *Afishi Doma pechati*, Leningrad, 1928, no. 2, pp. 11–13. English version: *Black Coat*, p. 248.
7. We may note the similarity between Kharms and Camus in their conceptions of the absurd (on this see Jaccard, 1985, and Jaccard's essay in the present volume). The absurd in Kharms's prose clearly takes on the characteristic features of an existentialist category.
8. *Polët*, p. 353; *Plummeting*, p. 27.
9. Jaccard, 1985, p. 290.
10. Published in *Krokodil*, 33, November 1988, 8.
11. It is interesting to compare this with the emblematisation of names in Platonov's novel *Chevengur* (the peasants Franz Mering, Fëdor Dostoevskii) and with the theme of the anonymity of being in the same novel (before the assertion of their new names, the peasants live 'as though nameless').
12. '*Traktat bolee ili menee po konspektu Emersona*' is published in Jaccard, 1985, pp. 311–12.

# Part IV: The Poetic Works

# 10 On One Enigmatic Poem by Daniil Kharms[1]

## Lazar Fleishman

> We said, and it's obvious,
> We can't see an hour back.
> We thought – for us
> It's very lonely.
> We little enough in a moment
> Can grasp with an eye.
> And only one sound
> Does our beggarly hearing sense.
> And a pathetic part of science
> Does our spirit comprehend.
> We said, and it's obvious,
> All this is very insulting.
> 
> A. Vvedensky, 'Invitation to me to think' (Vved. I, p. 127)

The rapid process of getting to grips with the literary heritage of the OBERIU group, which has marked scholarship in the field of modern Russian literature over the last two decades, caught researchers unawares. On the one hand, they have been confronted by a huge body of newly discovered texts of obvious originality, whose organic kinship with the poetic trends of the Russian avantgarde is plain to see. On the other hand, it was soon obvious that scholarly techniques (even those based on avantgarde poetics) were inapplicable when it came to describing a considerable part of OBERIU work. While the prose and dramatic pieces of Kharms and Vvedensky fitted comparatively easily into the classifications available to literary scholars and were immediately labelled a phenomenon analogous to the 'literature of the absurd' which had chronologically anticipated it,[2] – the verse texts of the Oberiuty could not be handled, and still cannot be handled, with the tools at present available to the literary historian. Specific discussion of individual texts has, in OBERIU studies, been limited to prose works, whereas for the analysis of the recently published poems by Kharms and Vvedensky (and of Vaginov), commentators have invariably been faced with the absence of any 'key' which would unlock the meaning of these works. Hence the seemingly deep-rooted feeling that it is fruitless to search for a 'key' to the understanding of the works of the Oberiuty. And, however apparent – particularly in the early phase of their work[3] – the link between the OBERIU poets and the traditions of 'trans-sense' poetry [*zaum'*] (Kruchënykh, Tufanov, Terent'ev[4]), this fact brings no relief at all to the literary historian. One of the central points of the celebrated OBERIU manifesto of 1928 was a clear demarcation from *zaum'*:

> Some people even now call us *zaumniki*. It is difficult to decide whether that is because of a complete misunderstanding or a hopeless failure to grasp the principles of literary art. No school is more alien to us than *zaum'*. We, people who are real and concrete to the marrow of our bones, are the first enemies of those who castrate the word and make it into a powerless and senseless cur. In our work we broaden and deepen the meaning of the object and of the word, but we do not destroy it in any way.
>
> (adapted from *Black Coat*, pp. 247–8)

The poetical practice of Kharms and Vvedensky in this period bears unambiguous witness to their withdrawal from *zaum'*. It is beyond doubt that this move was not dictated by external pressure or by 'opportunistic' considerations: for this breakaway did not legitimise the Oberiuty in the literary world of the twenties and thirties and did not make their work any more understandable to the reader.

Because of this, the discovery of the 'content level' and its relation to the 'expression level' remains, to this day, the central problem in any description of Oberiuty versifying. The prevailing tendency nowadays is to designate the general qualities of Oberiuty poetics by the soothing term 'nonsense', and to attempt to classify various types of 'nonsense'; but this tendency only highlights the failure to achieve any detailed analysis of any one text on its own merits. Thus we have a situation, whereby general characteristics – correct or otherwise as they may be – have forged ahead of any possibility of testing them out on specific material.

The present brief study proposes one approach to the decoding of the poetic utterances of the Oberiuty. Its aim is to attempt to separate the 'rational' and the 'meaningful', from the deliberately '*zaum'*-quality', and to show this as an accepted characteristic of Oberiuty poetics. We have chosen for analysis Kharms's poem '*I rasrushenie*' [Ist Destruction'], written after the break with *zaum'*, but before

# On One Enigmatic Poem by Daniil Kharms 161

Kharms turned to the 'philosophical' and 'religious' notions which filled his lyrics of the thirties and which require special examination. The poem, from the Kharms archive, was published in the ongoing scholarly edition of his works edited by Meilakh and Erl (*Sob. proizv.*, II, pp. 13–14), but without any commentary (other than a textological one).

### Ist DESTRUCTION

A week – is briefly the way of the spirit.
A week – is a landmark, the sign of seven.
A week – is a giant's fig.
A week – is indivisible into letters.
So indivisible is the week
for doing it divides days into bits,
in the weekday doings of wild will
our body longs for bed.

For us a week is long drawn out,
we go out on a Monday,
we work away until Saturday,
doing all our doings on weekdays.

But shortening the week,
We shall increase our peace:
In the span of an equal stretch
a little trunk in just four days. –
You see, a day of free jokes
by the year catching up on things,
you see, the new week
has become divisible by reason,
like a palm of five fingers –
time has started to flow inexorably.
And so we construct time's score
By the law of our bodies.
Time anew is flowing
for convenience of our doings.
The week – has become divisible by us.
The week – is a five-day badge.
The week – is a giant's fig.
The week – flies on its way like a bullet.

Hurray, short week,
you have lost it all!
And now we can get down to the next destruction.

*that's all*
(Begun 6 November – finished
20/21 November 1929.)

Like other works of Kharms's post-*zaum'* period, this poem, cannot fail to evoke bewilderment. Despite the evident inner form and completeness of the text,[5] signalled by the 'framing' stage direction (*vsë*), which Kharms frequently employed in such instances, the content of the chain of what would seem to be meaningful verbal constructions making up the poem remains elusive. The title, and its relation to the thesis of the 'indivisibility of the week' [*nedelimost' nedeli*], are even more unclear. In its turn, this last thesis seems no more than punning wordplay. What is striking, though, is that the 'destruction' here described is, for some reason, termed 'first'.

An answer to these questions must be sought in the specific historical circumstances to which this enigmatic poem is a response. The first year of the 'five year plan' was accompanied by persistent calls for daily life to be completely transformed, for the socialist 'reconstruction' of life. One element of this movement was the attempt to reform the calendar and to convert to a new system of counting the years. These calls were motivated by three distinct types of consideration. The primary impulse stemmed from the need to extirpate the age-old traditions of observing 'religious festivals'. In connection with this, on the eve of Easter 1929, a columnist in the Moscow *Izvestiia* demanded that the seven-day week be changed for a six-day one, as a means of taking Sunday 'resurrections' out of circulation and of totally secularising reality:

> According to the Soviet constitution, religion is a private matter for believers. Clearly, it would seem, religious festivals of any type must also be a private matter for believers. According to the legal labour code, no 'festivals' exist and there are only *days of rest*.
>
> However, *in point of fact, we do observe precisely religious festivals, since the overwhelming majority of rest days fall on religious festivals* [italics as quoted by Fleishman, here and below: Ed.]. Suffice it to say that fifty-two Sundays are observed in a year, not to mention Easter, Christmas and so on. It may be said that this

is an accidental coincidence between rest days and religious festivals and that only believers attach religious significance to rest days.

But, in the first place, this can not be an accidental coincidence because the coincidence is almost total. And, secondly, even accidental coincidences between rest days and religious festivals may be interpreted as a concession by Soviet society to backward, ignorant strata of the population, contaminated by all kinds of prejudices.[6]

According to the author, the reform proposed by him – a change to a six-day week – 'will not in the least degree break' the calendar system, 'leaving the same months and dates in the year. *It comes down only to throwing out one day in the present week*'. The project was therefore taken to be insufficiently revolutionary. The well-known Party publicist M. Ol'minsky advanced a counter-balancing idea of a complete reform of the calendar with the aim of achieving total eradication of the old prejudices. According to his plan, the first day in the new calendar had to be the October Revolution of 1917[7] – by analogy with the calendar of the French Republic, brought in by the Convention in 1793 and maintained over a period of twelve years.

On the crest of the wave of the anti-religious campaign and of the demands for a calendar system which would accord with the epoch-making significance of revolution, there were advanced also more prosaic considerations in favour of calendar reform – references to the practical needs of the spread of 'socialist competition'. The newspaper *Komsomol'skaia Pravda* affirmed that 'the regular stoppage of our factories and plants every "seventh day" – a Sunday – **lowers** the pace of socialist construction' and proposed going over to **the** 'uninterrupted week'.[8] Argument over this new idea instantly took on epidemic proportions and the initiators of this considered it essential to play down the 'atheistic' tone. Replying to readers' questions, the inventor of the uninterrupted week ['*nepreryvka*'], Iu. Larin,[9] declared: 'abolition of the seventh day – Sunday – is called for not from religious considerations, but for considerations of production. It is simply an accidental coincidence that it is Sunday which would be lost'.[10] On 24 September, the Council of People's Commissars approved the conversion from 1 October of all enterprises and institutions of the Soviet Union to 'uninterrupted production' on the basis of a 'five-day' cycle (four working days, plus one day off).[11] A few weeks later there followed an announcement that a new calendar was in preparation, which, in accordance with Ol'minsky's initiative, would begin counting the years from 1917 and make the year begin on 7 November.[12]

If to us now these events[13] seem a transitory humorous episode in the annals of Soviet history, to the contemporary eye-witness they assumed catastrophic, almost eschatological, significance.[14] The historical backdrop given here enables us to decode Kharms's poem. It was begun hot on the heels of the introduction of the 'five-day-cycle', on the eve of the first of the remaining (in the sense of general, for the whole population) 'rest days',[15] – all other days off were 'sliding' ones and were distributed in each instance only as a 'fifth part' of days worked.[16] Hence the mention of a 'trunk in four days' and the motif of 'divisibility' of the new week. The *first* destruction is so called by Kharms, evidently, because the new departure, removing in practice 'Saturdays' and 'Sundays', in November 1929 had still not been crowned by the confirmation of the new calendar. This question was still in a state of discussion,[17] but the 'Godless' direction[18] of the outlined measures (despite the protestations of Larin) appeared irreversible, just as it was clear that the very term 'Sunday' was becoming unmentionable.[19] It may be supposed that comparison of the shortened week with the flight of a 'bullet' represents the motif of the interdiction of Sunday ['resurrection'] turned inside out and refers to the timing of the creation of man in the Bible on the 'sixth day'.[20] Connected also with the biblical subtext is the parodic motif of the 'giant's fig',[21] which has a dual application: it simultaneously refers to the story in Genesis of the creation – now overturned by revolutionary reality – and to that hysterical mania about giants which had enveloped (as they then liked to keep saying) 'a sixth part of the terrestrial globe'.

However tempting it may be to read into Kharms's poem a touch of political satire, of oppositional invective,[22] its content does not provide reliable grounds for such an interpretation. It is not possible to draw directly from this poem any conclusions about the 'negative' attitude of the author towards the enacted reforms. On the contrary, one may suppose that the Oberiuty poet might have been drawn by the element of attraction, amazement, eccentricity in the state-wide – almost even 'global' – scale contained in the experiment being undertaken. The leap from an age-old tradition (line 8 – 'our body longs for bed'[23]) to a new norm, 'day of free jokes', obviously provoked in the author of 'Ist Destruction' a compound reaction of cynical scepticism and merry curiosity, as a part of which 'the palm of five fingers' irrepressibly tightens into a 'fig'.

The calendar 'revolution' stimulated Kharms also to the idea with which the work '*Sablia*' ['The Sabre'], written at the same time, opens (*Polët*, p. 433): 'Life is divided into working and non-working time. Non-working time creates schemes, pipes. Working time fills these pipes.'

In this way, the externally *zaum'*-like poem[24] acquires a fully rational interpretation. At the same time it becomes clear that 'neighbouring' poems by Kharms too can be comparatively simply decoded by analogous means: in the same volume (*Sob. proizv.*, II, numbers 80 and 81), '*Neva techët vdol' akademii*' ['The Neva flows past the Academy'] and '*Tiul'panov sredi khoreev*' ['Tulips among the trochees'] represent sketches of the October (1929) flood in Leningrad and the destruction which arose from it. Evidently also the 'apocalyptic' *terzetti* '*Vse, vse derev'ia pif*' ['All, all trees are piff'] (*Polët*, II, number 79) should also be placed in the same historical context.

*Translated by Neil Cornwell*

NOTES

1. This article was first published in *Stanford Slavic Studies*, vol. 1, 1987. Thanks are due to the editors and author for permission to translate and republish.
2. Revzina and Revzin, 1971, p. 254; Gibian, *Russia's Lost Lit.*; Meilakh, 1978, p. 388. Cf. Revzina, 1978, pp. 397–8.
3. Meilakh, 'Foreword' to Vved. I, pp. xv–xvii; Aleksandrov, 1980.
4. On Terent'ev, see Tat'iana Nikol'skaia, 'Igor' Terent'ev v Tiflise', in *L'avanguardia a Tiflis*, ed. Luigi Magarotto *et al.* (Venice, 1982) pp. 189–209; Rozemari Tsigler [Rosemarie Ziegler], 'Poetika A. E. Kruchënykh pory "41°"'. Uroven' zvuka', in ibid., pp. 231–58.
5. Publications of recent years have demonstrated the difficulty of distinguishing completed works from abandoned experiments in the notebooks of Kharms. Vvedenskii used the word '*konets*' [the end] as his crowning stage-direction.
6. P. Baranchikov, 'Ne prazdniki, a dni otdykha. Shestidnevnaia nedelia vmesto semidnevnoi', *Izvestiia*, 1929, no. 86 (3622), 14 April, p. 3.
7. M. Ol'minskii, 'Proletarskii schët vremeni. Na obsuzhdenie', *Komsomol'skaia Pravda*, 1929, no. 102 (1189), 8 May, p. 3. See the remarks of Kim Oktiabrëv in the selection of readers' letters headed 'Pochemu

my do sikh por schitaem s "rozhdestva Khristova"? Pora pokonchit' s popovskim letochisleniem', ibid., no. 127 (1214), 6 June, p. 3.
8. 'Organizuem bespreryvnuiu rabochuiu nedeliu', *Komsomol'skaia Pravda*, 1929, no. 121 (1208), 30 May, p. 4.
9. On him see Roy A. Medvedev, *Nikolai Bukharin: The Last Years*, trans. A. D. P. Briggs (Norton: New York and London), 1980, pp. 108–10. On Larin's unrestrained passion for fantastic reforms, see the memoirs of A. Gurovich, 'Vysshii Sovet Narodnogo Khoziaistva. Iz vpechatlenii goda sluzhby', *Arkhiv Russkoi Revoliutsii*, VI (Berlin, 1922) pp. 323–4.
10. 'Berëm vremia za gorlo!', *Komsomol'skaia Pravda*, 1929, no. 144 (1231), 27 June, p. 4.
11. In this connection it was also proposed to renounce the old names of the days of the week. According to one variant debated the new designations were to be: 'Marx', 'Lenin', 'Komintern', 'Industrializatsiia', 'Kommuna' ('Dni sovetskoi nedeli', *Poslednie Novosti*, Paris, no. 3120, 7 October 1929, p. 1). The well-known philosopher E. Kol'man wrote: 'Thanks to the system of uninterrupted work, general rest-days are disappearing and thereby the names of the days themselves are losing sense. This is a shattering blow to fetishism, to sanctified age-old tradition and religious custom, and to religion itself. Here the change of organization of the technical process itself, the change in the organization of people in production in the most radical irretrievable way is breaking down the foundations of religion and stagnation': E. Kol'man, 'Zametku o nepreryvke', *Molodaia gvardiia*, 1929, no. 20, October, p. 54. This may be compared with Hugo Huppert, 'Werksonntag. Ein Stück neue Kultur', *Das neue Russland*, VII, (Berlin, 1930) Heft 3–4, p. 50.
12. '6 nedel' v mesiatse. Reforma kalendaria SSSR', *Poslednie Novosti*, no. 3112, 29 October 1929, p. 1; F. Dan, 'K reforme kalendaria', *Sotsialisticheskii Vestnik*, 1930, no. 3 (217), 8 February, pp. 4–6. The new calendar, introduced in 1930, was abolished (as was the five-dayweek) in 1931: see I. P. Ermolaev, *Istoricheskaia khronologiia* (Kazan', 1980) pp. 115–16; S. I. Seleshnikov, *Istoriia kalendaria i khronologii*, 3rd. ed., (Moscow, 1977) pp. 169–71. Celebration of New Year, officially banned from this time – see Kharms's poem '*My (dva tozhdestvennykh cheloveka)*', *Sob. proizv.*, II, 17 – was restored on the eve of 1 January 1936: see L. Fleishman, *Boris Pasternak v tridtsatye gody* (Jersualem, 1984) p. 275.
13. They figured in Maiakovskii's *Bania*, when, in the well-known 'March of time', there occurs the slogan: '*Naliag strana, skorei moia, na nepreryvnyi god*'; see Vl. Maiakovskii, 'Marsh vremeni. Otryvok Bani', *Komsomol'skaia Pravda*, 1929, no. 218 (1305), 21 September, p. 1.
14. Stalin called the change to the five-day-week one of the three main elements (along with 'self-criticism' and 'socialist competition') of the new life. See I. V. Stalin, 'God velikogo pereloma', *Sochinenia*, vol. 12, April 1929 – June 1930, Moscow, 1949, p. 120.
15. 7 and 8 November, 22 January, 1 and 2 May: Seleshnikov, p. 170.

16. Western observers predicted catastrophic results for this reform. Compare this slightly later report from Russia:

> The introduction of the uninterrupted week has destroyed "festive days" [*prazdniki*] – days of *common* rest. The old type of Sundays has disappeared, when trade ceased in the city, traffic lessened etc. Now our life is one big weekday. Although rest days are frequent (every fifth day), only perhaps manual workers and lower grades of employees take advantage of them. For all practical purposes, we hardly ever have rest days. It is rare that rest days would coincide in the same apartment. . . . From the economic viewpoint, its introduction has brought ruin. A holiday after four days means that a fifth of the work force is constantly resting, that is to say there's a twenty per cent cut in production. Add in the general fall in productivity on the day following a holiday and you will get some idea of how the productivity of labour has gone down. It seems to me that the worst "saboteur" could not have thought up anything worse.

'Pis'mo iz Moskvy', *Poslednie Novosti*, no. 3405, 19 June 1930, p. 4. Cf. Eugene Lyons, *Assignment in Utopia* (New York, 1937) pp. 210–11. The five-day-week was abolished after Stalin's speech of 23 June 1931, in which the uninterrupted labour system was deemed 'irresponsible'; this speech was considered a liberal turning point in the internal life of Soviet Russia: see 'Pokhorony nepreryvki', *Poslednie Novosti*, no. 3773, 22 July 1931, p. 2; G. Iavorskii, 'Nepreryvnaia nedelia i bor'ba s obezlichkoi v promyshlennosti', *Izvestiia*, 1931, no. 210 (4408), 23 July, p. 2; P. Garvi, 'Bunt mashin', *Sotsialisticheskii Vestnik*, 1931, no. 10 (248), 23 May, p. 9.

17. 'Zapozdalye triuki', *Poslednie Novosti*, no. 3115, 2 October 1929, p. 1.
18. 'Time exists, and therefore so does worship. All times are marked by the liturgy and, when religious foundations fall apart, then "the time is out of joint", in Shakespeare's words': Father Pavel Florenskii, 'Izbogoslovskogo naslediia', *Bogoslovskie trudy*, 17, Moscow, 1977, p. 133. Compare Kharms's definition of the week: 'briefly, the way of the spirit'. We may recall that 'the year of the great change' was accompanied by massive destruction of churches and monasteries and the public *autos da fé* of icons. Almost the last action of A. V. Lunacharskii in the post of Commissar for Enlightenment was the decree for the removal from 1 September of the Gospels from all libraries: see 'Otstavka Lunacharskogo. Naznachenie Bubnova', *Rul'* (Berlin), no. 2665, 1 September 1929, p. 1.
19. 'Sovetskaia "sreda" vzamën starogo voskresen'ia', *Izvestiia*, 1929, no. 126 (3662), 5 June, p. 1. It is remarkable that when the GPU's discovery of a counter-revolutionary plot in Leningrad was announced in September, the new villainous group was given the name '*Voskresenie*' ['Resurrection']: see '70 novykh zhertv GPU: "Kontrrevoliutsionnaia organizatsia", "Voskresenie"', *Vozrozhdenie* (Paris), 1929, no. 1567, 16 September. In this light, a phrase of Pasternak's in

*Okhrannaia gramota* [*Safe Conduct*] takes on a clearly ironic sense: 'And it is true, the confrontation of faith in Sunday [*voskresen'e*] with the age of the Renaissance is a unique phenomenon and a central one for all European culture'.

20. Lines 23–24: '*Tak my stroim vremia schët / Po zakonu nashikh tel'* ['And so we construct time's score / by the law of our bodies'] refer to the leitmotif of 'additive-subtractive' manipulations with the human body in OBERIU texts: see Fleishman, in Oleinikov, *Stikhotvoreniia*, pp. 7–8.

21. The juxtaposition in Kharms of the 'inexorable' flow of time and 'the palm of five fingers' may be compared with a similar image in the journalism of the day. 'We have a sensation of highly condensed and compressed time. Here, where we recently had heaps of time, years, ages have slipped through widespread fingers, neglected in shaggy, unkempt slow-wittedness, now, today, we have learned to sense keenly its weight, its density and movement. Never, anywhere was time valued as it now is here': L. Kassil', 'Na zlobu dnia sed'mogo', *Molodaia gvardiia*, 1930, no. 1 (January), p. 101.

22. In this connection we may take note of a previously unnoticed fact: it so happened that in 1929 Kharms was a close observer of one of the most unruly scandals of Soviet history of that time. His first wife, Ester, was the daughter of the revolutionary and political émigré A. I. Rusakov (Ioselevich), who had returned from France to Petrograd in 1919 (see Aleksandrov, 1980, p. 69) and who in 1928–29, together with his family, became the victim of GPU provocation. His elder daughter Liubov' was the wife of Viktor Serge (V. L. Kibal'chich), a leading figure [and writer! Ed.] of the European communist movement, who had settled in the USSR and sided with the Trotskyist opposition. (Later, in 1933, his name became famous when he was arrested and sent without trial into exile. Gor'kii, Rolland and Gide were involved in appeals for his release. After pressure from the European left intelligentsia he was allowed to leave the country in April 1936: see 'Viktor Serzh', *Biulleten' oppozitsii (bol'shevikov-lenintsev*, no. 50, May 1936, pp. 19–20.) Another daughter married the French communist and later Slavic scholar Pierre Pascal. The 'Rusakov affair' gained international publicity thanks to the account by Panaït Istrati ('L'affaire Roussakov ou l'URSS d'aujourd'hui', *Nouvelle Revue Française*, t. XXXIII, October 1929, pp. 437–76; see also P. Istrati, *Vers l'autre flamme. Après seize mois dans l'URSS*, Paris, 1929). See Fleishman, 1987, pp. 256–7, n. 26 for more documentation.

23. The key to interpreting this phrase could be a passage from the same article by Kassil': 'The uninterrupted production week has unseated our time from its calendary saddle. With the destruction of the sleepy flop, which the seventh day, Sunday, had been, the country is in a state of constant wakefulness': L. Kassil', op. cit., p. 99.

24. According to Ia. Druskin, Vvedenskii once said: 'I don't understand why my stuff is called *zaum'*; in my view, the editorial in the paper is *zaum'*': Ia. Druskin, 'Poetika bessmyslitsy', in *Sob. proizv.*, V (forthcoming).

# 11 'I Razrushenie'
## Daniil Kharms

I  РАЗРУШЕНИЕ

Неделя – вкратце духа путь.
Неделя – вешка, знак семи.
Неделя – великана дуля.
Неделя – в буквах неделима.
Так неделимая неделя
для дела дни на доли делит,
в буднях дела дикой воли
наше тело в ложе тянет.

Нам неделя длится долго.
мы уходим в понедельник,
мы трудимся до субботы,
совершая дело в будни.

Но неделю сокращая,
Увеличим свой покой:
через равный промежуток
сундучок в четыре дня. –
Видишь, день свободных шуток
годом дело догоня,
видишь, новая неделя
стала разумом делима,
как ладонь из пяти пальцев –
стало время течь неумолимо.

Так мы строим время счет
По закону наших тел.
Время заново течет
для удобства наших дел.
Неделя – стала нами делима.
Неделя – дней значок пяти.
Неделя – великана дуля.
Неделя – в путь летит как пуля.

Ура, короткая неделя,
ты все утратила!
И теперь можно приступать к следующему разрушению.

*все*

**Начато 6 ноября – кончено
20/21 ноября 1929 года.**

# 12 Kharms's '1st Destruction'
Jerzy Faryno

The historico-ideological reality lying behind Kharms's poem '1st Destruction' has been explained and reconstructed in detail by Lazar Fleishman in his article of 1987 [translated and reprinted above, Ed.]. Without such a reconstruction, much in this poem would have remained not entirely comprehensible. First and foremost at least an elementary knowledge of the history of the Soviet calendar is called for here; namely, the fact that from October 1930 the Soviet Union converted to a five-day week of four working days and one day off and to a new system of year-counting, starting from 1917 and not from the birth of Christ (the new year was to be observed on 7 November; this system was abolished in June 1931; for details, see Fleishman, above; Seleshnikov, 1977, pp. 169–71). As Fleishman has shown, this calendar system in particular entered the structure of '1st Destruction'.

Without a knowledge of both extra-textual calendar systems, this poem obviously loses its quality of 'actuality' for the reader. But, on the other hand, such knowledge does not constitute the content of the poem in question, but only its artistic material or, so to speak, the object being modelled.

The traditional seven-day week is modelled here as an indivisible temporal unit, where *nedelimost'* [indivisibility] is made explicit from the verbal forms *nedelia – ne delit'* ['week' – 'not to divide']. The attribute *znak semi* [sign of seven] goes back on the one hand to the seven-day composition of the traditional week and, on the other, to the older name for the week, *sedmitsa*. In return, the phrases *vkrattse dukha put'* [briefly the way of the spirit] and *nashe telo v lozhe tianet* [our body longs for bed] activate a conception of the week as being completed by a 'resurrection' [*voskresenie*: cf. *voksresen'e*, Sunday, Ed.], that is to say by the Christian sign of 'the resurrection from the dead'. Therefore *nedelia* as *vkrattse dukha put'* may be interpreted here as a model of the Christian way of life. The etymology of *ne-deli/ ne-deleniia*, as of *dolia* [fate] and *delo* [affair, 'doing'], derives from *nedelia* in its sense as lot/fate (*dolia=uchast'=sud'ba*), but also of 'labour' [*trud*] in this world. *Znak semi*, in its turn, actualises the archaic conception of the universe, of the cosmos as a seven-part structure. In this respect, *nedelia* achieves the status of a model for the cosmos.

This model is further determined by the attributes *velikana dulia* [giant's fig] and *v bukvakh nedelima* [indivisible into letters]. *Dulia*, that is also to say 'pear' [*grusha*], is the standard symbol of 'the vale of life, the vale of tears'. In Christian painting the pear is equivalent to the apple or the pomegranate held by the Child in pictures featuring the Madonna (particularly significant in this respect is the 'surrealistic' pear standing on the frame in front of the Madonna with Child in Giovanni Bellini's picture, kept in Bergamo at the Carrara Academy). *Dulia* as 'fig' or [obscene] gesture [*kukish*] is reminiscent of the Fall of man and of the expulsion from paradise. But apart from that, *dulia-kukish* in folk culture serves as an apotropaic gesture – for the averting of evil powers (in this instance it is the equivalent of the 'knot', the 'tying up', called upon to preserve the integrity of an object or the justice of a trial).

*Velikan* [giant] in this context is undoubtedly the Creator of this world and 'week' is his creation, in other words the whole world of creatures. *Bukva* [letter] is 'the law'. Here, of course, this is God's Law, directing in particular man to labour by the sweat of his brow and keep holy the seventh day (the Sabbath in the biblical-Judaic system), repeating by this the act of creation of the world and the cessation of all activities on the seventh day. Therefore in the final line of the first verse, '*nashe telo v lozhe tianet*' [our body longs for / is drawn to / bed] reads like a return to the primeval state of the world, and as 'death', which presupposes resurrection [*voskresenie/voskresen'e*] to [in?] that other world, forfeited by man in the dim past (and, in the biblical context, to Abraham's bosom).

'We' [*my*] in Kharms are weighed down by this model of '*nedelia-mir*' and the word 'we' introduces a new model, dividing the previous cosmos into temporal units of four-days plus one day off. '*Sunduchok v chetyre dnia*' [a little trunk in four days], with its 'four', refers to another four-part model of the world, one which correlates above all with the earthly world, with its earthly organisation, and also with 'death'. *Sunduchok* [trunk or box] in itself is a repetition of the symbolism of 'four'. In Kharms's own story 'Sunduk' ['The Trunk'] (*Polët*, pp. 363–4; *Plummeting*, pp. 15–16) *sunduk* represents death, and the disappearance of the trunk proves to be a triumph over death ('So, life has triumphed over death by means unknown to me'). But, apart from the meaning of coffin, *sunduchok* in the poem under discussion is loaded too with the meaning of mobility and wandering which is then verbalised in motifs of time displaced, its *is-* and *vytekanie* [expiry, running out] and its 'inexorability-ruthlessness' [*neumolimost'-besposhchadnost'*] ('*stalo vremia tech' neumolimo*', with the latent presence of a link with *molit'/molitva*, and '*Nedelia – v put' letit kak pulia*', with its repetition of *PUt'/PUlia*, by which *put'* announces 'killing' and thereby activates the ancient mythologeme of 'road-way = place of death').

*Sunduchok* as a sign of 'wandering' results in the last verse in the meaning '*utrata/poteria*' [loss] ('*Ura, korotkaia nedelia, ty vsë utratila!*'), and *pulia* takes on the sense of 'destruction' ('*I teper' mozhno pristupit' k sleduiushchemu razrusheniiu*') [see translation included in Fleishman above, Ed.].

If *nedelia* in the first model presupposed 'resurrection', a second birth through earthly death, then in the second model, the four-part one, the result is the opposite: *sleduiushchee razrushenie* or 'second death', which is unambiguously connected with the second – definitive – death of the Apocalypse (cf. the correspondence of the first and last models of the poem with the first and last books of the Bible, i.e. with Genesis and Revelation).

The repetition of '*Nedelia – velikana dulia*' in the fourth verse may now be read not only in its *kukish* gesture sense, but in the wider context as 'the laughter of the Lord' (cf. the motif of laughter in the Book of Job, 8:21; 22:19). The earlier 'seven', now substituted by the number 'five', and *znak* by *znachok*, is no less than the change from macrocosm to microcosm, God to man (the number 'five' is widely known in European symbolism to stand for man). 'Man' becomes a measure of things and the world in this model: '*novaia nedelia / stala razumom delima, / kak ladon' iz piati pal'tsev*' and '*Tak my stroim vremia schët / Po zakonu nashikh tel. / ... dlia udobstva nashikh del'*. Now the previous *bukva* is changed to *pal'tsy*, behest is now 'by the law of bodies', and *dukh* has become *razum*, but this 'reason' is no longer the *dikaia volia* (= *vol'naia volia*, or completely free will) of biblical man, but mockery: the day of rest is no longer a day of respect for the Creator, but a 'day of free jokes'. Thus the division of the established world order ominously turns, with the downfall of the world, its *razrushenie* and non-existence, into a 'second death' (cf. Book of Revelation, 2:11, 20:6, 20:13–15).

*Translated by Neil Cornwell*

## REFERENCES

S. I. Seleshnikov, 1977: *Istoriia kalendaria i khronologiia*. 3rd edition. Moscow.

L. Fleishman, 1987: See Fleishman's article translated above (first published in Russian 1987).

# 13 Daniil Kharms's Poetic System: Text, Context, Intertext
## Nina Perlina

Now that the legacy of the OBERIU group has been published and with it a whole body of memoir and research literature on the authors Vvedensky, Oleinikov, Vaginov, Zabolotsky, Kharms and their writings, we have come to realise that it is fruitless to approach their literature by reducing *zaum'* to mere nonsense and by denying that there is a system of aesthetically organised poetics in the intentional alogicality of their writings.[1] Recent research has paved the way to a study of the structure and poetics of the absurd, the philosophy of *zaum'*, or, to use Kharms's own precise though cunning definition, the system of 'third cis-finitum logic' i.e. logic which is finite in this world.[2]

The most typical and most constant features of Kharms's poetics can be summarised into three obvious characteristics:

(1) An extremely close tie between his works and the cultural context;
(2) A re-arrangement of the normal components of the context, an intentional violation of its aesthetic, logical, and causal associations, and a re-creation of the contextual whole according to a new and previously undetermined model;
(3) A rejection of causal motivations and of the hierarchical submission of different text-elements, both in relation to each other and in relation to the surrounding context, i.e. the conscious and consistent substitution of synchrony for diachrony on all levels of the text.

In Kharms's poems, paraphrases of the Gospels, allusions to Biblical texts and poetic versions of them coexist on an equal footing with travesties of nursery lullabies and children's counting songs. In the extremely condensed verbal space of his texts we find an abundance of hidden quotations from Goethe and the Russian

Goetheans, allusions to Russian and European Romanticism, direct, parodied or re-emphasised quotations from Pushkin, Dostoevsky and the Russian Symbolists.[3] The close ties in Kharms's writing with the poetics of Khlebnikov and the numerous references to the works of his fellow Oberiuty are just as obvious.[4] No less significant are the references to a wide aesthetic, cultural, historical, scientific and philosophical context: to painting, the theatre, to art history, and to the philosophy and theory of the humanities. Commentators have more than once pointed out that in Kharms's writings we can detect rejoinders from undeveloped dialogues with the philosopher Druskin, and that the titles of his poems refer explicitly or implicitly to the history of science and of philosophy.[5] The *zaum'* of the Oberiuty is a profoundly cultural poetic phenomenon steeped in intellectual associations. *Zaum'* is not a poetic imitation of nonsense language, but a meta-reasoning, a meta-logic (in the same way that metaphysics is not a repudiation of physics and meta-poetics is not a rejection of poetics).

The new correlation between text and context, which Daniil Kharms and his friends are responsible for, weakens the sense of the poetic subtext. Because their texts are charged with allusions, and because they consciously overlook the hierarchy of poetic values, the key words are *a priori* made equal to all other semantic components of the text. So either all the words in the poem can be understood as signal-words and the poem itself as a coded text, or the weakening of the semantic and syntagmatic role of the subtext is compensated for by the appearance of a new, additional element in the poetic system. This crucial shift in the text-subtext-context correlation, and the expansion of the extra-textual poetic, cultural and historical space in which Kharms's works function, prompts us to introduce the notion of intertext as a new element.

Kharms's poetic system apparently takes its bearings not only from the broad cultural, aesthetic and historical context (a space which has already been spiritually, ideologically and aesthetically interpreted and diachronically organised), but also from the intertext. By intertext we mean a conglomerate of internally diverse phenomena, not ordered hierarchically but separately dispersed in time and space, which represents a kind of 'rough draft of culture' or cultural synchrony. To borrow the terminology from Viktor Vinogradov's formalist works, we might say that the relationship of context to intertext is similar to that between poetic language and the national lexicon. Like poetic language, context is a specially selected and hierarchically organised system which has been projected on to the broad unstructured background of the intertext, or lexicon. The difference between intertext and context can also be looked at as the difference between what is unacknowledged and what is acknowledged, or as material needing to be organised, recorded and interpreted is to be distinguished from material which has already been interpreted, organised and memorised.

Granted this provisional definition of intertext is accepted, we can further argue that the essence of Kharms's poetic innovations lies in his translation of intertext into context, and the subsequent introduction of re-accentuated, semantically enriched and restructured discrete elements of the cultural chaos into the poetically organised structure, i.e. into the texts of his poems. The fact that OBERIU texts relate to the intertext does not preclude relationships between text and context (or cultural memory); rather it makes these connections freer. Since a poetic text is structurally organised, while the intertext is a discrete category manifesting synchronicity, any element of a text, i.e. of an organised structure, can be associated with the intertext either through causal relationships and logico-semantic poetic associations (i.e. the extrapolation of the principle of poetic structure on to the intertext), or through external comparisons, alogical and non-logical juxtapositions (i.e. the interpolation of free discrete components into the poetic structure). The links between text and intertext enrich the semantic significance of the elements that make up the poetic utterance, since, by analogy with the separate components of the intertext, the elements of the text acquire new, supplementary semantic meanings.

The connections which introduce elements of the intertext into the text reorganise the free elements into polysemic, structured semantic complexes and broaden the syntagmatic potentialities of the poetic text. Yet this reorientation towards structuredness is a-causal,[6] for it is based on external analogies and not on relationships of causality. The connections which are directed into the text from without semanticise the chance associations between the elements coming from outside the text and the elements already there. As a result, within the text, rhythmico-acoustic similarities come to seem like semantically significant complexes: Konstantin Vaginov made use of this principle in his programmatic *Attempts to Unite Words by means of Rhythm*.[7] These mechanical devices, for instance the repetition of one and the same sounds, acquire a quasi-semantic meaning. The sound-meaning transformation can be treated as analogous to glossolalia features in Khlebnikov's *korneslovie*.[8] In extreme cases lexically meaningless sound combinations are perceived as words in inverted commas, as quotations from unknown languages.[9] In many instances, however, the systematisation of binary links between text and intertext would be impossible without the context. The context serves as an organic barrier between text and intertext; its verbal fabrics, however, consist of the same material as the material of the text and intertext (the language and meaning of the text, the language and meaning of the texts which form part of the context, the language and meaning of the isolated texts which still dwell in the intertext and have not yet been drawn into contextual associations).

In the works of the Oberiuty, the contact between text and intertext took place through the laws of aesthetics, of form, of history and so on; the members of the group took these laws in one way or another from the surrounding culture (i.e. the context) and then modified them each in his own way for his own poetic practice. We can identify several clusters of such contextual influences. The elements of the context, like the intertext, penetrated the OBERIU writings from the outside and fused organically with the poetic text. The intertext and material from the context were processed and absorbed in accordance with linguistic and aesthetic laws formulated within the context. For instance in Vaginov's ironic tone we can readily detect a parody of Shklovsky's ideas about collage and the novella of incidents both on the level of the plot of his novel and as an element of its architectonics, i.e. its poetics.[10] The parodic reproduction of the 'material' and the 'text' of writings by the hero, Svistonov, is presented in full accord with the ideas of the Formalist theorists, Shklovsky and Tynianov. Kharms's and Vvedensky's theory of *zaum'* is to a large extent a derivation of the ideas about 'inner form', the 'self-valuable word', and the 'resurrection of the word' (i.e. the poetic innovations and theoretical observations of Khlebnikov, Shklovsky and Kruchënykh, combined with Potebnia's ideas).[11] The artistic practice of Kharms, Vvedensky and, as Lazar Fleishman suggests, of Oleinikov, also echoes some of the ideas of Marr's linguistic theories.[12] Particularly important are Marr's theory of the four elements *sal, ber, rosh, ion*, which he thought were the universal generative models of language and the semantic matrices to be discovered in the substratum of any language, and also his theory of 'hand or kinetic speech', i.e. the system of social communication which is realised first by gesture and body movement, and only later by acoustic signals, or words.

The OBERIU writers, and Kharms and Zabolotsky more than the others, were drawn to discreteness and synchronicity: they loved juxtaposing heterogeneous components. This is why they could combine elements from profoundly heterogeneous, disparate and antagonistic individual and cultural contexts in their poetry and system of imagery. For instance Kharms's notion of the mythologeme parodied some of Pëtr Bogatyrëv's ethnographical and folkloristic discoveries about magic actions, incantations, and divination which were accompanied by various intelligible and unintelligible verbal formulae. Bogatyrëv is well-known as one of the initiators of the synchronic (static) approach to the study of ethnographic and folklore facts. On the other hand, the poetic semantics of the mythologeme in Kharms's writings can well be compared with Olga Freidenberg's proposed explanations for the semantics of metaphor in ritual actions and folklore plots, and she was a stalwart supporter of the idea of diachrony in all her researches into the field of culture.[13] As regards theory of literature, by the end of the 1920s and beginning of the 1930s it had become unthinkable to combine the synchronic with the diachronic method (Bogatyrëv wrote a masterly polemic on this subject).[14] As regards poetic practice neither Kharms, nor Oleinikov, nor Zabolotsky, nor Vvedensky had the least difficulty in combining and juxtaposing the uncombinable.

We must stress that artistic eclecticism was alien to all the Oberiuty, and that for all their writings, both literary and theoretical, the principle of synchrony was the determining and dominant one. One of the points of the OBERIU programme was to relate notions of 'reality' and 'the real' to synchrony, and to attempt to make sense of this philosophical category as a 'confrontation of verbal meanings'.[15] All Kharms's provocative innovations which so shocked the public, like using several acting areas (the stage, the top of a wardrobe, and a town crossroads) in one and the same play can be explained by his intense interest in the real and multifarious manifestations of synchrony.[16] The stress the Oberiuty laid on notions of 'the whole as an aggregate' and on 'the unpredetermined sequence of units'[17] explain their aesthetic predilections and tastes (their attraction to Meyerhold's stage principles, according to which each production should present the whole of Gogol, the whole of Griboedov and not just one particular play; their working contacts with the artists

Malevich and Filonov). To an even greater extent this stress is felt in their own writings:

> We are expanding the meaning of object, word and action. This work advances in different directions, each one of us has his own artistic persona ... Each one of us knows himself and each one of us knows how he is linked with the others.[18]

On the theoretical level this self-definition by the OBERIU is extremely important. It is implicitly suggesting that their constant reminiscences and borrowings from each other's work are made according to principles which, in the nineteenth and early twentieth centuries, had played no part in literature: such borrowings occurred only within the narrow domain of personally-exchanged poetic epistles not intended for publication; or, if they did occur in literature, then they were carefully concealed by the authors themselves. For instance, Kharms's numerous reminiscences and paraphrases from Zabolotsky's poetry are important not as quotations, but as components of 'a new feeling about life and its objects' (a point promulgated in the manifesto). This is why in Kharms's poem 'A Solitary Beduin, looking at the Flying Sand' (*'Odinokii beduin, gliadia na letiashchii pesok'*) we find an obvious imitation of Zabolotsky's poetic lexis and style:

> Ptichka tam v pesok popala,/ vverkh zhivotikom lezhit,
> Ptichka bednaia propala,/ dazhe kon' moi ne gliadit.
> [The little bird has fallen there in the sand/
> it is lying with its little stomach up.
> The poor little bird is dead,
> even my horse is not looking.] (*Sob. proizv.*, II, p. 20)

but this coexists with poetic inversions from Pushkin's poem 'Devils' (*'Besy'*) which are introduced into the poetic text from the zone of the intertext on the principle of a-causality. Kharms has: *'Von pesok letit, araby,/ochi nam zasypet on'* ['There the sand is flying, Arabs/ it will cover our eyes'], and Pushkin has: *'Mchatsia tuchi, v'iutsia tuchi, .. V'iuga mne slipaet ochi'* ['Clouds are rushing, clouds are whirling .. The blizzard is sticking up my eyes']. Kharms has 'a choir of Beduin and archangels', Pushkin has the song of the devils.[19]

In classical Russian literature and culture of the nineteenth century this kind of overlapping and borrowing would have been unthinkable. Even Pushkin's glaring self-quotation from the *Gavriliada* in the first canto of *Eugene Onegin*: *I derzost'yu nevinnost' izumlyat'*;

*Shutya nevinnost' izumlyat'* ['To astound innocence with an impertinence', 'to astound innocence with a joke'] passed unnoticed by even his closest contemporaries in spite of the similarity of the intratextual situations. No less glaring is the word-by-word coincidence in the description of the emotional state of the two heroines: Karamzin's Natalia from his tale 'Natal'ia, the boyar's daughter', and Pushkin's Tatiana from *Eugene Onegin*. Unlike the Kharms-Zabolotsky situation, where what is common is a similar sequence of poetic associations and not literal quotations, we find in Pushkin word for word similarity with Karamzin's text: in Karamzin's story the old nurse calls Natalia 'her little early bird' (cf. in *Eugene Onegin* 'O my little early bird'), Karamzin says of his heroine that 'her heart fluttered and said: "It is he"' (cf. in *Eugene Onegin*: 'She said: "It is he"'). Yet there is no conclusive evidence that Karamzin's tale forms part of the poetic subtext to Pushkin's novel in verse, *Eugene Onegin*.[20]

So the essential distinguishing mark of OBERIU poetics, and one which the members of the group insisted on as their own innovation, was the freedom to make literary associations on many levels and to organise them on a synchronic principle. On the level of culture and aesthetics this innovation led them to break down the normal relationships between poetic text, subtext and context, and to have recourse to the broad and totally unlimited zone of the intertext. The Oberiuty, being members of a literary movement of the 1920s, rather sensed the consequence of their innovations intuitively, than gave it theoretical formulation. Yet it is the recourse which their poetic texts make to the broad intertextual space, and the different ways they had of translating elements of context and intertext into an artistic text which most clearly shows up the poetic individuality of each of these writers.

Our analysis of five of Daniil Kharms's poems, which follows, aims to test the validity of our proposed ideas about the nature of the binary two-way correlations of text/context and of text/intertext, and about the restructuring of the diachronic order into the synchronic. The end result of these restructurings was the new programmatic idea of the Oberiuty about poetry as such and about the poetics of the individual poetic text. Instead of creating a closed, self-sufficient poetic whole, Kharms concentrated his attention on 'the confrontation of several objects and the interrelationships between them'. Kharms himself later defined his attitude to the poetic text:

at the moment of action an object takes on new concrete outlines full of real meaning. The action, though changed into a new key, preserves its 'classical' imprint and at the same time represents the wide open space of the OBERIU feeling for the world.[21]

In other words, as the fragmentation of the individual text increases, the linkages between the poetic whole and the external contextual space and the intertext intensifies. On the one hand, Kharms often deliberately emphasised the fragmentary character of his verses by the expressive finality of the ending 'that's all' [*vsë*]. On the other hand, since he consciously built his poetics on the 'confrontation of several objects and the interrelationships between them', the multiplicity of fragments increased the possibility of confrontations, correlations and contacts between the text and the cultural-aesthetic space set outside it. The poems (Nos 89 ['There lived a miller' of 13 January 1930], 120 ['He and the mill/eress' of 26–28 December 1930], as well as Nos 121 ['The vitalist and Ivan Struchkov'], 164 ['*AnDor*'], 204 ['*Ohne mel'nitsa*'] and 220 ['Where the mill is there are the rapids']) have been chosen to illustrate the theoretical ideas outlined above.

Commentators have pointed out the wide and deliberately unharmonised range of associations in poems Nos 89 and 120.[22] In poem No 89 the daughter of the miller is called Agnessa, a name which has associations with several unconnected cultural spheres. A West European name from the point of view of onomastics, it is also, according to the laws of folk etymology, and because of its phonetic assonances which are supported by the rhythm and rhyme, a homomorph to words with the root *ogon'* (fire): Agnessa-'Ognessa' (see the line 'her pupils shine like fires' [*eë zrachki blestiat ogniami*]). Like other legendary forest dwellers, she is a sorceress, and the text of the poem thus draws in a large contextual and intertextual element of Slavonic folklore. We can make the link between the text of Kharms's poem and folk legends about forest maidens, water-spirits and sorceresses. By rhyme and sound association, 'Agnessa ... from the depths of the woods' (*Agnessa ... iz nedr lesa*) is an allusion to Kuprin's tale *Olesia*.[23] The chain Agnessa – Olesia – sorceress, daughter of the sorcerer-miller, branches out into a cluster of semantic meanings, the threads of which lead into the zone of the intertext. There are accentuated associations with the theme of water-spirits and sorcery in works that range from Ablesimov's comic opera 'The Sorcerer-Miller, the Deceiver and the Matchmaker' (see the line: 'and the miller is happy. He is a sorcerer' [*i mel'nik schastliv. On koldun*]) to Pushkin, Gogol, Ukrainian and European folk music and songs and their Romantic interpretation (Schubert's song-cycle *Die schöne Müllerin*). The metonymic series: the mill – the sails of the mill – the winged miller suggest an allusion to Pushkin's poem 'Rusalka', to its operatic version by Dargomyzhsky and to the legendary renown of Chaliapine in the role of the raven-miller (lines 17–20 of Kharms's poem: 'ah if only the wind would suddenly blow/ and the mill-sails turned/ then priest Agnessa and the gossip/ would fly together on the roof of the mill. .'). The European connotations of the heroine's name make it possible to relate lines 10–11 ('Agnessa plants a bean in the miller's Adam's apple in the morning') to the Western tradition of carnival eroticism and sorcery (the bean as a carnival sexual symbol: the Bean King, divination with beans). The rhythmic pattern and lexis of lines 12–14 ('Agnessa growls. The miller leapt/ but the priest comes through the door./ Long Agnessa sits down') prompts the association with the tale of 'The Priest and his Servant Balda' and with Pushkin's folk ballad 'The Bridegroom' (this would explain the tendency towards ballad metre and the thematically undeveloped scenes of marriage-making and of revenge on the miller for his cruelty in lines 6, 16).

This far from complete analysis of one of Kharms's poems is enough to show that traditional poetic theories cannot cope with such an overload of cultural and aesthetic associations, which was one of the points of the OBERIU programme they put into practice. Kharms's poetic system is a stable one precisely because in conditions of synchrony the poetic linkages remain free and in a double sense not obligatory.

First of all because, for an adequate understanding of the poem, there is no need to resurrect the *entire* network of associations; and secondly because, if they are resurrected, the allusions and poetic associations do not disrupt the architectonics of the text and do not turn the artistic structure into chaos. Quite the contrary: the text-intertext and text-context relationships give an added semantic significance to the utterances and word-combinations which would have no meaning if they were taken in isolation.

The heroine of the poem 'He and the Mill/eress' (*On i mel'nitsa*) is, as commentators have remarked, both the *water-mill* (*mel'nitsa*), i.e. a mechanical apparatus, and a milleress, in this case the *miller's daughter* [*mel'nitsa*] (*Sob. proizv.*, II, 197) (in the latter case the word, a neologism, is formed by analogy with lexico-morphological models such as *umnik/umnitsa* [clever man/clever woman]). The combination of a nominal lexical meaning with a newly acquired one generates, through poetic semanticisation, a cluster of absurd ambivalent combinations: to grind [*molot'*] grain is useful work done by the mill-stones; to chatter [*molot' iazykom*] is a useless empty pastime (see the hero's response in line 16: 'no point, no point' [*zria, zria*]). Because we cannot distinguish the semantic meanings 'woman'/'machine' in the word *mel'nitsa*, or 'to work productively'/ 'to work with the tongue' in the word *molot'*, we can semanticise several subsequent absurd utterances:

THE MILL/ERESS: The noise of the water has taken away my memory.
HE: I see the path of the iron horse-tram (lines 3–4).

It is obviously absurd to look for the tracks of a horse-tram by the banks of a river. But in the arsenal of Russian folk proverbs are several such combinations which have the general theme of nonsense and absurdity: 'Where the horse goes with its hoof, there goes the crayfish with its claw'. The verbal level of the proverb which associates the idea of the river with a horse trail is paradoxically preserved in the text of Kharms's poem. Once more we must stress that on the level of text-subtext-context such associations are unthinkable. But on the level text-intertext they are an extravagant surprise and prepare a chain of new semantic and syntagmatic, i.e. inter-generic, transformations. From one implicitly assumed folk proverb the thread leads on further to lines 6–7:

THE MILL/ERESS: Under the lime tree.
There even my father broke his leg.

(cf. 'the devil will break his leg'). And since the father with the broken leg is still the same miller, the fairytale wizard and forest dweller, the phrase 'under the lime tree' would seem to be a reminiscence of the Russian tale of the bear with the limewood leg.[24]

The dialogue in the poem 'He and the Mill/eress' ('MILL/ERESS: O yes, he is teaching the cows the alphabet/HE: Why teach creatures/ signs?/ Who is the dawn of wisdom for creatures?/MILL/ERESS: A reading primer./ HE: No point, no point') is a variation on the shocking themes in Zabolotsky's long poem 'The Triumph of Agriculture'. Kharms repeats Zabolotsky's typical motifs of a neo-vitalist Utopia sustained in grotesquely emotional tones:

Take heart, wise cows...
Here we shall build you shelters
With great bowls of flour...
We'll completely do away with the old world
And in a great chorus we will pronounce
the letter A for the first time.[25]

Other reminiscences of the theme of neo-vitalism are to be found in lines 25–30 ('In the moth/and even in the fly/ there are various vessels/ disposed in the ear/on the back of the head...') and also in the exchanges of lines 33–4 which at first glance seem to be absurd ('What's that sticking out of your boots?/ Bean pods [*struchki*]'). These lines relate to the poem 'The vitalist and Ivan *Struchkov*' which was written on the same day as 'He and the Mill/eress' (*Sob. proizv.*, II, 86 and 198). From the biographical point of view, i.e. in the zone of the cultural context and intertext, Kharms's interest in vitalism derives from his passion for Goethe, and can be explained by the fact that he knew N. O. Lossky's philosophical brochure *Contemporary Vitalism* (1922) and was interested in the polemics between the adherents of philosophical materialism and scientific materialism which came to a head at the end of the twenties. The brochure *Vitalism, Mechanical Materialism and Marxism* published in 1930 by I. Agol, who was president of the Society of Militant Atheists, played a part in these debates which were memorable for the violence of their tone.[26]

Through their connections with discrete, unorganised and logically incompatible zones of the intertext, lines 17–24, 31–2, 36–8 acquire added ambivalent semantic connotations (lines 17–24: MILL/ ERESS: Lift the moth to your glasses. Are you short-sighted? HE: Very. I see among a thousand objects... MILL/ERESS: Excuse me, among how many? HE: Among a thousand objects only very large things. Lines 31–2: HE: Wait, my pupils are covered in sweat. Lines 36–38: HE: Hey you! My frames have cracked! MILL/ERESS: I'll tell you: the eye is not given to us for all kinds of amusements). It is traditional for the word 'shortsightedness' to have the meanings both of 'poor vision' and 'lack of foresight, stupidity'. But in the late twenties the expression 'shortsightedness, lack of foresight' had, in the language of the press, an ominous connotation of political threat. At the same time the word 'glasses', which traditionally from the time of the Middle Ages connoted stupidity, became in the slang of illiterate Soviet citizens a metonymy for an intellectual of the old days: 'still wearing glasses, still wearing a hat'.

The hero's exclamation in line 42: 'I've gone blind' can be interpreted in three ways: he has gone blind because his pupils are covered in sweat (metonymically his eyes like his glasses imply his stupidity), and because 'his frames have cracked' (still wearing glasses!), and he is blind from lust.

In 1931 Kharms wrote two more poems about a mill: Nos 204 and 210. No 204 entitled '*Ohne mel'nitsa*' ('Ohne mill/eress') was written on the same page of the notebook as '*AnDor*' (No 164) (*Sob. proizv.*, III, 81, 97, 11, 210). Both titles use the device of borrowing a word from another language and then adapting this foreign sound-complex to Russian lexis. This is a case when the relationship of the text to the intertext is glaringly apparent. We might term this device a play with folk etymology or with what is known to be a false etymology. '*Ohne mel'nitsa*', i.e. in German 'without a mel'nitsa' sounds in spoken Russian like '*on-i-mel'nitsa*' (the title of No 120, discussed above). The seemingly senseless '*AnDor*' can be interpreted by analogy with the German *ander* (other), (ibid., III, 165–6) even though the assonance is not a perfect one.

The analysis of poem No 164 which we propose illustrates an instance when a lexically empty sound-complex is semanticised as it revolves between text and intertext. Each new contact of the *zaum'* word with the intertext evidently adds additional logico-semantic and poetic meanings to its sound matter. To start with we must agree with the proposed etymology of '*AnDor*' from the German word for 'other'. But since the first part of the poem (lines 1–21) concerns a game with a ball, most likely either the village game of *lapta* or football (lines 19–21: 'the red one jumps round with his hands claps the airborne blue one at the goal-post'), the title AnDor can be etymologically related to the German *An Tor* (at the goal-post). This interpretation accords also with the graphic representation of the *zaum'* word with the capital letter in the middle and also with the presence in the text of the word *kalitka*, a synonym of goal.

The second half of the poem (lines 22–40) differs from the first both rhythmically and thematically. Instead of the fun and animation of a game, joyfulness, and time that passes swiftly, there is a slowing down of the tempo, and sleepy immobility: 'Then quite the opposite/ he lies down in the palace [*dvorets*] /and slowly groans' (lines 22/24). The word *dvorets*, which nominally refers to the residence of an important person, a tsar, tsarevna or prince, paradoxically preserves the connotation not of a court-retinue, but of a court-space beyond the gates [*dvor* means yard or courtyard, trans.]. The word 'magical' (*volshebnyi*), which is many times repeated in different combinations (lines 31, 32, 33, 34, 35, 36, 37 [twice], 38, 39), establishes firm associations with the context of the fairytale, mystery, mystery story: the 'magic night' (lines 31, 32) is the quintessence of a folklore and a Romantic mythologeme; the 'magic cat' (line 34) refers us to Hoffmann and the world of sorcery; the 'magic old man' (line 34), the 'magic yardman' (line 35) are the guard at the magic doors or enchanted gates; the 'magic fircone' is the magic seed of fairytales; there are also the 'magic horse' with its 'magic bridle' (line 37), the 'magic bird' and 'magic flower' and the 'magic singing' (lines 38–39) etc. But under the paradigmatic pressure of the magic mythologeme we can glimpse an allusion to a Biblical text: 'So [Saul] said to his servants, "Find a woman who has a familiar spirit, and I will go and enquire through her". They told him there was such a woman at En-dor' (1 Samuel 28.7). On the text-intertext level there is a connection between the magic of fairy-tale beings and objects and the witch of En-dor. But, once arisen, the correlation of text and intertext is applied to the whole poem, including the title, and implicitly prompts one more semantic interpretation, namely that AnDor is En-dor. This last interpretation is the most convincing since from the geographical description of Biblical places we know that En-dor (the source Dor) is a village in Palestine not far from the town of Tabor. If the *zaum'* word AnDor is raised to this etymological model then its graphics can be explained and its mythological meaning brought out.

In this way as a result of repeated revolutions between text and intertext the lexically indeterminate sound-complex acquires polysemy in which we can find a dominant and a marginal 'lexical meaning'. The reconstruction of the semantics and etymology of the lexeme AnDor which does not exist in Russian can be envisioned as follows:

AnDor – *ander* ('other')
AnDor – *an Tor* ('at the gates/goal'), on the boundary of this space and *the other* space
AnDor – En-dor (the source Dor), the village where Saul conjured up the ghost of Samuel who appeared to him from *the other* world.

Of course we must never forget when discussing Kharms's poetics how strong the play principle is in his practice. His experiments with the structural organisation and semanticisation of *zaum'* constantly come up against his desire to 'shake the dictionary' (ibid., III, 167). In this antinomic paradoxality – enriching the dictionary by shaking it – lay the innovatory, creative element of his play. In the immediate context, Kharms's playful poetic practice found its back-up in various philological theories.

We can reconstruct historical semantics and mythologemes such as 'AnDor – En-dor' without going into the extremes of theories such as Olga Freidenberg's or Marr's. Freidenberg's theory, when applied to Kharms's poetic practice, can suggest historical roots for *zaum'* lexemes and discover the mythopoetic genesis of *zaum'*. Followers of Bakhtin's ideas about heteroglossia and carnival ambivalence will be attracted by the playful reaccentuation and the travestied forms of another's language in one's own: AnDor – *an Tor* – En-dor, or *ohne mel'nitsa – on-i-mel'nitsa*.

A final point: we remarked above that Kharms was acquainted with the theories of neo-vitalism, hylozoizm, and intuitivism, which leads us to conclude that he shared Bergson's conception of culture, creative evolution and cultural memory.[27] The foundation of Bergson's philosophy and aesthetics was the principle of the juxtaposition and correlation of elements, in other words, the consistent reorganisation of diachrony into synchrony. The central concept of Bergson's intuitivism, 'memory of the future', could not have failed to have attracted the attention of Kharms and his friends, both on account of its philosophical content and as a striking oxymoron. The idea of the present as an ungraspable, unfixed category which merely makes possible the realisation of the past in the future, and the notion of the discrete in the really developing open and incomplete process of life, wholly accorded with the programmatic pronouncements and poetic practice of the Oberiuty.

*Translated by Ann Shukman*

NOTES

1. Quotations from the writings of the OBERIU group are from the following editions: Daniil Kharms, *Sob. proizv.*, I–IV; K. Vaginov, *Sobranie stikhotvorenii* ed. L. Chertkov, preface W. Kazack (Munich: Otto Sagner, 1982); id., *Trudy i dni Svistonova* (Leningrad, 1929); Aleksandr Vvedenskii, Vved., I–II; N. Zabolotskii, *Izbrannye proizvedeniia v dvukh tomakh* (Moscow, 1972); Oleinikov, 1975.

2. *Sob. proizv.*, II: 43–4 (No 105), II: 45 (No 106), II: 177–8. See Nakhimovsky, 1982, 44–60: the illustrations she provides of Kharms's violations of the lexical, grammatical, and lexico-semantic norms of Russian are convincing; her conclusion that the 'meaning' in Kharms's poetic lexicon is an implicitly assumed fictive value (p. 55) needs further explication. See also Stoimenoff, 1984, 32, 45–55. The author proposes a complex analysis of *zaum'* which takes account among other things of the stanzaic, rhythmical, and lexico-stylistic combinations and speaks of the changing perspective and unmotivated emotional stoppages within a single poetic text.
3. See, for example, '*Zloe sobranie nevernykh*', *Sob. proizv.*, II, 24, a text of twelve lines which includes paraphrases from the Bible (Psalm 1.1, Matthew 26.11), a word-for-word quotation from Matthew 26.22, an allusion to Pushkin's *Mozart and Salieri*, to a painting by Leonardo da Vinci (details of 'The Last Supper' which make up the level of description), and a semantic neologism, typical of Kharms, created according to Khlebnikov's *korneslovie* model (lines 10, 12): *Odin umyë, drugoi TUpitsa, tretii gLUP ... Ia TULUP* ['One is clever, another is a blockhead, a third is stupid ... I'm a sheepskin coat'].
4. Fleishman, 1975, p. 3. V. P. Grigor'ev's books propose a methodology for studying the poetic language and lexis of Khlebnikov: *Grammatika idiostilia Velemira Khlebnikova* (Moscow, 1983) pp. 83–119; and, *Slovotvorchestvo i smezhnye problemy iazyka poeta* (Moscow, 1986) pp. 85–124. Khlebnikov's principle of word-creation (more than 50 'languages', more than 20 'principles' – i.e. in Grigor'ev's definition, philosophical metalinguistic concepts) had an important influence on the OBERIU's declared thesis of 'widening the confines of object and word'. But the Oberiuty did not share Khlebnikov's systematic and all-rounded realisations of phonetic, etymological, lexicographical, historical and mytho-poetic 'principles'.
5. Fleishman, op. cit., traces the line linking the poetry of the Oberiuty with that of Khlebnikov and Pasternak and remarks on the interest shown by the Oberiuty in modern philosophical, linguistic and aesthetic theories. See also Meilakh, introduction to Vved. I, xiv; Darra Goldstein, 'Zabolotskii and Filonov' (forthcoming in *Slavic Review*); and her monograph, *Play for Mortal Stakes: The Life and Long Poems of Nikolai Zabolotsky* (in press).
6. The term is taken from O. M. Freidenberg, *Poetika siuzheta i zhanra: Period antichnoi literatury* (Leningrad, 1936), pp. 20–33, 224–55. The notion of a-causality assumes that the imagery-principle and the concept-principle in the verbal utterance are fused and inseparable, and that the idea of the world when all its component elements were held to be contiguous but not causally interrelated, has been preserved as a kind of cultural experience. Freidenberg, for instance, explained the poetic formula 'grey-bearded old man' used in the ancient Greek epics to refer to the sea not by a causal linkage (as the face of old man Neptune the sea-god is covered with a curly grey beard, so the surface [the face] of the sea is covered with a grey beard of waves). In the Homeric tradition this representation of the sea came about by a

juxtaposition of the idea of the sea, his element, which by contiguity acquired all the emblematic features of the divinity. Freidenberg's folklore theory is an effective method for the interpretation of many of Kharms's poetic innovations.

7. Vaginov, *Sobranie stikhotvorenii*, 119–175. See also, in *Sob. proizv.*, II, 194–5, the editors' reference to the description of the 'zaumniki' in Vaginov's *Kozlinaia pesnia* (Leningrad, 1928) p. 97.
8. Khlebnikov's theory of 'personal language' as 'subjective' language involved sound-patterning, *zaum'* and the 'language of the gods', i.e. the unconscious longing of people and gods for a single means of communication. See, V. Grigor'ev, 'Voobrazhaemaia filologiia Velemira Khlebnikova' in *Stilistika khudozhestvennoi rechi*, ed. S. G. Barkhudarov (Kalinin, 1982) p. 34.
9. The mechanics of this sort of intratextual semanticisation can be explained by using Uspenskii's approach. See his 'Grammaticheskaia pravil'nost' i ponimanie', in *Mezhvuzovskaia konferentsiia po porozhdaiushchim grammatikam* (Tartu, 1967) pp. 101–6.
10. Vaginov, *Trudy i dni Svistonova*, 5–21, 141–51. On this see Perlina, 'K. Vaginov', in *Histoire de la littérature russe*, eds. Efim Etkind and Georges Nivat (Paris: Fayard, 1986) vol. 4.
11. On the evolution of the notion of *zaum'* among the zaumniki poets, and on the various ways of interpreting 'the word as such', see Fleishman, 1975, 4–9.
12. Among N. Ia. Marr's works we should point to his article 'Why it is so difficult to become a theoretical linguist', *Iazykovedenie i materializm* (Leningrad: 1929) pp. 1–56. The question whether Kharms knew of the Japhetic theory has not been studied. On a superficial level the coincidence is striking. Most likely the travestied representation of the ancient Egyptian pantheon in 'Lapa' (*Sob. proizv.*, II, 87–108) originates in Marr's famous article 'Ishtar (from the goddess of matriarchal Afreurasia to the love-heroine of feudal Europe)' *Iafeticheskii sbornik*, 5 (1926) 109–178. If we are making comparisons we should also note the Japhetological definition of symbiosis as the simultaneous coexistence of cultural experiences of different epochs and developmental stages in human thinking. O. A. Dobiash-Rozhdestvenskaia, for instance, in her article 'The cult of waters on the perifery of Gaul and the legend of the Celtic maidens', *Iafeticheskii sbornik*, 5, (1926) 128, treats symbiosis in this way: 'the symbiosis of the mountain peak, of the source and of the Mother-Goddess who, in this triple definition, was the powerful and protective divinity of the place'. Compare in Kharms the image of the woman-mill as heroine which we discuss below.
13. Compare for instance P. Bogatyrëv, 'Magic actions, rituals and beliefs of Transcarpathia', in his *Voprosy teorii narodnogo iskusstva* (Moscow, 1971, first published in French in 1929), with Freidenberg, 'The semantics of architecture of the puppet theatre', *Dekorativnoe iskusstvo*, 2 (1976) 41–4 (a fragment from her paper 'Semantics of the structure of the puppet theatre', 1926). On the theoretical differences between supporters of the synchronic and the diachronic approach,

see Nina Perlina, 'Olga Freidenberg on Myth, Folklore and Literature', *Slavic Review*, forthcoming.
14. Bogatyrëv, op. cit., 172–9.
15. The OBERIU Manifesto, in Vved., II, 243.
16. Ibid., II, 238–49. See also Meilakh, introduction, xvii, xxi–xxii.
17. Fleishman, 1975, 7.
18. Vved., II, 244.
19. A. S. Pushkin, *Polnoe sobranie sochinenii v desiati tomakh* (Leningrad, 1977) III, pp. 167–8.
20. N. M. Karamzin, *Izbrannye proizvedeniia v dvukh tomakh* (Moscow, 1964) I, 627, 632; Pushkin, op. cit., V, 63, 51 (Alexander Pushkin, *Eugene Onegin*, translated by Charles Johnston, Harmondsworth: Penguin, 1977).
21. Vved., II, 244.
22. *Sob. proizv.*, II, 195–7. Poem numbers are as in this edition.
23. A. I. Kuprin, *Sobranie sochinenii v shesti tomakh* (Moscow, 1957) II, 249–329. The heroine of Kuprin's melodramatic tale, Olesia, a beauty from Polese and a sorceress, lives concealed in the 'depths of the forest' ['*v nedrakh lesa*'] and lovingly tends the wild birds and animals.
24. The tale 'The Bear', no 57–8 in A. N. Afanas'ev, *Narodnye russkie skazki* (Moscow, 1957) I, 83–4.
25. Zabolotskii, op. cit., I, 144; Goldstein, *Play for Mortal Stakes*, chapters II and IV.
26. Meilakh in Vved. I, xiv has pointed out that the Oberiuty were familiar with Losskii's works. We can add to his evidence the fact that in 1920–1 Losskii organised a proseminar at Petrograd University on 'Materialism, hylozoizm and vitalism' and a few months before he was expelled from the Soviet Union published a brochure, *Sovremennyi vitalizm* (Petrograd, 1922). Losskii found a general philosophical basis for hylozoism and vitalism in intuitivism. His book *Intuitivnaia filosofiia Anri Bergsona* of 1911 was published in its third edition in 1922. On this see N. Losskii, *Vospominaniya* (Munich, 1968) 212. I. Agol, *Vitalism, mekhanicheskii materializm, marksizm* (Moscow, 1930) sharply criticises the ideas of the German neo-vitalist, Hans Driesch, and his Russian translator, the well-known histologist and geneticist, A. G. Gurvich.
27. In the 1910s Bergson's writings 'Creative Evolution', 'Matter and Memory' and his essay on laughter were reprinted many times in Russian. Losskii gives a summary of Bergson's intuitivist conceptions in the fourth chapter of his brochure. *The Intuitive Philosophy of Henri Bergson* (see n. 26), 42–68.

# Part V:
# The Theatrical Works

# 14 The Oberiuty and the Theatricalisation of Life
## Tat'iana Nikol'skaia

Creative lifestyle, the transformation of 'the forms of private life into a fact of art' was an integral part of OBERIU creativity.[1] The theatricality of life had played an important role in the activities of the avantgarde groups which preceded the Oberiuty – the Futurists and the Imaginists. Thus the Cubo-Futurists, in the first years of their existence, in contrast to the tinted faces of the decadents went in for daubing themselves like savages and sporting a radish or a carrot in their buttonhole rather than the dandyish chrysanthemum. For purposes of self-promotion, they arranged processions in costume around the streets; provoking scandals, they would appear at their evening performances in outlandish garb. The Imaginists attracted attention to themselves by shock tactics: sticking up notices declaring total war on other literary groups, and renaming Moscow streets in their own honour.

In the case of the Oberiuty, the theatricalisation of life was in many respects different. By their frequently preposterous outer appearance and by their absurd behaviour, they were striving not so much to shock as to perplex the public by the alogicality of what was happening, to give a twist in the public's consciousness to normal causal-investigatory notions, having exposed reality in all its illogicality. At the same time, this creative lifestyle was for the Oberiuty a 'theatre for themselves', in which not the least significant role was played by self-irony.

If among the Futurists the most consistent theatricalisers of life were V. Kamensky and 'the Futurist of life' V. Gol'tsshmidt, then in the case of the Oberiuty this role unquestionably belonged to Daniil Kharms. Everyone who knew Kharms agrees in affirming that extravagant behaviour was for him the natural norm. According to A. Poret's memoirs: 'It seemed that he consisted entirely of jokes, he did not conceive of his existence otherwise. Eccentricity was his nature and essential to him.'[2] It would be possible to put together an entire anthology of anecdotes about Kharms, covering the various sides of his creative lifesyle. We shall here detail just a few of them. V. Sterligov used to tell how Kharms appeared before the medical commission to determine fitness for military service wearing a tie and top hat, a large pectoral cross and carrying a cane, but with no other clothes on. On another occasion, Kharms strolled down the street for a bet in a rimless straw hat, a jacket without a shirt, military breeches and bedroom slippers, holding a butterfly net. During a serious conversation, Kharms would juggle with celluloid balls with aplomb and inherent artistry, even pulling them out of his mouth. When he walked along Nevsky Prospect past Troitskaia Street, he would invariably lie down for a minute on his stomach on the pavement and then, as though nothing had happened, just walk on.

A. Poret recalls how Kharms played a trick on a doctor, who had been insistently advising him that 'a bit more fresh air' was the best treatment for pneumonia. When on the appointed day the doctor arrived to visit the patient, 'the windows were stuck up tight with paper, the smell was abominable, on the patient's head was a woman's bonnet with a fringe, and unmatching gloves on his hands'. The flabbergasted and incensed doctor quickly fled the room. In reply to Poret's question as to how Kharms had managed to achieve such a stink, 'Daniil Ivanovich's face lit up and he pulled a box of old cabbage stalks from under the bed ... Then he opened the window wide and threw the box out, having already placed in it the now superfluous props, the bonnet and so on, and having painstakingly tied the whole thing up with string'.[3] Prankish preparation for a meeting with another doctor is recorded in Kharms's notebook:[4]

what to say to the doctor:
1. Pain in left wrist, palm, (ha)
2. A throttling feeling around the neck, as though trousers with brass buttons were tied round it.
3. Bruises on right and left legs.
4. Feeling as sick as if looking at a filthy beard.
5. The fleas are biting.

Such a performance given by one actor for a single spectator is reminiscent of the sketches advocated by that theorist of the theatricalisation of life, Nikolai Evreinov. If Evreinov had known Kharms, then the latter could have been the hero of his book *The Theatricality of Life*, which glorifies the poet who can achieve a complete fusion of life and creativity.[5]

Kharms was the unfailing initiator of collective pranks and games. One of these games consisted of blindfolding someone and taking them thus to the most unexpected and, as a rule, to them the most unpleasant place: 'We used to take fat people with a bad heart to St Isaac's cathedral, up the narrow staircase', recalls A. Poret, 'or we would bring dashing carousers to a retired old music teacher, to drink weak tea with her, and they would sit there, submissively sour, looking through old albums of photographs of pupils and dead relatives.'[6] A distinctive peculiarity of such amusements was that of multiple repetition. In the course of almost two years, Kharms together with Poret, kept playing on a famous organist of the city, a good friend of theirs, the trick of bringing to each of his concerts 'abandoned babies', dolls, which they would leave in the foyer of the conservatory with a note saying something like 'take care of our love-child', to be delivered to the musician.

Kharms was not only a practitioner but a theoretician of the theatricality of life. As A. Gerasimova has remarked, Kharms's treatise 'A Tract More or Less Summarising Emerson' is 'an original textbook in the art of creative lifestyle'.[7] Under the light touch of Kharms, the theatricality of life took on a programmatic purpose amid the activities of the Oberiuty. This is attested by the plans for the conducting of evenings and debates to be found in Kharms's notebooks. For example: 'For the Litfond evening ... drinking and eating on stage';[8] at a debate: 'Charcoal moustaches, eat soup';[9] at a performance: 'Eat soup. Drink violet and green liquid'.[10] Kharms planned too the propagation of 'real art' in restaurants, gaming clubs and cinemas:

> Around the Restaurants
> Coffee with cucumbers.
> Tea with eggs.
> On given signals, draw milk through a pipe.
> Seven glasses of tea for three.
> Semolina.                    Turnip
> Millet gruel.
> Herring and milk.
> Tea and carrots.
>
> ---
>
> The buffet.
> Bar.
> Fëdorov's
> The Vladimirskii club.
> The Roof.
> The Grand Palais foyer.[11]

Read the alphabet.
Black list.
Pour out from paper.
Sit with closed eyes.
Have across the shoulder an embroidered patch.
Cut up cucumbers with scissors.
Warm up one's own food.
Play tin soldiers over beer.
Tie on serviettes and feed each other.
Arrive in armour.
All three stutter.
Dark glasses.[12]

As we can see, at the core of this 'programme' are idiosyncratic mini-happenings based on minor contraventions of the generally accepted norms of behaviour, of the usual juxtaposition of associations, and on children's games. The quality of juvenility is especially underlined by the porridge [semolina, gruel], by the tying on of the serviettes, or rather bibs, and by the mutual feeding.

The theatricalised performances of the Oberiuty, with antics and happenings organically interwoven into the artistic texture along with vocal creativity, bore some resemblance to the performances of the West-European Dadaists,[13] a fact which was noted even by the Soviet press of those years.[14] Such a format to OBERIU evenings, painstakingly thought out in advance, also had points of contact with Marinetti's 'Music-Hall' manifesto, which contained an appeal for 'the destruction of logic in performances, and for the domination on the stage of the implausible and the ridiculous'.[15]

Many of Kharms's antics, such as the stroll for a bet mentioned above, the re-hanging of pictures upside down to check the owners' reaction, or lack of it, the distribution of notes in concert halls, informing unknown people as well as close acquaintances that Kharms was changing his name to 'Charms' – all these are anticipatory of the activities of Western and Soviet conceptualists.[16]

*Translated by Neil Cornwell*

## NOTES

1. Aleksandrov, 1968, p. 300.
2. Poret, 1986, p. 348.
3. Poret, 1986, p. 352.
4. Kharms, 'Zapisnaia knizhka', no. 14, 1928. Deep thanks are expressed to V. Erl' for providing access to the text of Kharms's notebooks.
5. It is quite possible that Kharms was acquainted with Evreinov's works. At the beginning of the 1920s he could have seen on the Petrograd stage Evreinov's sensational play *Samoe glavnoe* ('The Most Important Thing'), about actors on the stage of life, which ran for more than 100 performances in the Free Comedy theatre.
6. Poret, 1986, p. 352.
7. Gerasimova, 1988a, p. 51.
8. Kharms, 'Zapisnaia knizhka', no. 16, 1928.
9. Kharms, 'Zapisnaia knizhka', no. 14, 1928.
10. Ibid.
11. The references here are to Fëdorov's, on Ekatorinskaia (Malaia Sadovaia) Street, a popular restaurant in the NEP years; the gaming club on Vladimirskii Prospect; the restaurant on the roof of the Evropeiskaia hotel; the foyer of the cinema on Rakov Street.
12. Kharms, 'Zapisnaia knizhka', no. 13, 1928.
13. See Nakhimovsky, 1982, p. 1; and Gibian, in *Black Coat*, p. 39. The latter also mentions similarities between the creative lifestyle of Kharms and the behaviour of such western avantgardists as Alfred Jarry, Francis Picabia, Guillaume Apollinaire and Tristan Tzara (*Black Coat*, p. 6).
14. D. Tolmachev, 'Dadaisty v Leningrade', *Zhizn' iskusstv*, 1927, no. 44, p. 14.
15. Quoted from F. Marinetti, *Futurizm* (Moscow, 1914) p. 287.
16. A range of Leningrad and Moscow avantgardist groups now consider Kharms to be their inspiration: for example 'New Artists' ('*Novye khudozhniki*') and 'Popular Mechanics' ('*Populiarnaia mekhanika*'). One informal Leningrad group arranged 'happenings' on Kharms's birthday in the yard of the building in which he lived. In this article we have deliberately not dealt with the esoteric sources of Kharms's creative lifestyle, which compare in part with the mystical strivings of the early surrealists. This would have to be a subject for separate research.

# 15 Kharms's Play *Elizaveta Bam*
## Mikhail Meilakh

'Elizaveta Bam was written at the request of the theatre section of OBERIU by section member, D. Kharms': so runs the wording of the fourth chapter of the article 'OBERIU' which is often erroneously referred to as the OBERIU declaration or manifesto.[1] Kharms wrote the play in an extremely short time, twelve days in December 1927, especially for the forthcoming OBERIU evening 'Three Left Hours' scheduled for the stage of the Leningrad Press Club (House of Print) where the play was in fact put on. The production was by Kharms himself with two fellow-members of OBERIU. To quote the article again, 'the composition of the show was the work of I. Bakhterev, Bor. Levin and Daniil Kharms'.[2] Kharms had already spent two years with these two (Bakhterev was also an artist and the stage designer) working together in the field of the new theatre.

### THE DRAMATIC PRINCIPLES OF OBERIU

Many elements of the earlier 'Radix' poetics were operative in OBERIU theatre, including the use of montage [*montirovanie*] in conjunction with the actors who introduce an element of improvisation, and the notion of the 'bit' [*kusok*], which is a scene in itself and yet subject to the total scenic action. This essentially modernistic poetics of 'threading theatrical elements together' is explained in the fourth chapter of the article 'OBERIU'. The Oberiuty rejected literary drama, in which all the elements are subordinate to the dramatic plot, that is the play which is 'a tale told by people about something that happened', and in which everything is done on the stage in order 'to explain the meaning and the course of the events more clearly, more comprehensibly, and in a more life-like way'. Theatre, said the Oberiuty, has nothing to do with that. Citing examples of absurdist scenic actions (an actor representing a politician who walks across the stage on all fours and howls like a wolf, or an actor representing a Russian peasant who delivers a speech in

Latin; or the example of the chair which appears on stage with a samovar standing on it, its lid opening to reveal not steam but two naked hands), the authors declare that the series of 'separate moments' arranged by the producer are what makes up the theatrical presentation. This has its own kind of plot-line and its own kind of scenic meaning. In contrast to the *dramatic plot*, the OBERIU concentrate all their attention on the *scenic plot*:

> This is a plot which only the theatre can present. The plot of a theatrical representation is theatrical, just as the plot of a musical work is musical. They each represent one thing – the world of phenomena, though, depending on the material, they each express it in its own way...
> When you come to see us, forget everything that you have been used to seeing in all other theatres. Perhaps much of it will seem absurd. We take a plot, a dramatic one. First it is developed simply, then it is suddenly interrupted by plainly absurd, seemingly irrelevant objects. You are amazed. You want to find the laws of normality and logic which you think you see in life. But you will not find them here. Why? Because an object and a phenomenon transferred from life onto the stage are no more dependent on the laws of 'life' and acquire laws of another kind, those of theatre. We are not going to explain what they are. To understand the laws of a theatrical presentation you have to see it. All we can say is that our aim is to present the world of concrete objects on the stage in their mutual interaction and confrontations. This is what we have been aiming at in our production of *Elizaveta Bam*. The *dramatic* plot of the play is shattered by many seemingly irrelevant themes which isolate the object as a separately existing whole, without any connections with the rest; so the viewer will not see a clearly delineated *dramatic* plot, for it as it were flickers behind the back of the action. In its place is the *scenic* plot, which emerges spontaneously from all the elements of our show.

The principles of OBERIU theatre which were put into practice in the staging of *Elizaveta Bam*, are also evident from Kharms's production notes; these are preserved on his copy of the play, which makes this a document invaluable for reconstructing the production. Kharms evidently wrote in these numerous stage directions on his copy of the play (though they may of course also be by Bakhterev and Levin) either while working out the production scenario or during rehearsals (the notes were certainly made at different times using different pencils).

The whole play was divided up by the author into nineteen producer's 'bits', each of which was to be acted in its own autonomous way. These are variously marked 'realistic melodrama', 'genre of realistic comedy', 'absurdly comic naive' 'realistic' 'rhythmic (Radix)' 'A displacement of heights', 'pastoral', 'Monologue aside, double-intentioned bit', 'speech' and so on. So the staging of the play involved a kind of parodic retrospective of all possible theatrical genres, 'made strange' both by the text of the play and by all kinds of eccentricities, bouffonades, musical accompaniments and so on, which, in their sequence, create the thread of the scenic action running through the work. Stressing the primacy of the scenic plot as something which arises spontaneously from the separate theatrical elements, the authors of the article 'OBERIU' say:

> Moreover, some elements of the show are valuable in themselves and precious. They carry on their own existence without submitting to the click of the theatrical metronome. The corner of a golden frame sticks out – it is alive as an object of art; a snatch of a poem is recited – it is independent in its meaning and at the same time – irrespective of what it wants – it moves the scenic plot of the play forward. The scenery, the movements of the actors, a bottle thrown down, the hem of a costume are just as much a part of the action as the people who are shaking their heads and speaking words and phrases.

The 'theatrical elements' which, although subject to the scenic plot, are the substance of the theatrical action in itself, have another function as well: they are bearers of information in abbreviated form of whole cultural layers to which the spectators are meant to refer. The special kind of 'symbolisation' characteristic of the style-markers of the bits, which point to the cultural and artistic realia behind these headings is apparent also in other units of the show which are not especially marked. For example, the old-fashioned romance sung by Mummy in the third bit, or its *contrepartie* in the ninth bit; the typically Karmsian plot-defying tale of Nicky and the apples (in fact a tale 'about nothing'); the note 'Bobchinsky' in the second bit which associates the doubles Ivan Ivanovich and Pëtr Nikolaevich with Gogol's characters in *The Government Inspector*. Even the farcical elements, the clowning and the eccentricities, which are so widely used in the play have a similar function; and from a larger perspective, so do fragments such as the opening and final scenes before the doors, the roots of which lie in classical comedy, where in their turn they are connected with archaic ritual structures; also the romantically mythologised poetic fragments about 'the little house on the hill' with its squeaking door and the mice where no one lives (episodes which bear an amazing similarity to the motif of the Chapel Perilous taken from the stories of the Holy Grail in T. S. Eliot's *The Wasteland*); or finally the central episode of the play, the 'battle of the two heroes' which is deeply archetypical and foretold by a verbal duel which lapses into magic *zaum'*. This kind of 'symbolisation' is at first glance paradoxical, given the orientation of OBERIU (the Union of *real art*), a post-Futurist movement, towards an original treatment of 'realism';[3] but in fact this 'symbolisation' is an organic part of OBERIU poetics, modernistic *par excellence* and with its connections with other avant-garde twentieth-century art movements.

Along with the general theatrical principles of 'Radix' the OBERIU theatre took over many details from the earlier 'My mother's all in watches'. These included the role of Elizaveta herself, which in both productions was played by the professional actress, A. Ia. Gol'dfarb (at that time the wife of L. S. Lipavsky, she acted under the pseudonym of Grin); that of Mummy which was acted by Babaeva, an actress from 'Mastfora' (N. M. Foregger's studio), a heavily-built tall woman, the oldest in the troupe; that of Daddy which was played by E. I. Vigiliansky who taught at the school in Tsarskoe Selo which Kharms had attended. He was a poet who began as a post-Acmeist and later joined Tufanov's group (in 1925 at a poetry evening, Kharms introduced him to Vvedensky). By a whim of fate, the 'Radix' rehearsals took place in the same White Hall of INKhYK where a few years previously Tatlin had presented Khlebnikov's 'Zangezi', and the production of Elizaveta Bam took place on the stage of the Press Club still adorned with the scenery for Terent'ev's production of *The Government Inspector*.

Our present task is, despite the abundant difficulties, to give as full an account as possible of the history of the production of *Elizaveta Bam*.

## THE PRODUCTION OF THE PLAY

Production of *Elizaveta Bam* started the very day that Kharms finished writing it, as we know from his notebooks.[4] For the production and indeed for the entire OBERIU evening, the members of the group were indebted to the director of the Press Club, A. A.

Baskakov, a sympathiser with left art, who in the autumn of 1927 had offered the group a place in the artistic sections of the Club and had agreed to a 'large-scale concert evening' on the stage of his theatre, in order 'to show the latest currents in art'.[5] (The black lacquered cupboards left behind from Terent'ev's production were used by the Oberiuty for the first, poetry, hour and Kharms, as always, sat on one of them.[6]) The quite fictional allocation of posts in the OBERIU theatre, somewhat comic in its bureaucratic pedantry, was an effort at a kind of establishment in the new organisational set-up.[7]

The play was in fact typed out at the expense of the Press Club. As regards the recruitment of actors, we have already pointed out that the three main roles were taken by actors who moved straight to OBERIU from 'Radix'. New actors were given the roles of Ivan Ivanovich and Pëtr Nikolaevich: the first was played by Pavel Manevich, a worker from the Putilov factory who was a talented amateur comedian, and the second by the children's writer, Varshavsky; both of them had been students together with the producers at the Institute of Art History.

**The Staging**

The staging by I. Bakhterev made use of abstract scenery on the left and right of the stage: this consisted of small side-screens with oddly cut indentations. These side-screens were mounted on skis and on them they could recede, as happens in the third bit, *bring in* objects, *swallow things and people up* (a table in the sixth bit, Daddy and Mummy in the eighth and seventeenth bits and so on), *spin round* 'from room to countryside' (eighth bit), and 'from countryside to room' (seventeenth bit). The difference between the *narrow room* of the first two and last two scenes, which were a stylisation of a provincial melodrama, and the *deep room* of the other scenes, as also between this set and the 'forest' of the pastoral scenes, was achieved by a receding back-drop and the receding side-screens. As well as the moveable side-screens there were:

> rolls [of paper] hanging over the door (the door, which was a very large double one crowned with a port-hole and framed with magnificent panels, stood in the centre) and as required these rolls were unrolled to cover its upper part, like a 'lintel', which was quite absurd and unexpected considering the tiny window in the centre. These rolls however would not always obey the producer's com-

mands: they were moved by strings which got tangled up or broke and so on – so that when the scene should have changed back to its original appearance [eighteenth bit, M.M.] these untidily hanging paper ribbons got in the way.[8]

Kharms recorded the scene changes as follows:

*Scenery*
1. Narrow room – 1 and 2
2. Deep room – 3, 4, 5, 6, 7, and 8.
3. Forest – 9, 10, 11, 12, 13, 14, 15, 16, and (17).
4. Small room – 18
5. Everything together – 19.

Evidently the team were not successful in bringing off the intended staging of the last scene ('the operatic ending') and the play ended in exactly the same provincial petty bourgeois room as it opened with and as was seen in the previous bit. The only essential difference lay in the fact that during the last bit the lights were slowly dimmed and the final lines were spoken in complete darkness.

Kharms gives a vast list of props:

For the forthcoming '3 left hours' evening the following props are needed:
1. A tricycle
2. Some pieces of coloured material, though I think we just need sheets.
3. A siren (mouth operated)
4. A samovar
5. 2 wineglasses
6. Fencing swords
7. A crutch
8. An abacus
9. A pen
10. A log and a saw
11. A little box
12. A lantern

The tricycle was intended for the master of ceremonies, S. Tsimbal, who was supposed to ride around on it 'in improbable lines and figures'; this, however, he did not do as the evening was compèred by Vvedensky. The pieces of material were intended either for a curtain (the play in fact went on without one) or for the back-drop (designed by Bakhterev). The other objects (apart from the abacus) were used directly in the production: the siren in bit 13, the samovar and wine glasses in bit 11, the swords in bit 15 (where they are referred to as sabres in the text and as rapiers in the stage directions), the crutch in bit 2, the pen in bit 6 and probably also 10, the log and saw in bit 5, the little box in bit 9. Pëtr Nikolaevich is lit by the lantern in bit 13.

**The Music**

The mention of the siren brings us to the most important 'theatrical element', the music used in the production. The poster mentions P. Vul'fius, a school friend of Kharms, who at that time was teaching the history of Western music in the Institute of History of the Arts.[9] Unfortunately he was not able to remember anything about the production when we met him shortly before his death in 1979 (in the thirties he had been arrested and spent seventeen years in camps and exile). We do not know for certain whether any original music was written for the production[10] or whether the music was a selection from existing works.[11]

Let us try to summarise as far as we can the little evidence we have about the music of the production. It opened with an overture as we know from the stage directions in bit 12: 'Off-stage a choir sings to the tune of the overture', and 'choir (to the music of the tune of the overture)'. Hence we know there was a choir, whose composition is detailed in Kharms's notebook: 'Choir: women 10 (5–10), men – 10–15'. Other notes reveal traces of conversations about taking on musicians; the minimal composition of the orchestra we know from the text of the play (pipes, a grand piano, a violin, drum, siren). Besides these, there were supposed to be kettle drums and a bell, the sound of which was to enframe the 'battle of the two heroes'.[12] A bell, however, was not to be found and it was replaced, according to Bakhterev, by something rather unsuitable.

The first reference to a musical accompaniment in Kharms's production copy of the play (not counting the songs which the actors sing during the play) relates to the middle of the play, bit 12, where besides the directions we have just quoted is also another one: 'Music strikes up'. At this point the choir part is interrupted by the orchestral or instrumental part which concludes with a repetition [? M.M.] of the overture.

In discussing the music we are entering the field of suppositions and guesswork, supported, however, by a few indications in the text. There are grounds for supposing that the musical side of the production was to a large extent coordinated with the rhythms of the verse: for instance the fragments of *zaum'* are often marked with accents and supplied with directions such as 'with an alliterative ring' (bit 1), 'Rhythmic (Radix), author's rhythm'; 'measured verse'; 'melodiously' (bit 4); we may suppose also that the music was coordinated with the long drawn out lines such as 'Let's go, nu-u-u-u' (bit 4), 'Oo-oo-oo-oo' (bit 8 and the whole of 9 with the stress on the vowels). The function of the musical instruments in places is particularly interesting (in bit 13 it is the violin, siren and drum): they appear as personages in dialogue with the characters of the play at its most dramatic moments (see text of play below).

That is all we know about the music in the production. We can only suggest that it was used much more than might be implied from Kharms's notes (it seems that there was a separate musical text of the play). Most likely Mummy's performance of the romance 'Morning has broken' [*Chaika*] [so-called in our translation, Ed.] had a musical accompaniment, as did Ivan Ivanovich's song, 'Pussy Cat' [*Murkakosechka*]. Most likely too there was a musical accompaniment for the rhythmical and dynamic fragments of the production; and the last scene was as we have mentioned supposed to have been an 'operatic ending'.

Even our meagre knowledge allows us to conclude that the OBERIU theatre was continuing the traditions of 'Radix' in as far as we can reconstruct them. There was also improvisation in the play: Bakhterev recalls that during the performance of the seventh bit, when a voice off-stage and the musical instruments harmonise with the voice of the actor, he took it into his head to take part. He ran up to the choir, found a double-bass standing there and began to pluck the strings which worked in with the production very effectively.

REACTIONS TO THE PLAY

The 'Three Left Hours' at which *Elizaveta Bam* was staged was the only performance on that scale by the OBERIU and, since they were historically speaking the last group of left art in Russia, this occasion was destined to be also the very last large-scale performance by Russian left art. Times were coming when even the word 'group' was to be dangerous, and the word 'grouplet' [*gruppka*] even worse. (This was the word used two years later by the newspaper *Smena* [Shift] to refer to the Oberiuty in a violent article called 'Reactionary juggling' in which their poetry was openly described as counter-revolutionary and 'a protest against the dictatorship of the proletariat'.[13] And eighteen months later, at a poetry discussion at the Union of Writers, Aseev was to accuse Zabolotsky, Vvedensky and Kharms of 'sterility', 'creative paralysis' and of being 'far from the problems of building socialism'.[14] (Soon after this speech came the first arrest and exile of Kharms and Vvedensky. Zabolotsky's time had not yet come.) But for the time being the reviews in the press were, though hostile, comparatively 'vegetarian', to use Akhmatova's epithet. In the autumn of 1927 when OBERIU had just taken on its new shape, an article by D. Tolmachev appeared in *Life of Art* where our authors were described as 'the pettiest and last of the imitators of Khlebnikov, still dreaming of the dictatorship of *zaum'* in poetry'.[15] No less hostile was Lidiia Lesnaia's review of the 'Three Left Hours' in which *Elizaveta Bam* was described as 'blatant and cynical chaos in which no-one could understand anything' and the whole evening as 'something unprintable'.[16] It may have been in response to this article that Kharms wrote his 'Explanatory Note on the Production of *Elizaveta Bam*', which is referred to in his notes but which has been lost.[17] The unfavourable reception given to the evening in the press evidently brought all kinds of difficulties for its promoters.[18]

Was the production of *Elizaveta Bam* a success? Lidiia Lesnaia's review says that the reaction of the audience was entirely hostile, but we cannot really judge how the evening was received from this tendentious remark or from the few contemporary recollections of it. In order to imagine what happened in the audience, let us attempt to reconstruct the composition of the audience that evening. Here again we rely on Kharms's notebooks with his mania for lists and numbers, and in this case on the list of those who were to be sent the following invitation:

Press Club<br>
Fontanka 21<br>
Invitation<br>
OBERIU requests the pleasure of your company at<br>
'Three Left Hours'<br>
on 24th January 1928.

            Performance commences at 7.30
Stamp                                       Signature

  The simplest estimates of the composition of the lists of invitees and of those who received complimentary tickets (the participants and the actors engaged in the production) show that nearly seventy places in the hall were reserved for a public who were for the most part the strength of left art in Leningrad and certainly sympathetic to the OBERIU. The lists include the names of the artists Matiushin, Sokolov, Lebedev, Mansurov, Ermolaeva, Suetin, Sterligov, the writers Kliuev, Lipavsky, Marshak, Rozhdestvensky, the music critic Sollertinsky. A special list included those invited to take part in the dispute – among them in the section headed 'Literature' were Stepanov, Petnikov, Eikhenbaum, Tufanov, Livshits; in the 'Theatre' section were Terent'ev, in the 'Cinema' section, the *feksy*; in the artistic section, Malevich and Filonov. Of course these lists refer only to the people invited and not to those who actually attended, but in any event a large part of the audience was made up of sympathisers (and we must add the many people who were invited personally to these lists). Three days before the performance, in expectation of the usual uproar that greeted any left performance, Kharms noted under the date 21 January: 'Call on V. Ulishin about the claque'. Nonetheless, the Oberiuty tried to publicise the evening as widely as possible. An announcement was twice printed in the newspapers and twice in *Notices of the Press Club*, and Kharms indicates about thirty places where the fifty posters were to be distributed and displayed (the remainder were evidently posted around the town); these places included publishing houses, the Public Library, the University, embassies, the House of Arts, the Library of new books, the Conservatory, the Philharmonia, 'Life of Art'; as well as the Industrial Bank, the North-West Trade organization, the North-West Union, and lawyers' and businessmen's clubs.

The negative reaction to the performance on the night may well have originated (as it was to later) from the students who attended the 'workers' faculty' (*rabfak*) courses associated with the campaign for the liquidation of illiteracy. In B. F. Semënov's memoirs, for instance, 'The hall were some 150 students of *rabfak* age had gathered was hardly silent. In the back rows, people kept laughing, the rare applause was interspersed with whistles'.[19] On the subject of students, in December 1927 Kharms had noted that Kliuev had invited him and Vvedensky 'to read verses to some students, who unlike the others were fairly civilised'; the article 'Reactionary juggling', referred to above, was on the other hand published because, after the OBERIU evening, the 'proletarian students responded to the provocation by the infamous OBERIU, decided to record their opinion in the proper manner by drawing up a resolution and sending it to the Union of Writers'. It was this denunciation, and the denunciatory article in *Smena* which it provoked, that put an end to the theatricalised performances of the OBERIU and to their drama.

But this happened in 1930. And in the meantime the semi-official condemnation of the production of *Elizaveta Bam* in *Red Newspaper* in 1928 did not stop Baskakov, the director of the Press Club, who sympathised with the OBERIU, from suggesting to them that they prepare a new production on the occasion of the transfer of the Club to the Mariinsky Palace (no wonder that Baskakov was later to be accused of Trotskyism and arrested). Bakhterev remembers that the text of this new play, entitled *A Winter's Walk* [*Zimniaia progulka*], was written by him and Kharms in two weeks and that the role of the notorious red-beard, taken over, along with several other production points from the theatre of 'Radix', was played by the same Doivber Levin. We have so much material relating to the production of *Elizaveta Bam*, yet virtually nothing relating to *A Winter's Walk* seems to have survived and even Kharms's eloquent notebooks contain merely isolated jottings about it.[20]

So ended the story of OBERIU theatre which reached its culmination in the production of *Elizaveta Bam*. As we have mentioned, the dramatic efforts of the group frequently took the form of theatricalised evenings (many such evenings were held in the period between the two OBERIU productions of 1928).

Kharms's notebooks show that by the end of 1928 these projects were no more than dreams, but Kharms still hoped for theatricalised evenings at which his own poetry and that of the OBERIU would be recited, 'theatricalised happenings' performed and even an entire 'OBERIU show' put on. At those evenings which could still take place, however, excerpts from *Elizaveta Bam* and *A Winter's Walk* were performed by Kharms himself.[21]


THE TEXT OF THE PLAY

We come now to a consideration of the textual history of *Elizaveta Bam* and the problems attendant on it. The conditions of literary and social life at the end of the twenties, which led to the persecution of the OBERIU and eventually to the arrest in 1931 of Vvedensky and Kharms, were such that *Elizaveta Bam* could not, of course, be published. Kharms, however, regularly included the play in the lists for projected anthologies which he recorded in his notebooks. The play was included in a manuscript anthology given to P. A. Mansurov, who emigrated in August 1928,[22] and in a collection entitled *The Bath of Archimedes* [*Vanna Arkhimeda*] which was to consist of writings by the prose-writers L. Dobychin and Iurii Olesha, the Formalist literary scholars and by the OBERIU poets,[23] and finally it was included also in an anthology of the same title consisting only of OBERIU works. This was when the play was sent to *New Lef* (see below).

It took V. A. Kaverin forty years to include five quotations from the play in his memoirs.[24] Over the last decade two attempts have been made to publish the complete play abroad but both publications are unsatisfactory. The reasons for this are that the publishers used defective 'wandering' copies of the play, and overlooked wholly or in part the only authorised copy which had been preserved by N. I. Khardzhiev. This is what Khardzhiev has to say:

> The fate of Kharms's play has been an 'absurd' one.
>
> Two identical life-time typescripts of the text were preserved (from one original).
>
> In 1928 one of these typescripts was sent by the author (together with several works by Kharms and Vvedensky) to the editors of *New Lef*, where I discovered it in the so-called 'editorial basket' of the journal. It was normal practice to destroy many of the manuscripts sent to *New Lef* and only those few manuscripts of undoubted artistic worth were put in the basket. The Oberiuty sent in their work not for publication (only works by Lef writers were published in the slim journal) but to keep the journal informed of the latest developments in literature.
>
> The typescript preserved in the archives of *New Lef* was incomplete: the last page was missing.
>
> In the early sixties this copy was given by me to N. Stepanov (at his request) as he proposed to use two or three quotations from the play in his memoirs of Zabolotsky. Unless my memory deceives me these quotations did not appear in the memoirs and, unfortunately, Stepanov did not return the typescript to me but passed it round for circulation by hand. This was the version in which Kharms's play was translated into English and Polish: see the translation by Z. Fedeckij and W. Woroszylskij in the journal *Dialog* (1966) and the translation by George Gibian in his book *Russia's Lost Literature of the Absurd* (1971).
>
> *Elizaveta Bam* was produced without the ending on the stage of the Polish student theatre 'Gong-2' in Lublin.

The second typescript of the play which Kharms gave me in the early thirties is complete. This copy has numerous producer's notes written by the author, who was also the producer. So the sole surviving authorised typescript of *Elizaveta Bam* contains, besides the basic literary text, also the stage interpretation of it. When giving me the play Kharms said that the production notes could be used for a production but should not be included in the basic text. [Unpublished note.]

We should note that this final copy of the play, besides being enriched with Kharms's own production notes, is the ultimate version since it was undoubtedly completed in the course of the production.[25]


THE PLAY ITSELF

The plot of *Elizaveta Bam* may have been in part suggested by the recent arrest of the producer of the 'Radix' theatre, Kharms's friend, G. N. Katsman (his arrest on 16 April 1927 is noted in Kharms's notebook), and more broadly by the atmosphere of post-revolutionary Russia which strongly coloured Kharms's prose. Looked at from an even wider perspective, the motif of being accused of a crime which has not been committed, or indeed of which one is not even aware, is one of the themes of the period and forms the plot of several works of twentieth-century literature, such as Kafka's *The Trial* written ten years earlier, and Nabokov's *Invitation to a Beheading* written ten years later. From the biographical angle the motif was prophetic for Kharms himself, who was arrested twice and who died in prison during the blockade of Leningrad.[26]

The motif of the crime which Elizaveta Bam has allegedly committed is made absurd almost from the very beginning of the play, and this finds scenic expression in the movement from 'realistic melodrama' of the first bit, to the 'realist, comic' genre, and then to the 'absurdly comic, naive'. To Elizaveta Bam's question, 'Why am I a criminal?' (or earlier, '... what am I accused of?') one of the people following her says, 'Because you have no voice', a statement in which cause and effect have changed places (though in a preceding line it appears that Elizaveta Bam is alleged to have committed 'a vile crime'). The accusation of 'having no voice' suggests an existentialist theme (compare in bit 7, Ivan Ivanovich's twice repeated line, 'I speak therefore I am') and can be compared with the accusation of 'epistemological vileness' made against the hero of *Invitation to a Beheading*. Elizaveta Bam rejects the accusation and suggests that her accusers 'check it with the clock'. This nonsense phrase serves as a kind of operator marking the shift of the action into eccentricity, farce and the absurd. Pëtr Nikolaevich and Ivan Ivanovich who appear behind her, one on a crutch and the other with a bandaged cheek, argue, turn into conjurers, pay Elizaveta Bam compliments, and finally ask to be allowed to go home because their children are waiting for them. In the next scenes they again seek out Elizaveta (and find her) 'in order to kill her'. In the scene where Pëtr Nikolaevich gives the mysterious description of 'the little house with the squeaking door' and the mice and the cockroaches, it turns out, finally, that Elizaveta's crime is the murder of Pëtr Nikolaevich; and in the following no less mysterious, ecstatic scene, entitled 'A displacement of heights' (in which Elizaveta rises up and Ivan Ivanovich sinks down) she apears in a demonic guise as the howling 'she-wolf'. After several eccentric scenes with dialogue made up of absurd truisms and clichés, comes the dramatic culmination of the play, on the threshold of which Pëtr Nikolaevich, standing alone on the proscenium, again has a dialogue with the musical instruments (as he had done previously during the tale of the little house). The ensuing dialogue with Ivan Ivanovich, in which both return to the motif of the little house on the hill, has a more 'cosmic' tone, and the theme of time introduced in it leads to the theme of the imminent death of Elizaveta ('But remember that tomorrow night Elizaveta Bam will die').

The cosmic theme is continued in the verbal duel between Pëtr Nikolaevich and Ivan Ivanovich, who echoes him, and Daddy, who comes to rescue Elizaveta. Pëtr Nikolaevich grows to the size of a universal wizard who moves the seas, destroys the forests and mountains, etc. In the ensuing 'battle of two heroes' his weapon is the word ('let's join battle, sorcerer, you by word and I by arm') and, fully in accord with archaic models, he tries to conquer his opponent with magic spells like the "binding song" with which in Aeschylus' *Eumenides* the Furies bind Orestes' limbs; the chant is first in *zaum'* and then calls him to watch 'the movement of the iron centres and the curdling of deathly powers'.[27] Daddy's answering speech with its images of day shaded by birds which cover the sun and the noise of hoofbeats in the forest, is a no less astonishing glimpse of the world of mythopoetic imagery on Kharms's part. In the course of the battle, with its reminiscences of Hamlet's battle with Laertes, Daddy, who praises in his war-song 'iron-carborundum' [*zhelezo-karborund*] (a word introduced into Futurist usage by Kruchënykh), feathers and stone, finally defeats his opponent after praising the stone from under which 'water runs to meet the dead enemy'. The fallen Pëtr Nikolaevich asks Elizaveta's forgiveness, urging her to come to his house on the hill and there 'fall back' and he remembers to mention its inhabitants, the cockroaches and mice.

The epic feel of the 'battle of the two heroes' (Kharms called it ballad-like) is further 'made strange' by the extreme physiological domesticity of the following two scenes which return us to the situation of the opening of the play. Pëtr Nikolaevich and Ivan Ivanovich poke their heads round the door dressed as firemen who now openly accuse Elizaveta of the murder of 'Pëtr Nikolaevich Krupernak'. Elizaveta opens the door and falls into their power, shouting, however, that she has never killed anyone and could not kill anyone. Her last words are about a cockroach from the little house on the hill (which has been mentioned in each of the preceding references to the motif of the little house) which now acquires the threatening form of an executioner. 'Cockroach Cockroachovich, in his shirt with the reddish collar and an axe in his hands'.[28] The final words of Pëtr Nikolaevich with their poetically strange conversational semantics are spoken in total darkness.

The overall composition of the play encloses a constant chain of transformations on the part of the participants. This affects primarily the doubles, Ivan Ivanovich and Pëtr Nikolaevich. The latter was, according to the play, apparently murdered by Elizaveta before the start of the action,[29] and in the course of the play is killed by her father. The motif of the double comes over in part by the particular disposition of their lines and by Kharms's production notes to those moments when Elizaveta is first accused of murder. At a certain moment during the first telling of the tale of the little house on the hill by Pëtr Nikolaevich his words 'But once I woke up . . .' are continued by Ivan Ivanovich ('. . . and I saw . . .'); at this point Kharms noted 'they cover each other' and there follows the mysterious, existentialist line of Ivan Ivanovich, 'I speak, therefore I am'. The most significant transformation of Pëtr Nikolaevich is his change into a wizard; besides which, Pëtr Nikolaevich and Ivan Ivanovich arriving 'on important business' begin, already in the opening 'realistic' scenes to treat Elizaveta Bam deferentially: Ivan Ivanovich asks permission to go home to his large family, not to mention all the absurd eccentricities associated with them, the game of 'mob-mob' [*piatnashki*] and the classics, etc. The penultimate scene in which Mummy, who up till now has not spoken, begins suddenly to speak in vulgar street language, assumes that Elizaveta is not her daughter, while Pëtr, supposedly killed by her, is her son. The status of Elizaveta is also a fluid one; at one moment she talks of her husband who has been delayed somewhere, then she fools around like a little girl, then she acts like a demonic she-wolf. It is a telling point that one moment Ivan Ivanovich refers to her as Elizaveta Cockroachovna . . . Edwardovna . . . Mikhailovna. An extreme degree of this kind of fluidity, changeability, inconstancy in the image of his heroes is inherent in the typical Kharmsian category of 'disappearance', 'emptying', 'emptiness', which, with its far-reaching epistemological and ontological consequences,[30] is bound up with the OBERIU-*chinar* poetics 'of the battle against meanings'[31] (including 'semantic emptying'). In fact, on the plot level too, many of Kharms's characters disappear, become invisible[32] and so on, which is the final limit of transformation as such.

This category, which is expressed by various means in the play, is insisted on in Pëtr Nikolaevich's first story about the 'little' house, where he 'lived alone' and where apart from him 'there were only mice and cockroaches' (see below on the Anchorite Cockroach). This category is made explicit in the word 'nothing' ('I used to sleep and would be afraid of nothing more') which is picked up and repeated by the Voice off-stage, Mummy, Ivan Ivanovich and by Pëtr Nikolaevich himself, and which is rhythmically picked up by the pipes off-stage and by the piano (as the text specifically indicates). The same word, repeated after several sentences is again picked up by the pipes alone, and is associated with phrases such as 'nothing more', 'nobody else', 'there's nobody'. A little further on, Elizaveta Bam, in answer to the question why she killed Pëtr Nikolaevich, answers, 'Hurray, I didn't kill anyone' (she repeats the same words in the last scene, the one of her arrest), and later, 'Hurray I haven't said a thing'; this is confirmed by Ivan Ivanovich ('No, no, not a thing, not a thing'), whose earlier lines, spoken at the moment when Pëtr Nikolaevich, who allegedly has been killed by Elizaveta, takes his place, derive 'existence' from 'speaking' ('I speak therefore I am'); very curious is the fact that the situation is soon realised in the *zaum'* exchange between Elizaveta and Ivan Ivanovich ('gug-ga, psh, psh' and so on). The same category is manifest on different levels in the curtailing of words (in the pastoral bit), 'Ivan-Iva-ah', 'a box made of woo-oo-ooh' and so on, and, in the same bit, the typically Kharmsian plot-destroying tale of

Nicky and the apples.[33] It is also developed in Pëtr Nikolaevich's second verse tale about 'the little house on the hill':

> No one resides therein[34]/and the door doesn't open,/
> therein only mice rub flour between their palms,/
> therein only the lamp shines as rosemary/
> the livelong day sits the anchorite cockroach on the stove./
> But who then lights the lamp?/No one, it burns by itself./

The cockroach, who in general is associated with neglect, is here defined as an 'anchorite' [*pustynnik*] (a word which had come into usage in left art since the publication in 1912 of Kruchënykh's book illustrated by Goncharova, *Pustynniki. Pustynnitsa* [Anchorites. Anchoress]) and this phrase is repeated in Pëtr Nikolaevich's farewell to Elizaveta:

> And then will run all over you/and up and down your arms,/
> the mice so wild and after that/
> the anchorite cockroach.

Again this category is made explicit in the father's remark about Elizaveta: 'O women, they have little conception,/ and in their conceptions they have a vacuum [*pustotu*]'.

The apotheosis of this category is, however, the fading of the light during the last scene of the play when the 'anchorite cockroach' from the hill takes on the ominous shape of executioner, and Pëtr Nikolaevich invites Elizaveta to follow him, to execution or to the kingdom of the dead, 'having stretched out your arms and extinguished your fixed stare'.

These are some of the salient motifs of this play which, because of its essential syncretism and also because it was both in intention and in realisation a programmatic event, was the apotheosis of all the OBERIU stood for. Subsequently, the OBERIU-*chinary*, Kharms and Vvedensky, were to follow independent and individual paths and their later work cannot be reduced either to OBERIU world-view or to OBERIU poetics. Yet a whole range of motifs and devices typical of *Elizaveta Bam*, which was the first largescale work that the young Khams completed, were to be developed in his later writings.

*Translated by Ann Shukman*

This article was first published in *Stanford Slavic Studies*, vol. 1, 1987. Thanks are due to the editors and author for permission to abridge, translate and republish.

# NOTES

1. *Afishi Doma pechati* [Posters of the House of Print], 2, 1928, p. 12. Reprinted in Milner-Gulland (1970); and *Izb.* (1974), pp. 287–98; English translation in *Black Coat*, pp. 245–54. Translations of quotes given here are by Ann Shukman.
2. Ibid.
3. I. V. Bakhterev, in one of his conversations with Vl. Erl', characteristically emphasised that in none of the theatrical events should one look for symbolism, still less, a subtext, for these were both phenomena which Kharms and his associates treated as a failure and which they were constantly struggling against. What happens on stage, said Bakhterev, is the plot of the play, is the most real life, perhaps even more real than all the rest.
4. Notebook No. 11, which we refer to here and below, contains his notes for late December 1927 and early January 1928 and has particularly interesting material on the history of the play's staging:

    *Agenda for Saturday 24th Dec.*
    Play reading.
    Talk with House of Press about money for typing the play.
    Apportion the jobs
       a) for calling the actors
       b) for putting together the plan of the show.
    *Urgent tasks.*
       1) Typing 10 copies of the play.
       2) Find 1 male actor, 1 woman, and a deputy producer.

5. Poster for the evening.
6. This image, which may well derive from Chekhov ('deeply respected cupboard') was a key word in OBERIU 'literary life': see the famous OBERIU slogan 'art is a cupboard'. The image of the cupboard as a quintessence of 'thing-ism' is found in Vvedensky (see Vved. I, 130 and notes). Among Kharms's notes is the title of a projected article 'Zero and cupboard' notebook No. 18, 1929). The cupboard was associated also in Kharms with the image of the *trunk*.
7. Literary Director D. Kharms.
   Chief Stage Designer – I Bakhterev.
   Chief Producer – S. Tsimbal.
   Chairman of the Theatrical Council – B. Levin.
   Director of Music – P. Vul'fius. (Notebook 11)
8. Recollections of I. Bakhterev, taken down by Vl. Erl'.
9. See also, M. Druskin, *Issledovaniia. Vospominaniia* (Moscow-Leningrad, 1977) p. 253.
10. See Kharms's later note (notebook 14, October 1928), 'Get Vul'fius to write the music for the melodeclamation'. Vul'fius was also indicated as the composer for *Zimniaia progulka* [*A Winter's Walk*].
11. See Kharms's note relating to the play in which he enumerates the pizzicato from *The Little Hunchback Horse* [*Konëk-gorbunok*] and

The Futile Warning [*Tshchetnaia predostorozhnost'*], Chopin's Adagio, and a polka by Rachmaninov. However it is not clear whether these works were supposed to be played during the show, and if so, whether they in fact were.

12. From the notebook: 'Get an order ... for kettle drums in the Press Club ... Get a bell'. The bell is referred to in bit 15 and also on the posters ('The start will be announced by a bell').
13. *Smena*, 9 April 1930, No. 81. This article is reprinted in Vved. II, Appendix X, No. 28, pp. 247–9.
14. N. Aseev, 'Segodnyaschii den' sovetskoi poezii', *Krasnaia Nov'*, 2, 1931, pp. 163–4. Reprinted in Vved. II, pp. 249–50.
15. D. Tolmachev, 'Dadaisty v Leningrade', *Zhizn' iskusstva*, 44, 1st November 1927, p. 14.
16. Lidiia Lesnaia, 'Ytuerebo', *Krasnaia gazeta*, 25 January 1928 (evening edition) No 24 (1694). Reprinted in Vved. II, pp. 246–7.
17. We do not even know if this article actually was written: the title is mentioned in a list of articles in Notebook No 12. Of these the only one we know is the first one, 'Objects and figures'. The other articles mentioned include 'The history of OBERIU', 'I and Shura' (i.e. Vvedensky), etc.
18. See Kharms's note (Notebook No 12) about the agenda of one of the OBERIU meetings which was to be held soon after the 'Three Left Hours' evening: 'Discuss the position in Press Club'.
19. B. F. Semënov, 'Dalëkoe – riadom', *Neva*, 9, 1979, p. 184.
20. 'For the evening of Litfond: Read *A Winter's Walk* ...' (November 1928); '25 Tuesday – evening in Press Club. Our play.' Notebook No. 16.
21. Notebooks Nos 13, 14, 16, 19, 20.
22. See Vved. II, Appendix X, No. 21, p. 247.
23. Ibid. I, p. xxiii.
24. V. Kaverin, 'V starom dome', *Zvezda*, 10, 1971. These memoirs were later reprinted in his book, *Osveshchënnye okna*.
25. Many of the stage directions which formally refer to the stage actions in fact explain not only the staging but also the text itself. Such are 'A log is carried to the front of the stage', and 'while P. N. and I. I. are running they saw up this log', which explain the line 'the log is sawed up' in bit 5; or 'Enter P. N. and I. I. dressed as firemen' at the end. [For this reason, we have retained the stage notes in the translation which follows. Ed.]
26. Kharms was first arrested along with Vvedensky and several left artists on the eve of the New Year 1932. See Vved. I, p. xxiv. Ten years later he was arrested again [See Introduction and Chronology for further details, Ed.].
27. See previously in the verbal duel of the antagonists the purely incantatory semantics of joints bound [?] with red lashes. Cf. *zaum'* with a similar function in Elizaveta's speech in her demonized form in the 'displacement of heights' scene. In both places the *zaum'* is accompanied by a magic raising of the hands. Kharms's notebooks testify to his interest in magic.

# Kharms's Play Elizaveta Bam 219

28. An inverted form of this image (the cockroach as the victim of the 'knives, axes' of executioners and vivisectionists) is to be found in Oleinikov's 'Cockroach' ('Tarakan', Oleinikov, pp. 80–2). The connection between Oleinikov's image and the verses of Captain Lebiadkin has often been discussed: G. V. Filippov, 'O traditsiiakh Dostoevskogo v russkoi poezii 20–30 godov (Kapitan Lebiadkin i oberiuty)', *Nauchnaia konferentsiia, posviashchënnaia 150-letiiu so dnia rozhdeniia F. M. Dostoevskogo i N. A. Nekrasova* (Novgorod, 1971) pp. 20–2; Fleishman, in Oleinikov, pp. 17–18; S. V. Poliakova, 'Dve zametki o poezii Nikolaia Oleinikova', *Neue russische Literatur*, No. 2–3, 1980; Serman 1981. But there is also another inverted reference to Lebiadkin's cockroach in *Elizaveta Bam*. In general insects were important inhabitants of the poetic world of the Chinar-Oberiut poets, not only for Oleinikov but also Vvedensky (see Vved. I, pp. 34–5, 87, 113, 130, 133, etc.) and Zabolotsky, in his 'School for Beetles' and others.
29. Can this be related to the folklore motif of the return of the murdered person to avenge his murder? (see also note 34).
30. These can be interpreted as desired either in Advaitist (Shunyat) terminology, or in a New Testament, kenotic sense.
31. See 'Prayer before sleep' [*'Molitva pered snom'*], Sob, proizv. III, p. 22.
32. For instance the 'young man who surprised the watchman' from the tale of that title in *Sluchai*, and the hero of the story 'Makarov and Petersen', with the explanation taken from the book *Malgil*: 'Gradually a person loses his shape and becomes a "sphere" . . .' A character in one of Kharms's little fragments shatters 'into a thousand little balls', the draughtsmen 'shamed by their ignorance' melt into the air, and in the story 'Optical illusion' (*Sluchai* No. 6) a certain Semën Semënovich sees a peasant in a pine tree threatening him with his fist when he puts his glasses on, but when he takes them off 'he sees that there is no one sitting in the pine tree' (see *Polët; Black Coat; Plummeting*, for texts in Russian and English).
33. There are quite a few such stories 'about nothing' in Kharms; for instance, the stories 'Petrakov' and 'A Meeting' (in *Sluchai*) which both end with the words 'That's about all' (See *Polët* and *Black Coat*). Then there are the stories 'about no one', about the red-haired man who had no ears, eyes, hands, legs and so on, 'He had nothing! So we can't understand who we are talking about', and the related story 'On phenomena and existences No 2' (see *Polët* and *Plummeting*).
34. Compare in the first tale, 'then I lived . . .' Perhaps one possible interpretation of the image of Pëtr Nikolaevich is to see him as murdered by Elizaveta and returning to take vengeance on her? This interpretation would explain why Ivan Ivanovich who completes Pëtr's sentences and speaks for him, says, 'I speak, therefore I am'; it would also explain the motif of his transformation into a wizard, etc. This, however, is only one possible reading of this highly complex work.

# 16 *Yelizaveta Bam*: A Dramatic Work. A new translation from the definitive text by Neil Cornwell

Daniil Kharms

DRAMATIS PERSONAE

Yelizaveta [Elizabeth] Bam
Pyotr Nikolayevich [First Voice]
Ivan Ivanovich [Second Voice]
Daddy
Mummy
Beggar
various voices, noises, instruments, a choir etc. – offstage, or from the hall

(DECOR – STAGE: A SHALLOW, SIMPLE ROOM)

**1st bit. Realistic melodrama**

*Yelizaveta Bam* Now, I'm afraid, the door will open and they'll come in . . . They'll definitely come in, to catch me and wipe me from the face of the earth. (*quietly*) What have I done! What have I done! If only I knew . . . Run away? (*a footstep*) But run away where? This door opens on to the staircase, and I'll meet them on the staircase. Through the window? (*looks out of the window*) Ooh-er, it's so high! I couldn't jump! So what shall I do? . . . Oh!, someone's footsteps! It's them. I'll lock the door and won't open it. Let them knock as long as they like.
(*Knock at the door, then a Voice threateningly*):

Elizabeth Bam, open up!
Elizabeth Bam, open up!
*Distant Voice: (Behind stage)*
What's she up to in there, won't she open the door?
*Voice behind the door:*     She'll open it. Yelizaveta Bam, open up!
*Eliz. Bam throws herself onto the bed and covers her ears*
*Voices behind the door:*
*First:*     Elizabeth Bam, I am ordering you to open up immediately!
*Second (quietly):*     You tell her that if she doesn't we'll break the door down. Let me try.
*First (loudly):*     We'll break the door down if you don't open up right away.
*Second (quietly):*     Perhaps she's not here?
*First (quietly):*     She's here. Where else would she be? She ran up the staircase. There's only one door here. Where else could she get to? *(loudly)* Yelizaveta Bam – it's speaking to you I am
*(Eliz. Bam raises her head)*
*(with an alliterative ring)*, for the last time, open the door. *(a pause)* Break it down.
*(They try to break the door down. Eliz. Bam runs to the middle of the stage, listening)*
*Second:*     Haven't you got a knife?
*(A bang at the door. Eliz. Bam listens, her shoulder thrust forward)*
*First:*     No, use your shoulder.
*Second:*     It won't give. Wait a minute, I'll try again.
*(The door creaks, but doesn't break)*
*El. Bam:*     I won't open the door to you until you tell me what you intend to do with me.
*(The knocking quietens at El. Bam's retort)*
*First voice:*     You know yourself what you are in for.
*El. Bam:*     No, I don't. Are you going to kill me?
*First:*     *(together)*     You are liable to stringent punishment!
*Second:*     You won't get away from us, whatever happens!
*El. Bam:*     Perhaps you would tell me what offence I have committed.
*First:*     You know yourself.
*El. Bam:*     No, I don't know. *(stamps her foot)*
*First:*     Excuse us if we don't believe you.
*Second:*     You are a criminal.

*El. Bam:* Ha, ha ha! And if you kill me, do you think your conscience will be clear?
(*Runs across*)
*First:* We'll take care of it, in due conformity with our conscience.
*El. Bam:* In that case then, alas, you can't have any conscience.

**2nd bit. The genre of realistic comedy**

*Second:* What do you mean, no conscience? Pyotr Nikolayevich, she says that we have no conscience.
(*El. Bam, standing, hands on thighs and neck craned to the door*)
*El. Bam:* You, Ivan Ivanovich, have no conscience whatsoever. You are just a scoundrel.
*Second:* Who's a scoundrel? Me? I am? I am a scoundrel?!
*First:* Now, hang on a minute, Ivan Ivanovich!
Elizabeth Bam, I order you to . . .
*Second:* No, Pyotr Nikolayevich, would you say that I am the scoundrel here?
*First:* Hang on a minute before you take umbrage! Yelizaveta Bam, I'm ord . . .
*Second:* No, just a mo, Pyotr Nikolayevich. Are you going to tell me that I'm a scoundrel?
*First:* Leave it off, will you!
*Second:* You mean, you do think I'm a scoundrel?
*First:* Yes, a scoundrel!!!
*Second:* So that's it, you think I'm a scoundrel! Is that what you said?
(*El. Bam runs about the stage*)
*First:* You'd better just bugger off then, you dunderhead! And you're supposed to be conducting a responsible inquiry. The first word that's said to you and you go up the wall. What does that make you? Just an idiot!
*Second:* And you're a charlatan!
*First:* Just bugger off!
*El. Bam:* Ivan Ivanovich is a scoundrel!
*Second:* I won't forgive you for this!
*First:* I'll throw you down the staircase in a minute!
(*El. Bam opens the door. Ivan Ivanovich stands there on crutches, and Pyotr Nikolayevich is sitting on a chair with a bandaged cheek*)
*Ivan Ivanovich:* Just you try it!
*Pyotr Nikolayevich:* I will, I will, I will, I will!

## Yelizaveta Bam: *A Dramatic Work*

*El. Bam:*     No chance!
*Pyotr Nik.:*     I've no chance, you mean?
*El. Bam:* (*together*)     Yes
*Ivan Iv.:*     You! You! You mean him, don't you?
(*Ivan Iv. points to Pyotr Nik.*)
*El. Bam:*     Him!
*Pyotr Nik.:*     Elizabeth Bam, how dare you speak like that!
*El. Bam:*     Why shouldn't I?
*Pyotr Nik:*     Because you have lost all right of reply. You have committed a vile crime. It's not for you to be impertinent to me. You are a criminal!
*El. Bam:*     Why?
*Pyotr Nik.:*     What do you mean, why?
El. Bam:     Why am I a criminal?
*Pyotr Nik.:*     Because you have lost all right of reply.
*Ivan Iv.:*     Lost all right of reply.
*El. Bam:*     I haven't lost any such thing. You can check by the clock.
(*The stage backcloth moves back, letting I.I. and P.N. through the door*)

**3rd bit. Absurdly comic-naive**

*Pyotr Nik.:*     It won't come to that. I have placed a guard on the door, and at the slightest push Ivan Ivanovich will hiccup an aside.
*El. Bam:*     A demonstration, please, a demonstration.
*Pyotr Nik.:*     Just look, then. I suggest you avert your eyes.
(*P.N. comes to the proscenium, I.I. follows him*)
     One, two, three.
(*touches the pedestal, I.I. hiccups loudly, Pyotr turns the pedestal over*)
*El. Bam:*     And again, please.
(*They repeat it. P.N. again touches the pedestal and I.I. again hiccups.*)
     How do you do it?
*Pyotr Nik.:*     It's very simple. Ivan Ivanovich, demonstrate.
*Ivan Iv.:*     With pleasure.
(*Gets down on his hands and knees and kicks one leg in the air*)
*El. Bam:*     Oh, it's charming, it's so good (*Shouts*) Mum! Come here! The conjurers have arrived! My mother will be here in just a moment . . . You must meet her, Pyotr Nikolayevich! Ivan Ivanovich! Are you going to show us something?

*Ivan Iv.:* With pleasure.
*Pyotr Nik.:* Allez-oop!
(*I.I. tries to stand on his head, but topples*)
*Pyotr Nik.:* He'll do it now, right away.
(*On stage come Daddy and Mummy, who sit down and watch*)
*Ivan Iv.:* (*sitting on the floor*) There's nothing to lean on here.
*El. Bam* (*flirtingly*): Would you like a towel perhaps?
*Ivan Iv.:* What for?
*El. Bam:* Oh, not for anything in particular. Tee-hee-hee.
*Ivan Iv.:* I say, you do have an extraordinarily pleasant appearance.
*El. Bam:* Oh really? Why is that?
*Ivan Iv.:* Ee-ee-ee-ee-, because you're a forget-me-not (*loudly hiccups*).
*El. Bam:* I'm a forget-me-not? Really? And you are a tulip (*in a nasal tone*).
*Ivan Iv.:* What?
*El. Bam:* A tulip.
*Ivan Iv.:* (*in some perplexity*) Thank you very much, I'm sure.
*El. Bam* (*nasally*): Allow me to pluck you.
*Daddy* (*in a bass voice*): Elizabeth, don't be silly.
*El. Bam* (*to father*): Daddy, I'll stop right away. (*squatting, her hands resting on her knees; to I.I., nasally*) Get down on your hands and knees.
(*P.N. goes over to Daddy and Mummy. Mummy, displeased at something, moves downstage*)
*Ivan Iv.:* If you will allow me, Elizabeth Cockroach, I had better be getting home. My wife's waiting for me at home. She has lots of children, Elizabeth Cockroach. Forgive me for boring you so. Don't forget me. I'm the sort of person everyone sends on errands. Why, one wonders? Am I a thief, or something? Certainly not! Yelizaveta Edwardovna, I'm an honest man. I have a wife at home. My wife has children, lots of them. Nice children. They keep holding a matchbox in their teeth, every one of them. Please forgive me. I'm going home, Yelizaveta Mikhaylovna.
(*I.I. puts on his fur coat and goes out. El. Bam ties a rope to Mummy's leg – the other end she ties to a chair. They all remain silent.*)
*Mummy* (*sings to music*): Morning has broken
Like the first morning.
Blackbird has spoken
Like the first bird.

*(Mummy finishes her song and goes back to her place, dragging the chair behind her)*
*Pyotr Nik.:*     Well, here we are!
*Daddy:*     Thank God for that!
*(They leave the stage)*


**4th bit. Realistic. Everyday comic genre.**

*El. Bam:*     And you, Mummy, are you really not going out?
*Mummy:*     Do you feel like it?
*El. Bam:*     Awfully.
*Mummy:*     No, I'm not going.
*El. Bam:*     Let's go, come on.
*Mummy:*     Well, let's go then, let's go.
*(They go out. The stage is empty.)*


**5th bit. Rhythmic (RADIX), author's rhythm.**

*Ivan Iv.* and *Pyotr Nik.* (*running in*):
    Oh where, where, where
    is Yelizaveta Bam,
       Yelizaveta Bam.
       Yelizaveta Bam.
*Pyotr Nik.:*     Here, here, here.
*Ivan Iv.:*     There, there, there.
*Pyotr N.* (*syncopated verse*):     Oh, Ivan Ivanovich, what is our result?
*Ivan Iv.:*     Why, Pyotr Nikolayevich, we're under lock and key.
*Pyotr N.:*     Well, that is just outrageous! It's not me that you should clout!
*Ivan Iv.:*     Here's a pound for you, and it's five minus five for me!
*Pyotr N.* (*melodiously*): Where, oh where is Elizabeth Bam?
*Ivan Iv.:*     Why do you want her, you big ham?
*Pyotr Nik.:*     Oh, to kill her!
*Ivan Iv.:*     Well, now, Elizabeth Bam
    Is sitting there: if you want her, scram!
*Pyotr Nik.:*     We'd better start running then, feller!
*(Both start running on the spot. A log is brought on frontstage and while P.N. and I.I. are running, the log is being sawn.)*

*Both:* Hop, hop
move your stumps
the sun is setting
over the humps
big clouds of rosy hue
puff, puff
of chuff-chuff
toowit-towoo
the owl does coo
   that log! –
   – it's all sawn through.

**6th bit. Everyday RADIX**

(*A flap is moved back and behind the flap sits Eliz. Bam*)
*El. Bam:* Are you looking for me?
*Pyotr Nik.:* Yes, you! Van'ka, she's here!
*Ivan Iv.:* Where, where, where?
*Pyotr Nik.:* ere, under the thingamy!
(*On stage comes a beggar.*)
*Ivan Iv.:* Pull her out here!
*Pyotr Nik.:* She won't come!
*Beggar* (*to El. Bam*): Comrade, help me out.
*Ivan Iv.* (*stammering*): Next time I'll have have experience. I've just been watching points.
*El. Bam* (*to beggar*): I have nothing.
*Beggar:* Just a kopek.
*El. Bam:* Ask that bloke over there (*pointing at P.N.*).
(*A table is wheeled out on stage; El. Bam brings a chair over to it and sits down*)
*Pyotr Nik.* (*to Ivan Iv., stammering*): You look what you are doing!
*Ivan Iv.* (*stammering*): I'm digging up roots.
*Beggar:* Help me out, comrades.
*Pyotr Nik.* (*to beggar*): Come on. Get in there.
*Ivan Iv.:* Hold on to the pebbles with your hands.
(*The beggar climbs under the flap*)
*Pyotr Nik.:* That's not bad, he can do it.
*El. Bam:* You sit down, too. Why don't you?
(*Pause*)
*Ivan Iv.:* Thank you.

Yelizaveta Bam: *A Dramatic Work* 227

*Pyotr Nik.:* Let's sit down.
(*They sit down; silence; they eat soup.*)
*El. Bam:* My husband is late, it seems. Where's he got to now?
*Pyotr Nik.:* He'll come (*jumps up and runs around the stage*). Mob-mob! Chur-choora!
*Ivan Iv.:* Ha, ha, ha (*runs after P.N.*). Where's the 'den'?
*El. Bam:* Here, behind this line.
(*Daddy comes on stage with a feather in his hand.*)
*Pyotr Nik.* (*taps I.I.*): You're 'it'.
*El. Bam:* Ivan Ivanych, run over here!
*Ivan Iv.:* Ha, ha, ha, I've no legs!
*Pyotr Nik.:* Go on, like that, on all fours!
*Daddy:* Concerning whom it was written.
*El. Bam:* Who's 'it'?
*Ivan Iv.:* I am, hah, ha, ha, the one in the trousers!
*Pyotr N. & El. Bam:* Ha, ha, ha, ha . . .!
*Daddy:* Copernicus was a very great scientist.
*Ivan Iv.* (*falling to the floor*): I've got hair on my head!
*Pyotr N. & El. Bam:* Ha, ha, ha, ha, hahahaha!
*Ivan Iv.:* I'm completely lying on the floor!
(*On stage comes Mummy.*)
*Pyotr N. & El. Bam:* Ha, ha, ha, ha, ha!
*El. Bam:* Oh, oh, it's too much!
*Daddy:* When you're buying a bird, make sure it hasn't got teeth. If it's got teeth, it isn't a bird.

**7th bit. Solemn melodrama, with undertones of RADIX**

*Pyotr Nik.* (*raising his hand*): I must ask you to listen properly to my words. I want to prove to you that every misfortune comes unexpectedly.
When I was still a very young man I lived in a small house with a squeaking door. I lived alone in that house. Apart from me there were only mice and cockroaches. You get cockroaches everywhere; when night came on I would lock the door and put out the lamp. I used to sleep, and would be afraid of nothing more.
*Voice off:* Nothing!
*Mummy:* Nothing!
(*Pipe sounds offstage: three notes:*) ♩ ♪ ♩
*Ivan Iv.:* Nothing!
(*Piano is played: three notes:*) ♩ ♪ ♩

*Pyotr Nik.:* Nothing more!
(*A pause*)
I had nothing to be afraid of. Really. Robbers could have come and gone through the whole house. What would they have found? Nothing more.
(*Pipe sounds off: three notes:*) ♩ ♪ ♩
(*Pause*)
*Pyotr Nik.:* And who else could get to me at night? Nobody else? At all?
*Voice Off:* Well, was there nobody else?
*Pyotr Nik.:* At all?
But on one occasion, I'm just waking up . . .
(*P.N. and I.I. merge together*)
*Ivan Iv.:* . . . and I see the door, open, and in the doorway stands some woman or other. I look her right in the eyes. She just stands there. It was light enough. It must have been getting on towards morning. Anyway, I saw her face quite clearly. And this is who it was (*points at El. Bam*). At that time she looked like . . .
*Everyone:* Like me!
*Ivan Iv.:* . . . I speak, therefore I am.
*El. Bam:* What are you saying?
*Ivan Iv.:* I speak, therefore I am. It had to be done now. She's listening to me.
(*Everyone, apart from El. Bam and I.I., leaves the stage*)
I asked her what she had done it with. She says they were fighting with spadroons. It was a fair fight, but she's not to blame for killing him. Listen to me, why did you kill Pyotr Nikolayevich?
*El. Bam:* Hurray, I didn't kill anyone!
*Ivan Iv.:* To cut him down, just like that! The treachery in that! Hurray! you did it, but why?

**8th bit. A displacement of heights**

*El. Bam* (*exits to the side, from where*): Ooh, ooh, ooh-oo-oo.
*Ivan Iv.:* She-wolf.
*El. Bam:* Ooh-oo-oo-oo.
*Ivan Iv.:* She-ee-ee-wolf.
*El. Bam* (*shaking*): Oo-oo-oo-prunes.
*Ivan Iv.:* Your gr-r-r-eat grandmother. (*lowers his arm*)
*El. Bam:* Triumph!
*Ivan Iv.:* You're destroyed for ever. (*lowers his finger*)

*El. Bam:* A black horse, and on the horse a soldier!
*Ivan Iv.* (*strikes a match*): My darling Yelizaveta! (*I.I.'s hands shake*)
*El. Bam:* My shoulders, like rising suns! (*climbs on chair*)
*Ivan Iv.* (*squatting*): My legs, like cucumbers!
*El. Bam* (*climbing higher*): Hurray! I haven't said a thing!
*Ivan Iv.* (*lying down on the floor*): No, no, not a thing, not a thing, gug-ga, psh-psh.
*El. Bam* (*raising her arm*): Koo-nee-ma-ga-nee-lee-va-nee-ba-ooh, ooh!
*Ivan Iv.* (*lying on the floor*): Pussy-cat, pussy-cat
taking the milk to task
on the cushion she jumped
on the stove she jumped
jump, jump
skip, skip
*El. Bam* (*shouts*): Gee, a gate! A shirt! a rope!
*Ivan Iv.* (*getting up*): Two carpenters come running up and ask: what's up?
*El. Bam:* Rissoles! Varvara Semyonna!
*Ivan Iv.:* A dancer on the wi-ire!
*El Bam* (*springing up from chair*): I'm all a-glitter!
*Ivan Iv.* (*runs to back of room*): The cubic capacity of this room has not been fully calculated by us.
(*The scenery revolves from living room to countryside. The coulisses give way to Daddy and Mummy*)
*El. Bam* (*runs to the other end of the stage*): It's a family affair!

## 9th bit. Pastoral bit

*Ivan Iv.* (*jumping onto chair*): The prosperity of the Pennsylvanian shepherd and shep-uh-uh!
*El. Bam* (*jumping onto other chair*): Ivan Iva-ah!
*Daddy* (*showing a box*): A box made of woo-oo-ooh!
*Ivan Iv.* (*from the chair*): So lo-o-ong!
*Daddy:* Here, have a lo-oo-oo!
*Mummy:* Coo-ee-ee-ee!
*El. Bam:* I've found a brown-cap mush-er-roo-oo-ooh!
*Ivan Iv.:* Let's go down to the lake!
*Daddy:* Coo-ee-ee-ee!

*El. Bam:* Coo-ee-ee-ee!
*Ivan Iv.:* I met Nicky yesterday!
*Mummy:* Really-ee-ee-ee!
*Ivan Iv.:* Yes, I did. I met him, I met him. I saw Nicky walking along, carrying some apples. You bought them, did you, I asked? Yes, he said, I bought them. Then he just walked on.
*Daddy:* You don't say-ay-ay!
*Ivan Iv.:* So yes, I asked him: what, did you buy those apples, then, or steal them? And he said: why should I steal them? I bought them. And he just walked off on his way.
*Mummy:* Where did he walk off to?
*Ivan Iv.:* I don't know. He didn't steal them, didn't buy them. Just walked on.

**10th bit. Monologue aside, double-intentioned bit**

*Daddy:* With this not particularly amiable salutation, her sister conducted her to a more open spot, where stacked in a pile were golden tables and armchairs and a complement of about fifteen young maidens, babbling gaily amongst themselves and sitting wherever they could. All these maidens were badly in need of a hot smoothing-iron and all were distinguished by a strange manner of rolling their eyes, not for an instant ceasing to babble.
(*A maid comes in, carrying out a table-cloth and a basket of provisions.*)

**11th bit. Speech**

*Ivan Iv.:* My friends, we are all gathered. Hooray!
*El. Bam:* Hooray!
*Mummy & Daddy:* Hooray!
*Ivan Iv.* (*shaking and striking a match*): I want you to know that since I was born thirty-eight years have passed.
*Mummy & Daddy:* Hooray!
*Ivan Iv.:* Comrades. I have a home. My wife is waiting at home. She has lots of kids. I've counted them – there are ten of them.
*Mummy* (*straight out, on the spot*): Darya, Marya, Fyodor, Pelageya, Nina, Alexander and four others.
*Daddy:* Are they all boys?

Yelizaveta Bam: *A Dramatic Work* 231

**12th bit. The Chinar-ish bit.**

*El. Bam: (running round the stage):* I've broken away from everywhere!
Broken away and started to run!
Broken away and, so, run!
*Mummy (running after El. Bam):* Sup some soup?
*Daddy:* Sup some meat? *(running)*
*Mummy:* Sup some flour?
*(Entracte-cataract)*
*Ivan Iv.:* Sup some swede?
*El. Bam:* Sup some mutton?
*Daddy:* Sup some rissoles?
*Mummy:* Oh, my legs are getting tired!
*Ivan Iv.:* Oh, my arms are getting tired!
*El. Bam:* Oh, my scissors are getting tired!
*Daddy:* Oh, my springs are getting tired!
*(Behind stage a choir sings to the tune of the overture)*
*Mummy:* The door's open onto the balcony!
*Ivan Iv.:* I'd like to jump up to the third floor!
*El. Bam:* Broken away and started to run!
Broken away and, so, run!
*(Music strikes up)*
*Daddy:* Help, my right hand and my nose are the same as my left hand and ear!
*(All, one after the other, run from the stage)*
*Choir (to the music of the tune of the overture):*
Fare thee well, then.

Upstairs there speaks a pine,
and all round it speaks darkly.
On the pine, there speaks a bed
and in the bed lies a spouse.
Fare thee well, then.

Once we ran to
♩ ♪ ♩ an endless house.
And out of the window upstairs there looks

though his glasses a young old man.
Fare thee well, then.

♫ ♩ ♪
♫ ♩ ♪

There then opened the gates,
and there showed themselves  ♪ ♩ ♪
(*Overture: the lights dim.*)

**13th bit. RADIX**

(*Only Pyotr Nikolayevich is illuminated*)
*Ivan Iv.:*    Now you are broken
  your chair is broken.
*Violin:*    Pa pa pée pa
  pa pa pée pa
*Pyotr Nik.:*    Rise like Berlin
  put on your pelerine.
*Violin:*    pa pa pée pa
  pa pa pée pa
*Pyotr Nik.:*    Eight minutes
  fly past unnoticed.
*Violin:*    pa pa pée pa pa
  pa pa pée
*Pyotr Nik.:*    You are made to see
  you arouse the laboureres
  the platoon or the compan-ee
  to carry the machine gun.
*Drum:*    I--I-    ♩ ♫ ♩ ♪
  I--I-    ♩ ♫ ♩ ♪
  I--I--I-I    ♩ ♫ ♩ ♫ ♩ ♪ ♩
*Pyotr Nik.:*    The tatters, they flew
  week after week.
*Siren & Drum:*    Vee-a-a-boom, boom
  Vee-a-a-boom.
(*The light gradually becomes brighter*)
*Pyotr Nik.:*    The droopish bridge didn't notice
  the captain-like shuntish noise.
*Siren:*    vée-a, vée-a, vée-a, vée-a
*Pyotr Nik.:*    Help me now, please help me
  I've salad and water hanging over me.
(*Full light*)

*Violin:* pa pa pée pa
   pa pa pée pa
(*The coulisse gives way to Ivan Ivanovich*)

**14th bit. Classical inspiration**

*Ivan Iv.:*   Tell me, Pyotr Nikolayevich,
   Have you been there, on yonder hill?
*Pyotr Nik.:*   I'm just back from there.
      It's wonderful there.
(*Declamation*)
      Flowers are growing. The trees are rustling.
      There stands a poor hut – a small wooden house,
      in the hut a low light burns,
      over the light swarm thunderflies,
      at windows knock the gnats of the night.
      Now and then who flutters in and out under the roof,
      but that old brigand, the night-jar.
      The dog agitates the air with its chain
      and barks all before it into the void,
      while in reply unprepossessing dragon-flies
      murmur their spells in every key.
*Ivan Iv.:*   And in this small house, all of wood
      which we call out a poor hut,
      in which a low light shines and shifts,
      who, pray, in this small house resides?
*Pyotr Nik.:*   No one resides therein
      and the door doesn't open,
      therein only mice rub flour between their palms,
      therein only the lamp shines as rosemary
      the livelong day sits the anchorite cockroach on the
      stove.
*Ivan Iv.:*   But who then lights the lamp?
*Pyotr Nik.:*   No one, it burns by itself.
*Ivan Iv.:*   But that surely cannot be!
*Pyotr Nik.:*   Empty, stupid words!
      There is an infinite movement,
      the breathing of the lighter elements,
      planetary motion, the earth's rotation,
      the crazed alternation of day and night,
      the combination of remote nature,

the anger and strength of untamed beasts
and the subjugation by man
of the laws of light and wave.
*Ivan Iv.: (lighting a match)*:     Now I realise, realise, realise.
I give my thanks and squat
and as always take an interest –
What time is it? Tell me.
*Pyotr Nik.:*     Four. Oh, it's time for dinner!
Ivan Ivanovich, let's go,
but remember that tomorrow night
Yelizaveta Bam will die.
*Daddy (entering)*:     Which is Yelizaveta Bam,
who is daughter to me,
whom you want
on the very next night
to kill and string up on that pine,
who is so slender,
so all the beasts around should know
and the entire country.
But I am ordering you
by the might of my arm
to forget Elizabeth Bam,
all laws notwithstanding.
*Pyotr Nik.:*     Just try to stop us,
I'll crush you in an instant,
and then with gilded lashes
I'll break all your joints.
You'll be slit up, puffed up
and floated downwind like a fowl.
*Ivan Iv.:*     He knows what's what,
he's my guv'nor and my friend,
with a single movement of the wing
he moves the seas,
with a single swing of his axe
he cuts down forest and mountains –
with just his breath
he is ubiquitously elusive.
*Daddy:*     Let us join battle, sorcerer,
you by word and I by arm,
a minute will pass, an hour will pass,
and yet another more.

Perished be you, perished be me,
quiet let it be 'til – wham!
may then she rejoice, daughter mine,
Yelizaveta Bam.

**15th bit. Balladic inspiration**


BATTLE OF THE TWO HEROES

(*Two chairs are brought on stage*)
Ivan Iv.:   The battle of the two heroes!
   Text – by Immanuel Krasdeiteirich.
   Music – by Veliopag, the Netherlandish shepherd.
   Movement – by an unknown wayfarer.
   The bell will announce the start.
*Voices from various parts of the hall:*
   The battle of the two heroes!
   Text – by Immanuel Krasdeiteirich!
   Music – by Veliopag, the Netherlandish shepherd!
   Movement – by an unknown wayfarer!
   The bell will announce the start!
   The battle of the two heroes!
      (etc.)
*Bell:*   Boom, boom, boom, boom, boom.
*Pyotr Nik.:*   Kurybéer daramóur
   dín-dee-ree
   slakatéer paka-rádagou
   da kée chéerie kíri-kíri
   zan-dudéela khaba-cooler
      hey-ell
   khánchoo aná coodie
   stóom chi na lákoodie
   para voo-ee na lée tenner
      hey-ell
   chápoo áchapáli
   chapátali már
   nabalóchéená
(*Raises his arm*)   hey-ell
*Daddy:*   Let it fly off to the sun,
   that wingèd parrot,

let it fade, the golden
widened day, let it.
Let there through the forest peal
the beats of hoof and hunk,
and with a squeal comes from the wheel
that fundamental trunk.
While the knight at table sits
touching his pointed ends
he'll raise his goblet up and then
o'er goblet he will cry:
I lift this cup
to my rapturous lips,
I toast the very best of all,
to Yelizaveta Bam!
Whose very hands, so spick and span
caressed my robes and furs . . .
Live, Elizabeth Bam, live on,
a hundred thousand years!
*Pyotr Nik.:*  Well, sir, let's begin.
I beg you to follow closely
the wavering of our sabres –
which one whither throws its point
and which takes where its direction.
(*Strikes*)
*Ivan Iv.:*  Thus I record a thrust on the left!
*Daddy* (*thrusting*):  I cut to the side, I cut to the right,
save himself who may!
The oak grove rustles with all its might,
grow, gardens, while ye may.
*Pyotr Nik.:*  Spend less time looking around
and watch rather the movement
of the iron centres and the curdling
of deathly powers.
(*Daddy raises his rapier and waves it in declamatory time*)
*Daddy:*  Praise be to iron – carborundum!
It holds pavements together
and, shining by electricity,
tears asunder the enemy!
Praise be to iron! Our battle song!
It alarms the brigand,
bears the infant into youth,

tears asunder the enemy!
Oh battle song! Glory to the feathers!
Through the air they fly,
they fill in the eyes of the faithless,
tear asunder the enemy!
Oh glory to the feathers! Wisdom to the stone.
It lies neath the portentous pine,
from under it water runs
to meet the dead enemy.
(*Pyotr Nik. falls*)
*Pyotr Nik.:*   I've fallen, stricken, to the earth
farewell, Yelizaveta Bam,
come down to my place on the hill,
and fall back with a slam.
And then will run all over you
and up and down your arms,
the mice so wild and after that
the anchorite cockroach – wham!
(*A bell rings*)
You hear now how the bell tolls
on the rooftop, bim and bang.
Forgive me and excuse me please,
Yelizaveta Bam.
*Ivan Iv.:*   The battle of the two heroes is over.
(*Pyotr Nik. is carried out*)

**16th bit. Chimes**

*El. Bam* (*entering*):   Ah, Daddy, here you are. I am glad.
I've just been to the shop,
I've just been buying sweets,
I wanted there to be cake for tea.
*Daddy* (*opening the gate*):   Phoo, I'm just about worn out.
*El. Bam:*   But what have you been doing?
*Daddy:*   I've been, er, cutting the wood and I'm totally worn out.
*El. Bam:*   Ivan Ivanovich, go down to the barroom and bring us a bottle of beer and some peas.
*Ivan Iv.:*   Aha! peas and a half bottle of beer, go down to the bar, and from there, back here.
*El. Bam:*   Not half a bottle, a bottle of beer, and don't go to the bar, go for the peas!

*Ivan Iv.:* Right away, I'll hide my fur coat in the barroom and I'll put a half pea-pod on my head.
*El. Bam:* Oh no, don't do that, just hurry up, or my Dad will have dropped from cutting wood.
*Daddy:* Oh women! They have little conception, and in their conceptions they have a vacuum.


**17th bit. Physiological inspiration**

*Mummy:* (*entering*): Comrades. This Jezebel done my son in.
(*Two heads poke out from the wings*)
*Heads:* Who did? Who did?
*Mummy:* This one here, with her very lips!
*El. Bam:* Mummy, Mummy, what are you saying?
(*Ivan Ivanovich strikes a match*)
*Mummy:* All because of you his life ended as a dead loss.
*El. Bam:* Just tell me, who are you talking about?
*Mummy* (*stone faced*): Eek! Eek! Ee-eek!
*El Bam:* She's gone mad!
(*Daddy gets a handkerchief and dances on the spot*)
*Mummy:* I'm a cuttle-fish.
(*The decor begins to turn from countryside into a room. The wings absorb Mummy and Daddy.*)
*El. Bam:* They'll be here in a moment. What have I done!
*Mummy:* 3 × 27 = 81


**18th bit. Realistic dry-official**

(*Scene is as at the beginning*)
*El. Bam:* They'll definitely come, to catch me and wipe me from the face of the earth. Run away. I should run away. But run away where? This door leads to the staircase, and I'll meet them on the staircase. Through the window? (*looks out of the window*) Oh-oh, I couldn't jump. It's very high. So what shall I do? Oh! someone's footsteps. It's them. I'll lock the door and won't open it. Let them knock as long as they like.
(*Locks the door*)
*Knock, then Voice:* Elizabeth Bam, in the name of the law, I order you to open this door.
(*Silence*)

*First Voice:* I order you to open this door!
(*Silence*)
*Second Voice* (*quietly*): Let's break down the door.
*First Voice:* Elizabeth Bam, open up, otherwise we'll break in ourselves!
*El. Bam:* What do you intend to do with me?
*First Voice:* You are liable to stringent punishment.
*El. Bam:* For what? Why don't you want to tell me what I have done?
*First Voice:* You are accused of the murder of Pyotr Nikolayevich Krupernák.
*Second Voice:* And for that you will answer.
*El. Bam:* But I haven't killed anyone!
*First Voice:* That the court will decide.
(*El. Bam opens the door. PN and II enter dressed as firemen.*)
*El. Bam:* I am in your power
*Pyotr Nik.:* You are arrested, in the name of the law.
*Ivan Iv.* (*lighting a match*): Follow us.

**19th bit. Operatic ending:**

*El. Bam* (*shouts*): Truss me up! Pull me by my locks! Thread me through the trough! I haven't killed anyone! I couldn't kill anyone!
(*Movement of the coulisses [flap], objects, backcloth and people.*)
*Pyotr Nik.:* Elizabeth Bam, calm down!
*Ivan Iv.:* Look into the distance in front of you. (*loudly hiccups*)
*El. Bam:* And in the little house on the hill a light is already burning. The mice are twitching their whiskers, twitching them. And on the stove sits Cockroach Cockroachovich, in his shirt with the reddish collar and an axe in his hands.
*Pyotr Nik.:* Yelizaveta Bam. Having stretched your arms and extinguished your fixed stare, start walking after me, preserving the equilibrium of your joints and the celebration of your sinews. Follow me.
(*Exeunt slowly. Darkness*)


CURTAIN

Written 12 to 24 December, 1927
Daniil Kharms

## NOTE

Readers of this play (the original text is to be found in Meilakh, 1987, and subsequent Soviet reprintings in *Rodnik*, 1988, and *Polët*: we are grateful to the editors of *Stanford Slavic Studies* for permission to translate) are referred to Mikhail Meilakh's essay preceding the play in this volume. Those wishing to look further into *Elizaveta Bam* are referred to the full text of Meilakh's 1987 article and its accompanying commentary (not translated here). It may also be noted that a more everyday transliteration system, which hopefully facilitates pronunciation of names, has been used for the text of the play than pertains elsewhere in this volume.

# Part VI:
# Conclusion and Apparatus

# 17 Beyond the Turning-Point: An Afterword
Robin Milner-Gulland

These words (*vdali za povorotom*) conclude what may well be Daniil Kharms's most remarkable achievement, the cycle of thirty short pieces called *Sluchai* (*Incidents*). The last episode recounts a bitter, if one-sided, altercation between Pakin and Rakukin, to which Rakukin's sole contribution is the one significant word *Veriu* ('I believe', *Polët*, p. 395). Rakukin dies, and his soul is led by the 'angel of death' into a further realm of 'space beyond the turning-point' (to quote Neil Cornwell's perceptive English version, *Plummeting*, p. 46). The *Sluchai* cycle was finished in 1939, and its ending – lifting earthbound squalor and comically unmotivated violence into unexpected transcendentalism – may seem typical of 'late' Kharms. Yet eight years before he ended a short verse dialogue ('*A nu-ka pokazhi mne ruku*': *Sob. proizv.*, III:165) thus:

> He – Soon we shall construct a rapid raft
> and we shall float along the winding river.
> We shall moor instantly at the angelic gates.
> She – Where?
> He – Beyond the turning-point.

In another poem of the same period (*Voda i Khniu*, *Sob. proizv.*, III:170), 'beyond the turning-point' becomes a thrice-repeated motif in the dialogue between a dead girl and the river that drowned her. The later appearance of this little phrase, it should be observed, throws retrospective light on its earlier uses, and all are illuminated by (and illuminate) a religio-philosophical diary entry for 25 May 1938, which reads in part: 'There is one straight line on which lies everything earthly. And only that which does not lie on this line can bear witness to immortality'.[1] In various genres and over many years Kharms reworked motifs, phrases, names and situations – for this is only one small example among many – allowing us, through them, to enter the intricate pathways of his world of perceptions. Without making some attempt to follow these paths we can claim no more than a nodding acquaintanceship with Kharms.

If I use the phrase of my title as a peg on which to hang some reflections on the possible future directions of Kharms studies, it is also partly because it can evoke another connotation. The general appreciation and scholarly investigation of his legacy seem themselves to have reached a turning-point, which the appearance of the present volume indeed signals. The recent and welcome opening up of publication policy in the Soviet Union means that Kharms can now be printed, read and discussed in his own land. A substantial one-volume selection of his work (*Polët*, over 500 pages) has now appeared there. We also have the complete poetic works – specially valuable for its critical apparatus – in four volumes (*Sob. proizv.*, the Meilakh and Erl edition). It would seem that most, if not all the important dramatic and prose works, together with abundant letters and diary-entries, have seen print. One of our contributors (A. Anemone) draws attention to a sense of Kharms scholarship being poised on the threshold of a major breakthrough. With the feast of Kharmsiana (studies, memoirs etc., as well as original texts) now available, it might seem churlish to demand more. But some of us without regular archival access will be unable to rest content until every word left by Kharms is published (and even then – a topic that I shall return to later – we shall no doubt demand facsimiles of the manuscripts). The reason is simple, and relates to the often-quoted characterisation of Kharms by Vvedensky, cited by Druskin, 'Kharms does not create art, but himself *is* art'. One may be wary of 'biographism' and still admit that the necessary context for Kharms's achievement is his life taken as a whole (he himself, adopting a multitude of *personae*, seems to have clearly understood this). There are important parallels with two writers whose names are frequently and rightly mentioned in connection with Kharms. One is Kafka, who once responded to a correspondent incautious enough to have shown his handwriting to a graphologist, who detected in it 'literary interests', by declaring 'I have no literary interests, but am made of literature; I am nothing else'.[2] The other is Khlebnikov, all of whose work is now normally taken as a totality by specialists, whether it is 'literary' in the ordinary sense or not.

Here a note of warning should be sounded. There are several potential ways in which Kharms can be 'sentimentalised', and one of them is to regard him as a naive and unworldly genius from whose pen flowed a spontaneous but ill-regulated torrent of semi-comprehensible word-weaving with occasional, rather haphazard, flashes of brilliance. Recent investigations, not to mention the various memoirs left by his friend Druskin, tend towards a very different picture. Kharms was a thoroughly professional, self-aware writer, whose works (even the most apparently 'artless') went through various drafts, who distinguished between unfinished, or fragmentary, and finished products – and usually dated the latter precisely. His intermingling of genres, tones of voice, points of view or registers of language does not mean that his feeling for any of these categories was weak: rather, the opposite. With hindsight, we may be tempted to read him as a particularly twentieth-century and Russian type of *poète maudit*, and imagine that he had no hope of publishing 'adult' work after 1927; *he*, though, seems to have counted on readers (even if only his friends, or ultimately just himself) and to have treated them with respect. The consequence of this for us, and our approach to him, is important. We must cease to regard these as semi-finished or throwaway works, or to assume his effects are uncalculated or his obscurities simply aleatoric wellings-up of the subconscious, or that there is much – anything – in his finished works that we can dismiss as 'meaningless'. We must work hard on him.

\* \* \*

Since the emergence of Kharms from obscurity in the late 1960s, we have witnessed successively the rediscovery of Kharms the *oberiu* and children's author, Kharms the humourist, Kharms the dramatist, Kharms the prose-writer – his achievement in this area not really understood until the late 1980s, as the essays in our volume bear witness – and Kharms the speculative religio-philosophical thinker. Can we doubt that the 1990s will see the resurrection of Kharms the poet? After all his verse output (of course known to, but generally marginalised by, commentators up to now) is a constant if fluctuating element throughout his literary activity, pervades his drama and constitutes the largest single element in his heritage. He seems to have seen his role in life as primarily *stikhoslozhenie*.[3] He must, formally, be one of the most varied poets to have written in any language. Much of his verse is so free that no hard and fast distinction can be drawn between the most prosaic of his poems and the most poetic, or stylised, items among his prose. Yet he is also at all times a master of tighter structures, and not only in the pieces that he labelled *U.K.R.*, 'exercise in classical measures'. A broad study of his metrics would be rewarding.

Dynamic and memorable as some of his early works are, Kharms's poetry seems to have reached its peak, quantitatively and in my judgement qualitatively, after the OBERIU period, when his talent was no longer being so largely channeled into theatrical activities. His *annus mirabilis* as a poet was 1931 (year of the *Khniu* and, in part, *Mel'nitsa* cycles) – though this was made apparent only by the splendid third volume of the Meilakh-Erl edition (1980), since the previous anthology of Kharms's work (Gibian's *Izb.*, 1974) contained only one piece from the period. After his short imprisonment in 1932 (during which, with some relief, he was forbidden to write: see our Chronology, 1931), his poetic productivity lessened, and soon prose acquired a growing, though never exclusive importance.

Kharms's most characteristic poetry, with its freedom of form, its abrupt and seemingly unmotivated transitions from plane to plane of diction, its atmosphere of a private fantasy-world, peopled by a cast of improbable and inexplicable characters, may often seem singularly (and deliberately) resistant to analysis. No wonder this has not been much attempted. Yet, as Perlina's, Fleishman's and Faryno's contributions show, seemingly esoteric material can be much less obscure than it seems, and indeed can yield many riches. To tap them will involve scholars of the next decade in a more comprehenisve quest: the exploration of Kharms's entire poetics, the mapping out of his world as a writer and the identification of its landmarks. I shall devote most of the remainder of this essay to some preliminary observations on Kharms's multifaceted poetics.

\* \* \*

In general terms, of course, Kharms belongs to the poetic world of modernism, as his 'collage' techniques, oddities and crudities of lexis, *sdvigi* (dislocations), sometimes fractured syntax, parodistic and bathetic effects and phonetic experimentation, often reaching into 'transrational' word-invention, all bear ample witness. Indeed, if we feel we can cope with Mallarmé or Pound, Eliot or Joyce, Kharms's modernity need hold no terrors for us, while his timeless qualities of wit and anarchic grotesquerie are likely to captivate us from the outset. Yet we may also feel that there is a particularly personal Kharmsian core of impenetrability to which we cannot have immediate – or perhaps any – access; or (to change metaphors) that the real landmarks of Kharms's poetic world are not fully recognisable as such to outsiders.

We are here faced with what V. P. Grigor'ev, writing on Khlebnikov (of whom more later), calls an 'idiolect' (*idiostil'*):[4] an individual patterning of language. Some years ago, in a study of Kharms and his fellow writers that touched on these points, I introduced a comparison with a 'Wittgensteinian' reading of Kafka (Milner-Gulland, 1984). I make no apologies for returning to this, though from a somewhat different angle. In both writers' work a distinct type of 'language game' seems to be being played. The situation I have in mind is admirably stated by a contemporary Kafka specialist:

> A language-game may be played by fixing, in some arbitrary way, the rules for the use of certain words ... The words to which Kafka assigns special, fixed meanings are obvious enough: castle, trial, arrest, official, beetle, stoker, hunger, artist, and so on. The whole point of these words is that we should not be able to establish, in any other way than is laid down, what these words mean ... Now, the words that Kafka has fixed in this inscrutable way are the foundation stones of his story, though we may not at once realise this.[5]

The attentive reader of Kharms will not take long to recognise a similar set of words, some of which recur with astonishing frequency in all areas of his work. Among them one might list (with some metonymic variants in brackets): *chasy* (*tsiferblat*), *shkap/shkaf*, *sunduk* (*chemodan*), *kasha, lampa, kolpak* (*shliapa*), *okno* (*fortochka*), *shar, starukha, dvornik, mukha* (*zhuk*), *babochka* (*motilëk*), *mel'nitsa, voda* (*reka*); more could doubtless be identified, including maybe parts of the human body and parts of speech other than nouns.

Three further observations about this aspect of Kharms's poetics deserve to be made. First, though clearly these mostly very solid and ordinary objects may play a symbolic role, we are not dealing with the Symbolism of a previous generation: they are not treated as 'objective correlatives' in Eliot's sense; they are not the furniture of symbolisation so much as of mythology, thus becoming 'mythologemes'. Secondly, this mythologising, though private, is not exclusive to Kharms: to some extent his close colleagues Oleinikov, Vvedensky and Zabolotsky evidently shared it. Thirdly, Kharms appears to give an almost comparable semantic load to some proper names (as does Kafka, too, to 'K').

This last point deserves some amplification. Naming in Kharms is of great importance, and many names occur more than once in different works: prose, verse or drama. Mariia/Masha (connoting amiability: note his *alter ego* in children's writing, *umnaia* Masha);

Pëtr/Petia (often with sinister overtones: *'groznyi* Pëtr Palych'); Oknov; Kozlov; Myshin; Komarov/Kamarov; Makarov and doubtless others. His choices of names veer, often surprisingly, from the most banal to the highly peculiar. Strange and un-Russian as names like 'Mys Afilei', 'Faol' or 'Khniu' are, however, I suspect they are more than just phantasy-coinages. 'Khniu' has a vaguely oriental sound; it might well derive from 'Khu', mentioned in Khlebnikov's story *Ka*, and defined by his recent editors as an 'element of human existence in Egyptian mythology, the incarnation of a human being beyond the grave';[6] perhaps too the initial 'Kh-' is self-referential. Part of the attractiveness of Kharms's poetic world is its diverse and ubiquitous population, in which figures from the 'real' world (Pushkin, Gogol, Michaelangelo, a vast range of historical characters, the author's friends and contemporaries), oddly metamorphosed yet vivid, as in a dream, move with complete naturalness. Among them, of course, is the discreet but pervasive author-figure himself in his various *personae*. His considerable range of guises and pseudonyms deserves special study. Arguments as to whether the name 'Kharms' itself derives from 'Holmes', 'Harms', or 'Charms' are beside the point: clearly it suggests all these, and maybe other words as well, but is designedly reducible to none of them alone. I do not, incidentally, think his choice of other pseudonyms is merely fanciful or random: 'Shardam' suggests 'shaman'; 'Dandan' is Frenchified (from the audacious Danton? cross with 'Dindon', a turkey-cock!?), a gesture to his French-speaking wife; 'Dania' is for friends, 'Daniil' often for God – the identification with the prophet Daniel would not have escaped him, and indeed glimmers unmistakably through the line '*Ia vsë obdumal, vzvesil, pereschital i peremnozhil*' in the splendid conversational poem '*Skazhu tebe po sovesti*' (*Sob. proizv.*, III:179; see also the first item in our Chronology).

\* \* \*

The period of Kharms's greatest flowering as a poet, 1930–1, coincides with the main impact on him and his friends of the legacy of Velimir Khlebnikov, who had died in 1922. They freely admitted Khlebnikov's mastery and their regard for him, and it may seem odd that it took them several years to experience his influence comprehensively. But in the 1920s Khlebnikov was still imperfectly known, on the whole through his pre-Revolutionary publications and through Tatlin's important staging of *Zangezi* in 1923. In the years around 1930, however, the standard five-volume edition of his (more-or-less) complete works appeared: its compiler, the young critic N. Stepanov, got to know the Oberiuty at one of their readings and shared his knowledge of the Khlebnikov archive with them. Here we should observe that though there is a Khlebnikov quotation in a Kharms poem, *Dachnaia noch'* of 1926 (*Sob. proizv.* I:12), it appears to be an isolated instance (the tiny poem dedicated to him – '*Nogu na nogu zalozhiv / Velimir sidit. On zhiv.*' – is misdated '1926', *Sob. proizv.*, I:15; it in fact refers to an illustration in a Khlebnikov volume of 1930). After 1930, however, Kharms's poems and plays have many Khlebnikovian echoes. The strangest is perhaps the poem he oddly called *Nóchnyi obysk* (*Sob. proizv.*, II:152), which, though much shorter, takes up motifs from Khlebnikov's *poema Nochnóy obysk*. Khlebnikov appears in person as a heavenly rider in the verse play *Lapa* (*Sob. proizv.*, II:122). On several occasions when Kharms uses the word *doski* ('boards', but also the 'Tables of Destiny' and perhaps 'icons') a Khlebnikovian reminiscence is evidently intentional – particularly when it is associated with *babochki*, or with *glaza*, as it had been in Khlebnikov's fine *poema Kamennaia baba*.

Such reminiscences may be a notable tribute to an older master, but do they imply any closer identity of poetic method? Here Meilakh and Erl sound a cautionary note in their comment on *Lapa* (*Sob. proizv.*, II, p. 203): 'It should incidentally be noted that D. Kh. and Vvedensky, deeply as they respected the great poet, strove at the same time to overcome the influence of his poetics'. Certainly the younger poets had their own most distinctive personalities and forged individual styles that would not be mistaken for Khlebnikov's or anyone else's. Their differences are evident: Kharms was remote from Khlebnikov's Slavophilism and Eurasianism (so intense that he would admit no words of Western European origin into his work), for example, while Khlebnikov had little interest in the urban *byt* of Kharms's stories, nor indeed in the Kharmsian fundamental categories of 'humour' and 'sacredness'. Nevertheless, I believe that researchers of the 1970s–80s into Khlebnikov's 'idiolect' and general poetics can draw attention to some deep-seated similarities that may also assist our purpose of 'mapping' Kharms's poetic universe.

The aspect of Khlebnikov's poetics that has inspired the most fertile recent investigations (and has led to a greatly enlarged appreciation of his profundity and originality) is often called by scholars, following Jakobson, 'polysemy' or 'polysemantics'. This has been defined by a contemporary specialist in relation to Khlebnikov as 'a use of the word that actualizes potential meanings and overcomes the univocity of verbal messages':[7] through the multivalent resources of language, harnessed to various modes of symbolisation (the mathematical, pictorial, religious, mythopoeic, musical etc.) he felt he could make direct contact with, and lay bare, the hidden balance and interconnectedness of the cosmos. It is a poetics of transitions and metamorphoses. It relies, as Khlebnikov himself often hinted, on double meanings – sometimes obvious, more often hidden – encoded into the structure of words. The 'particular entrancement (*chary*) of things', as he once put it, rests in their being 'full of secret sound, calling forth corresponding vibrations (*drozhaniia*) in ourselves'.[8] Words have a 'daylight' existence, but in addition a 'starry intelligence' that the brightness of everyday meaning blots out, and it is part of the poet's business to reveal and make use of this 'constellation' of multiple significances. Recent investigations into some of these 'constellations' – the interaction of phonetic, semantic and sometimes visual associations – have revealed a web of interconnected codes at work in Khlebnikov's poetry.[9] The word-play, phonetic patterning etc that have always been part of the stock in-trade of poetry are given the urgency and status of vital clues to meaning, and are buttressed by metonymies, paronomasia, sound repetitions (not only through rhyme), anagrams, palindromes, the splitting of words into component parts, riddles, number-symbolism, neologistic transformations and – most notoriously – various kinds of *zaum'*, or transrational language.

Instinctively or by design, Kharms seems to have adopted a similar associative and transformational poetic system. Obviously there are differences – Khlebnikov, unlike Kharms, put his poetics at the service of a large theory of history; Kharms's metaphysical strivings centred, unlike Khlebnikov's, on the concept of *chudo* (miracle), as Druskin has made clear – but in both we have the remarkable interplay of the domestic and the cosmic, mediated through the battery of linguistic devices mentioned above. But whereas Khlebnikov deliberately limited himself to non-Western linguistic roots, which he then enriched through neologism into a sort of 'super-Slav' linguistic medium, Kharms – fluent in German, with a reading knowledge of English and French – was ready to make often sly use too of scraps, reminiscences and distortions of these tongues: the upshot is often hilarious (as in the line ' "*Vous aitez enfen*" – *znachit*: "*Vy geroi*" ', *Sob. proizv.*, I:33), with a lurking hint of the sinister (an ancient Russian response to foreign sounds). The comic and sinister are splendidly combined in the title of that extraordinary piece of black humour, *Istoriia sdygr appr* (*Polët*, pp. 298–307), suggesting quasi-English 'digger-upper', but (it seems to me) also 'Stick 'em up!'. The 'foreignness' of his own *nom-de-plume* adds a dimension of poignancy to the deadpan diary entry where Kharms records his father's judgement that 'as long as I remain Kharms I shall be the victim of ill fortune' (see Introduction).

\* \* \*

The strange mixed German-Russian title of the poetic fragment *Ohne mel'nitsa* (1931, *Sob. proizv.*, III:204) has been noted more than once (see Nina Perlina's essay in this volume). It may serve as the starting-point for a curious journey in the sort of associative poetics that Kharms probably inherited from Khlebnikov, hovering between metonymy and phonetics, involving metamorphosis, mythopoeia, the encoding of a known person into an apparently fantastical narrative and transrational variations on his name. As Perlina notes, *Ohne mel'nitsa* (literally 'Without Mill') is a transparent pun on the Russian '*On i mel'nitsa*'; this phrase in turn is the title of a verse dialogue dating from the end of 1930. *Mel'nitsa* is characteristically both 'the mill', as one would expect, and its metamorphosis into human form as the 'miller's daughter' (who appears more recognisably in the earlier '*Zhil mel'nik / doch' ego Agnessa...*', *Sob. proizv.*, II:89). Such metamorphosis – the 'reification' of a human being or part of one, and conversely the 'animation' of a machine – is not uncharacteristic of Kharms, and is indeed a highly interesting (Gogolian, modern and even Khlebnikovian) aspect of his poetics. *Mel'nitsa* appears to be a semantically loaded noun – a mythologeme – noted already as characteristic of Kharms's work: the mill runs on one or other of the fundamental elements, air or water, as basic human 'provider'. The miller ('winged' in '*Zhil mel'nik*') takes on an archetypal folkloric role as magician; the miller's daughter is an elusive love-object and perhaps sorceress.

The poem *Ohne mel'nitsa* is an unpunctuated fragment, only thirty-five words long, whose narrative thread remains unclear, though evidently violent and sinister (arms and a body are broken). In the context of the other 'mill' poems, however, the sense of the title-riddle must be 'without a love-object', or 'lovelessness' (a theme which had a personal resonance for Kharms in 1931, when he parted from his first wife Esther, to whom he seems to have attributed magical properties). Worthy of attention though in this enigmatic fragment are first the name of its 'hero' (mentioned twice), 'Androniy'; and secondly, its precise location among Kharms's manuscripts. It is traced by the editors to page 22 of Kharms's *Grossbuch*; on the right-hand side of the same page (and on its reverse) is the major poem *AnDor* (see *Sob. proizv.*, III, p. 210).[10] This strange mystificatory title is related by Meilakh and Erl to the German word *ander* (other), and by Perlina also to the German *an Tor* (at the gate or goal) and, very plausibly in view of the poem's magical subject-matter, to the famous Witch of Endor in the First Book of Samuel (though an English speaker might also read into it the words 'and/or'). But the manuscript propinquity of *Ohne mel'nitsa* can leave little doubt that the primary reference of *AnDor* (though not excluding the others) is to the figure Androniy of the immediately preceding poem, whose predicament is perhaps magically transformed in *AnDor* (making the second poem a 'spell' against lovelessness).

We have not yet done, however, with the unexplained name Androniy. A small metamorphosis turns it, via the closely related form 'Andronik', and by reversal of its elements, into the name 'Nikandr'. In this new guise it becomes a thread linking the mill poems with the cycle Kharms began immediately afterwards (spring 1931), dedicated to the drowned girl Khniu: the watery element in both cycles is significant. In the first Khniu poem (*Voda i Khniu*, *Sob. proizv.*, III:170), Nikandr makes a sudden, disruptive appearance as Khniu's cynical fiancé ('*devits nasiluiu, igraia / s nimi v poddavki*'). I do not doubt that a real person, however transmogrified, was encoded into the figure of Nikandr – and that that person was none other than the poem's dedicatee, Nikolai Makarovich Oleinikov. By all accounts, Oleinikov, a close colleague of Kharms and other former Oberiuty at Detgiz, was a remarkable personality:[11] a Cossack by origin, fond of living dangerously, a pungent wit and fervent amorist, a mathematician and above all a brilliant and alarming parodistic poet.[12] The syllable 'nik', occurring in both his first name and surname, is a blatant clue; the matter is clinched in the second Khniu poem (*Khniu – drug lampy*, *Sob. proizv.*, III:171) with the intrusion of a mysterious 'makander', derived evidently from Oleinikov's patronymic and his nom-de-plume 'Makar Svirepii' (note too Kharms's fondness for the surname Makarov). The historical Nicander, incidentally, was a Greek poet whose 'style is harsh and obscure; two of his poems, one on *Venomous Animals* and another on *Poisons and their Antidotes*, are still extant';[13] Oleinikov, bard of the cockroach, the fly and the beetle, would have approved. 'Nikandr' is certainly a high-profile name, formed from Greek elements meaning 'victorious' and 'male'. In a draft for the poem Kharms generates a fantastical set of variant names: Nikandr, Pukandr, *'Fukandr nebesnogo umnozheniia'* (how colloquially did he know English?), Stokandr, Kukandr, Mikandr, Dukandr (*Sob. proizv.*, III, p. 182; MS in Leningrad Public Library, F1232: 124/117). 'Nikandr Andreevich' is also the dedicatee of a 'pseudo-missive' relating to his supposed marriage (Leningrad Public Library MS F1232: 230), dated 1933 – the patronymic representing yet another link in the 'AnDor' chain of names.

Several times in Kharms's writing Oleinikov is mentioned by name, and he was obviously a figure who haunted him. The most direct portrait of him is in a quasi-classical epigrammatic poem of 1935 (*Oleinikovu, 'Konduktor chisel, druzhby zloi nasmeshnik...', Sob. proizv.*, IV:294), originally intended as part of an *Epistle to my Friends*, that plays on the alarming and ambiguous qualities of his character. In the same year Kharms wrote the famous 'Missive to Kazimir' (*Na smert' Kazimira Malevicha, Sob. proizv.*, IV:298) that he read over Malevich's coffin at the latter's funeral: the first draft of this strange and minatory work, it transpires, was addressed not to the dead Malevich at all, but to the living Oleinikov (see *Polët*, p. 519; one wonders whether Kharms sensed the ominous side of this when Oleinikov was arrested in 1937 and subsequently shot). The poem seems to fit both of these proud, domineering and brilliant figures. But the last personification of Oleinikov in Kharms's writing is the most memorable. He appears as a leading figure – perhaps the narrator's *alter ego* – in the masterly late story *Starukha* (1939): in the first draft under his real name and patronymic, in the finished manuscript as 'Sakerdon Mikhailovich' (see *Polët*, p. 531). It will not escape the alert clue-hunter that the unusual name Sakerdon (Latin *sacerdos*, priest) contains within it the letters ANDOR (is indeed a near anagram of 'Andronikos'). At the time when Kharms wrote *Starukha*, he was much enthused with Meyrink's novellistic retelling of an old Prague Jewish folk legend, *The Golem*: Aleksandrov notes the opening detail of the clock without hands as a motif from *The Golem* (ibid.). What no commentators seem to have noticed is that in the narrator's dream Sakerdon Mikhailovich himself becomes a Golem, a 'man of clay' waiting to be animated when the Divine Name (the Shem) is put into his mouth and then wreak havoc among the tormentors of the Chosen People.[14]

I have lingered over some of the transformations of Oleinikov and his name in Kharms's work as a single illustration of a poetic procedure well attested in Khlebnikov (in his encodings of friends, the Siniakovy sisters for example, and his hero and perceived counterpart Stenka Razin).[15] It draws attention also to a fascinating area of study about which surely more will be discovered: the interrelationships between the tight-knit group of writers and friends at whose centre Kharms stood. Suffice it here to say that in the early thirties these were evidently close (though not without strain) and are reflected in both overt and concealed references, dedications and textual echoes. There are striking parallels too in the explorations of style, genre and subject-matter between Kharms, Zabolotsky and Vvedensky, even though the latter two had quarrelled. In the poem *Khniu* (the third of the cycle), Kharms not only mentions and discusses the remaining 'five *oberiuty*', but has thematic echoes from Zabolotsky's *Shkola zhukov*; other Zabolotsky poems too are echoed at various times, though it is not always clear in which direction influence is flowing. Zabolotsky too transmuted Oleinikov into the eponymous hero of his long poem *Lodeinikov* (a name by which he was known). But the most memorable and significant group portrait of the friends who constituted themselves for a time as 'the club of semi-literate scholars' is in Zabolotsky's poem *Vremia*, whose four characters (Iraklii, Tikhon, Lev and Foma) represent stylised images of, respectively: Oleinikov, the club's host Leonid Savel'ev, Kharms and Zabolotsky himself.[16] Important Kharmsian mythologemes – *chasy, sunduk* – play a key role in the poem's narrative action, at the climax of which Lev takes Iraklii's gun and 'destroys time' by shooting the clock. Were these nicknames in general use among the friends? Certainly Zabolotsky was jocularly known as 'Foma' in his family: perhaps occurrences of the name Foma/Fomka/Fomin in Kharms (and Vvedensky) at the time should be read in such a light. It would be intriguing if the Kharms line '*Gde mërtvyi lev sil'nee zhivoi sobaki*' were a self-reference to Daniel, by metonymy with the lions' den?; but the irony could easily have been directed at Lev Tolstoy. Since Kharms's work also appears to be saturated with references to Iakov Druskin, to the Lipavskys (Leonid and Tamara – whose name is nicely encoded in one poem as 'Aromat'), to the artists Pëtr Sokolov and Alisa Poret, to his first and second wives, and doubtless others, there would seem to be plenty for literary biographers still to do.

The riddles, anagrams, paronomasia, 'sliced-up' words, non-standard exclamations, noises etc. that play an important role in Khlebnikov's 'polysemantics' all, I believe, have a significant place in Kharms's poetics too, though it would be an ambitious specialist endeavour to make a comprehensive analysis and categorisation of them. They shade into the semantic-phonetic area in which Kharms most obviously follows Khlebnikov: that of neologistic word formation and transrationality. Commentators have tended to ignore or play down the sheer quantity of *zaumnii iazyk* (broadly defined) in Kharms's work; perhaps they have been puzzled or misled by the somewhat over-defensive blast against *zaum'* in the OBERIU declaration; but this is primarily a polemic against A. Tufanov and others who would 'emasculate the word'.[17] On the contrary, Kharms's *zaum'*, like Khlebnikov's, is urgently concerned with meaning (Grigor'ev has pointed out how profoundly anti-Formalist Khlebnikov is in this respect).[18] When a comprehensive history of Russian modernist *zaum'*, in all its variety, comes to be written, Kharms must hold a major place. His *zaum'* is far from identical with Khlebnikov's (even if it is in debt to his example), and is no less rich. Kharms is obviously less interested than Khlebnikov in neologisms generated from Slavonic roots, prefixes and suffixes (though there are examples, in *Sob. proizv.*, I:47 and again in *Sablia*, as well as generative forms like *vladyka / mladyka*). By contrast, many of his word experiments (including imagined proper names) have a 'foreign' coloration. We also find, for example, the sounds made by children, animals, guns, natural objects (particularly water); and a category not, I think, previously mentioned by commentators, that of musical notes, including real or imaginary elements of sol-fa notation. There is a nice example in the short poem *'Vam poverit"* (1930, *Sob. proizv.*, II:97):

> И нет во мне той милой склонности
> греть ваши ноги о девушка,
> тона девичьего «до» нести
> вашего голоса девушка. ...
> До вашего дома
> иду по досочке, ...

We observe *do* picking up semantic coloration (implying a feminine principle?); this will appear again, later the same year, in the incantatory *Vecherniaia pesn'* ... (*'Doch' docheri docherei ...'*, *Sob. proizv.*, II:111), with its mysterious repeated word *doto*. Such a process, of course, is thoroughly Khlebnikovian. The decomposition of words into component syllables which could then look like, or also be, other words, sol-fa notes or expressive *zaum'* noises evidently fascinated Kharms. There is a witty example in *Stolknovenie duba s mudretsom* (*Sob. proizv.* I:47): 'Do / mi / sol' / do be la / dobela / vystirat' vystirat' / v bane mu / dre / tsa'. Such free-floating syllables can become a shorthand language, and we observe it in the process of formation in the moving short poem '*Na siianii dnia mesiatsa iunia*' (*Sob. proizv.* III:178), with abbreviations such as *tkim, dkhaniiu* ('*takim*', '*dykhaniiu*'). Kharms's minimalism (later to bear fruit of a different kind in *Sluchai*) can be seen here. Maybe he found something not only meaningfully fundamental but sacred in the shortest elements of language: note the remarkable last line of *Néteper'* (*Sob. proizv.* II:107): 'Eto, to, tut, tam, byt', Ia, My, Bog'.

We cannot leave the important topic of the role of Kharms's *zaum'* in his poetics without mentioning the significant fact that the same transrational words are often used more than once in his works and may, indeed, have been employed by Khlebnikov or others before him. In *Vecherniaia pesn'* ..., for example, we encounter the elements *pe* and *trr* that four years later are re-employed (and explained) in the 'Missive to Kazimir'. Do they have the same semantic values? (if not, why not?) The latter poem introduces a third piece of *zaum'*, *agalton* (explained as 'your slender memory'). This is no mere sliced-off phoneme, and one has to suspect an encoding: I propose it as an anagram of 'naglota', a neologism (midway between *naglost'* and *nagota*) that I think – on the basis of his interest in generating *-ota* nouns – Kharms would have relished. But there may well be a better explanation. To return to the re-used transrational words: by repetition they change their status significantly, from 'nonce-words' to a deliberate enhancement of the vocabulary. Kharms becomes a new Adam, affixing permanent names to things that had never had them.

Khlebnikov had been a signatory to the manifesto *The Letter as Such* (1913), an important, often disregarded statement that proclaimed the primacy of handwriting over print, and in so doing gave theoretical justification to the notable efflorescence of Russian modernist hand-produced book design. Kharms – not only, I think, because he could not be published – was a notable follower of this tradition. We have to welcome the many facsimiles provided by recent editors while hoping ideally to see all his manuscripts in photomechanical reprints. Kharms (like Zabolotsky but not, it seems, Vvedensky) expended much care over the appearance of his manuscripts. The visual aspect of his work is an integral part of his poetics. Kharms himself explained the rebus he called 'the window', ⊟ as referring to his first wife Esther.[19] But there are many other symbols, hieroglyphs, whole secret alphabets; they may be no more than playful sidelines, yet if Kharms was truly 'all art', nothing about him is irrelevant. The importance of lay-out is evident from *I Razrushenie*, a poem analysed earlier in this volume. Its riddling first element (presumably to be pronounced '*odno*' or '*pervoe*') can be read equally as the pre-Revolutionary letter 'I', which had been 'destroyed' in 1918. The poem ends with a block of seven lines, so encoding the seven-day week that the poem's purpose is to uphold. The importance of orthography is illustrated by the fact that Kharms sometimes reverts to pre-Revolutionary script: notably in a considerable group of poems dating from about the time when the seven-day week was restored (see *Sob. proizv.*, III:225–36). As is the case with Khlebnikov,[20] Kharms may have found the very form of digits and letters semantically significant: the fragmentary poem introducing Hrabanus Maurus (*Sob. soch.* III:252) derives the digit 'three' from a bisected heart: ⟨β. Words, diagrams, colours and private mysticism come together in a remarkable notebook of 1937 (Leningrad Public Library, MS F1232:375), where light and deep yellow, green, blue and red are equated with states (from 'highest' to 'lowest') of the spirit.

The question of the 'architecture' of Kharms's works, whether verse, prose, drama or generically mixed, is of great significance if we are to assess his qualities justly. Earlier in this essay, the belief was expressed that, despite appearances, he was a master of form. Important in this context is the excessively belated realisation that the *Sluchai* miniatures form a consciously shaped cycle, carefully selected, arranged and presented by Kharms as if for publication. The perspicacious and detailed study here by Aizlewood shows that, as a cycle, they constitute a major work of modern European literature, greater than the sum of its parts, comparable in a twentieth-century Russian context only to Babel's *Konarmiia* (which, interestingly, is also a collection of over thirty diverse 'miniatures', narrating horrific events in deadpan, non-judgemental style, constituting a 'casebook' with subtexts: some influence is certainly possible). The cycle emerges as a many-sided investigation of the category of 'happening' or 'incidence' (or, to be more precise, of our 'narrativising' of it). Threads however stretch out to link it with the rest of his *oeuvre*: names of characters, titles of individual episodes ('Makarov and Petersen. No. 3' refers us to two other stories 'On

Phenomena and Existences'; 'Blue Notebook No. 10', as title of the first episode, leads us in to the 'casebook', as it were, from the author's external case notes; incidentally, the colour clash between *golubaia* and *ryzhii* would not have escaped Kharms, and again evokes Khlebnikovian echoes). The titles of episodes can indeed have hidden subtleties: it has not, I believe, been pointed out that the episode mysteriously called 'Sonnet' contains fourteen sentences, with a natural 8:6 division, echoing normal sonnet form. *Sluchai*, as an apparent jumble of fragments with a hidden unity, opposes and complements the other late masterpiece, *Starukha*, an apparently unified and well-articulated short story whose coherence is stealthily undermined in a variety of ways – not least by the disruptive shifts of point-of-view (in the paragraph after the narrator leaves Sakerdon Mikhailovich's room and the latter, left alone, is described from a 'God's-eye-view' as if dead) and of narrative manner (in the play-like dialogue outside the bakery).

\* \* \*

Few problems within the general area of the structuring of literature have so exercised modern writers as that of endings. The artificiality and unacceptability of neat or pointed endings to short stories or novels was already evident by the time of Chekhov, whose natural existentialism demanded open-ended narratives, apparently free of the author's monologic control. For Kafka, endings were a particular source of agonising, and he became, intentionally or not, one of the modern masters of the fragment as genre. To many readers (and to his editors) the works of Khlebnikov have, in their totality, seemed fragments of an imagined cosmic epic where any beginnings or endings can be no more than provisional. One way round the problem of the ending, however, was sometimes adopted by Kafka: 'harnessing traditional types of ending to more complex effects than they had engendered hitherto', reminding one 'of the moralising fable's didactic conclusion', as at the end of *A Country Doctor*: 'Once one has followed the false ringing of the night-bell – one can never make amends for it'.[21] Many of Kharms's later stories and *sluchai* gleefully take up this device of the 'parody-moral', sententious, facetious or banal, that may nevertheless subtextually open up new questions about the significance of the preceding action. One example among many is *The Fate of a Professor's Wife*, one of Kharms's finest stories, a whole psychological novel in two and a half pages, brutally undermined by its sententious yet resonant conclusion: 'This professor's wife is merely a pitiful example of how many unfortunates there are in life who do not occupy in life the position that they ought to occupy' (*Plummeting*, p. 61; *Polët*, p. 330).

It is clear that, in his poetry too, Kharms felt the difficulty of achieving an appropriate sense of finality: hence the OBERIU habit (kept up into the early 1930s) of signing off with the pseudo-naive 'All'. He later adopts a more subtle device: that of dissolving the rhythms of the poetry in a deliberately prosaic and, usually, extended last line (*I Razrushenie* provides a good example). But nowhere, I think, is the problem of ending so acute and so ambiguously resolved as in *Starukha*. On the surface *Starukha* is a well-made tale, for all its fantastical elements, and ostensibly ends (a little too neatly, even sentimentally?) with the narrator's dropping to his knees and uttering a prayer: some commentators describe it in these terms. But this is not in fact the end of the story (nor are the narrator's words actually a prayer – a blessing, perhaps of incantatory effect, rather).[22] After a caesura of dots we have the anticlimactic final (though pretending not to be final) sentence: 'At this I temporarily close my manuscript, considering that it is anyhow too long-drawn-out' (*Polët*, p. 430; cf. *Black Coat*, p. 153). This is an outrageous borrowing from the end of Dostoevsky's *Notes from Underground*, ironising retrospectively many elements of the tale, and is only the last of the pastiche effects and intertextual echoes with which this deceptive tale is rich.

\* \* \*

If the immediate context for Kharms's poetics (as with Khlebnikov) is the totality of his life and work, great importance attaches to his philosophy, religion, perceptual world and thought-processes. It cannot be doubted that this will prove a most productive and tantalising area of future research. The field is vast, difficult and little explored, though Druskin and other memoirists have given useful signposts for future investigations. It would be inappropriate here to attempt to do more than sketch some personal reactions to the problems involved, and thoughts on the matters that seem particularly to deserve to be followed up.

Interested as Kharms was in philosophy, it would probably be a mistake to try to extract a coherent philosophical outlook from his works (as Druskin indicates): his speculative pieces, if deprived of their literary dimension, may seem merely lightweight or whimsical.

What we *can* extract from them is a strong sense of (often disrupted) world-order, contrasting such qualities as smoothness and roundness with 'rockiness', height with depth (water generally representing the crucial, transparent yet palpable dividing line between the latter two, cf. *Sob. proizv.* III:242), wholeness with dislocation (often concretised in the 'separation' of various parts of the body). He is not really a 'philosophical poet' either, at least not in the grand tradition of such as Lucretius, Dante, Pope or Goethe – in which his colleague Zabolotsky had a more recognisable place (at least in his work of the 1930s).[23] Yet the philosophical implications of his imaginative work are a subtext that is often, if unclearly, sensed, and sometimes surfaces to open up new vistas on the text itself – as when we learn that 'Blue Notebook No. 10' originally bore the laconic gloss 'against Kant' (*Polët*, p. 528). What aspect of Kant's teaching is attacked is not specified; one assumes Kharms refers to the notion of the *Ding an sich*, 'thing in itself': yet Kharms had expressed an essentialism as thoroughgoing as Kant's in the short piece '*Predmety i figury...*' of 1927.[24] Perhaps the years and the new climate of the times changed his views. In any case, as I have attempted to argue earlier (Milner-Gulland, 1984), Kharms is most fundamentally a philosophical poet not in his ideas but in his poetic practice, representing a language game or semantic experiment that investigates 'the meaning of meaning'.

Beyond philosophy in the strict sense lie more private and obscure reaches of Kharms's poetic world. Russia has not produced much great religious poetry and, in an early-Soviet context, Kharms is quite remarkable for his achievements in that direction alone. Some of his verse prayers are very moving, and seem to breathe the purest Christian piety, making impressively well-calculated use of Church Slavonic diction. Yet his religion – or the reflection of it in his writings – emerges as almost as idiosyncratic and disturbing as Gogol's. It seems entirely personal, without any hint of communality. Its preferred medium of expression is the prayer, most often for literary inspiration. It embraces an ideal of holiness from which the individual can only fall short, existing in an ever-growing sense of his own turpitude, a Fall continually re-enacted. It justifies itself primarily through a promise of immortality (see the narrator's conversation in *Starukha* with Sakerdon, or 'priest') that can never be guaranteed.

In Kharms's scheme of things religion seems to be contiguous with poetry and magic: it is no accident that he refers to the 'four kinds of word-machine at present known to me: poems, prayers, songs and

*Beyond the Turning-Point: An Afterword* 261

spells (*zagovory*)' (*Polët*, p. 513). This association is of course an age-old one and equally imbued the work and world-outlook of Khlebnikov (though the latter was not, like Kharms, overtly Christian). 'Word-machine' is incidentally a most interesting expression: it seems to evoke, and perhaps mock, the general interest of the age in things mechanical and scientific, in 'social engineering', but it could well conceal a reference to the 'magic mill', the Sampo of the northern epic *Kalevala*, which Kharms's artist friends of the School of Filonov were at the time illustrating for an ambitious Academia edition.[25] In any case, it presupposes a view of literature not as mere object of aesthetic contemplation, but as an active and probably supernatural force in the world. The association of religion, magic and world-order clearly lies behind Kharms's interest in cabbalistic and Pythagorean thought, as his remarkable 'list of interests' (see Chronology, 1933) testifies. When, delving into a book of wisdom, Makarov causes Petersen (in *Sluchai*) to vanish, the word he utters, 'MALGIL' may well evoke *mogila* ('grave'), as Aleksandrov suggests (and indeed *magiia*, 'magic'):[26] but it is also a tetragrammaton of four consonants, like the Hebrew name of God. (The characteristic note of irony or even buffoonery does not preclude serious import or deeply-felt motivation, as always in the poetics of Kharms and his circle.) I do not doubt that a search of Kharms's work for cabbalistic and similar occult references would produce much of significance.[27]

The most interesting result of his cabbalistic and Pythagorean interests (relating also to his devotion to music: cf. letter to Pugachëva, *Polët*, p. 486) is Kharms's concern with numbers and their power. Here the connection with Khlebnikov is close, since the latter had a consuming interest in numerology: one of his most haunting creations is the figure of 'Chislobog', god of numbers and time, and one of the poet's alter egos.[28] Yet there is also a difference, since Khlebnikov (like Oleinikov) was a practised mathematician, obsessed with often complicated calculations that he believed would reveal hidden but objective laws governing human destiny (once he had predicted the Revolution of 1917 there was no stopping him). He also sensed a basic dialectical contradiction between the principles of 'twoness' and 'threeness' in all aspects of the world – considering the former embodied order and harmony, the latter destabilisation (Kharms, more dynamic and restless, inclined towards 'threeness'). For Kharms, numbers had a fundamental, inherently numinous quality, their very arbitrariness perhaps a sign of their superhuman significance. *I Razrushenie* (see Fleishman and Faryno here) clearly owes its serious subtext to a sense of the outrage, even blasphemy, of human 'division' of the God-given 'indivisible' seven-day week. Numbers are ubiquitous in Kharms, particularly in the form of times on the clock or watch: note too the frequent, very precise dates given at the end of his works (they thus become the 'happenings', *sluchai*, of his individual biography). 'Sonnet', of course, is grounded in the spooky arbitrariness of our system of digits; its fourteen-sentence structure (mentioned earlier) is perhaps echoed when, in the last paragraph of the whole cycle, Rakukin's soul emerges 'fourteen or so minutes' after his death. The magic of numbers is directly evoked in '*Korotkaia molniia proletela...*' (*Sob. proizv.*, III:211) in connection with 'Nikolai Makarovich', i.e. Oleinikov; indirectly in the delightful poem '*Ia znaiu pochemu dorogi...*' (*Sob. proizv.*, III:175) where the poet alters the course of the natural world by lifting his notebook and reading 'seventeen words composed by me yesterday', after which he is 'extremely happy'. Note also the role of 'zero' as a symbol of circularity and hence perfection (*Sob. proizv.*, IV:278). Closely related to numerology is the theme of measurement, as in *Izmerenie veshchei* and *Sablia* (*Polët*, pp. 73–7; 433–9).

\* \* \*

Placing Kharms in the broad contexts of contemporary and past Russian literature, or of the European modern movement as a whole, has lured commentators ever since his 'adult' works began to be rediscovered. Such efforts may continue fruitfully, but as his heritage becomes more deeply understood he may well be seen as extremely elusive in this respect. The same has happened with regard to the two writers with whom I have most consistently compared Kharms here: Khlebnikov and Kafka. Neither seemed 'problematic' to their contemporaries (i.e. among the Russian Futurists, or the progressive young Prague writers) to the degree they have since. Nowadays we have decoded much of the obscurity, but at the same time feel the unique originality of each all the more strongly. The same will surely happen with Kharms. We are likely to hear less about how he fits into broad movements, and more of the quiddity of his particular vision, the locus of meaning in individual works, and the areas in which his methods and intentions coincided (or contrasted) with other figures – and not just writers.

Nevertheless, Kharms's relationship with his particular circle of friends and colleagues remains of interest, though in ways more complex than earlier apparent. Particularly teasing are his relations with Zabolotsky and Oleinikov: some idea of a hidden dialogue going on with each during the 1930s has already been suggested. Perhaps strangely, given the propensity of some commentators to treat them almost as twins, I find in Kharms's work fewer evident traces of Vvedensky. From time to time, though, emphatic four-foot iambic rhythms in Kharms have a Vvedenskian ring, as do some of his neologisms. A generally parallel development in the literary interests of Kharms, Vvedensky and Zabolotsky in the thirties can be seen. Just as close to Kharms as these poets, however, were the thinkers Lipavsky and Druskin. It is clear that Kharms developed his concept of the *vestnik* ('messenger') from Druskin, leading to the memorable prose piece '*O tom, kak menia posetili vestniki*' (*Polët*, pp. 503–4) and to this remarkable self-definition: 'Druskin spoke about *vestniki*. I am a *vestnik*'. The word is a translation of the Greek *angellos*, 'angel', such a figure having much in common with the 'angelic' figures of Rilke's *Duino Elegies* (not completed until the 1920s – would Druskin or Kharms have known them?).

Artists and musicians figured prominently in the Leningrad cultural milieu of the 1920s–30s. Shostakovich (Kharms's near contemporary) came close to writing operas based upon works by both Oleinikov and Kharms, shortly after setting Gogol's *The Nose*.[29] Particularly significant is Kharms's relationship to the three giants of the Russian artistic avant-garde (all of an older generation and previously close to Khlebnikov): Filonov, Malevich and Tatlin. Filonov, whose ascetic life and dedication was an awe-inspiring example (to Zabolotsky particularly and to his disciples, the 'Filonovtsy', some of whom Kharms knew well),[30] emerges as a magus-figure ('*Skazhu tebe po sovetsti*', *Sob. proizv.*, III:179). Malevich, who once might have joined OBERIU and later became the object of Kharms's celebrated obituary poem, was close to him not only in the purity and minimalism of his Suprematist paintings, but even more so in the 'alogism' of his slightly earlier works. When Kharms writes of the association of a comet and a spoon in the sky (with Michaelangelo! – *Polët*, pp. 315–16; *Plummeting*, pp. 47–8), is this not a reminiscence of the well-known Malevich painting 'An Englishman in Moscow'? Tatlin – the youngest of the three and close friend of Khlebnikov – produced memorable illustrations in 1929 to a Kharms children's work (see *Polët*, pp. 257, 261). A recent paper by John Bowlt suggests close connections between their conceptual worlds, a desire on the part of each to push logic to, or rather beyond, its limits.[31]

In the world of European modernism, the most interesting comparisons to be made with Kharms are, I believe, not so much (as was earlier thought) with the Dada movement, or dramatists such as Ionesco or Beckett – though the world of Beckett's *plays* has connections with that of Kharms's *prose* – as with other great originals whose temperaments seem to have matched his. A quirky or comic surface concealing spiritual strivings, a propensity for the 'uncanonical', for the apparently naive, for ceaseless conceptual innovation, for puns and 'serious play' – which might appear clowning – of all kinds: such characteristics bring him particularly close, I think, to the composer Erik Satie and the artist Marcel Duchamp (whose ambiguous attitude to the machine is very Kharmsian); but again we must return, for Kharms's nearest 'double', to the figure of Franz Kafka. Here I mean not the qualities vulgarly known as 'Kafkaesque', which I take to be an atmosphere of ineluctable menace compounded by inpenetrable bureaucracy – actually a minor dimension of Kafka's work, largely confined to the unfinished *The Trial*. Occasionally Kafka's works (notably *In the Penal Colony*) have scenes of unmotivated or ill-motivated savagery that match some of Kharms's post-1935 prose; more characteristic of both is a sinister jauntiness devoid of psychologism ('Never again psychology!' as Kafka wrote) and morality. But such qualities are not exclusive to Kharms and Kafka and perhaps not part of their deeper essence. Their real closeness comes in the aspects of their poetics discussed earlier in this essay and in what seem to me basic similarities of character and outlook. Both were splendid aphoristic notebook, diary and letter writers; both had an extraordinary, yet unpompous sense of the significance of their work: Kafka would have understood Kharms's sentiment that for every vain word one would answer at the Day of Judgement; Kharms would have sympathised with Kafka's uncertainty as to whether his talent was the gift of God or the Devil. Kharms's remark of 1933 that a poem should be such that it would smash the window if thrown at it (*Polët*, p. 484; *Plummeting*, p. 90) matches Kafka's sense of literature as an ice-axe to unlock the frozen sea within us. Kharms's address to his creations as 'my sons and daughters' echoes Kafka's short piece *Eleven Sons*, allegorising his own previous works; each end stories (*Son* by Kharms, *Metamorphosis* and *A Fasting Showman* by Kafka) with the curious motif of an emaciated hero dying and being thrown out with the rubbish; both writers fantasised about opening up their own heads to observe thought processes within. Kharms's short piece 'I Had Raised Dust'

(*Plummeting*, p. 26) – one example among many – is thoroughly Kafkian in its dreamlike breathlessness; and it was Kafka (though how Kharmsianly!) who said 'There exist only miracles'. Both are among the great minimalists of modern literature, to which their concentrated miniature prose pieces may be their most remarkable single contribution. The reader who knows either, beyond any direct correspondences, will simply feel on familiar territory when encountering the other.

No doubt other literary links can be sought out: in Borges's brief story *The God's Script*, for example, we find the Kharmsian motifs both of the spell of a certain number (fourteen) of unspecified words that will change the order of the world, and that of the miracle-worker who chooses not to perform a miracle. But the final subject that (it seems to me) demands thorough study if we are to place Kharms in context is close to home: the Bakhtin circle of the late 1920s in Leningrad. How its philosophical-religious and anthropological-aesthetic concerns penetrated Leningrad artistic and intellectual life is a story that has yet to be fully told, but can now at last be properly investigated.[32] Indirect links with Kharms and his friends were undoubtedly present (Iudina and Sollertinsky being two names which come to mind). Beyond that, worthwhile would be a consistent Bakhtinian reading of Kharms, as several of the contributions to our volume hint. Kharms is one of the most thoroughly dialogical of writers; a chronotope-based study would also greatly help our understanding of Kharms's personal world. Bakhtin himself knew of the Oberiuty and apparently welcomed the carnivalistic element which their lives and work contributed to the atmosphere of their city.

It would be as regrettable if future scholarship were to 'domesticate' Kharms as (in Ken Hirschkop's view) it has Bakhtin.[33] His restless genius must never be allowed to seem tame or mundane. But, as the present volume should demonstrate, Kharms is so substantial a figure that any such risk has to be taken, rather than leaving him on the margins of literature as no more than a historical curiosity. It is a miracle (the elusive miracle that he himself expected, perhaps, but whose circumstances he could hardly have wished for) that we are able to talk about him at all, that his archive has come down to us intact;[34] such a miracle demands that his stature be properly recognised by all fortunate enough to benefit from it. When Khlebnikov, Kharms and his colleagues appear on the syllabuses as the true giants of the new Russian literature, we shall know that an intellectual turning-point really has been reached.

## NOTES

1. *Knizhnoe obozrenie*, 3 (1990) 9.
2. Franz Kafka, *Letters to Felice* (New York: Schocken, 1973), p. 304.
3. Cf. prayer of 13 May 1935, *Knizhnoe obozrenie*, 3 (1990) 9.
4. V. P. Grigor'ev, *Grammatika idiostilia* (Moscow, 1983); and his 'K dialektike voobrazhaemoi filologii', in W. Weststeijn (ed.), *Velimir Chlebnikov (1885–1922): Myth and Reality* (Amsterdam: Rodopi, 1986).
5. A. K. Thorlby, 'Anti-Mimesis: Kafka and Wittgenstein', in F. Kuna (ed.), *On Kafka: Semi-Centenary Perspectives* (London: Elek, 1976) p. 74.
6. V. Khlebnikov, *Tvoreniia*, eds M. Poliakov et al. (Moscow, 1986) p. 700.
7. B. Lönnqvist, 'Chlebnikov's Double Speech', in Weststeijn (note 4 above), p. 292.
8. V. Khlebnikov, *Sobranie sochinenii*, ed. V. Markov (Munich: Fink, 1968–72) II. iv. 115–17.
9. R. R. Milner-Gulland, 'Eyes and Icons: Some Visual-Verbal Constellations in the Work of Khlebnikov', in M. Falchikov et al. (eds), *Words and Images: Essays in Honour of D. Ward* (Letchworth: Astra, 1989).
10. *AnDor*, *Sob. proizv.* III: 164. It also appears in *Polët*, (no. 12, pp. 78–9), but as '*Miach letel s tremia krestami*', i.e. without the title '*AnDor*'; it is dated '1930' (which must be intentional, since it is placed among 1930 poems). This discrepancy (among others) between two indispensable editions shows that even now that we have scholarly publications of Kharms, all is not plain sailing for the student without access to the manuscripts.
11. See reminiscences of Oleinikov in several contributions to *My znali Evgeniia Shvartsa* (Moscow-Leningrad, 1966).
12. R. R. Milner-Gulland, 'Grandsons of Kozma Prutkov', in R. Freeborn et al (eds), *Russian and Slavic Literatures* (Columbus, Ohio: Slavica, 1976).
13. Rev. Dr. Brewer, *A Guide to Grecian History* (London, no date) p. 423.
14. See account by J. Urzidil, 'Two Recollections', in J. P. Stern (ed.), *The World of Franz Kafka* (London: Weidenfeld and Nicolson, 1980); and in *There Goes Kafka!* (Detroit, 1968), ch. 7.
15. Lönnqvist (see note 7 above), pp. 302–6; see also R. Vroon, *Velimir Khlebnikov's Shorter Poems: A Key to the Coinages* (Ann Arbor: Michigan Slavic Materials, 1983); and Milner-Gulland (note 9 above).
16. R. Milner-Gulland, 'Zabolotsky's *Vremya*', *Essays in Poetics*, 6:1 (1981); identifications confirmed in letter to author from E. V. Zabolotskaia, widow of the poet, dated 17.VI.77. Although she is positive that 'Iraklii' represented Oleinikov, one cannot help being also reminded of Iraklii Andronikov (for a couple of years a younger colleague at Detgiz) – whose significant surname could well have associatively inspired the 'AnDor/Andronii' chain of encodings discussed above.

Beyond the Turning-Point: An Afterword 267

17. See, for example, Aleksandrov, 1968.
18. Grigor'ev, in Weststeijn (see note 4 above), p. 322.
19. Letter to R. I. Poliakova, Polët, p. 459; note that Stoimenoff (1984, pp. 77–87) gives examples of the visual dimension of Kharms's texts.
20. See Milner-Gulland (note 9 above).
21. J. J. White, 'Endings and Non-Endings in Kafka's Fiction', in Kuna (see note 5 above), p. 156.
22. Note the use of the same formula at the head of the draft (really an independent work) of Sob. proizv. III:228 (p. 223).
23. See R. R. Milner-Gulland, 'Zabolotsky: Philosopher-Poet', Soviet Studies (April, 1971).
24. Published in Levin, 1978, pp. 299–300.
25. R. R. Milner-Gulland, 'Masters of Analytic Art: Filonov, his School and the Kalevala', Leonardo, XVI:1 (1982); on science, see note in Sob. proizv. III, pp. 168–9.
26. Polët, p. 530; the unusual name 'Petersen' could have been inspired by the N. Peterson who edited, and perhaps partly wrote, the works of the strange and influential turn-of-the-century philosopher Nikolai Fëdorov.
27. Meilakh and Erl' (Sob. proizv. II, p. 212) draw attention to the cabbalistic connections of Kharms's interest in letters and alphabets. This too is a Khlebnikovian concern. Note Zabolotsky's fine poem of esoteric wisdom of this period, Tsaritsa mukh.
28. R. Vroon, 'Chlebnikov and his Doubles', in Weststeijn (see note 4 above), pp. 257–8; also R. Cooke, Velimir Khlebnikov (Cambridge: Cambridge University Press, 1987), passim, particularly ch. 4.
29. Fëdorov, 1976; Kharms in his diary wavers amusingly as to his opinion of Shostakovich's genius: Knizhnoe obozrenie, 3 (1990) 9.
30. J. Bowlt and N. Misler, A Hero and His Fate (Austin: University of Texas Press, 1983); see also Milner-Gulland (note 25 above).
31. J. E. Bowlt, 'Tatlin and his Anti-Tale', paper read to Tatlin conference, Düsseldorf, November 1989 (publication forthcoming).
32. See though, for a short account, K. Clark and M. Holquist, Mikhail Bakhtin (Cambridge: Mass.: Harvard University Press, 1984).
33. K. Hirschkop, 'The Domestication of M. M. Bakhtin', Essays in Poetics, 11:1 (1986).
34. See L. Druskina, 'Bylo takoe sodruzhestvo...', Avrora, 6 (1989).

# 18 Selected Bibliography
## Neil Cornwell and Julian Graffy

The main existing Kharms bibliography (including lifetime publications, republications, foreign and translated publications, as well as works on or referring to Kharms) is to be found in Jaccard, 1985 (see below). The present bibliography repeats some essential items to be found in Jaccard (in particular, items referred to in notes to the current essays) but concentrates mainly on items not included by Jaccard and items which have appeared since his bibliography.

### MAIN COLLECTIONS OF KHARMS'S WORK

*Izbrannoe.* Ed. and introduced George Gibian (Würzburg: jal-verlag, 1974), pp. 300 [*Izb.*].
*Sobranie proizvedenii.* Ed. Mikhail Meilakh and Vladimir Erl' (Bremen: K-Presse, 1978– ). [*Sob. proizv.*] Four vols so far:
I    Stikhotvoreniia 1926–1929. Komediia goroda Peterburga (1978, pp. 200)
II   Stikhotvoreniia 1929–1930. Lapa. Gvidon (1978, pp. 221)
III  Stikhotvoreniia 1931–1933 (1980, pp. 237)
IV   Stikhotvoreniia 1933–1939. U.K.R. Spasenie. Alfavitnyi ukazatel' stikhotvorenii (1988, pp. 227).
*Polët v nebesa: Stikhi. Proza. Dramy. Pis'ma.* Ed. and introduced A. A. Aleksandrov (Leningrad: Sovetskii pisatel', 1988), pp. 560 [*Polët*].
*Sluchai. Rasskazy i stseny.* Introduced A. P'ianov (Moscow: Izd. TsK KPSS Pravda, 1989), pp. 48.

### MAIN COLLECTIONS OF KHARMS'S CHILDREN'S WORKS

*Igra* (Moscow: Detskii mir, 1962).
*Chto eto bylo?* (Moscow: Malysh, 1967).
*Dvenadtsat' povarov* (Moscow: Malysh, 1972).
*Stikhi* (Moscow: Sovetskaia Rossiia, 1981).
*Zagadochnyi sluchai* (Cheliabinsk: Iuzhno-Ural'skoe knizhnoe izdatel'stvo, 1989).
*Vrun* (Leningrad: Detskaia literatura, 1989).
*Letiat po nebu shariki: Stikhi, Pesenki, Skazki, Rasskazy,* (Krasnoiarsk: Krasnoiarskoe knizhnoe izdatel'stvo, 1990), pp. 253.

### MAIN ENGLISH TRANSLATIONS

'Daniil Kharms' ['Fire', 'For a long time I looked at the green trees...', 'Death of the Wild Warrior', 'Nicholas II'], translated by Robin Milner-Gulland, *Modern Poetry in Translation*, 6 (1970), pages unnumbered.

George Gibian (ed. and trans.), *Russia's Lost Literature of the Absurd – A Literary Discovery: Selected Works of Daniil Kharms and Alexander Vvedensky* (Ithaca and London: Cornell UP, 1971), pp. ix + 208 [*Russia's Lost Lit.*].
Revised and expanded as: id. *The Man in [with] the Black Coat – Russia's Literature of the Absurd. Selected Works of Daniil Kharms and Alexander Vvedensky* (Evanston, Ill.: Northwestern UP, 1987), pp. x + 258 [*Black Coat*].
Neil Cornwell (ed. and trans.), Daniil Kharms, *The Plummeting Old Women*, with Afterword by Hugh Maxton (Dublin: Lilliput, 1989), pp. vi + 101 [*Plummeting*].

## SELECTED MISCELLANEOUS PUBLICATIONS

| | |
|---|---|
| 1971 | 'Rasskazy', *Grani*, 81, pp. 65–83 (22 stories). |
| 1973 | 'Iumoristicheskie paradoksy Daniila Kharmsa', published A. Aleksandrov, *Voprosy literatury*, 11, 296–304 ('Kak ia rastrepal odnu kompaniiu' and 2 letters). |
| 1979–80 | 'Neizdannoe', published Gleb Urman, *NRL: Neue Russische Literatur*, Almanach 2–3, pp. 135–42 ('Sablia', 'Cisfinitum', 'Nul' i nol'', 'O kruge'). |
| 1980 | 'Neizvestnye stranitsy', published Gleb Urman, *Vremia i My*, 53, 182–91 ('O tom kak menia posetili vestniki', 'Veshch'' and 4 poems). |
| | 'Proza', published Il'ia Levin, *Kontinent*, 24, 271–95 (14 stories). |
| | 'Rasskazy', published Il'ia Levin, *Soviet Union/Union Soviètique*, 7, 1–2, 228–37 (9 stories). |
| 1982 | 'Rasskazy' (republication, in a different order, of Levin's 9 stories above), in *Russica –81: literaturnyi sbornik* (New York: Russica), pp. 353–60. |
| 1983 | 'Arkhiv fortochki: Daniil Kharms, Aleksandr Vvedenskii', *Poiski*, 5–6, 439–43 (includes letter from Kharms to Vvedenskii). |
| 1985 | 'Iz rukopisei Daniila Kharmsa', published I. F. Petrovichev, *Russkaia mysl'*, 3550, 3 January, Literary Supplement, 1, p. viii (letter and 3 stories). |
| | 'De la réalité au texte: l'absurde chez Daniil Harms', Jaccard, 1985 (see below: contains significant unpublished fictional and philosophical texts). |
| 1986 | 'Daniil Kharms (1905–1942): "Stolbtsy" i "Razgovory" Daniila Kharmsa', introduced An. Aleksandrov, in *Den' poezii 1986*, Leningrad, pp. 378–85 (5 poems). |
| | 'Chitaia Daniila Kharmsa', commentary Valerii Sazhin, *Daugava*, 10, 110–15 ('Veshch'', 'Sonet' and letter to Lipavskiis). |
| 1987 | 'Elizaveta Bam', definitive text and commentary, published M. Meilakh (see Meilakh, 1987, below), *Stanford Slavic Studies*, vol. I, 205–46. |
| | 'Sluchai', publication N. Bogomolov, *Knizhnoe obozrenie*, 14, 3 April, [supplementary pagination] pp. 36–40 (17 stories). |

'Vospominaniia odnogo mudrogo starika', published V. Glotser, *Literaturnaia gazeta*, 25, 17 June, p. 16.
' "... I emu v rot zaletela kukushka" (iz prozy i poezii Daniila Kharmsa', introduction and publication Vladimir Glotser, *Voprosy literatury*, 8, 262–75 (10 stories and 6 poems).
'Iz neopublikovannogo', introduction and publication N. A. Bogomolov, *Druzhba narodov*, 10, 176–7 (5 poems).
'Vo-pervykh i vo-vtorykh', pp. 239–46 of L. Zhadova, 'Rabota Tatlina v knige', *Iskusstvo knigi*, 10, '1972–80', 235–48.
'Neopublikovannye rasskazy i stsenki', publication Vladimir Glotser, *Iunost'*, 10, 93–5 (8 stories).
' "Moi tvoreniia, synov'ia i docheri moi..." ', introduction and publication Vladimir Glotser, *V Mire knig*, 12, 83–8 (11 stories).
'Rasskazy', publication Valerii Sazhin, *Daugava*, 12, 120–2 (3 stories).

1988   'Daniil Kharms. Iz literaturnogo naslediia', publication Vladimir Glotser, *Knizhnoe obozrenie*, 1, 1 January, p. 7 (5 stories).
'Znak pri pomoshchi glaza', introduction and publication Anna Gerasimova, *Pamir*, 2, 141–9 (9 poems and 2 stories).
'Ia dumal o tom, kak prekrasno vsë pervoe!', introduction and publication Vladimir Glotser, *Novyi mir*, 4, 129–59 (9 letters to K. V. Pugachëva, 'Starukha', 8 poems).
[Three poems], *Ogonëk*, 17, 16.
'Elizaveta Bam', introduction and publication Mikhail Meilakh and Vladimir Erl', *Rodnik*, 5, 28–32.
'Logika alogizma', introduction Aleksandr Kobrinskii, *Neva*, 6, 204–5 (2 stories and 3 poems).
' "Da, ia poet zabytyi nebom...": k vykhodu v svet chetvërtogo toma Sobraniia proizvedenii Daniila Kharmsa' (review of *Sob. proizv.* IV, plus appendix: from notebooks, diaries and poems omitted from *Sob. proizv.* IV), publication Jean-Philippe Jaccard, *Russkaia mysl'*, 3730, 24 June, Literary Supplement, 6, pp. xi–xii.
'Daniil Kharms: Rasskazy iz tsikla "Sluchai" ', publication and afterword Mikhail Meilakh, *Raduga* (Tallinn), 7, 28–38 (10 stories).
'Daniil Kharms', introduction and publication Vladimir Glotser, *Nedelia*, 29, 22 ('Avtobiografiia' and 3 stories).
'Prazdnik', 'Shapka' (with A. Aleksandrov's note 'Sud'ba chudodeia' and M. Blok's memoir 'Zhizn' v nelepom polozhenii', *Leningradskaia pravda*, 243, 21 October, pp. 2–3.
'Daniil Kharms', publication Vladimir Glotser, *Knizhnoe obozrenie*, 43, 28 October, p. 10 (4 stories and 4 poems).
'Daniil Kharms', publication Vladimir Glotser, *Krokodil*, 33, November, pp. 8–9 (8 stories).

1989   [Eight Poems] *Avrora*, 6, 121–3.
1990   'Dnevniki Daniila Kharmsa. Iz dnevnika 1933–1938 gody', publication Vladimir Glotser, *Knizhnoe obozrenie*, 3, 19 January, pp. 8–9.

# Selected Bibliography

'Pomekha?' 'Pushkin i Gogol'', *Teatral'naia zhizn'*, 1, 22–3.
'Vechnyi tarakan' / 'Letanie bez kryl zhestokaia zabava', *Iskusstvo Leningrada*, 2, 79–91 (includes 7 poems by Kharms with commentary by A. B. Ustinov, pp. 82–5, and works by Bakhterev).
'Neskol'ko slov ob absurde: pis'ma D. I. Kharmsa, A. I. Panteleevu', publication Evgenii Pritsker. *Russkaia mysl'*, 3834, 6 July, Literary Supplement, 10, p. xiii (3 letters).

## CRITICISM, MEMOIRS ETC. ON KHARMS

(some of which include substantial Kharms quotations, including main publications of works of or on other Oberiuty of relevance to Kharms)

Aizlewood, Robin (1990) ' "Guilt without Guilt" in Kharms's Story "The Old Woman"', *Scottish Slavonic Review*, 14, 199–217.
Akopian, L. O. and Grigor'ian, M. V. (1989) 'Kharakternye osobennosti kompozitsii prozaicheskikh miniatur D. Kharmsa', in O. G. Revzina and T. A. Mikhailova (eds), *Problemy poeticheskogo iazyka. Konferentsiia molodykh uchënykh. Tezisy dokladov. Tom 1. Obshchee i russkoe stikhovedenie* (Moscow), pp. 3–4.
Aleksandrov, Anatolii (1968) 'OBERIU. Predvaritel'nye zametki', *Československá rusistika*, 13, 5, 296–303.
Aleksandrov, Anatolii (1973) 'Iumoristicheskie paradoksy Daniila Kharmsa', *Voprosy literatury*, 11, 296 (introductory note).
Aleksandrov, Anatolii (1980) 'Materialy D. I. Kharmsa v rukopisnom otdele Pushkinskogo Doma', in *Ezhegodnik rukopisnogo otdela Pushkinskogo Doma 1978* (Leningrad), pp. 64–79.
Aleksandrov, Anatolii (1984) 'Uchitel'', uchenik...', *Detskaia literatura*, 2, 42–5.
Aleksandrov, Anatolii (1985) 'Ob odnom stikhotvorenii Daniila Kharmsa: k 80-letiiu so dnia rozhdeniia', *Detskaia literatura*, 12, 37–9
Aleksandrov, Anatolii (1988a) ' "V shirokikh shliapakh, dlinnykh pidzhakakh...": Poety OBERIU', in *Den' poezii, Leningrad* (Leningrad), pp. 229–34.
Aleksandrov, Anatolii (1988b) 'Chudodei. Lichnost' i tvorchestvo Daniila Kharmsa', introduction to *Polët*, pp. 7–41.
Aleksandrov, Anatolii (1990) 'Mesto smerti Daniila Kharmsa – ?', *Literaturnaia gazeta* (5282), 8, 21 February, p. 5.
Aleksandrov, A. and Meilakh, M. (1967) 'Tvorchestvo Daniila Kharmsa', in *Materialy XXII nauchnoi studencheskoi konferentsii* (Tartu), pp. 101–4.
Bakhterev, Igor' (1984) 'Kogda my byli molodymi (Nevydumannyi rasskaz)', in Zabolotskaia (1984 – see below), pp. 57–100.
Belen'kaia, L. N. (1984) 'Master iz "Solnechnoi sistemy"', in I. P. Lupanova (ed.), *Problemy detskoi literatury* (Petrozavodsk), pp. 99–110.
Cassedy, Steven (1984) 'Daniil Kharms's Parody of Dostoevskii: Anti-Tragedy as Political Comment', *Canadian-American Slavic Studies*, 18, 3, 268–84.

Chances, Ellen (1982) 'Čexov and Xarms: Story/Anti-Story', *Russian Language Journal*, XXXVI, 123–4, 181–92.

Chances, Ellen (1985) 'Daniil Charms' "Old Woman" Climbs Her Family Tree: 'Starukha" and the Russian Literary Past', *Russian Literature*, XVII, 353–66.

Cheron, George (1983) 'Mixail Kuzmin and the Oberiuty: An Overview', *Wiener Slawistischer Almanach*, 12, 87–101.

Cornwell, Neil (1989) Introduction to *Plummeting* (see above), pp. 1–8.

Druskin, Iakov (1985) 'Chinari: glava iz knigi Iakova Semënovicha Druskina (1902–1980), *Son i iav'*, 1968' and 'Stadii ponimaniia', *Wiener Slawistischer Almanach*, 15, 381–403 and 405–13.

Druskin, Iakov (1988) *Vblizi vestnikov*, compiled Henry Orlov (Washington, D.C.: Frager).

Druskin, Iakov (1989) 'Chinari', *Avrora*, 6, 103–15.

Druskina, Lidiia (1989) 'Bylo takoe sodruzhestvo...', *Avrora*, 6, 100–31 (includes Druskin, 1989; and Lipavskii, 1989).

Fëdorov, G. (1976) 'Vokrug i posle "Nosa"', *Sovetskaia muzyka*, vol. 38, 9, 47–9.

Flaker, Aleksandr (1969) 'O rasskazakh Daniila Kharmsa', *Československá rusistika*, 14, 2, 78–84.

Flaker, Aleksandr (1984) 'OBERIU' and 'Harmsova poetika apsurda' in his *Ruska avangarda* (Zagreb: SN Liber/Globus), pp. 361–76.

Fleishman, Lazar' (1975) 'Marginalii k istorii russkogo avangarda (Oleinikov, oberiuty)', in Oleinikov (1975) – see below), pp. 3–18.

Fleishman, Lazar' (1987) 'Ob odnom zagadochnom stikhotvorenii Daniila Kharmsa', *Stanford Slavic Studies*, I, 247–58.

Gerasimova, Anna (1988a) 'OBERIU (problema smeshnogo)', *Voprosy literatury*, 4, 48–79.

Gerasimova, Anna (1988b) 'On tak i ostalsia rebënkom', *Detskaia literatura*, 4, 32–5.

Gernet, N. V. (1988) 'O Kharmse', *Neva*, 2, 201–4.

Giaquinta, Rosanna (1982) 'Su alcuni aspetti del teatro *Oberiu*', *Annali di Ca' Foscari*, XXI, 1–2, 85–97.

Giaquinta, Rosanna (1983) 'I poemi drammatici di Aleksandr Vvedenskij *Minin i Požarskij* e *Krugom vozmožno Bog*', *Annali di Ca' Foscari*, XXII, 1–2, 67–81.

Giaquinta, Rosanna (1987) 'Introduzione' to '"La vecchia", racconto di Daniil Charms', *Lettere internazionale*, 13, pp. 39–45 (39).

Giaquinta, Rosanna (1985–1988) 'OBERIU: per una rassegna della critica', *Ricerche Slavistiche*, vol. XXXII–XXXV, 213–52 [contains considerable bibliographical detail].

Giaquinta, Rosanna (1990) 'Daniil Charms: prosa senza poesia', in Daniil Charms, *Casi*, edited and translated Rosanna Giaquinta (Milan: Adelphi), 307–30.

Gibian, George (1971) Introduction to *Russia's Lost Lit.* (see above), pp. 3–38.

Gibian, George (1974) Introduction to *Izbrannoe* (see above), pp. 9–43.

Gibian, George (1987) 'Introduction: Daniil Kharms and Alexander Vvedensky' to *Black Coat* (see above), pp. 1–42.

Ginzburg, Lidiia (1982) *O starom i novom. Stat'i i ocherki* (Leningrad).
Ginzburg, Lidiia (1989) *Chelovek za pis'mennym stolom: esse. Iz vospominanii. Chetyre povestvovaniia* (Leningrad).
Glotser, Vladimir (1988a) 'Ia dumal o tom, kak prekrasno vsë pervoe', *Novyi mir*, 4, 129–32.
Glotser, Vladimir (1988b) 'Legends and the truth about Daniil Kharms' / 'Legendy i pravda o Daniile Kharmse', *Moscow News / Moskovskie novosti*, 35, 16.
Glotser, Vladimir (1989) 'Kharms sobiraet knigu', *Russkaia literatura*, 1, 206–12.
Iudina, M. V. [on] (1979) *Mariia Veniaminovna Iudina. Stat'i. Vospominaniia. Materialy* (Moscow), pp. 262–77.
Jaccard, Jean-Philippe (1985) 'De la réalité au texte: l'absurde chez Daniil Kharms' and 'Bibliographie', *Cahiers du monde russe et soviétique*, XXVI, 3–4, pp. 269–312 and 493–522.
Jaccard, Jean-Philippe (1988a) 'Daniil Harms dans le contexte de la littérature de l'absurde russe et européenne', in Peter Brang (ed.), *Schweizerische Beiträge zum X. Internationalen Slavistenkongress in Sofia, September 1988* (Bern: Peter Lang), pp. 145–69.
Jaccard, Jean-Philippe (1988b) 'Daniil Harms (1905–1942)', in Efim Etkind et al. (eds), *Histoire de la littérature russe. Le XXᵉ siècle\*\*. La Révolution et les années vingt* (Paris, Fayard), pp. 732–41.
Jaccard, Jean-Philippe (1989) [Zhakkar, Zhan-Filipp] 'Polët bez polëta', *Russkaia mysl'*, 3781, 23 June, Literary Supplement 8, p. xi (review of *Polët*).
Jaccard, Jean-Philippe (1990) 'Daniil Kharms: teatr absurda – real'nyi teatr (Prochtenie p'esy *Elizaveta Bam*)', *Russian Literature*, XXVII, 1, 21–40.
Jovanovič, Milivoe (1981a) ' "Situatsiia Raskol'nikova" i eë otgoloski v russkoi sovetskoi proze (parodiinyi aspekt)', *Zbornik za slavistiku*, 21, 45–57.
Jovanovič, Milivoe (1981b) 'Daniil Harms kao parodičar', *Umjetnost riječi*, XXV, 367–77.
Jovanovič, Milivoe (1983) 'A. Vvedenskii – parodist: k razboru "Ëlki u Ivanovykh" ', *Wiener Slawistischer Almanach*, 12, 71–86.
Kalashnikova, R. B. (1984) 'Oberiuty i V. Khlebnikov (Zvukovaia organizatsiia stikha)', in I. P. Lupanova (ed.), *Problemy detskoi literatury* (Petrozavodsk), pp. 90–8.
Kalashnikova, R. B. (1987) 'Shkola i "antishkola" Daniila Kharmsa', in I. P. Lupanova (ed.), *Problemy detskoi literatury* (Petrozavodsk), pp. 38–49.
Kalashnikova, R. B. (1989) 'Daniil Kharms i narodnaia schitalka', in *Problemy detskoi literatury* (Petrozavodsk), pp. 24–33.
Kasack, W. (1976) 'Daniil Charms. Absurde Kunst in der Sowjetunion', *Die Welt der Slaven*, 21, 70–80.
Kaverin, V. (1971/1982) 'V starom dome ("On liubil udivliat'")', *Zvezda*, 10, 1971, 138–86. Also in his *Vechernii den'* (Moscow, 1980), pp. 331–5; and his *Sobranie sochinenii v vos'mi tomakh*, vol. 6 (Moscow), 1982.
Kaverin, V. (1973) *Sobesednik. Vospominaniia i portrety* (Moscow), pp. 60–80.
Kobrinskii, A. A. (1988) 'Tsikl Daniila Kharmsa "Sluchai" kak edinoe

tseloe', in *Materialy XXVI vsesoiuznoi nauchnoi studencheskoi konferentsii: 'Student i nauchno-tekhnicheskii progress'*. *Filologiia* (Novosibirsk), pp. 64–9.
Kobrinskii, A. A. (1989). 'Psikhologizm, alogizm i absurdizm v proze Daniila Kharmsa (O perspektivnykh napravleniiakh izucheniia arkhivnogo fonda Ia. S. Druskina)', in *Problemy istochnikovedcheskogo izucheniia istorii russkoi i sovetskoi literatury*, ed. V. N. Sazhin (Leningrad: Gos. publ. biblioteka imeni M. E. Saltykova-Schedrina), pp. 167–90.
Kobrinskii, A. A. and Meilakh, M. (1990) 'Neudachnyi spektakl'', *Literaturnoe obozrenie*, 9, 81–5.
Kotrelev, N. (1988) [Undated letter] *Sovetskaia bibliografiia*, 4, 87–9.
Kublanovskii, Iu. (1988) 'Pozdnii Kharms: k vykhodu v svet 4-go toma sobraniia proizvedenii', *Russkaia mysl'*, 2 September, p. 10.
Levin, Il'ia (1978) 'The Fifth Meaning of the Motor-Car: Malevich and the Oberiuty', *Soviet Union / Union Soviétique*, 5, 2, 287–300.
Levin, Il'ia (1980) 'Mir vymyshlennyi i mir sozdannyi', *Kontinent*, 24, 271–5.
Lifshits, V. (1969) 'Mozhet byt', prigoditsia', *Voprosy literatury*, 1, 241–3.
Lipavskii, Leonid (1989) 'Iz razgovorov "chinarei"', *Avrora*, 6, 124–31.
Loseff, Lev (1984) *On The Beneficence of Censorship* (Arbeiten und Texte zur Slavistik, 31, Munich), pp. 205–10 and 244–6.
Martini, A. (1981) 'Retheatralisierung des Theaters: D. Charms "Elizaveta Bam"', *Zeitschrift für Slavische Philologie*, 42, 146–66.
Maxton, Hugh (1989) 'Kharms and Myles: An Afterword' to *Plummeting* (see above), pp. 93–100.
Meilakh, Mikhail (1974/1978) 'Semanticheskii eksperiment v poeticheskoi rechi', *Russian Linguistics*, 1, 1974, 271–6. Reprinted *Russian Literature*, VI, 4, 1978, 389–95.
Meilakh, Mikhail (1980) 'Predislovie' to Vved. I (see below), pp. ix–xxxii.
Meilakh, Mikhail (1987) 'O "Elizavete Bam" Daniila Kharmsa (predystoriia, istoriia postanovki, p'esa, tekst)', *Stanford Slavic Studies*, I, 163–246.
Meilakh, Mikhail (1989) 'Daniil Kharms: Anecdota posthuma (Posmertnye anekdoty Daniila Kharmsa)', *Russkaia mysl'*, 3781, 23 June, Literary Supplement 8, pp. x–xi.
M. M. (1990) 'Oberiuty v Amsterdame', *Russkaia mysl'*, 3827, 11 May, p. 10.
Milner-Gulland, R. R. (1970) '"Left Art" in Leningrad: The OBERIU Declaration', *Oxford Slavonic Papers*, New Series, III, 65–74.
Milner-Gulland, R. R. (1984) '"Kovarnye stikhi": Notes on Daniil Kharms and Aleksandr Vvedensky', *Essays in Poetics*, 9, 1, 16–37.
Müller-Scholle, Christine (1986) 'Daniil Charms. Jelisaweta Bam', in Bodo Zelinsky (ed.), *Das russiche Drama* (Düsseldorf), pp. 280–91.
Naiman, A. (1989) *Rasskazy o Anne Akhmatovoi: iz knigi: konets pervoi poloviny XX veka* (Moscow).
Nakhimovsky, Alice Stone (1978) 'The Ordinary, the Sacred and the Grotesque in Daniil Kharms's *The Old Woman*', *Slavic Review*, 37, 203–16.
Nakhimovsky, Alice Stone (1982) *Laughter in the Void: An introduction to the writings of Daniil Kharms and Alexander Vvedenskii* (Vienna: Wiener Slawistischer Almanach, Sonderband 5).

Nikitaev, Aleksandr (1989) 'Tainopis' Daniila Kharmsa. Opyt deshifrovki', *Daugava*, 8, 95–9.
Nivat, Georges (1982) 'Le crayon vert de Kharms' in his *Vers la fin du mythe russe* (Lausanne, L'Age d'Homme), pp. 233–6.
'Olegri' [Oleg Ris] (1982) 'Literaturnye penaty na fontanke', *Neva*, 3, 198–200.
Oleinikov, N. M. (1975) *Stikhotvoreniia*, introduction L. S. Fleishman (Bremen: K-Presse) [Oleinikov].
Oleinikov, N. M. (1988) *Peremena familii*, edited Vladimir Glotser (Moscow).
Poret, A. (1980) 'Vospominaniia o Daniile Kharmse', in *Panorama iskusstv*, vol. 3 (Moscow), pp. 345–59.
Revzina, O. G. (1978) 'Kachestvennaia i funktsional'naia kharakeristika vremeni v poezii A. I. Vvedenskogo', *Russian Literature*, VI, 4, 397–401.
Revzina, O. G. and Revzin, I. I. (1971) 'Semioticheskii eksperiment na stsene (Narushenie postulata normal'nogo obshcheniia kak dramaticheskii priëm)', in *Trudy po znakovym sistemam*, vol. 5 (Tartu), pp. 232–54.
Roberts, Graham (forthcoming) 'A matter of (dis)course: metafiction in the works of Daniil Kharms' (paper delivered to Fourth ICSEES International Conference, Harrogate, July 1990, publication due in forthcoming proceedings).
Sazhin, V. (1985) 'Literaturnye i fol'klornye traditsii v tvorchestve D. I. Kharmsa', in *Literaturnyi protsess i razvitie russkoi kul'tury XVIII–XXvv. Tezisy nauchnoi konferentsii* (Tallinn), pp. 57–61.
Sazhin, V. (1986) 'Chitaia Daniila Kharmsa', *Daugava*, 10, 110–15.
Sazhin, V. (1988) ' "Chinari – literaturnoe ob''edinenie 1920–1930–x godov (istochniki dlia izucheniia)', in M. O. Chudakova (ed.), *Chetvërtye Tynianovskie chteniia. Tezisy dokladov i materialy dlia obsuzhdeniia* (Riga), pp. 23–4.
Scotto, Susan D. (1986) 'Xarms and Hamsun: *Staruxa* Solves a Mystery?', *Comparative Literature Studies*, 23, 282–96.
Semënov, Boris F. (1977) 'Chudak istinnyi i radostnyi', *Avrora*, 4, 69–75 (substantially reprinted in Semënov, 1982).
Semënov, Boris F. (1979) 'Dalëkoe – riadom', *Neva*, 9, 180–5.
Semënov, Boris F. (1982) 'Daniil Ivanovich Kharms' and 'Poet Aleksandr Vvedenskii', in his *Vremia moikh druzei. Vospominaniia* (Leningrad), pp. 258–77; and 278–89.
Serman, Il'ia Z. (1981) 'Stikhi Kapitana Lebiadkina i poeziia XX veka', *Revue des Etudes Slaves*, 53, 597–605.
Shklovskii, Viktor (1967/1973) 'O tsvetnykh snakh', *Literaturnaia gazeta*, 47, 22 November, p. 16. Reprinted in *Klub 12 stul'ev* (Moscow).
Shukman, Ann (1988) 'Towards a poetics of the absurd: the prose writings of Daniil Kharms', in Henri Broms and Rebecca Kaufmann (eds), *Semiotics of Culture. Proceedings of the 25th Symposium of the Tartu-Moscow School of Semiotics. Imatra, Finland, 27–29 July 1987* (Helsinki), pp. 81–95. [This is in fact a revised version of Shukman, 1989]
Shukman, Ann (1989) 'Towards a Poetics of the Absurd: The Prose Writings of Daniil Kharms', in Catriona Kelly et al. (eds), *Discontinuous Discourses in Modern Russian Literature* (London: Macmillan), pp. 60–72.

Shvarts, Evgenii (1990) *Zhivu bespokoino ... Iz dnevnikov* (Leningrad: Sovetskii pisatel').
Sigov, Sergej (1986) 'Istoki poetiki OBERIU', *Russian Literature*, XX, pp. 87–95.
Smirnov, Igor (1988) 'L'Obériou', in Efim Etkind et al. (eds), *Histoire de la littérature russe. Le XX$^e$ siècle**. La Révolution et les années vingt* (Paris, Fayard), pp. 697–710.
Sokol, Elena (1975) 'Observations on the prose of Daniil Kharms', *Proceedings of the Pacific Northwest Conference of Foreign Languages*, 26, 1, 179–83.
Sokol, Elena (1984) 'The Oberiu Poets', in her *Russian Poetry for Children* (Knoxville: U of Tennessee P), pp. 122–51.
St., F. (1988) '*Le Cas Harms*, de Slobodan D. Pesic', *Cahiers du cinéma*, 409, June, p. 15.
Stelleman, Jenny (1985) 'An Analysis of *Elizaveta Bam*', *Russian Literature*, XVII, 319–52.
Sterligov, V. V. (1990) 'Prostota – khuzhe vorovstva: pis'ma V. V. Sterligova A. I. Panteleevu', publication Evgenii Pritsker. *Russkaia mysl'*, 3834, 6 July, Literary Supplement, 10, pp. xii–xiii [letters about Kharms].
Stoimenoff, Ljubomir (1984) *Grundlagen und Verfahren des sprachlichen Experiments im Frühwerk von Daniil J. Charms. (Ein Beitrag zur Definition der 'oberiutischen Ästhetik')*, SS, 19 (Frankfurt: Peter Lang).
Sysoev, V. (1985) 'Noch'. Neskol'ko rasskazov o Daniile Kharmse', *Literaturnoe izdanie A–Ia*, 1, 27–35.
Vishevsky, Anatoly (1986) 'Tradition in the Topsy-Turvy World of Parody: analysis of two *OBERIU* plays', *Slavic and East European Journal*, 30, 355–66.
Vizhar, Kolen (1987) 'Tëtushka Daniila Pervogo', introduced by Stefano Garzonio, *Europa Orientalis*, 6, 219–35.
Vul'fius, P. A. (1980) *Stat'i. Vospominaniia. Publitsistika* (Leningrad).
Vvedenskii, Aleksandr (1980/1984) *Polnoe sobranie sochinenii*, ed. Mikhail Meilakh (Ardis: Ann Arbor), 2 vols. [Vved. I and II].
Woroszylska, Natalia (1987) 'Realizacja założeń programowych grupy Oberiu w opowiadaniach dla dzieci Daniela Charmsa', *Prace Naukowe Uniwersytetu Śląskiego* Katowice, 794, *Rusycystyczne Studia Literaturoznawcze*, 10, 95–108.
Zabolotskaia, A. V. et al. (eds) (1984) *Vospominaniia o N. Zabolotskom*, 2nd. ed. (Moscow).
Zabolotskii, Nikolai Alekseevich (1981) 'The Story of my Imprisonment', edited and translated by Robin Milner-Gulland, *Times Literary Supplement*, 9 October, p. 1179.
Zhukova, Lidiia (1983) 'Oberiuty', in her *Epilogi*, kn. 1–aia (New York: Chalidze), pp. 222–7 (plus chapters on 'Oleinikov' and 'Proshchanie s soboi').
Ziegler, Rosemarie (1982) 'Die Modellierung des dramatischen Raumes in Daniil Charms' "Architektor" (1 Teil)', *Wiener Slawistischer Almanach*, 10, 351–64.
Zolotonosov, Mikhail (1989) 'Muzyka vo l'du', *Iskusstvo Leningrada*, 1, 37–41; 45–56.

# Selected Bibliography

## ADDENDUM

Morev, G. A. [ed.] (1990) *Mikhail Kuzmin i russkaia kul'tura XX veka: tezisy i materialy konferentsii 15–17 maia 1990g.* (Leningrad: Sovet po istorii mirovoy kul'tury AN SSSR) [includes items relevant to Kharms by: B. M. Konstriktor, V. N. Sazhin, and A. B. Ustinov, including three letters from Kharms to A. I. Panteleev, pp. 131–3].

# Index

Adamov, A.   50
Aeschylus   213
Aizlewood, R.   11, 21, *97–122*, 130, 257
Agol, I.   185, 191
Akhmatova, A.   7, 8, 208
Aleksandrov, A.   4, 10, 19, 20, *32–46*, 74, 80, 90, 91, 117, 121, 130, 137, 165, 199, 253, 267
Andersen, H.   23
Andronikov, I.   40, 266
Anemone, A.   11, *71–93*, 103, 118, 244
Apollinaire, G.   68, 199
Artaud, A.   147
Aseev, N.   208, 218

Babel, I.   257
Bacon, F.   23
Bakhterev, I.   5, 6, 20, 34, 35, 36, 37, 38, 200, 201, 204, 205, 206, 207, 210, 217
Bakhtin, M.   75, 77, 79, 93, 104, 119, 147, 151–2, 155, 188, 265, 267
Baranchikov, P.   165
Barthes, R.   66, 70, 87, 92
Baskakov, A.   204, 210
Baudelaire, C.   132
Beckett, S.   12, 19, 50, 52, 58, 61, 63, 64–6, 69, 70, 71, 120, 264
Bellini, G.   172
Bem, A.   146, 148
Bergson, H.   188, 191
Blake, W.   12
Bogatyrëv, P.   179, 190, 191
Borges, J-L.   12, 135, 140, 265
Bowlt, J.   263, 267
Bréton, A.   12, 13–14, 21
Brod, M.   12, 15, 20, 21
Brooke-Rose, C.   134, 144, 148
Bulgakov, M.   3, 89, 123, 130
Busch, W.   43, 44

Caillois, R.   133, 148
Calvino, I.   15
Camus, A.   14, 50, 52, 67, 155
Carroll, L.   12, 13
Castex, P-G.   134, 137, 142, 147, 148
Cassedy, S.   146
Cervantes, M. de   15
Chaliapine, F.   183
Chances, E.   68, 71, 78, 118, 146
Chekhov, A. P.   3, 11, 68, 92, 98, 100, 118, 217, 258
Cheron, G.   118
'Chinari'   5, 20, 34, 35–6, 117, 118, 119, 120, 215, 216, 219
*Chizh*   39, 42, 43, 44, 68, 91
Chopin, F.   121, 218
Christ [Christianity]   26, 75, 76, 90–1, 120, 171–3, 260–1
Cooke, R.   267
Cornwell, N.   *3–21*, 67, 146, 148, 220–40, 243
Crosby, D.   21

Dadaists, the   6, 12, 55, 198, 264
Dal, V.   98, 118
Dali, S.   13
Dargomyzhsky   183
Dobychin, L.   38, 211
Dostoevsky, F.   11, 12, 51, 68, 73, 85, 86, 89, 101, 115, 132, 137–8, 145, 146, 147, 151, 176, 259
Doyle, Sir A. Conan   4
Driesch, H.   191
Druskin, Ia.   6, 9–10, 12, 14, 19, 20, 21, *22–31*, 34, 41, 43, 72, 73, 90, 98, 101, 106–7, 109, 110, 117, 118, 120–1, 141–2, 145–6, 147, 151, 168, 176, 244, 245, 250, 254, 259, 263
Druskin, M.   217
Druskina, L.   117, 267
Duchamp, M.   264

# Index

Eagleton, T.   79, 87, 92, 93
Eikhenbaum, B.   38, 209
Eisenstein, S.   6
Eliot, T. S.   203, 246, 247
Erl', V.   10, 67, 68, 161, 199, 217, 244, 246, 249, 252, 267
Ermolaev, V.   39
Esslin, M.   66, 93
Evenbakh, E.   38, 39, 40
Evreinov, N.   196, 199
Ëzh   37, 68

Faryno, J.   119, *171–4*, 246, 261
Fëdorov, G.   20, 267
Fëdorov, N.   267
Feofan, Bishop   31
Fichte, J.   28
Filippov, G.   219
Filonov, P.   5, 180, 209, 261, 263, 267
Flaker, A.   71, 77, 78, 83, 84, 89, 90, 91, 92, 118, 131, 147
Fleishman, L.   11, 18, 19, 20, 71, 89, 99, 101, 102, 103, 118, 119, *159–68*, 171–4, 178, 189, 190, 191, 219, 246, 261
Florensky, P.   167
Forsh, O.   80–1, 82
Freidenberg, O.   179, 188, 189–90, 190–1
Freud, S. [Freudian]   13, 16, 23, 138–9, 145, 147, 148
Futurists, the [see also *zaum'*]   5, 6, 12, 195, 203, 214

Galich, A.   xii, xiii, xiv, 19
García Márquez, G.   135
Garshin, V.   11
Gerasimova, A.   73–4, 77, 90, 98, 118, 197, 199
Gernet, N.   39, 42, 45, 46
Giquinta, R.   11, *132–48*
Gibian, G.   4, 21, 67, 71, 88, 165, 199, 246
Gide, A.   168
Ginzburg, L.   5, 20, 36, 38
Glotser, V.   8, 10, 11, 20, 90, 117
Goethe, J.   12, 175–6, 185, 260

Gogol', N.   11, 12, 18, 24, 25, 26, 44, 51, 53–4, 58–63, 67, 68, 69, 72, 77, 78–9, 82, 98, 101, 103, 104, 117, 118, 140, 179, 182, 202, 248, 251, 260, 263
Goldstein, D.   189
Gol'tsshmidt, V.   195
Goncharov, I.   134
Goncharova, N.   216
Gorbachëv, M.   10
Gor'ky, M.   168
Griboedov, A.   179
Grigor'ev, V.   189, 190, 246–7, 255, 266, 267
Grin, A. [Gol'dfarb, A.]   38, 203
Grinberg, V.   45
Gurovich, A.   166

Hamsun, K.   12, 15–16, 21, 27, 44
Heidegger, M.   120
Hirschkop, K.   265, 267
Hoffmann, E. T. A.   135, 138, 140, 187
House of Print (Press Club/*Dom pechati*)   6, 35, 37, 38, 200, 203–4, 208, 210, 217, 218
Hoyles, J.   21

Ioffe, N.   35–6
Imaginists, the,   195
Ionesco, E.   49, 50, 53, 56, 57, 66, 68, 69, 264
Irwin, W. R.   134, 148
Istrati, P.   168
Iudina, M.   265
Iuvachëv, D. I. [original name of D. I. Kharms]   3, 4, 32, 46
Iuvachëv, I. P.   3, 20, 33

Jaccard, J-P.   8, 11, 12, 14, 19, 20, 21, *49–70*, 101, 105, 118, 120, 121, 147, 151, 153, 155
Jackson, R.   134, 148
Jakobson, R.   104–5, 118, 249
Jarry, A.   199
Jovanović, M.   146
Joyce, J.   18, 246

Kafka, F.   12, 15, 20–1, 50, 71,
    89, 133, 140, 143, 147, 148, 212,
    244, 247, 258, 262, 264–5, 266,
    267
Kamensky, V.   195
Kant, I.   107, 260
Karamzin, N.   181, 191
Kasack, W.   131
Kassil, L.   168
Katsman, G.   5, 32, 212
Kaverin, V.   38, 211, 218
Kayser, W.   147, 148
Kent, L. J.   140, 147, 148
Khardzhiev, N.   211–12
Khlebnikov, V.   8, 12, 20, 38, 55,
    68, 118, 176, 178, 189, 190, 203,
    208, 244, 246, 248–51, 254, 255,
    256, 257, 258, 259, 261, 262, 263,
    265, 266, 267
Kierkegaard, S.   23, 120
Kipling, R.   12
Kliuev, N.   33, 209
Kobrinsky, A.   11, 21, 90, 117,
    121, *149–55*
Koliubakina, Nadezhda I.   3
Koliubakina, Natalia I.   4, 32
Kol'man, E.   166
Kon, L.   43
Kropachev, N.   37
Kruchënykh, A.   55, 68, 91, 93,
    160, 165, 178, 214, 216
Kublanovsky, Iu.   20
Kuprin, A.   182, 191
Kuzmin, M.   118

Larin, Iu.   163, 164, 166
Lear, E.   12, 50
Lesnaia, L.   37, 208, 218
Levin, B. 'Doivber'   5, 6, 38, 39,
    40, 200, 201, 210, 217
Levin, I.   67, 69, 79, 82, 88, 90,
    92, 267
Levitin, M.   68–9
Likhachëv, D.   75, 76, 85, 91, 93
Lipavskaia, T.   27, 117, 254
Lipavsky, L.   5, 6, 40, 41, 73, 77,
    90, 107, 110, 117, 141, 203, 209,
    254, 263
Livshts, V.   20

Lomonosov, M.   12
Lönnqvist, B.   266
Lossky, N.   185, 191
Lotman, Iu.   76–7, 91, 93
Lovecraft, H. P.   133, 148
Lunacharsky, A.   8, 167
Lyons, E.   167

Magarotto, L.   165
Maiakovsky, V.   166
Malevich, K.   5, 25, 35, 36, 41,
    42, 44, 180, 209, 253, 263
Malich, Marina V.   7, 42, 43, 46
Mallarmé, S.   246
Mandel'shtam, O.   109, 120
Manevich, P.   204
Mann, T.   92
Mann, Iu.   135, 143, 148
Mansurov, P.   44, 45, 209, 211
Marinetti, F.   198
Marr, N.   178, 188, 190
Marshak, S.   7, 209
Marx, K. [Marxist etc.]   13, 35, 185
Matveev, G. N.   33
Mauthner, F.   14
Maxton, H.   21
Medvedev, R.   166
Meilakh, M.   9, 10, 11, 19, 20, 67,
    74, 90, 106, 117, 118, 120, 121,
    161, 165, 189, 191, *200–19*, 240,
    244, 246, 249, 252, 267
Meyerhold, V.   179
Meyrink, G.   12, 253
Michaelangelo   248, 263
Michalkski, M.   11, *123–31*
Michaux, H.   51, 67
Milhaud, D.   34
Milne, A. A.   12
Milner-Gulland, R.   viii, 20, 21,
    68, 74, 79, 80–1, 91, 92, 97, 117,
    118, 121, 217, *243–67*
Miroliubov, I. P. [pseud. of I. P.
    Iuvachëv]   3
Mozart, W.   28

Nabokov, V.   212
Nadson, S.   33
Nakhimovsky, A.   20, 78, 89, 90,
    91, 92, 121, 143, 189, 199

Nietzsche, F. 14
Nikol'skaia, T. 7, 165, *195–9*
Nil'vich, L. 39, 93

OBERIU 5–7, 10, 11, 13, 15, 17, 21, 36–9, 56, 68, 71–4, 77, 78, 80–1, 86, 88, 89, 91, 92–3, 97, 102–3, 113, 117–18, 119, 121, 145, 152, 155, 159–60, 164, 168, 175–83, 188–9, 191, 195–9, 200–19, 220–40, 246, 249, 252, 255, 259, 263, 265
O'Brien, F. 2, 21
Olegri 20
Oleinikov, N. 5, 6, 8, 9, 29, 36, 39, 40, 41, 42, 43, 73, 117, 119, 168, 175, 178, 179, 188, 219, 247, 252–4, 261, 263, 266
Olesha, Iu. 11, 12, 38, 89, 211
Olimpov, K. 5
Ol'minsky, M. 163, 164, 165
Orwell, G. 18, 86

Palmer, J. 16–17, 21
Panchenko, A. 75, 76, 85, 91, 93
Panteleev, L. 45
Pascal, P. 168
Passage, C. 147, 148
Pasternak, B. 5, 20, 118, 167–8, 189
Perlina, N. 11, *175–91*, 246, 252
Pešić, S. 123–31
Petrov, V. N. 44–5
Petrovsky, Iu. 146, 148
Picabia, F. 199
Plato 14
Platonov, A. 12, 89, 155
Poe, A. E. 16, 135
Poliakova, R. 33, 267
Poliakova, S. V. 219
Poret, A. 40, 46, 119, 120, 195, 196, 197, 199, 254
Potebnia, A. 178
Poulenc, F. 34
Pound, E. 246
Press Club [see House of Print]
Propp, V. 121
Prutkov, K. 12, 120, 266

Pugachëva, K. 42, 97, 261
Pushkin, A. 18, 26, 68, 78–9, 82, 91, 103, 132, 151, 176, 180–1, 182, 183, 189, 191, 248
Pythagoras 42, 261

Rabkin, E. 133, 148
Rachmaninov, S. 218
'Radiks' [Radix] 5, 34, 36, 200, 202, 203, 204, 207, 210, 212
Razumovsky, A. 37, 39
Revzin, I. 104, 119, 165
Revzina, O. 104, 119, 165
Rilke, R. M. 263
Rolland, R. 168
Rusakov, A. 9, 168
Rusakova, Ester A. Marcel- 4, 9, 33, 168, 251–2

Sade, Marquis de 13
Safonova, E. 38, 39, 40
Sartre, J-P. 25
Satie, E. 34
Savelev, L. (see also Lipavsky) 5, 73, 254
Sazhin, V. 146
Schubert, F. 183
Scotto, S. 21
Sebeok, T. 119
Seleshnikov, S. 166, 171, 174
Semënov, B. 20, 43, 209, 218
Serge, V. 9, 20, 168
Serman, I. 219
Shklovsky, V. 36, 38, 53, 68, 74–5, 86, 178
Shostakovich, D. 8, 263, 267
Shukman, A. 104, 118
Shvarts, E. 39, 40, 68, 266
Siniakovy sisters, the 254
Siniavksy, A. 11, 12, 91, 93
Smirnov, I. 106
Smith, G. S. 19
Sokolov, P. 40, 209, 254
Sollertinsky, I. 43, 209, 265
Solov'ëv, V. 134–5, 146, 148
Solzhenitsyn, A. 11
Stalin, J. [Stalinism] 18, 26, 73, 85–7, 88–9, 92, 102, 119, 126, 129–30, 166, 167

Stelleman, J.   118
Stepanov, N.   209, 249
Sterligov, V.   195, 209
Stoimenoff, L.   189, 267
surrealists, the   12–14, 21, 145–6
Swift, J.   13

Tatlin, V.   39, 203, 248, 263, 267
Terent'ev, I.   160, 165, 203, 204, 209
Terts, A. [see Siniavksy]
Thompson, E.   76, 93
Thorlby, A.   266
Tikhonov, A.   33, 38
Tiutchev, F.   33
Todorov, T.   133, 134, 140, 143, 144, 146, 147, 148
Tolmachev, D.   199, 208, 218
Tolstoy, A. K.   134
Tolstoy, A. N.   80–1, 82
Tolstoy, L. N.   3, 254
Trenin, V.   45
Tsimbal, S.   5, 35, 205, 217
Tufanov, A.   5, 33, 34, 55, 68, 160, 203, 209, 255
Turgenev, I.   11
Tynianov, Iu.   38, 178
Tzara, T.   55, 199

Uspensky, B.   76–7, 91, 93, 190

Vaginov, K.   5, 6, 37, 159, 175, 177, 178, 190
Vax, L.   134, 137, 147, 148
Vazarin, Z.   91, 93
Vigiliansky, E.   34, 38, 203
Vinogradov, V.   176
Vishevsky, A.   71–2, 74, 78, 90, 121

Vladimirov, Iu,   6, 39
Voinovich, V.   12
Voloshinov, V.   119
Vroon, R.   266, 267
Vul'fius, R.   38, 206, 217
Vvedensky, A.   5, 6, 7, 8, 10, 12, 23, 27, 29, 33, 34, 35, 36, 37, 38, 39, 40, 41, 45, 73, 79, 89, 90, 92, 105, 106, 113, 115, 117, 118, 120, 121, 136, 144–5, 146, 152, 159, 160, 165, 168, 175, 178, 179, 188, 191, 203, 205, 208, 209, 210, 216, 217, 218, 219, 244, 247, 249, 254, 256, 263

Wasiolek, E.   85, 93
Wittgenstein, L.   247, 266
Wright, E.   16, 21

Zabolotskaia, E.   266
Zabolotsky, N.   5, 6, 9, 20, 31, 34, 36, 37, 38, 39, 40, 41, 73, 117, 125, 127, 175, 179, 180, 181, 184, 188, 189, 191, 208, 219, 247, 254, 256, 260, 263, 266, 267
Zamiatin, E.   11, 89
Zarikovsky, A.   91, 93
zaum' [zaumniki]   5, 6, 55, 68, 160, 175–6, 178, 186–8, 189, 190, 203, 208, 213, 215, 250, 255–6
Zegzhda, N.   33
Zheleznev, L.   35–6
Zhitkov, B.   36, 39, 40, 41, 43
Zhukova, L.   20
Ziegler, R.   165
Zolla, E.   138, 147, 148
Zolotonosov, M.   119
Zoshchenko, M.   11, 12, 39, 88